PUTIN'S PLAYBOOK

PUTIN'S PLAYBOOK

Russia's Secret Plan to Defeat America

REBEKAH KOFFLER

REGNERY GATEWAY
Washington, D.C.

Regnery Gateway™ is a trademark of Salem Communications Holding Corporation
Regnery® is a registered trademark and its colophon is a trademark of Salem Communications Holding Corporation

ISBN: 978-1-68451-003-0
eISBN: 978-1-68451-022-1

Published in the United States by
Regnery Gateway,
An imprint of Regnery Publishing,
A Division of Salem Media Group
Washington, D.C.
www.Regnery.com

Manufactured in the United States of America

10 9 8 7 6 5 4 3 2

Books are available in quantity for promotional or premium use. For information on discounts and terms, please visit our website: www.Regnery.com.

For my parents, Valentina and Vladimir

DISCLAIMER

Based on open source information and the author's personal experience, the views and analytic assessments in *Putin's Playbook* are the author's only. These views and assessments do not represent the views of any government agency or organization. Some names have been changed for privacy reasons.

Contents

The Defense Intelligence Agency and Central Intelligence Agency conducted an extensive prepublication review of *Putin's Playbook* and redacted significant portions of the typescript. The author strongly disagrees with these redactions as unnecessary and unjustified but has complied with them. The blacked-out portions of what follows are the result of these redactions.

Why I Wrote This Book

M isunderstanding Russia and its president, Vladimir Putin, is dangerous. Russia is not merely intent on interfering with our elections. Russia is determined to weaken the United States and defeat us—if necessary, by using military force. This is Putin's playbook. Many Americans, worn out by upheaval from the coronavirus and constant political and social strife, are eager to restore some sense of normalcy and equanimity to their lives. And, after four years of exhausting federal investigations that stemmed from the alleged collusion between the Trump campaign and Russia, many lost interest in Russia and its foreign policy. And yet now it is more important than ever to understand Moscow's role in "Russiagate," which has torn our country apart, and President Putin's intentions toward America in the future.

Understandably, it is tempting to close the "Russiagate" chapter of America's life. After all, the multi-year, multi-million-dollar investigation by Special Prosecutor Robert Mueller concluded that not a single American, let alone the U.S. president himself, conspired with the Russians to steal the 2016 election.[1] Former president Donald Trump, whose entire term was darkened by the shadow of the unfounded "collusion" allegations, famously tweeted in relief at the conclusion of the Mueller probe, "No collusion. Game Over."[2] Many Republicans and the former president's supporters celebrated his innocence and vindication. Democrats and those who hate Trump got busy looking for other ways to resist and discredit the president.

Russian president Vladimir Putin, who has consistently denied interference in our election, mocked the Mueller probe, saying, "The mountain gave birth to a mole."[3] His spokesman Dmitry Peskov triumphantly proclaimed: "It's impossible to find a black cat in a dark room, especially if it's not there."[4]

The "witch hunt," as Trump called it, turned out to be just that. As evidenced by the Justice Department's findings, a small but powerful group within the American law enforcement and intelligence apparatus orchestrated an unprecedented intrusion into the electoral process by weaponizing the highly sensitive Foreign Intelligence and Surveillance Act (FISA) and other powers against American citizens. They sought to penetrate a presidential candidate's campaign on the pretext of counterintelligence concerns in order to discredit Trump and eventually remove him from office. In the process, these apparatchiks destroyed the lives and careers of innocent Americans like General Michael Flynn, the former national security advisor and my boss in his earlier role as director of the Defense Intelligence Agency. As newly declassified documents reveal, this 33-year U.S. Army veteran, who risked his life during the United States' war on terror to protect his country, was deliberately ensnared in an elaborate dragnet by the FBI, which destroyed his career, family, and reputation. The American intelligence and security apparatus unleashed the full power of the state against Flynn and others.

But just because the "Trump-Putin collusion" turned out to be a hoax fabricated by the U.S. intelligence and security apparatchiks doesn't mean Russia did not have a hand in the disruption of the 2016 presidential election and the resulting upheaval in America. It certainly did. It worked so well for Putin that he went for seconds in 2020. Creating discord and disarray in America was Putin's plan both in the 2016 and 2020 elections, and Moscow believes it has been fulfilled—and then some. It remains Putin's plan for our future.

For the past thirty years, the failure to grasp this essential truth has caused the U.S. government to pursue a dangerously misguided policy toward Moscow. U.S. administrations have been stuck in an endless cycle of "resets" with Russia for too long, launching and re-launching misguided policies based more on wishful thinking than on realistic assessments of a sophisticated and strategic opponent. Such inept approaches to dealing with Moscow have brought a crisis in U.S.-Russian relations that could escalate even to the point of a nuclear war—a war that neither country wants, but one that Putin's Russia has been preparing to win.

Putin's Playbook reveals the blueprint and the array of tools that the Russian military and security apparatus has crafted (and that the Russian president has approved) to destabilize and defeat America.

As a Russian-born American citizen, I grew up behind the Iron Curtain and, in an unusual twist of fate, became a U.S. intelligence officer. This book describes for the first time the true Russian threat to America. I have seen this threat up close, and I understand both sides of this conflict from an intelligence perspective. *Putin's Playbook* reveals the Russian president's unique thought process, which is unmistakably Russian, and reveals his master plan for dominating America. And the plan involves much more than interfering with U.S. elections.

From 2008 through 2016, I served in the Defense Intelligence Agency, the Pentagon's military intelligence counterpart to the Central Intelligence Agency. My U.S. government superiors considered me one of the top three experts on Russian doctrine and strategy in the Intelligence Community (IC), including the CIA, and I was frequently summoned to brief senior U.S. and NATO generals, admirals, and policymakers. Some even called me a "national asset," which made me proud as someone who had chosen to be American.

I was never a political appointee, but a senior government analyst with expert knowledge of Russia. Unlike agency heads and other managers, who rarely obtain deep expertise and don't normally see original and unprocessed intelligence reports, my position was as an analytical "worker bee." It enabled me to work with raw intelligence, such as communications intercepts, satellite imagery, and reports from actual foreign spies. I dealt with highly sensitive information in the original foreign language, and sometimes even with the information before it officially became "intelligence." It wasn't uncommon for me to have special highly restricted access to information that even most three-star generals or senior government officials did not have. This was because, unlike mine, their jobs did not require them to work with raw intelligence reporting, nor could they read raw materials in the original language. Raw intelligence rarely comes in English!

The political appointees, whom we referred to ironically as the "Chiefs," made policy by reading finished intelligence, or FINTEL, which others and I crafted from raw intelligence, or "message traffic." Unlike the Chiefs, us "Indians"—as we called ourselves—were unconstrained by politics. When the Chiefs were called by *their* higher ups or Congress to brief or to testify, we prepped them, created their talking points, and accompanied them as "plus ones." The Chiefs, in turn, lent "top cover" to us if the policy "customer" did not like our analytic conclusions. Good Chiefs, as a rule, don't throw good Indians under the bus.

During my career, among those I briefed were CIA director John Brennan, DIA director Michael Flynn, Supreme Allied Commander

Europe (SACEUR) and head of the U.S. European Combatant Command General Philip Breedlove, and General Robert Kehler, the head of U.S. Strategic Command, or STRATCOM, the combatant command in Omaha, Nebraska, that oversees U.S. nuclear forces. STRATCOM tasked me and some of my colleagues to help devise a plan for defending America from a Russian nuclear strike. I also had the privilege of briefing vice chairman of the Joint Chiefs of Staff General Paul Selva as he prepared to take that position.

Having grown up in the USSR, I have firsthand experience of Russian-style totalitarian oppression. Unlike analysts who learned about Russia from textbooks without ever setting foot into the Bear's lair or even speaking the language, I am familiar with the mindset, behavior, and motivations of Russian leaders. I am fully bilingual, and I am a graduate of Moscow State Pedagogical University, where I completed a study of English that began in the third grade.

After the September 11 terrorist attacks, I was inspired by then president George W. Bush's call to serve, and I chose to enter public service as an intelligence officer. As an immigrant who enjoyed living the American dream as a business executive, I felt called to do whatever I could to prevent another attack on my adopted homeland.

Raised by anti-communist, America-loving parents, I was proud to serve as an American intelligence officer. I learned it was important to speak inconvenient truths about threats I uncovered, regardless of which political party was in charge. While my service in the Intelligence Community began during George W. Bush's administration, the bulk of my career as an intelligence officer was working with the Obama administration. And the inconvenient truth I learned was that the most dangerous threat to America during those years was Putin's Russia, despite Obama administration policies.

While there has always been mutual distrust and intense rivalry between Russia and America, it escalated in 2013, when Moscow ramped up its covert spy wars against the United States. What followed were signs of a troubling and expanding threat—whether it was Russian leaders' inflammatory rhetoric directed at Washington and NATO, the relentless cyber-hacking of our computer systems by Russian intelligence services, or the massive and provocative military drills by Russian armed forces, some daringly close to our homeland.

The Russian government during and after the 2016 U.S. presidential election stoked American racial divisions, ideological and political polarization, a profound distrust of government itself, and seething voter anger over the election results. The belief that Putin put Trump in office was fueled by a Russian intelligence operation. This operation and Russia's overall destabilization campaign against America are built upon Russia's sophisticated knowledge of existing tensions within American society and a deep understanding of how Americans think and behave. The 2016 covert operation helped to spur a so-called resistance campaign in America and the divisive twenty-five-million-dollar two-year probe by Mueller. Though the investigation found no evidence of collusion, out of nothing it generated questions about the legitimacy of Trump's victory in a manner unlike any election in recent memory, including George W. Bush's in 2000.

Some of the crises we have experienced are neither an accident nor a coincidence. It is Putin's playbook. As the often cynical and sometimes conspiratorial Russians like to say, "It is not by chance, Comrade!" (*Eto ne sluchayno, Tovarishch!*) As Mueller stated on the very first page of his 448-page report, "The Russian government interfered in the 2016 presidential election in sweeping and systematic fashion."[5] Indeed, Moscow unleashed in the run-up to the 2016 electoral season what we call in the intel world a "covert-influence campaign" aimed at dismantling our country.[6] Former CIA and NSA director General Michael Hayden has called this highly sophisticated operation "just about the most successful covert-influence campaign in history."[7]

This covert operation continued through the 2018 congressional elections and into the 2020 U.S. presidential elections. U.S. federal prosecutors, in charges against the finance chief of Putin's 2016 covert influence campaign, revealed that the 2016 operation was also intended to disrupt the November 2018 elections and "aggravate conflict between minorities and the rest of the population" by supporting radical groups.[8] Following the 2020 presidential election, U.S. Intelligence officials concluded that Putin directed election influence operations during the 2020 election campaign[9]—although, once again, there was foolhardy anti-Trump bias in the analysis.

Such campaigns are hardly a new phenomenon for American intelligence. The Soviet Union looked to undermine the United States throughout the decades-long Cold War. But what the intelligence and national security communities see today is "a significant escalation in directness, level of activity, and scope of effort."

Unlike other books on Russia that focus on certain aspects of the confrontation, such as the now disproven "Trump-Russia collusion," I have written this book to expose the full Russian strategy threatening to destroy America. The much-discussed election interference is important, of course, but it is only a single page in Putin's playbook.

I want to warn Americans how unprepared the U.S. government bureaucracy is to deal with Putin's playbook and how unaware it is in general that the playbook exists. For not only was Russia's intervention in the 2016 election not preempted or disrupted, our intelligence and security apparatus was played by Putin. The former KGB operative and his security services were able to outsmart their American counterparts because, based on my personal experience, there is a shortage of true Russia expertise in the U.S. government and a lack of a strategic approach to assessing foreign threats. The bureaucracy is much more interested in and adept at pursuing political infighting and waging personal vendettas than deciphering secrets about an adversary's schemes, which are camouflaged in the cloud of foreign language and elaborate deception techniques. Employees whose analytical judgments are at odds with the dominant bureaucratic party line, who rock the groupthink boat, are perceived as more of a potent threat by American apparatchiks than the geopolitical tricks of Putin, Kim Jong-un, or Xi Jinping.

Such deficiencies are dangerous for American security. Unwilling to contradict the Obama administration's erroneous view of Russia as a "regional power"[10] that would happily bend to America's will and "reset" into a malleable Washington buddy, ████████████ ██ ██ ██ ██ ██ ████████████████████████████████████ This was a mistake. DIA's mission was unique at the time. Unlike other intelligence agencies, ██ ██ ████████████████████████████████

So, as Putin purloined Ukraine's Crimea, intervened in Syria, and was gearing up to sabotage our 2016 presidential election, ██████████ ████████████████████████████████ The Pentagon's top intelligence officer for the Russian target, a man who was my mentor, was fired based on unfounded accusations of being a Russian spy. He was a retired U.S. Army officer and a Russian linguist who risked his life leading dangerous HUMINT operations against Moscow at the end of the Cold War and after the collapse of the Soviet regime. Never for a second did my close colleagues or I think that this American patriot was working for the Russians. 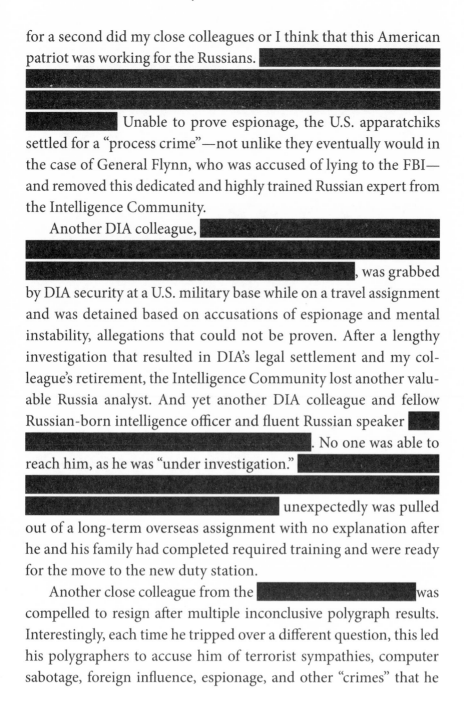 Unable to prove espionage, the U.S. apparatchiks settled for a "process crime"—not unlike they eventually would in the case of General Flynn, who was accused of lying to the FBI— and removed this dedicated and highly trained Russian expert from the Intelligence Community.

Another DIA colleague, , was grabbed by DIA security at a U.S. military base while on a travel assignment and was detained based on accusations of espionage and mental instability, allegations that could not be proven. After a lengthy investigation that resulted in DIA's legal settlement and my colleague's retirement, the Intelligence Community lost another valuable Russia analyst. And yet another DIA colleague and fellow Russian-born intelligence officer and fluent Russian speaker . No one was able to reach him, as he was "under investigation." unexpectedly was pulled out of a long-term overseas assignment with no explanation after he and his family had completed required training and were ready for the move to the new duty station.

Another close colleague from the was compelled to resign after multiple inconclusive polygraph results. Interestingly, each time he tripped over a different question, this led his polygraphers to accuse him of terrorist sympathies, computer sabotage, foreign influence, espionage, and other "crimes" that he didn't commit. I have no doubt in my mind that my friend was no foreign spy or saboteur, but a dedicated and talented American intelligence officer who became another victim of the government bureaucracy and DIA security. His polygraph troubles were likely related to anxiety and a heart condition from which he suffered in the aftermath of his father's death, as well as years of stress working at the Pentagon's J-2, which handles daily intelligence threats.

By early January 2017, when I was no longer with DIA, I was stunned to learn that my closest senior colleague, professional partner, and mentor had been suspiciously reassigned to a different intelligence target. He's a U.S. Army veteran and fluent Russian speaker who knows the Russian target inside and out, and he was involuntarily transferred from his position as the Pentagon's top intelligence analyst for Russia/Eurasia to a Latin American position. I still do not know the real reason why during the second term of the Obama administration, scores of Russia analysts were being forced out of the DIA. █████████████████ ███████████████████████████████ ███████ did not fit the original narrative of the friendly "reset" policy the Obama White House pursued. What is also clear to me is that Russia expertise became a liability rather than an asset for the Intelligence Community *nomenklatura*.

On January 6, 2017, U.S. intelligence made public a declassified version of a highly classified assessment entitled, "Assessing Russian Activities and Intentions in Recent U.S. Elections."[11] This document, which was presented to the American people as an Intelligence Community Assessment (ICA), was authored by only three of the seventeen U.S. intelligence agencies—CIA, FBI, and NSA—and not coordinated with the rest of the agencies, including DIA. These three agencies assessed "with high confidence" that "Russian President Vladimir Putin ordered an influence campaign in 2016 aimed at the U.S. presidential election."[12] They also claimed that President Putin and the Russian government did this to "help President-elect Trump's election chances" and "harm" Secretary Clinton's "electability and potential presidency."[13]

As an expert on Russian strategy and cyber doctrine, I categorically dispute the portion of the assessment concerning Russia's intentions to help then candidate Trump.

As Putin's playbook shows, Russia was trying not only to hurt both candidates Clinton and Trump, but to harm ordinary Americans by destabilizing our society through deceit, disinformation, and agitation. The Russians also knew, through their in-depth "study" of our society—i.e., by spying on our country and its citizens—that they could count on certain internal American help, witting or unwitting. As the Justice Department's investigations have shown, CIA, FBI, and DNI leadership played a critical, if unintentional, role in Putin's subversion strategy against America. Declassified transcripts of congressional testimonies of Obama administration members reveal that several of them vigorously promoted the "Russia-Trump collusion" narrative on cable TV shows while admitting to congressional investigators behind closed doors that no direct and specific evidence of such a conspiracy existed.[14]

The "Declassified Annex A" to the report by the DOJ's Office of the Inspector General also reveals that the FBI was concerned that the infamous Steele Dossier, which included numerous unsubstantiated and outlandish allegations of Russian collusion by Trump and his campaign, was instead disinformation planted by the Russian intelligence services.[15] And yet, the feds continued with their counterintelligence probe into the Trump campaign and dubious surveillance of its members, such as Carter Page. Intent on finding a crime instead of the truth, the FBI obtained authority several times from a secret U.S. court to spy on an innocent U.S. citizen, all based on deficient and partly "cooked" FISA applications. Instead of protecting Americans from Russia's interference in American politics, U.S. intelligence and law enforcement became an enabler and amplifier of Russian subversion of America.

The American people were, therefore, hit with a double-whammy—first by an external Russian adversary and then by internal American foes. These highly placed government functionaries, driven by their disdain for the unorthodox presidential candidate and desire to displace him, neglected their mission. Instead of identifying and neutralizing threats to American security, they became useful idiot soldiers in Putin's war on America.

Americans on both sides of the political spectrum have the incentive to divert the attention from the Russia issue. Democrats want to sweep under the rug not only that the Obama administration's security apparatus missed the Russian threat, but that it effectively served as a device in Putin's toolbox that was deployed to destabilize our country. Republicans are focused on probing the investigators of the fake Trump-Putin conspiracy theory. They are reluctant to relate the Russia issue and the 2016 elections because the faulty January 6, 2017, ICA created the perception that Trump was elected with Putin's help. The needs of both sides may create the impression that Russia had no role in the 2016 upheaval in American politics and society.

It would be at our own peril for Americans to ignore the Russian threat. Putin and his playbook are not going away any time soon. Having orchestrated a constitutional amendment allowing Russian presidents to serve more than two terms, the former KGB operative secured his presidency for life, or at minimum until 2036.[16] Even if Putin unexpectedly abandons the presidency due to illness or death, his successor will likely continue with his anti-American playbook. As readers will learn from this book, Russia's perception of America as its main enemy and Moscow's anti-American policy and strategy have been consistent for the last century, regardless of who sits at the top of the Russian government. It is time for America to develop a viable, reality-based policy rather than playing endless "reset" games or tit-for-tat "gotchas" with the Kremlin.

This will require strategic foresight and analytical competence with respect to Russia in our national security apparatus. It will also require our intelligence and law enforcement officials to spend the time, however long it takes, to identify, understand, and prevent foreign threats to America's security. They must not be allowed to waste enormous energy and resources staging feckless impeachment trials and pursuing personal vendettas against patriotic Americans whose politics, professional views, or personal style they don't like. Destroying dedicated public servants like General Flynn and many others, who were forced to defend themselves from false accusations or outright "framing," will not make our country safer—it will do the opposite, in fact.[17]

Such abuse of power and waste of government resources makes our country less safe, due to the loss of critical expertise and diversion of what resources and expertise are left from the true mission of intelligence. As we saw in 2020, the government was blindsided by the sudden spread of the coronavirus pandemic, which originated in China at the very moment it was preoccupied with the impeachment trial of President Trump. We will never know whether Americans would have had to endure the same level of devastation of its population and economy by COVID-19 if U.S. intelligence had provided adequate warning to the country about the impending pandemic.

Similarly, it is fair to ask what sort of quantity and quality of resources the U.S. intelligence had positioned against the Russian target in the run-up to the 2016 presidential election. What percentage of these resources was working the actual Russia threat, as opposed to digging into the non-existent crimes of U.S. citizens as part of the unfounded counterintelligence probe into the Trump campaign? The American people, whose confidence in the integrity of presidential elections has been shattered, deserve to know the answers to these questions.

It is important to point out to the readers that my book has no hidden political agenda. There is no intent to favor one political party or another in this book when it comes to my professional intelligence judgments on Russia and Putin. A threat is a threat. It doesn't change based on who holds the reins of power on Capitol Hill and in the White House. Both American political parties have pursued ineffective, sometimes foolish, and even dangerous Russia policies. As an author, I will do the same thing I did as an intelligence officer—speak the truth as I see it. The difference now is that my audience is the American public, in addition to U.S. and allied military and political leaders.

Putin's playbook also has profound implications for our economy and way of life. By supporting radical groups, the old judo-loving, former Soviet KGB agent from St. Petersburg is increasing the chances that socialism resurfaces in America. As I write, it is the presidential electoral season, and leading Democratic candidates are proudly proposing socialist ideas. It would be ironic if, through the clandestine actions of former communist Vladimir Putin, America were to join the ranks of failed socialist countries. Socialism is an evil system, which I grew up under. It is incompatible with freedom and democracy. Socialism is inhumane because it forces people to do unethical things out of desperation. It doesn't work because it is based on unrealistic theories that ignore human nature. It has failed everywhere, including in the USSR. And Putin knows it could also destroy America.

Socialism idealistically looks for government to create complete equality in society and to end suffering—a noble-sounding idea. To achieve this goal, a socialist government promises to give everyone life's necessities, regardless of an individual's ability to pay or desire to work. However, governments must find the money for all these necessities. Historically, they have confiscated wealth and income to pay for them. Ultimately, the government runs everything.

Lessons I learned as a child are worth repeating to younger Americans today. The first problem with socialism is not only that socialists eventually run out of other people's money, as Margaret Thatcher famously said in 1976; it is also that socialist societies stop producing wealth altogether. If individuals cannot keep the wealth they create, they stop creating it. In the USSR, we used to say, "They pretend to pay us, and we pretend to work." Most people made a rational decision to do mediocre work, because the same amount was paid regardless of how hard they worked.

Once the socialist state kills entrepreneurship, the society will stop innovating. Do you know why Americans have a potato peeler, garlic crusher, and apple cutter in their kitchens, for example, while Russians use a knife for everything? Because there was no financial incentive for Soviet citizens to create them. The same logic, tragically, would apply to creating blood pressure medicine and cures for cancer.

The second problem with socialism is that, as scarcity of goods grows, those in charge of wealth redistribution—the state—start taking care of their needs first, rationing goods and services for everyone except themselves. There comes a point when the society simply doesn't produce enough necessities, forcing ordinary people who are not part of the state apparatus to cheat and steal to survive. Two distinct classes of people form: those who are part of the government system, or the privileged, and everyone else, the oppressed.

In the Soviet Union, the Communist Party elites—we called them *apparatchiki,* because they were part of the state apparatus—had everything, and the rest of the people struggled. We lacked such basics as toothpaste, panty hose, toilet paper, and sanitary products. The party members, who formed under 10 percent of the Soviet adult population, shopped at different grocery stores, were treated at different medical facilities, and had other privileges. Everyone, for example, had "free" medical care, but you only went to see a doctor if there was an emergency. Going to a dentist was an especially terrifying experience; I would not hesitate to call it torture because teeth were drilled without Novocain. It's an unforgettable experience. The dentist's daughter needed her teeth fixed as well, I assumed. So, who can blame the dentist for hoarding Novocain for his family? My mother was stealing meat from the food factory where she worked to feed our family. My family was not particularly poor by Soviet standards, but there was nothing to buy. There were simply not enough goods and services for everyone, although they were all technically "free."

A third problem with socialism is the complete state control over the individual. In fact, being called an "individualist" has a derogatory connotation in Russian. Under socialism, since the state "takes care" of its people by providing everything "for free," it plays the dominant role in all spheres of life. It tells you what to do, where to live, what to wear, what to say, and what to think. The state censors everything. There is a law and a rule for everything. There is no free press, literature, or cinematography. No religion. No presumption of innocence. No real rights. No private property. Suppression of dissent is routine and brutal. Eventually, people start to self-censor to avoid persecution. You speak and appear to think "correctly."

Socialism creates a society of "one-percenters" and "ninety-nine-percenters," except the one-percenters are the ones who redistribute wealth, not the ones who create it. Having lived in a country where everything was "free," but nothing was available, I am terrified when

I hear proposals for a single-payer medical system, "Medicare for all," or "free college for all."

During the past few years, I have increasingly felt like I was back in the USSR. The rise of pervasive political correctness, growing intolerance towards religious people, and alienation of and even attacks on people whose views don't conform to the mainstream orthodoxy remind me of my childhood and youth in the USSR. I find myself repeating the same admonitions to my young children that my mother frequently gave to me and my sister: "Don't believe everything that you hear on TV, think for yourself, and keep your and your family's views private." Ironically, just like my parents tried to shield me from untruths and brainwashing by Soviet schools by explaining the vicissitudes of real life and the truth hiding behind Soviet indoctrination at our dinner table, I found myself pulling my children from public schools and placing them into religious schools in order to avoid heavy and biased government-sponsored indoctrination. It was painful for me to watch my little ones coming home and spouting how oppressive America is when I know firsthand what oppression really means. I also could not bear watching my kids coming home sad and confused because they were simply not old enough to be bombarded with all the sex-related ideas and concepts that the school pushed on them under the rubric of "family education." My American-born husband and I agreed that family education truly belongs within the family.

Following the 2020 presidential election, I cannot help but be alarmed by the monumental shift towards socialism and ever-increasing government control over many aspects of our lives. Big Tech and the mainstream media's taking on the roles of the government's mouthpieces and agents of influence is frightening. Silencing those who express "incorrect" opinions by deplatforming them on social media, banning their books, getting them fired from their jobs, and blacklisting them to ensure they cannot make a living—simply because they have strayed from the "party line"—is the method of totalitarian states to suppress dissent and ensure total control. I sincerely hope more and more of our citizens wake up and recognize these early markers of a Sovietization of America so that we can regain the freedom of the America that my mother sent me to at a young age. Socialism inevitably results in stagnation and tyranny. I hope Americans keep the right to bake a cake that doesn't violate their religious beliefs—or not bake it at all—maintain the freedom to express unpopular views without fear of being ostracized by fellow citizens or losing their jobs, continue to enjoy presumption of innocence and due process, and be free from unlawful government surveillance for having "incorrect" politics or working for the "wrong" presidential campaign.

Spreading socialism and intolerance in America is part of Putin's playbook, an ugly result of Russian election meddling.

Putin's Ministry of Truth produced a nifty name for Russia, calling it a "sovereign democracy." What it really means is that the sovereign rules from the top of the "democracy," wielding total control over lesser mortals. Similarly, in America today, many young people are so brainwashed by the public schools and universities that have been cultivating socialist ideas and the "us versus them" culture that they are unable to contemplate what a truly socialist government would do to them. For a sobering look at human impoverishment and psychological enslavement, every American should read Soviet dissident writer Yevgeny Zamyatin's magnum opus, *We*. It served as a blueprint for George Orwell's *Nineteen Eighty-Four*. Both books offer an eerie warning of what it feels like to live in a totalitarian system. The Soviet Union banned both books. The punishment for having one of them on you was imprisonment.

Today, we are living in a "new normal" of the Russian-American conflict, as the U.S. Intelligence Community has described it.[18] To cope with this reality, Americans and their leaders will need to learn how to recognize and respond to Putin-ordered anti-American activities.

It's time Americans learned the truth, uncomfortable as it may be: the Kremlin is not just considering or preparing for war—it is already at war with us. Although this war is mostly invisible so far, except to a select group of political and military experts, it could escalate into a direct military conflict at any time. Even test runs for actual Russian military attacks from the air and sea are underway, some very close to our borders.[19] This is why intelligence and national security leaders from both Democratic and Republican administrations have expressed deep concern about the Russian threat, even if policymakers haven't always been attentive.

These concerns have heightened dramatically since Moscow's escalation of cyberwarfare on U.S. soil. Recent cyberattacks have hit various sectors of the U.S. economy and our critical infrastructure, including nuclear facilities, and the beating heart of the U.S. government: the White House, the State Department, and the Pentagon.[20]

Until we clearly recognize its full extent, we cannot develop an effective counterstrategy against the Russian threat. To acknowledge it, Americans must stop politicizing the issue and conflating the Russian threat with political issues, like whether Donald Trump was placed in office by Putin. (He wasn't.) Until then, Russia will be able to continue putting us at each other's throats while patiently executing Putin's playbook.

The truth is Russia's mission was not to elect Trump in 2016 or 2020, even had Putin preferred him, but to disrupt the most important symbol of American democracy—the presidential election—and to generate chaos.[21] Putin's motive was mostly to shake our belief in the legitimacy of the American presidency, regardless of who occupied the White House.

Thus, the process was set in place to discredit our electoral process and foment massive discontent and confrontation. The angrier the divide, the more the extremists on either side hold sway. Putin's plan is working, even if he is only partially responsible. It's clear he is having an effect, given the total focus on Russia for the past four years.

Putin, of course, explicitly denies it all. But if you look carefully, you can see that he also implicitly admits it. A man with Putin's ego would not want to let such an achievement go uncredited.

A crafty former intelligence operative and Soviet apparatchik who ran the KGB's successor, the FSB, Putin is skilled in the art of intentional ambiguity, an integral feature of the Russian statecraft. During a press conference at the July 2018 Putin-Trump summit, the former KBG spy made remarks that subtly signaled the Kremlin's responsibility for the 2016 election interference—without acknowledging it directly.

In response to a reporter's question about why we should believe Putin that Russia didn't intervene in the 2016 election, Putin suggested that trust is not a concept that applies to great-power politics. "Where did you get this idea that President Trump trusts me or I trust him? He defends the interests of the United States of America, and I do defend the interests of the Russian Federation."[22]

Putin's dismissal of trust was, paradoxically, a moment of candor. From the Russian point of view, it is perfectly reasonable for the Kremlin to meddle in U.S. elections if it suits Russia's security interests. And it is also logical to Russians that the U.S. president—and the U.S. public—would not trust the Russian president's own assurances that his country didn't meddle.

Russia, like the United States, does not overtly acknowledge its intelligence operations. But Moscow regularly employs strategic ambiguity and signaling, such as Putin's denials, to confuse, as well as to warn, an adversary.

Such techniques come directly from Russian doctrinal writings, which are in this book to illustrate the grave threat. These Russian government materials—such as the Russian Military Doctrine,[23] National Security Strategy,[24] Foreign Policy Concept,[25] Information Security Doctrine,[26] as well as various presidential edicts—codify the Kremlin's views on the conduct of war. They serve as the guideposts for Moscow's military and political leaders, supplying the legal framework and justification for the use of Russian armed forces and its intelligence operations. They are also the basis for formulating military plans, including those that target the United States.

Because these documents are in Russian and are often filled with obscure military jargon, they are inaccessible to most Americans, as well as other U.S. intelligence analysts who often have an insufficient command of the Russian language and, in particular, the Russian military lexicon. Readers of this book will have access to information beyond the reach of most policymakers and even our so-called intelligence "professionals."

Even for those American-born analysts who speak Russian, it is extremely difficult to estimate Russia's geopolitical intentions and predict Putin's behavior. In a 2017 interview with an online publication, General Hayden lamented the challenge of understanding Putin's mindset. At the same time, Hayden revealed Russia was not as much of a priority as the Soviet Union was for U.S. intelligence, which had been focused on terrorism for more than a decade.[27] In my own experience as an intelligence analyst, my colleagues and ▮▮▮▮▮▮▮▮ ▮▮▮▮▮▮▮▮▮▮▮▮▮▮▮▮▮▮▮▮▮▮▮ as well as to get the attention of policymakers, especially during Obama's first term. The feeling within the IC bureaucracy and in the Pentagon's policy circles was that since the United States was not planning to go to war with

Russia, there was no need to worry about Russia's military doctrine and plans.

Two years after General Hayden admitted that collecting secrets on Russia had not been a priority for American intelligence for thirteen years—a period covering both Democratic and Republican administrations—President Trump's CIA director Gina Haspel made a stunning admission. In her unclassified remarks in April 2019, Ms. Haspel revealed that after years of heavy emphasis on counterterrorism in the wake of 9/11, the CIA had finally shifted its central focus to Russia and Iran.[28] This was nine years after Russia codified NATO as its primary national security danger in its 2010 Military Doctrine,[29] eleven years after Moscow invaded Georgia, and five years since Putin chopped off the Crimean part of Ukraine.

While General Hayden and Ms. Haspel deserve our gratitude for their years of government service, the ultimate reason that intelligence agencies exist is to avoid what we call "strategic surprise." It is impossible for intelligence analysts to detect an anomaly or a new development if they are not watching the target.

If the goal is only to issue a report two years later informing the American people that Russians interfered in the 2016 election, then we don't need seventeen intelligence agencies. The United States, however, keeps a robust intelligence apparatus, with unrivaled technological capability, to uncover and combat threats before they materialize.

America must take a much more serious and apolitical approach when dealing with Russia. Friendship should be the furthest from our minds. We cannot afford to base our relationship with Russia on sentiments or gimmicks, like looking into Putin's eyes and seeing his soul, as George W. Bush once said he did,[30] or giving the Russian foreign minister a Staples gadget bearing a mistranslation of the word "reset," like Hillary Clinton did.[31] We need to be prepared instead to win a war with Russia.

In writing about Putin's threat to the United States, I wanted also to write a story within a story about my personal battle to get our government to sharpen our intelligence analysis of Russia so we could understand what Putin has been up to and thwart him. I will talk about the struggles mission-driven, rank-and-file intelligence officers have with government careerists. That is not the primary purpose of this book, which is to provide a sobering analysis of the extraordinary peril Russia continues to pose to this country. But I also believe my story is a cautionary tale about how the inflexible and misguided bureaucracy that in many ways runs this country hampers our ability to nimbly face challenges from abroad.

At the DIA, I was in a unique position to understand Putin and his aims, because I am Russian-born and grew up in the culture and thinking that produced him. This led me to conclusions that sometimes differed starkly from colleagues who assumed Russians think like we do. They absolutely do not. In addition to holding a different frame of reference, I worked hard, to the point of dismaying government functionaries, who felt oddly threatened by a Russian-American woman's showing up at the office on a Sunday to put in the extra hours for the country she loves. I produced what I knew were original ideas, was frequently tapped for high-profile assignments because generals and diplomats wanted to hear my briefings, and did my best to tell the unvarnished truth as I understood it rather than simply telling others what they wanted to hear.

I learned that it is not uncommon even for our own U.S. government to take a page out of Putin's playbook. Some rogue bureaucrats routinely deploy Putin-style measures to destroy the lives and careers of fellow civil servants and other innocent Americans who find themselves on the wrong side of the party line. Politicizing intelligence analysis, weaponizing government activities such as the security clearance process, and even targeting U.S. citizens with unlawful government surveillance are some of these bureaucrats' most proficient weapons. Once the bureaucracy identifies you as someone who is unwilling to march in lockstep with the establishment, it begins to inexorably grind you down.

Putin knows well we won't easily defeat him if we continue to mimic what brought down the Soviet Union: an ever-expanding government ruled by apparatchiks more concerned with protecting their positions and pensions than safeguarding the United States of America.

It is my hope that *Putin's Playbook* will ignite a meaningful national conversation, one that goes beyond politics and juvenile, Russian-concocted "Steele Dossiers," about Russia's extraordinary threat to America today.

Characterizing this threat, in July 2018, former director of national intelligence (DNI) Dan Coats, in a reference to the signs of threat before the September 11 terrorist attacks, described Russia as projecting a similar "blinking red light."[32]

This book will reveal what that blinking red light is.

Why Can't We Be Friends?

"The United States will strive to weaken and dismember the rest of the world, and first of all the big Eurasia. This strategy is pursued by the White House regardless of whether it is occupied by the conservative or liberal administration or whether or not there is consensus among the elites."

—*A Russian analytic agency in the Russian publication* Foreign Policy

Russia is not America's friend. There are three basic reasons why.

First, there is a deeply rooted, century-long distrust between the two countries that's not easily erased.

Second, each country views itself as exceptional—anointed to shape the world in its own image.

And third, American and Russian leaders define their countries' national interests in such a way that places them on a geopolitical collision course.

The United States broke off diplomatic relations with Russia's new Bolshevik regime in December 1917, shortly after it seized power from

Czar Nicholas II during the bloody October Revolution. The United States did not recognize the new Soviet Union until Franklin Roosevelt became president in 1933. It was the last country in the world to do so.[1]

Throughout the post–World War II Cold War, Russia and the United States viewed one another as their chief adversaries, each fearing that the other would unleash a surprise nuclear attack. Global politics were shaped by this antagonistic relationship and largely governed by the doctrine of "mutually assured destruction," or MAD. According to MAD, the Soviet Union and the United States both maintained a portion of their vast nuclear arsenal on a hair-trigger, ensuring a retaliatory strike could swiftly be launched to wipe out the other nation—and the rest of the world with it.[2] This nuclear posture, whereby each superpower effectively held a "cocked and loaded" gun to the other's head, was supposed to make it unthinkable for either to launch a nuclear strike.

MAD or not, the Soviet Union, according to a former top-secret CIA report declassified in 1993, was prepared to wage and win a nuclear war.[3] This may help explain why the Soviets were willing to push confrontation to a very dangerous edge. The Cuban Missile Crisis of 1962, during which the Soviets placed nuclear weapons in Cuba to deter a U.S. invasion following a failed CIA operation to overthrow the Castro regime, is considered to be the closest the two superpowers came to a nuclear conflict.[4]

Growing up in Kazakhstan, I remember well fears of an American nuclear attack that the Soviet leadership instilled in us. I have memories of running outside in the middle of a school day, at the sound of a siren and hastily pulling on a gas mask with an elephant trunk hose—as though it would make a difference—to seek shelter in a nearby structure.

The legacy of this distrustful, hostile, and fearful relationship persists tenaciously to this day. Russia never abandoned its belief that the United States was its chief rival. Paid to be distrustful, national security officials in both countries continue to develop military capabilities and doctrines that would protect their respective countries from the other.

The Pentagon, after years of chasing ISIS and Al-Qaeda, has recently placed Russia back at the top of its threat list.[5] While the public's fear of nuclear war has subsided, the weapons are still there, ready to be launched within minutes. Russia and America have over 90 percent of the world's nuclear forces, and their systems are on high alert. The end of the world, it turns out, may well be nigh.

Just how entrenched distrust of Russians is within U.S. intelligence circles is seen in a statement made by former director of national intelligence James Clapper during an interview with NBC News. Commenting on Russia's intervention in the 2016 election, he accused the Russians of being genetically predisposed to lies and craftiness.[6]

While I am ethnically Russian, I was not offended by this remark. Although I might caution Mr. Clapper that it's not genetic, it is an aspect of Russian character. This is hardly surprising. The repressive society I grew up in was one where telling the truth could get you imprisoned—or worse. And my experience as a U.S. intelligence officer taught me that Ronald Reagan's famous maxim about dealing with the Russians, "trust but verify," was correct.

The cultures of Russia and the United States are marked by a deeply ingrained sense of uniqueness and superiority, which guides their approaches to national security.[7] Scientific researchers have discovered that cultural differences start emerging in humans as early as three years of age, shaping the way people perceive the world and their relationship to it.[8]

Russians are an enormously proud people. They inhabit the world's largest country, spanning 11 time zones and teeming with vast natural resources. Russians sent the first satellite and first human into space, invented the periodic table of elements, gave to the world the *Nutcracker* and *Swan Lake* ballets, and created some of the world's most profound literature. And, having sacrificed 20 million people in World War II, more than any other nation, Russia also views itself as the world's defender against fascism.

Throughout history, Russia's leaders have cultivated the idea of a unique, divinely inspired civilization, neither Eastern nor Western. This sense of imperial exceptionalism, even during communism, was passed down through generations. Russia was the "Third Rome," successor to the Byzantine Empire. Probably the most recognizable symbol of imperial and holy Russia is the sixteenth-century St. Basil's Cathedral on the Red Square in Moscow, built on orders of Ivan the Terrible, with its ornate, multicolor, onion-shaped domes and gilded Orthodox crosses.

Russia throughout its history has believed itself inscrutable to outsiders. Imperial czars and communist commissars alike played up Russian mystique and unpredictability, so eloquently memorialized by Winston Churchill, who proclaimed in 1939 that "Russia is a riddle wrapped in a mystery inside an enigma." Churchill also recommended a solution to the riddle that is a touchstone for this book: use Russia's national interests as a clue to its behavior.[9]

The Kremlin's current "Czar Vladimir" has revived Russia's sense of exceptionalism, significantly diminished by losing the Cold War and the USSR's collapse. Putin has resurrected the narrative of Russia's being a great power, or *derzhava*, destined by divine providence for leadership, particularly in Eurasia. He has pushed Russia's special "centuries-old" status and "active role" of peacekeeper and "balancing factor in the world civilization" as official Moscow policy.[10] In the old Russian czarist tradition of "gathering the lands," Putin has defined the establishment of dominance over the post-Soviet countries and the "consolidation of the Russian diaspora" as a key strategic priority under the rubric of "Eurasian integration."[11] He linked these ambitions to Russia's core national interest of staying a sovereign superpower in a "multi-polar" world.[12] The problem for U.S.-Russian relations is that achieving this requires Moscow to undermine U.S. foreign policy goals.

To ensure that his subjects view his agenda as sanctioned by the heavens, Putin revived the Russian Orthodox Church, which was decimated during Soviet times. Putin also revived the virulent anti-Americanism of the Cold War, contrasting the "decadent and chaotic West" with "traditional and iron-disciplined Russia." The Russian people, who suffered a crushing identity crisis after the Soviet Empire's collapse—a psychological calamity never fully appreciated by American policymakers—embraced Putin's call to reclaim Mother Russia's rightful place in the world.

Americans believe in the worth and dignity of the individual, a tradition emanating from the Founders, where everyone has God-given rights to life, liberty, and the pursuit of happiness. These concepts, so obvious to Americans, are alien to Russians, who don't share Americans' belief in individual freedoms and the sanctity of every life. Russians have been led to believe that an individual is subordinate to the state, that the well-being of a broader collective is superior to individual rights, and that a single life must be sacrificed if the Motherland decides that it would save or significantly benefit the collective. Russia, ravaged by wars and devastation throughout its one-thousand-year history, is hyper-focused on security. It views too much freedom as chaotic and destabilizing. Russia believes that tyrants like Saddam Hussein and Bashar al-Assad serve their own purpose in preserving security and the status quo. Stalin, who murdered millions of Soviet people, is still a popular Russian leader. These views are shocking and even abhorrent to Americans, whose national psyche was formed on the notion of natural and inalienable rights and freedoms. Aside from the Civil War, Americans have not experienced war's massive destruction on their soil, and even then not by a foreign power.

When American leaders pursue global human rights, aiding countries in building democracy or intervening on behalf of oppressed groups, they believe they are making the world a better place. But Russians, both the people and government officials, are deeply skeptical of Washington's motivations. They believe that America is "exporting" democracy to other countries through military interventions to control that country's politics and economy. This interpretation is consistent with Russia's worldview, where it is normal for big and powerful countries to dominate small neighboring ones. Small countries do not have a right to independence but should subordinate their national interests to a protectorate, such as Russia.

Conversely, when Russia uses military force and subterfuge to prevent its post-Soviet neighbors like Georgia and Ukraine from leaving its orbit and joining NATO and the European Union, American leaders don't accept that Russia wants to preserve a strategic buffer zone for security reasons. The United States believes that any country, regardless of its size, can pursue political and economic independence. Americans, therefore, view Moscow's actions towards post-Soviet states as authoritarian and immoral, rather than balance-of-power politics. Washington's morality-centered statecraft comes in conflict with Russian nationalism and realpolitik.

This stark contrast in outlook is found in the United States' refusal to accept Russia's annexation of Crimea or its quasi-occupation of eastern Ukraine, or in Moscow's development and fielding of treaty-breaking, ground-launched cruise missiles (GLCM) that would enable Russia to deliver short-notice nuclear strikes on Europe. In response, Barack Obama placed economic sanctions on Russia, which President Trump extended. Trump also authorized the sale of lethal weapons to Ukraine to help Kiev fight the Russians, a move the Obama Administration resisted out of concern for escalating the conflict further. Trump also announced his decision to withdraw from the Intermediate-Range Nuclear Forces Treaty (INF) in six months if Russia did not return to compliance, prompting Putin to suspend Russia's compliance with the treaty in what he called a "symmetric" response. With America's recent formal withdrawal from the Treaty, it has collapsed.[13]

No matter the pressure, Putin will not return Crimea to Ukraine, and he will not back down from his general stance toward Ukraine. Moscow interprets Washington's tough economic actions as part of a long-term strategy to destroy Russia.

In the aftermath of Latvia's, Estonia's, and Lithuania's escaping Russia's orbit by joining NATO, in addition to Poland's, Hungary's, Czech Republic's, Bulgaria's, Slovakia's, and Slovenia's joining the NATO club, Putin declared Ukraine a "red line" where he would stop Western expansion.[14] Driven by the centuries-old fear of hostile Western "encirclement," Russia, as early as 1993, six years before Putin became Russian president, designated NATO expansion close to its borders as a danger to its security that had to be countered.[15]

In his classified diplomatic cable in 1946, George Kennan, considered the most brilliant American diplomat of the modern era, who had a superb understanding of Russian behavior, described Moscow's worldview in the following way: "At the bottom of the Kremlin's neurotic view of world affairs is traditional and instinctive Russian sense of insecurity." Its origin lies in the "land which has never known a friendly neighbor." The "insecurity of a peaceful agricultural people trying to live on a vast exposed plain in the neighborhood of a fierce nomadic people" drove Russia's instinct to allow no compromise with a rival power.[16] The same mindset persists in today's Russia.

Putin will wage low-intensity conflict and tactical devastation in Ukraine and Georgia if NATO continues to court them for membership. Putin's strategy is to prevent the former Soviet Union countries from meeting the NATO membership criteria of having territorial integrity and being free of an ongoing conflict. Consistent with this strategy, Putin has chopped off parts of Georgia, Abkhazia, and South Ossetia into separate autonomous states, annexed Ukrainian Crimea, and since 2014 has been conducting destabilization operations through separatist proxies in eastern Ukraine. The conduct of this policy is brutal and deadly, with little regard to suffering.

Since the 1940s, American grand strategy has been centered on preventing the USSR and Russia from dominating Eurasia. Kennan, the founding father of this approach to Russia, recommended a "long-term, patient but firm and vigilant policy of containment" that was "designed to confront the Russians with unalterable counterforce at every point."[17] Consistent with this advice, Washington has managed a multi-dimensional policy of containment, democracy promotion, and strengthening of NATO both before and after the collapse of the Soviet Union. Ronald Reagan's White House, according to a declassified top secret strategy report, sought "to avoid a nuclear war while preventing a single hostile power or coalition of powers from dominating the Eurasian land-mass or other strategic regions" and "to assist democratic and nationalist movements where possible in the struggle against totalitarian regimes."[18]

Similarly, President George H. W. Bush's administration, faced with the collapse of the Soviet Union, sought to prevent the domination of former Soviet bloc countries by a hostile power and "the potential consolidation of control by such a hostile power over the resources" within what it viewed as a critical U.S. security region.[19] But Bush's Russia policy also sought to help Russia and Ukraine become "peaceful democracies and market-driven economies" by way of "demilitarization of their societies, conversion of defense industries to civilian enterprises, and reducing Russia's inventory of nuclear weapons."[20] This policy stemmed in part from concerns about the possibility of nuclear weapons falling into the wrong hands in the aftermath of the demise of the USSR. But Russians typically view any altruistic-sounding overtures as realpolitik dressed up in liberal rhetoric, a cleverly disguised attempt to alter the balance of power.

As George Kennan pointed out, the Russians, fearing our intentions, are fanatical in their belief that "with the [United States], there can be no permanent, peaceful coexistence." Therefore, it is "necessary that the internal harmony of our society be disrupted, our traditional way of life be destroyed, the international authority of our state be broken" for the Russians to feel secure.[21]

As soon as it had put behind the chaotic and economically devastating Boris Yeltsin era in the 1990s, Russia embarked on a new strategy in the 2000s, during Putin's first presidential term. Putin's Russia was "concentrating," or gathering strength, emulating the approach that Imperial Russia took after its defeat in the Crimean War of 1856. This strategy was succinctly captured in the historical phrase written in a circular to foreign powers by then foreign mi-nister Prince Gorchakov. He declared "*La Russie ne bouge pas; elle se recueille.*" It translates, "Russia is not angry; it is concentrating." American political scientist Paul Goble half-jokingly called it the Terminator Doctrine: "I'll be back."[22] Indeed, after a few years of "concentration," the moment it regained strength, Putin's Russia resurrected its role of a counterweight to American power, attempting to disrupt Washington's plans from nearby Ukraine, to near-abroad Syria, to far-off Venezuela.

There are no signs that either country is willing or considers it prudent to stop trying to tilt the balance of power in its own favor.

Putin, clearly aiming to diminish U.S. power projection, has made it Russia's official foreign policy "to counteract military interventions into sovereign states under the guise of responsibility to protect" human rights. In response, following several failed "resets" by the Obama administration, the United States has toughened its policy towards Russia under Trump, contrary to popular perceptions and false collusion narratives. The Trump administration's unclassified 2017 National Security Strategy accused Russia of being a revisionist power, one attempting to revise its standing in the world, creating instability in Eurasia—including Georgia and Ukraine—and thus increasing the probability of an armed conflict in Europe.[23]

Neither country feels that it has any incentives to moderate its behavior. The United States and China have strong economic ties that play a large role in their relationship. But Russia and America have no similar stake in their relationship. To the contrary, Putin was emboldened by the fact that the West did not isolate Russia after its seizure of Crimea. "The rest of the world sees Putin as someone with whom one can do business," former National Intelligence Officer for Russia/Eurasia Dr. Angela Stent points out in her recent book, *Putin's World*. China, Iran, and even Israel are just a few of the major international players who are not turned off by Russia's authoritarian tactics.[24]

Lessening the likelihood that the United States would seek rapprochement was the fact that if Trump had cooperated too closely with Putin, he would have opened himself up to charges that he was "colluding" politically with Russia. Nor still does there seem to be a willingness on either side to develop a deeper understanding of each other.

Sadly, even if Washington did extend an olive branch to Moscow, the gesture would not lead to a long-term improvement in the relationship. Friends and friendship are not part of Russia's lexicon when it comes to geopolitics. To put Russia on the couch for a moment, the fear-filled history that shaped Russia's national psyche means Moscow cannot have real friends in the way that America feels true kinship with Great Britain or Israel. Russia only has occasional transactional partners with whom it strikes advantageous deals. Or worse, it dominates former Soviet vassals, which newly "imperial" Russia considers junior partners rather than independent countries.

Stalin's repressions, including the barbaric practice of encouraging children to snitch on their parents, have wreaked havoc on the Russian psyche, which presumes that today's friend could be tomorrow's state police informer. "One is born alone and one dies alone" was my father's frequent admonition, warning me about the dangers of friendship. This is not to say that Russians are incapable of having deep and lasting friendships—they are. But as a people, Russians have unique reasons to fear friendships, particularly olive branches from foreigners. In response to a question from a reporter in the July 2018 summit with Trump about Russia's interference in the 2016 elections, Putin gave a backhanded acknowledgement that trust between presidents of two rival states like Russia and the United States was impossible.[25] The expectation in the Kremlin is that both countries, and presidents, would be doing whatever is necessary to defend and pursue their national interests. This does not exclude election interference, but it does exclude collusion based on trust or friendship.

Opposing concepts of trust explain why trying to normalize relations with Russia over decades have failed, despite the efforts of U.S. presidents since Roosevelt. Episodic and superficial easing of tensions has occurred from time to time. Though rare, we can even cooperate with Russia when mutual interests coincide, if we watch our backs.

But we cannot—ever—be friends.

CHAPTER 1

Russia's War on America

---

*"Russia is no longer a chopped-off map of the Soviet
Union but a confident great power, with a big future and
glorious people."*

—*Vladimir Putin*

I grew up in a blue-collar family in a small city founded by Russian emperor Peter the Great in Eastern Kazakhstan. At the time I was there, it was part of the Soviet Union. I didn't know it when I was young, but the city was filled with heavy industry, which was producing and processing toxic chemicals. The production of uranium, beryllium, and other rare metals was in support of a super-secret Soviet nuclear project. All I knew was that some of my friends' parents were "mailmen" (*pochtoviki*) because they worked at "mailboxes"—code-words for top-secret facilities and their employees—but I didn't dare ask what that meant. You didn't ask many questions as a Soviet citizen; you were told only what you needed to know.

I never knew why, but since I was little, my mother wanted me to go to America. She hired me a tutor to learn English, in addition to my English classes at school. America was supposed to be everything that the USSR wasn't: full of freedom, plenty of food to eat, clothes that had colors other than gray, and movies with happy endings. The Russian people loved America as much as the Soviet government hated it. They spent monthly salaries on blue jeans, grooved to the Eagles' "Hotel California," and secretly listened to the Voice of America. We were afraid of the American government, though, fearing that war would break out at any moment.

Just as my mother wanted, I finished high school with a gold medal—that is, first in my class—and was accepted to a university in Moscow to become a teacher or a translator of English and French. In my last two years of college, I worked as a tour guide during summer breaks, taking American and British tourists sightseeing around Moscow and to other cities in the USSR. Particularly struck by Americans, I noticed they smelled good, had super white teeth, always smiled, and had an attitude as though nothing was impossible.

I made great friends with them and was invited to come to America. That was in 1989, just before Mr. Gorbachev listened to Ronald Reagan and tore down "this Wall!" I was stunned in America; everyone here had a TV, a Walkman, a VCR, even a car! You could also choose to live in whichever city in America you wanted. Oddly, the sight of Red Delicious apples at the supermarket blew me away. They were clean, red, and shiny. They were fake, I thought; my friends, in a Potemkin village–like manner, had planted the apples to trick me into being overly impressed with America. No—the apples were real! Mother was right. Sometime later, her prediction came true: I became American, living in unimaginable freedom! I naively thought that this new and awe-inspiring feeling of liberty would last the rest of my life.

But to my surprise, the country I left to live in freedom has, in a sense, followed me here. It is working nonstop in multifarious ways to destroy the freedom we in the United States enjoy.

A "New" War, Twenty Years in the Making

Make no mistake: today, we are at war. The Kremlin's intervention in our 2016 election is only one page in an extensive "master plan" designed to keep America off-balance, or, if necessary, defeated militarily. The 2018 Annual Threat Assessment by former director of national intelligence Dan Coats notes: "Moscow will employ a variety of aggressive tactics…to weaken the United States and undermine Euro-Atlantic security." Among the tools Russia will use are influencing campaigns, "economic coercion, cyber operations…and measured military force."[1]

Moscow's desired strategic outcome is a weakened United States immersed in political dysfunction, torn by racial, religious, ethnic, and other social tensions, struggling economically, bogged down in external conflicts, and alienated from its allies. A distracted America, forced to deal with domestic and international problems, is far less likely to interfere with Putin's strategic ambitions.

In December 1991, the Soviet Union collapsed, and while nuclear weapons remained pointed at the United States, the hostile Soviet communist threat to America ended. Americans envisioned a future of friendship and cooperation with Russia, believing it would surely embrace democracy and (naively) join NATO. Instead, the post-Soviet Russian threat would be underway before the decade was out.

According to the U.S. Justice Department, during the 1990s, the Kremlin likely sent the redheaded "femme fatale" Anna Chapman and ten other Russian intelligence sleeper agents to infiltrate American society.[2] These deep-cover spies, called "illegals" in the parlance of Soviet and Russian Intelligence, conducted a sophisticated operation using false identities and posing as ordinary American families. The twenty-year intelligence operation was aimed at "searching and developing ties with U.S. policymaking circles" and sending intelligence reports about their sensitive activities in the United States back to Moscow.[3]

The intelligence on America, its citizens, and the American way of life that was collected by the Russian spies helped the Kremlin plan and execute its anti-American activities, including Russia's 2016 influence operation targeting the U.S. presidential elections.

In the late 1990s, Moscow launched a multiyear cyber operation—separate from the cyberattacks described earlier—nicknamed "Moonlight Maze" by U.S. investigators.[4] Vast amounts of critical, secret data were stolen from our military, government, and civilian networks, including from the U.S. Navy and Air Force.

But it still took Russia a decade to declare openly a state of conflict with the United States. During the Munich Security Conference in 2007, Putin vociferously denounced the United States and NATO in an inflammatory keynote speech in front of military, political, and business executives from more than forty countries.[5] He accused the United States and NATO of waging "illegitimate" wars, provoking an arms race, and causing extremism, terrorism, and general devastation across the world through destabilizing policies.[6]

Russia formalized the state of hostility in 2010 by designating, in the release of its second post-Soviet Military Doctrine, the United States and NATO as its primary security threat.[7] Moscow further codified this assessment in a series of other official documents, including the 2014 Military Doctrine,[8] the 2015 National Security Strategy,[9] and the 2016 Foreign Policy Concept.[10] These are what the Russian government calls "foundational strategic planning and military planning documents," developed every five to six years by the national security apparatus and approved directly by the Russian president. They serve as the basis for the Russian military's plans to neutralize assessed threats.

In preparation for a potential war with what Putin's generals frequently acknowledge as "the world's best military"—that is, the U.S. military—Russia developed a special doctrine and strategy and implemented an unprecedented military modernization with a price tag on the order of $650 billion.[11]

Practicing to Stage Cyber Doomsday

Most Americans will be surprised to learn that twenty-seven years after the end of the Cold War, our greatest antagonist of the twentieth century—which still considers itself America's archrival—is seeking a rematch. Humiliated by the collapse of the USSR, Russia is now ready for revenge.

As Americans—unless you are a military officer or an intelligence analyst—war is not something we think about in our daily lives. We are busy earning a living, inventing modern technologies, checking our social media, and enjoying our overpriced cappuccinos. Burnt out from brutal daily commutes, incessant text messages, and over-heated political debates, we hit the pillow, exhausted, only to repeat the routine the next morning. Perhaps this explains why hardly anyone noticed or cared much when, on October 3, 2018, a text message with the header "Presidential Alert" popped up on everyone's cellphone reading, "THIS IS A TEST of the National Wireless Emergency Alert System. No action needed."[12]

This surprising message was a test of the Integrated Public Alert and Warning System (IPAWS),[13] a communication capability administered by the Federal Emergency Management System (FEMA) intended to inform citizens about a major natural disaster, terrorist attack, massive cyberattack, or even a nuclear strike. It allows the president to address the nation during a national emergency. And once you see it for real, key government officials are already being evacuated to secret mountain bunkers and airborne command posts from which the president and our top military brass can respond to threats of a nuclear or other potential calamity.

The recent activation and testing of this modern doomsday alert, originally created during the Cold War to warn Americans about a Soviet nuclear strike, is a serious event. Eight to twelve minutes is all we'd have to find a shelter in the event of a real nuclear strike on American soil.[14]

Our national security apparatus no longer views such scenarios as merely hypothetical, even if you think we left them behind with the Cold War. Six months before the Presidential Alert message on your phone, the U.S. government issued a real alert on the website of U.S.-CERT, the United States Computer Emergency Readiness Team.[15] This is part of the national operations center responsible for monitoring cyber threats to our country. That day, the urgent DHS-FBI (Department of Homeland Security-Federal Bureau of Investigation) alert informed Americans that the Russian government had "since at least March 2016" been conducting cyber intrusions into America's most critical infrastructure.[16]

Facilities involving energy, water, aviation, commercial and manufacturing centers, the power grid—an existential necessity—and even the nuclear sector all have been under attack. These cyberattacks could have resulted in widespread blackouts, according to a *Wall Street Journal* report that cited DHS and cybersecurity industry experts.[17]

"They got to the point where they could have thrown switches" and disrupted power flows, warned Jonathan Homer, chief of industrial control system analysis for DHS.[18] At the time of this writing, it is unclear whether the Russians are still lurking within our critical systems. The likelihood that at least portions of our infrastructure are still compromised by the Russians is high. If so, they can wreak havoc at will, should they choose to do so.

Gaining access to these vital control systems could initiate a wide range of malicious activities—not just shutting down a power plant or even a grid, but also enabling major espionage operations and even triggering a nuclear explosion. Russian cyberhackers took screenshots of machinery used in energy and nuclear plants and stole detailed specifications that show how they operated, which suggests that one of the mission objectives was to conduct reconnaissance for future attacks.[19]

Russia had already crossed the cyber Rubicon by temporarily shutting down Ukraine's power grid in a crippling operation during Christmas of 2015, causing a blackout for 250,000 people in freezing temperatures.[20] This was the first recorded cyberattack on a power grid outside of a military conflict.[21] Imagine what would happen if something as essential as the U.S. power grid were disrupted! The most horrific dystopian movie you have ever seen would be an appropriate comparison.

Considered by U.S. intelligence to be the most formidable foreign cyber actor, Russia is continuously mining U.S. systems for vulnerabilities.[22] Russia, along with China, has stolen technical plans for nearly every major U.S. military system and will try to render our weaponry inoperable through cyberattacks during wartime.[23] That Putin and his cyber agents penetrated our electrical grid, election systems, and nuclear facilities keeps American generals and government officials awake at night.

In June 2018, top Trump administration officials were advised that the threat to the U.S. electric grid was so serious that the country needed to prepare for a catastrophic power outage, possibly caused by a cyberattack.[24] Even America's weapons arsenal, including the advanced Patriot missile system, the littoral combat ship, and the F-35 Joint Strike Fighter—capabilities that the United States would be reliant on in the event of a kinetic war with Russia—are vulnerable to cyberattacks, according to a recent U.S. Government Accountability Office audit.[25]

Although the very technology that ensures our survival had been penetrated, there has been little public discussion about it, perhaps because the Russians did not pull the trigger and cause a catastrophic event. Russia sometimes employs actions with limited consequences, what we intel folks call a "shot across the bow," to signal to its opponent that it possesses the capability to inflict devastating damage, even though it decides not do so. Surprisingly, the media's attention turned to the "more pressing" business of Russia's 2016 election interference and the alleged and now disproven Donald Trump–Vladimir Putin collusion story. The media's lust for political intrigue had once again eclipsed any serious coverage of a true threat to our existence.

What had occurred was not a series of random actions or Russian fun and games. Rather, the intrusions were a test run for a potential war. They were acts of sabotage designed to destabilize the United States, even during peacetime, by a country that views America as a strategic competitor at best and fears it as a powerful wartime adversary at worst.

The official journal of the Russian Ministry of Defense, *Military Thought* (*Voyennaya Mysl'*), has been read by very few Americans, even within the Intelligence Community, partly because so few intelligence officers speak fluent Russian—even those whose job it is to focus on Russia. The July 2015 issue discussed what the writers called the "Strategic Operation to Defeat Critical Infrastructure of the Adversary" (SOPKVOP in Russian transliteration), one of the key asymmetric strategies Moscow can use against the United States.[26]

Such strategic operations are no less than warfighting campaigns developed by the Russian General Staff and executed by their armed forces and the intelligence services to prevent, prosecute, or end a conflict.[27] Although intended for wartime, SOPKVOP operations also could be deployed during peacetime to "destabilize the opponent's social and political situation."[28]

It is my assessment that Russia has been conducting cyber penetration of America's critical infrastructure to test drive and eventually operationalize SOPKVOP. The U.S. government acknowledged that Russia's "destabilizing" cyber activities "jeopardized the safety and security of the United States and our allies" and were designed to "enable future offensive operations."[29] In other words, to prepare the battlefield for war.

Test Runs for Armageddon

Meanwhile, military steps far less subtle than cyber intrusions were activated. On March 1, 2018, Putin, in his annual State of the Nation address to the Federal Assembly, announced new weapons aimed at the United States, including next-generation nuclear missiles.[30]

To demonstrate that he meant business, Putin showed a video rendition of a nuclear strike on Florida, home to the U.S. Special Operations Command, the U.S. Central Command—which oversees Iraq and Afghanistan—and President Trump's "Winter White House" residence at Mar-a-Lago. The simulated attack was launched from a new Russian-based intercontinental ballistic missile (ICBM) complex known as "Sarmat"—nicknamed "Satan-2" by NATO—whose missiles, Putin claimed, were "immune to interception" by American missile defenses.[31]

"No one listened to us. Listen to us now," Putin warned.[32]

It was the latest iteration of the hostile anti-American Putin approach often echoed by Russian military and political elites. In 2014, for example, a Kremlin-backed journalist reminded us that "Russia is the only country in the world capable of turning America into nuclear ash."[33] In July 2018, a senior member of the Russian

Academy of Missile and Artillery Sciences stated in the military press that "only a weapon of Armageddon can stop the USA."[34]

In fact, Moscow views war with the United States in the long run as inevitable and regularly conducts practice runs for it.[35] Russian weapons systems are capable of striking targets throughout the United States and Canada from stand-off distances—that is, without entering U.S. sovereign airspace to deliver the weapons.[36]

Entering U.S. airspace or not, Russia is the only existential threat to our air domain, according to the U.S. Northern Command (USNORTHCOM), a combatant command that includes the North American Aerospace Defense Command (NORAD). This joint command is responsible for the defense of our nation's airspace.[37]

Fearing U.S. conventional superiority, Russia relies on its nuclear forces as a contingency weapon to prevail in any conflict. It is the only country in the world that can destroy American ICBMs on the ground by "precisely coordinating attacks with hundreds of high-yield and accurate warheads," according to the 2018 U.S. Nuclear Posture Review.[38]

While Moscow's cyberwarriors are busy mapping out access to our nuclear facilities, Russian military forces are becoming increasingly proficient at conducting nuclear sneak attacks on the U.S. homeland from the sky or the ocean.[39]

In 2007, after stunning Western officials at the Munich Security Conference by declaring an end to a U.S.-shaped world order,[40] Putin resumed the Cold War practice of running Russian strategic bomber patrols close to our homeland.[41] The flight over a U.S. military base on the Pacific Island of Guam by two nuclear-capable Tu-95 "Bear" bombers on August 8[42] was followed by a test of a powerful non-nuclear "vacuum" bomb on September 11 of that year.[43] To reinforce his earlier anti-American manifesto delivered in Germany, Putin was now flexing Russia's military and nuclear muscle on the anniversary of terrorist attacks on the U.S. homeland. The Russians named their bomb "the Father of All Bombs," claiming that it dwarfs a similar U.S. weapon called the Massive Ordnance Air Blast bomb, or MOAB, that U.S. designers dubbed the "Mother of All Bombs." Developed in 2005, the American MOAB, officially called GBU-43/B, was first used in combat on ISIS caves in Afghanistan in 2017, after President Trump granted U.S. military additional authorities, in order to speed up the defeat of the Islamist caliphate.[44]

Since Putin's renewal of patrols, Russian bombers capable of striking targets deep within the U.S. homeland have been conducting long-range sorties six to seven times per year, according to NORAD.[45] I had the privilege of briefing NORAD officials and the previous commander of NORTHCOM, which is nested in beautiful Colorado Springs and the spectacular snow-kissed Cheyenne Mountains, which reminded me of the mountains of my birthplace in Eastern Kazakhstan. Set up in 2002 in response to the 9/11 attacks, NORAD/NORTHCOM—in addition to monitoring missile threats to the U.S. homeland and Canada—also happens to track the arrival of Santa Claus and field phone calls from children all over the globe every Christmas.[46]

Russian bomber runs—intended to assess U.S. air defenses—have included breaches of the U.S. air defense zone (ADIZ) near Alaska and approaches as close as within forty miles of the coast of California. The U.S. Air Force usually scrambles F-22 fighter jets to intercept the Russian "Bears" and escort them out of the ADIZ. The Russians, who are big on symbolism, sometimes conduct such missions on major U.S. holidays or other significant days. On July 4, 2015, the Russian pilots announced themselves to U.S. airmen via radio communications by saying, "Good morning, American pilots. We are here to greet you on your Fourth of July, Independence Day."[47]

In 2009, building on Putin's renewed anti-U.S. Russian posture, President Medvedev, who was falsely considered by the U.S. national security establishment as the "good guy" in the Putin-Medvedev tandem, renewed Russia's patrols of strategic navy vessels close to U.S. shores. This was occurring even as President Obama's White House kept pressing the Russia "reset button." On August 4, 2009, in a symbolic and mocking gesture, Medvedev called President Obama to wish him a happy birthday, having sent a nuclear-powered attack submarine within two-hundred miles of the U.S. east coast a few days earlier.[48] In 2012, another Russian attack submarine armed with cruise missiles sailed, undetected for weeks, through U.S. strategic waters in the Gulf of Mexico, raising concerns within the Pentagon.[49]

Soon after that incident, I flew to U.S. Strategic Command in Omaha, Nebraska, the combatant command responsible for the U.S. nuclear mission. As part of the Intelligence Community interagency team, I briefed the STRATCOM commander, General Kehler. Due to classification restrictions, I cannot supply substantive details of those discussions, but you can imagine what that meeting was like, especially for my colleague from the Office of Naval Intelligence (ONI). ██████████████████████████████████████ ██ ██████████████████████████████████████ DNI, which coordinates the rest of the sixteen intelligence agencies, prefers reaching a consensus among intelligence agencies on key analytic issues before they are presented to policy or military leaders. So, dissent, although officially acceptable, is not encouraged and sometimes is looked down upon, especially when it is perceived as contradicting the existing administration's policy. This act of "sticking my neck out" on behalf of the DIA and other candid discussions with the general earned me, as I was told later by my superiors, the moniker "my favorite Russian spy" from the general.

In addition to the attack submarines, Russian spy ships and planes have been detected patrolling off the coasts of Florida,

Delaware, Connecticut, and Virginia—all near the areas that house notable U.S. military installations. These drills supply valuable training to Russian airmen and seamen for wartime operations against the United States. They also enable them to evaluate America's defenses and collect valuable intelligence on U.S. military installations. In the business, we call it "strategic targeting."

Until recently, Washington's weapon of choice against Moscow's cyber and nuclear threats has mostly been economic sanctions. The Trump administration—despite the media's portrayal of the president's being "soft" on Russia—has toughened the U.S. posture towards Moscow.[50] Trump expanded the use of sanctions initiated against Russia by Obama, indicted and expelled dozens of Russian "diplomats," indicted multiple organizations and individuals, approved lethal weapons' being sent to Ukraine to help fight Russian-backed forces, and adopted defense policies designed to mitigate the Russian threat.[51] Trump granted American cyber warriors the legal authority they needed to respond in kind to Moscow's cyber hacking.[52] In an unprecedented move in 2018, Trump, alleged to be Putin's "secret agent," also authorized an air strike on Russian military contractors who were supporting pro-Syrian government forces. These U.S. strikes killed scores of Putin's mercenaries.[53]

Pre-Trump, the U.S. national security community was concerned that offensive cyber operations launched by the American government against Russian systems would interfere with U.S. intelligence gathering operations in the cyber domain or would be met with an even stronger and possibly reckless retaliation by the Kremlin or other cyberthreat offenders. Obama's cyber policy restricted offensive cyber operations, possibly putting our cyber warriors at a disadvantage against our adversaries, out of concern for potentially unleashing a cyberwar with unpredictable and extremely dangerous outcomes.[54] The Trump administration has adopted a more aggressive cyber posture, allowing our military to better combat threats from sophisticated cyberthreat actors like Russia—but potentially increasing the risk of unintended escalation.[55] Only later will we know which U.S. policy approach is more effective at mitigating the Russian cyberthreat and whether either one of them changed Putin's calculus about waging cyberwarfare against us.

It Doesn't Take Much for the Entire System to Collapse

Russia's targeting strategy against the United States, such as the cyber intrusions into our nuclear sector and other critical infrastructure, is the result of years of comprehensive study of U.S. vulnerabilities by the Russian military and intelligence services. A January 2012 issue of a Russian military periodical, *Foreign Military Observer* (*Novoye Voyennoye Obozreniye*), reveals the military strategists' calculus for striking an adversary's civilian infrastructure during a conflict. You only need to defeat a "small number of key interconnected targets" that are vital to the functioning of the state, for the "entire system to collapse," it said.[56]

The article referenced a 2001 accident involving a train, which was transporting hazardous chemical materials and veered off the tracks in a Baltimore, Maryland tunnel. The accident burst a water pipe, causing a three-foot flood that disrupted Baltimore's mail carrier and telecommunications systems, which served major companies like WorldCom, Verizon, Nextel, and others. Disruption of train and auto transportation followed along the entire Baltimore-to-New York corridor. "Taking parts of the adversary's civilian infrastructure out of commission," the authors argue, will produce cascading destructive effects "harming the economy, healthcare, defense, and security of the entire state."[57]

Driven by Fear of America's Hostile Intentions

Why does Russia wish for the demise of America? Paradoxically, Moscow sees itself on the defensive. While its actions within its own borders and around the world can be outrageously and inexcusably oppressive and brutal, within the dark mindset of the Kremlin, these acts are justifiable.

Moscow considers the area within Eurasia that was once the Soviet Union as Russia's exclusive sphere of influence—a region that is critical for its security and therefore off limits to U.S. influence—a no-go zone for the West, in Russia's view. The freedom Washington has granted to the Baltic states to join NATO is considered an existential threat to the Kremlin. While it was the right thing to do, it made Russia more insecure and dangerous.

Deeply disturbed by U.S. involvement in conflicts in Kosovo, Iraq, Afghanistan, and Libya, and the Arab Spring uprising, Putin feared the U.S. might eventually intrude closer to Russia. He was known to be personally shaken by the disintegration of Yugoslavia and the brutal deaths of fellow strongmen Saddam Hussein and Muammar Gaddafi at the hands of their own citizens. Russian officials blamed Washington for the so called "color revolutions" that took place in Ukraine ("Orange"), Georgia ("Rose"), and Kyrgyzstan ("Tulip") in the early-to-mid 2000s, accusing the United States of "meddling" in its neighbors' internal affairs. It interpreted these events, and especially U.S. attempts to draw Georgia and Ukraine into NATO, as setting the stage for disintegration of Russia, which is itself an amalgamation of ethnic regions and republics. Some of these areas, such as Chechnya, are historically rebellious and ripe for secession.

In addition to history and culture, Russia's threat perceptions are also shaped by an ideology called Eurasianism.[58] The ideology, which has its roots in the 1920s, has recently been revived by Aleksandr Dugin, a Putin guru widely known for his anti-American views. This imperial, conservative, anti-Western ideology envisions Russia and the United States in an existential conflict for the control of Eurasia, the vast landmass that includes both Europe and Asia.[59] Russia in part justifies such claims by citing U.S. strategists who have advocated an assertive U.S. policy in Eurasia.[60]

Influenced by Cold War thinking, Moscow holds Washington responsible for the collapse of the Soviet Union, which the Russians believe was precipitated by America's outspending Russia on armaments and by a secret plot, which the Russians don't specify, orchestrated by the Central Intelligence Agency. Similarly, Russia's political and military elite believe Washington seeks to overthrow Putin's regime and, in the long run, dismember Russia in order to control Eurasia.[61]

They view Washington's promotion of democracy and advocacy for human rights, in addition to NATO's expansion into the post-Soviet space, as a ruse for installing anti-Russian and pro-Western governments in Eurasia, including Russia itself. Russia, therefore, rejects values we hold dear and views our embrace of them as cynical opportunism. Inflicting oppression in the name of stability, defense of its empire, and preservation of power for the ruling class defines Russian history.

The United States, under the leadership of Ronald Reagan, upgraded the Cold War policy of containment towards the Soviet Union with a proactive policy that sought the defeat of the USSR. This policy aimed to "weaken the USSR and its ruling elite, change the political and economic system to a more pluralistic one, and over time, reverse Soviet expansionism," according to the U.S. National Security Decision Directive (NSDD) from 1983 entitled "U.S. Relations with the USSR," which was declassified in 2008.[62] U.S. grand strategy in 1986, according to another previously top-secret document, sought to prevent "a single hostile power or coalition of powers from dominating the Eurasian land-mass…[and] assist democratic and nationalist movements where possible in the struggle against totalitarian regimes" by "providing material support to such movements" while remaining "the natural enemy of any country threatening independence of others."[63]

George H. W. Bush's defense policy and strategy, while acknowledging the reduction of the threat to U.S. and European security with the collapse of the USSR, aimed to prevent "re-emergence of a threat from the Soviet Union's successor state." Bush Sr.'s Pentagon sought to ensure that "no hostile power [be] able to consolidate resources within the former Soviet Union," as part of its broader goal to prevent "the emergence of any potential future global competitor." U.S. defense policy officials thought that the best way to achieve these goals was to encourage Russia and Ukraine to "demilitarize their society, convert their military industries to civilian production, eliminate or radically reduce their nuclear weapons…and prevent leakage of advanced military technology and expertise to other countries." Washington believed that turning Russia and the post-Soviet countries into "peaceful democracies with market-based economies" would promote peace and stability and enhance its own security since, according to this logic, democracies don't go to war with each other.[64] But Moscow, which for centuries has relied on authoritarian rule and military power for its security, internal stability, as well as expansion, considers such U.S. actions as deliberate attempts to weaken and defeat Russia.

Worst-Case-Scenario Mindset

Moscow's suspicions of U.S. intentions toward Russia and fears of regime overthrow were shaped by its turbulent past. Russians have a strong connection to their history, scarred with foreign invasions, wars, and revolutions that caused horrific economic devastation and loss of life. In the past hundred years, the country experienced four catastrophic events: the first World War; the Bolshevik revolution of 1917; World War II, which claimed the lives of twenty million Russians and is referred to as the Great Patriotic War; and the collapse of the USSR in 1991. These events forged strong imprints on the Russian national psyche, making Russians deeply suspicious of the West's intentions and obsessed with the idea of "encirclement" by hostile powers. Paranoia and presupposition of inevitable conflict are deeply rooted in Russian strategic and popular culture. Russians believe it is not a matter of if, but when, conflict will erupt. And so, they always prepare for the worst, especially when it comes to beefing up their military capability, which they make known to the world.

Moscow has adopted a "fear-equals-respect" mentality, often intimidating its perceived enemies with hostile rhetoric, demonstrations of powerful weaponry, and nuclear saber-rattling.

This outlook can be hard to understand for Americans, who are more optimistic and assume—or at least hope for—a peaceful future. But unlike Russia, America has not experienced a major war or revolution on its soil for over a century and a half. With the stark exception of the 9/11 attacks, Americans believe that wars happen "over there."

The Russians believe that only a strong, czar-like leader can protect Mother Russia from foreign invaders, supply domestic stability, and command respect internationally. This explains why, despite his authoritarian rule, Putin often earns high approval ratings, between 60 and 80 percent. It also explains why there are Russians who (oddly to Americans) support Joseph Stalin, even though he murdered millions of Soviet citizens. Most Russians will sacrifice what they feel they must, including personal freedoms, for stability and security.

They view democracy as chaotic and unstable because it allows individuals to challenge and change the state.

Russia interprets all geopolitical events through the prism of this "worst-case scenario" mindset. It is simply obsessed with the United States, which it fears as superior militarily, economically, and technologically. This can result in reactions to U.S. policies that are often the opposite of what Americans expect.

For example, America's military aid to Ukraine and U.S. sanctions on Russian companies and individuals—assessed as punishment for the Crimea annexation, the 2016 U.S. election interference, and the poisoning of a former Russian intelligence officer and his daughter in England—are completely misinterpreted by the Russians. Russians believe that by helping Ukraine militarily, the U.S. is weakening Russia by drawing it into an interstate conflict and that sanctions are a U.S. effort to undermine Putin, Russia's economy, and the ability to defend itself. And so, Russia fights back, working harder to limit its reliance on the U.S. dollar and the international financial system and accelerating its efforts to defeat America militarily.

East-West Existential Battle

In addition to the Russian home-grown philosophy of Eurasianism, the Western geopolitical concept of a "Eurasian Heartland" also animates Russia's fears of America's hostile intentions and fuels its anti-American strategy.[65] Its proponent, British geographer Halford Mackinder, put forth the thesis in 1904 that whoever controls Eurasia—which he called the World Island—commands the globe. Mackinder—widely thought of as the father of geopolitical studies—believed Eurasia is predetermined to play a dominant role in global politics because of its vast natural resources and central location on the globe. Indeed, it is from this "heart of the earth" that countless invasions and major wars, including the two World Wars, were initiated.[66]

Modified by Dutch-American John Spykman in 1930s, Mackinder's "Eurasian Heartland" theory provided the foundational basis for U.S. post-war grand strategy. Spykman was a balance-of-power realist, and convinced the U.S. national security establishment that to improve its chances of survival, America should get involved in Eurasian affairs to "defend forward" its security and interests. This strategy called for the prevention of an emerging rival power that could threaten America by creating U.S. strategic alliances and setting up military bases in Eurasia.[67] Eventually, this logic was applied to the development of containment strategy against the USSR after World War II.

Russia believes that Mackinder and Spykman's theories have shaped U.S. foreign policy and strategy towards the USSR and Russia. After fostering the breakup of the USSR, Moscow believes the United States now seeks Russia's containment and territorial fragmentation. The Russians see in current U.S. policy a reflection of what they perceive as America's anti-Russian strategy and "imperial ambitions" recommended by Zbigniew Brzezinski in the 1997 book, *The Grand Chess Board: American Primacy and Its Geostrategic Imperatives*.[68] A highly influential Polish-American geostrategist and national security advisor to President Jimmy Carter, Brzezinski was feared and hated by the Soviets as one of the architects of the successful American anti-Soviet strategy in Afghanistan, which contributed to the collapse of the USSR. In *The Grand Chess Board*, he echoed Mackinder and Spykman's strategic guidance, writing that the U.S. must "make certain that no state…gains the capacity to expel the United States from Eurasia or even to diminish significantly its decisive arbitrating role." He reminded U.S. policymakers that he "who controls Eurasia controls the world."[69]

Brzezinski also urged American global planners "as in chess…to think several moves ahead, anticipating possible countermoves" and to ensure that U.S. geostrategy has three distinct phases and perspectives: "short-term (five-plus years), medium-term (up to twenty-plus years), and long-run (beyond twenty years)." Such thinking is critical with respect to Russia, which thinks not only about tomorrow, but about the day and decade after tomorrow, and beyond. Perhaps blinded by a false sense of security in the aftermath of the collapse of the USSR, U.S. planners have lost the ability to focus on challenges beyond the immediate tasks—such as terrorism, Ebola, COVID-19, and other "issues du jour." They do not estimate dangers that lurk over the horizon and predict adversaries' future moves. These limitations have put us in the position of reacting to Putin's moves instead of expecting them.

More recently, in 2016, the Russian Center for Strategic Assessments and Forecasts, a think tank whose analysis reflects the perspective of Russian government officials, judged that "U.S. foreign policy for the past 20 years serves as confirmation of the Mackinder and Spykman theories embedded in these policies." As an example of such U.S. policies, the author listed U.S. wars in Afghanistan, Iraq, Yugoslavia, Libya, and Syria, as well as the conflict in Ukraine.[70] The authors cynically argue that Washington's true strategic goal of U.S. military involvement in these countries was to establish regional dominance for the purpose of securing control over resources and to create business opportunities.

In May 2014, another Russian think tank, whose analysis supports Putin's decision making, published a report, "Issues of Russia's Security in the Context of the Mackinder Concept." This report termed Mackinder's "Heartland" theory as reflecting a "geopolitical worldview that is hostile to Russia." The author justified Russia's annexation of Crimea as a step forced by "unprecedented Western pressure on Ukraine." He stressed the importance of "studying Western geopolitical concepts and developing our own responses to them," in order to keep Russia secure.[71] Russian analysts and military theorists follow U.S. strategic thinking closely on such topics as world politics, military strategy, technology, and economics. They try to understand how Americans think in order to harden the Russian people against foreign ideas they deem threatening to the Russian government—like free speech and other individual freedoms—and to find U.S. vulnerabilities to exploit in the future.

Putin is violently opposed to America's human rights policies and instead views U.S. strategy in Eurasia as an attempt to change the balance of power by weakening Russia forever. Putin sees the United States as the principal barrier to restoring Russia's great-power (*derzhava*) status and its sphere of influence in Eurasia.

Eurasianism, which is the opposing Russian philosophy to the Western "Heartland" theory, calls for the defeat of America and "decadent" Western liberal ideology. This task must be done so that Russia, which Eurasianists consider a unique civilization, can chart its own developmental path—a path distinctly different from that of Western democracies. With the cult of Lenin now abandoned along with communism, Eurasianism reestablishes the primacy of the Russian Orthodox Church, which Putin has weaponized against the West to achieve his ambitions for Russia.

The neo-Eurasianist Aleksandr Dugin, in his terrifying 1997 book *Foundations of Geopolitics*, which made him popular among Russian military and political elites, identifies America as "a total geopolitical rival of Russia." He prescribes that Russia "counteract U.S. policy at all levels and [in] all regions of the earth." Russia must "weaken, demoralize, [and] deceive, in order to win," he writes. "It is especially important to introduce geopolitical disorder into America's internal reality; to encourage separatism and ethnic, social, and racial conflicts; actively support dissident movements [and] extremist, racist groups and sects; and to destabilize internal processes."[72]

Dugin's Eurasianist ideas have found their way into key Russian doctrinal documents.[73] Evidently Dugin, who has been referred to by some as "Putin's Brain," has not only advised the Russian president but also the General Staff, which is in charge of developing Russia's warfighting doctrine and strategy.[74]

"The Bright and Shiny Object"

Russia's broad geopolitical goals, rooted in history, and Putin's strategic plan to bolster his regime must be understood by both ordinary Americans and national security officials tasked with defending us. Since the 1999 "Moonlight Maze," a multi-year Russian cyber operation targeting multiple U.S. government and military agencies, we have been "admiring the threat," as one former intelligence officer told me in frustration. "Reaping the benefits of the peace dividend," sarcastically commented another former senior career intelligence officer, referring to the savings on military spending our supposed new friendship with Russia allowed.[75]

Fellow former intelligence officers whom I interviewed for *Putin's Playbook* have been frustrated that the news cycle has been dominated for almost two years by the 2016 election intervention and the subsequently disproven "Russia collusion" theories, obscuring the full Russia story that includes Putin's plan to destabilize America.

"Everyone wants to talk about the damn election. It's not just the election, stupid!" vented a former senior career intelligence officer whose direct experience with the Russian target dates back to Soviet times. "It has become the bright and shiny object. That's all everyone wants to talk about when we begin to discuss Russia," he said of the election interference. "The minute you try to have a serious conversation about what the Russians are doing and our understanding of their actions and intentions," he complained, "we get irrelevant questions like 'What do they have on Trump?'"[76]

He warned that this would derail serious discussion and evaluation of Russia as an intelligence target, preventing our leadership from doing the job of protecting the country from foreign threats.

This veteran Russia expert, an old Cold Warrior, was equally disturbed that Americans still don't know that Russia and the United States are at war. "It's their country. Americans have a right to know. It's almost criminal that they still don't know that Russia is waging a war on us and that we are not fighting back," he asserted. Failure to recognize this conflict impairs our ability to develop an effective strategy for defending our country against it, in this former intel officer's opinion. "The damage [the Russians] do gets worse every day," he warned.[77]

The Threat Is with Us Now

Another former career senior intelligence officer who served during multiple administrations believes that Russia has developed a "deep understanding of how Americans think, what motivates us, our interests, and how open and democratic societies work." This enables Russia to "pursue its exceptionally well-defined targeting strategy against the United States."[78] He warned that the "Russian intelligence and security services are extraordinarily well prepared to counter U.S. interests and advance Russia's."[79]

Russia proved this with its 2016 election influence campaign. The Russians co-opted some of the most senior and well-known members of the American political media establishment, without their knowledge, in a fight they believed preserved American democracy against Donald Trump. Instead, it was a successful Russian effort to interfere in a democracy and sow discord.

The success of Moscow's scheme, however, was not an infiltration of the Trump presidential campaign, as the mass media tried to convince the American people for two years. The Kremlin's success was something entirely different. It shifted American focus away from the real Russian threat and toward fighting with each other.

Having an investigation looking to determine whether Trump conspired with a foreign power to steal an election makes an extraordinary allegation against a U.S. presidential candidate. Sending Americans on a two-year roller-coaster ride, with President Trump having to wage a daily battle to lift a cloud of suspicion off his presidency, is priceless for an old KGB operative like Putin.

Putin's winnings from his gamble continue to accumulate. What better outcome could Putin have sought than three years of turmoil and the impeachment of a U.S. president? But there was also an unseen benefit. After years of ignoring Putin's grievances and warnings—the attitude towards the Russian threat that afflicted the government bureaucracy throughout multiple U.S. administrations—the national security establishment finally got the Putin memo.

In August 2018, six weeks after Director of National Intelligence Coats's warning about the overwhelming Russian cyberthreats causing U.S. detection systems to start "blinking red," another dire warning was given by an American general about missile threats to America—this time from both the Russians and the Chinese. The NORAD/NORTHCOM commander, speaking at a National Guard Association conference, stated that the U.S. "homeland is no longer a sanctuary."[80]

In April 2019, Secretary General of NATO Jens Stoltenberg warned the U.S. Congress, in a high-profile speech at a joint session, not to be "naive" about the Kremlin's intentions with respect to NATO countries. He called out the threat posed by Russia, which included a massive military build-up, attacks on sovereign states, assassinations, election interference, and cyberattacks.[81]

In June 2019, DIA director General Robert Ashley, in response to a question posed to him at the Aspen Security Forum about what keeps him up at night, acknowledged that Russia has been in conflict, albeit of an unconventional character, with us "since 1991…since they recovered from the period of the Soviet Union."[82] The general placed Russia ahead of China as the more dangerous, near-term threat of an "existential" nature, due its possession of "thousands of nuclear weapons."[83] Ashley warned that Russia might "lash out" and act unpredictably because Putin feels "backed into a corner."[84]

I agree with DIA's current analysis, with an added observation: Putin, feeling cornered or acting as though he is cornered, is predictable. He will more likely than not surprise the West with another hostile act like the taking of Crimea during the next two years. It is not by chance that the old KGB man told us a story about a cornered rat in his autobiography. As a youngster, Putin and his friends would chase rats with a stick in the stairwell in his apartment building in St. Petersburg. Putin saw that when chased into a corner, with nowhere else to run, the rat started attacking him. "It threw itself at me. I was surprised and frightened. Now the rat was chasing me."[85] Using a similar analogy of counterattacking your adversary when pressured too hard by him, Putin in several of his speeches compared Russia with a spring that will eventually spring back because it is being compressed too hard. Might it be that the scheming Putin was laying the stage for blaming the United States and the West for provoking him to do whatever he may decide to do in the name of Russia's national interests?

There is no question that Russia's perceptions of the United States and NATO as threats are real. If they were not, DIA, which has the ability to compare the Russian leaders' public statements against clandestine reporting and intercepts, would not have included them as legitimate drivers of Putin's military policy in its 2017 unclassified report, *Russia: Military* Power.[86] However, I will go ahead and make this speculative assessment based on my Russian cultural background. Putin can and does masterfully play on Russia's genuine fears to achieve his strategic ambitions. "There is a joke in every joke" *(v kazhdoy shutke est' dolya shutki)* is another Russian saying, which means there is a kernel of truth in every joke.

Probably the most sobering of these warnings about Russian fears and intentions came from the speech of Marine general Robert Neller, during his December 2017 address to the U.S. Marine rotational force. Deployed to Norway as a deterrent to Russia, Neller ordered the Marines to be ready for the "big-ass war" that was coming.[87]

The Kremlin views Washington as the top security threat to Putin's regime. Justified or not, the notion that America wants to destroy Russia is what the Kremlin perceives. Convinced that it is fighting for its survival to avoid destruction by its archrival, Russia wants to destroy us first. Moscow will relentlessly pursue Putin's plan to steadily destabilize and subvert our country from within.

As you can tell by now, as Americans continue to fight one another with our eyes off the true target, we have already stumbled into what the U.S. Army calls "the gray zone" of warfare with Russia.[88] Abetted by Russian disinformation and the relentless focus by the press and Trump's political opponents on the faux collusion, the Russian threat is hidden from the American people. From where we are now, the risk of the escalation of current U.S.-Russian tensions to a direct kinetic military conflict is high. The most obvious and dangerous scenario of such a conflict is a nuclear strike that both Russian and U.S. doctrines endorse.[89] Whether we choose to acknowledge it or not, the threat exists. It is deadly and relentless, and, in the pages that follow, I will reveal it.

CHAPTER 2

Putin's Wish List: America's Nightmare

---

*"Judo teaches you to be in control, to feel the sharpness of
the moment, to see strong and weak points of the opponent, and to strive for the best outcome. Don't you agree:
all this knowledge, [these] abilities, and [these] skills are
simply a must for a politician?"*

—*Vladimir Putin*

Growing up with movies that emphasized patriotism and sacrifice displayed by brave Soviet soldiers during World War
II, I was fascinated by military and intelligence work. We
called it the "Great Patriotic War," in which we lost twenty million
people and suffered nearly total devastation.

As an eight-year-old, I was struck by a scene from the famous Soviet
espionage thriller *Seventeen Moments of Spring*. Katya Kozlova, a Soviet
deep-cover intelligence officer, was operating in Nazi Germany while
posing as a German citizen, Katherin Kinn. Her cover was blown when
German officers interrogated her. One German interrogator took Katya's
newborn baby out onto the balcony and unwrapped him naked in sub-
zero Berlin winter temperatures, trying to force Katya to talk. After

29

several long minutes of her baby boy's excruciating screaming, Katya fell unconscious. In the face of her baby's potential death, she would not compromise her deep-cover partner, also a Soviet intelligence officer, who had infiltrated high echelons of German intelligence, posing as a native German, Max von Otto Stierlitz.

As a young girl, I wanted to have the strength and the patriotism of Katya Kozlova. My mother, who was serving in a military unit as a civilian at the time, warned me that I was too idealistic, that the Soviet socialist system was rotten, and that eventually I would get hurt by my idealism. It was not until my college years, after realizing the hypocrisy, corruption, and tyranny of the Soviet system, that I fully accepted the uncomfortable truth. This terrible truth was that nothing within the oppressive and deceitful Soviet state, other than your family, was worth sacrificing yourself for.

Years later, as an American, having watched on television the second airplane commandeered by terrorists strike the World Trade Center, I knew I had to do something to help protect America. There were no unusual tensions in the Russian-American relations then. In fact, President Putin was the first foreign leader to call President Bush and express his sympathy—an act that I believe was genuine. Sooner or later, however, my Russian instincts told me the profound differences between Russia and America would emerge again. I thought American intelligence and security communities could use my firsthand knowledge of Russia and how the Russians think.

On November 1, 2001, I took a day off from work at WorldCom, a now defunct telecommunications company, to attend a conference called "Doing Business with the Federal Government" at a ritzy hotel in McLean, Virginia. It was an outreach by the government to the business community for ideas on how to better protect our homeland against the escalating terrorist threat. Dark-suited and clean-cut speakers from multiple federal agencies presented their most pressing security issues, which required innovative solutions. As the conference was coming to an end, I approached, a little nervous, one of the speakers, who struck me as especially candid about the government's shortcomings in being prepared for an unthinkable threat like the September 11 terrorist attacks.

He was an FBI special agent named Mark T., who directed the Bureau's Foreign Terrorist Taskforce. In a thirty-second elevator speech—with dozens of similarly patriotic Americans patiently queueing up to speak with him—I told agent T. that I hailed from Russia, had some unique skills that U.S. intelligence could use, and wanted to serve and protect my new homeland. In a no-nonsense manner, he looked me in the eyes, as if signaling, "I hear you, my fellow patriotic Russian-American," and handed me his business card, promising to connect me with his FBI colleague who was in need of someone just like me.

Impressed and comforted by the FBI agent's businesslike approach, I rushed home to inform my American-born and somewhat libertarian-minded husband that his impression of the government was incorrect. Skeptical from the very beginning about my desire to work for Uncle Sam, my husband thought that I was not cut out for nine-to-five government work. He blamed my adopted "overly free" American spirit and natural Russian low tolerance for bureaucratic nonsense—qualities that I inherited by living under the suffocating control of a communist state.

Determined to prove my husband wrong, I placed a call to agent Mark T. the same afternoon. This was the beginning of my journey to become a U.S. intelligence officer, an American Katya. I did not know at the time how long and arduous this journey would be.

Is Putin Insane?

Winston Churchill is not the only one who found Russia bewildering: "a riddle, wrapped in a mystery, inside an enigma," as he put it. Since Russia entered the headlines again, in the aftermath of Moscow's attempt to disrupt the 2016 U.S. presidential election, ordinary Americans and foreign affairs cognoscenti alike were puzzled by Russia's behavior. "Why did Russia do this? What does Russia want?" various news commentators often exclaim in response to Moscow's latest cyber hack or harassment of a U.S. combat ship or fighter jet. Russia has been upsetting things everywhere—in Georgia, Ukraine, Crimea, Syria, and the rest of Europe, they say. And now Venezuela! What is Putin up to in *our* own back yard?

Who is President Vladimir Vladimirovich Putin? What kind of person is he? What are his motivations and intentions? Why does he seem so angry with America and the West, acting as though he is eager to settle scores? Putin is viewed in the West as a villain, a revisionist who is nostalgic for the Soviet Empire, and a disruptor who is eager to do anything as long as it contradicts the interests of America and the West and upsets Washington's plans. Outraged by Putin's recent disruptions in the world, Western political leaders and security analysts consider him arrogant and reckless. The Russian president's state of mind has even been questioned. In the aftermath of Russia's annexation of Crimea, President Obama suggested that Putin acted irrationally, counter to his long-term interests. Former secretary of state Condoleezza Rice called Putin "wholly irrational," a "megalomaniac," and speculated that there is a "5 percent chance" that the Russian president is delusional.[1]

During my time as an intelligence officer, I sometimes briefed senior policy officials who seemed to think that if somehow Putin were to disappear or if someone else were at the helm of the Kremlin, all our Russia problems would go away. But is it really that simple? Is Putin just mindlessly inserting sticks in the spokes of Washington's wheel? Is he indeed irrational?

Unlike the case of the North Korean dictator Kim Jong-un— who has been publicly declared by the Central Intelligence Agency as "rational,"[2] even though he starves his people and murders family members—we have not heard any official views from American intelligence on the state of mind of the Russian president. A minor exception was a dubious-sounding study from 2008 contracted by the Pentagon, the authors of which—who never met Vladimir Putin—theorized that the Russian president has Asperger's syndrome, which the authors claim affects all of his decisions.[3]

Classified psychological profiles of foreign leaders developed by U.S. intelligence, most notably by the CIA's Center for Analysis of Personality and Political Behavior, are closely guarded secrets. As acknowledged by Dr. Jerrold Post, the center's founding director, who developed psychological profiles of Osama Bin Laden and Saddam Hussein, "These character portraits are used by American presidents during critical and historic events."[4] Figuring out what makes a foreign leader tick is part of gathering critical intelligence about an opponent. Done for the purpose of gaining leverage during negotiations or increasing the advantage for U.S. policy and decision-makers, it is a key mission of intelligence.

With that said, there is nothing insane about Putin. As frustrating as the Russian strongman's actions can be, his behavior is logical and not entirely unpredictable. There is a method for Vladimir's "madness." His logic, however, is Russian, and partly Soviet too—not American or Western. His actions reflect Russian cultural norms and standards of behavior. We can make sense of Putin's character and actions and explain why so many Russians continue to be on his side, having elected him four times.

Hooligan to Judo Man

Putin's worldview and character were shaped primarily by the following: his personal and family experience surviving World War II, and especially the blockade of Leningrad by the Germans; the collapse of the Soviet Union; his athletic training in judo; and, of course, his intelligence career. A former colonel in the KGB (Komitet Gosudarstvennoy Bezopasnosti; "Committee for State Security"), the Soviet State Security Service, Putin was born in post-war Leningrad (the Soviet-era name for St. Petersburg) and named after the Bolshevik leader Vladimir Lenin. Putin's father, an officer of the NKVD (Narodnyy Komissariat Vnutrennich Del; "People's Comissariat for Internal Affairs"), the Soviet Secret Police, fought in the Great Patriotic War. He conducted sabotage operations behind the German lines as part of a demolition battalion. The elder Putin was discharged before the war ended because of injuries that left him with a permanent limp. Vladimir Putin's mother barely escaped death during the 872-day siege of Leningrad by the Germans. Luckily, she was pulled from a pile of corpses barely alive because she moaned while regaining consciousness after fainting from hunger. Putin's one-year-old brother was not so lucky: he died of starvation during the blockade.

Putin grew up in poverty and lived in a government-owned communal housing unit shared by multiple unrelated families. He was a bad student, a street fighter, and a troublemaker (*khuligan*) until the sixth grade, according to his elementary school teacher and his own account. He later turned around and, in order to "maintain his social status," started doing well in school, began studying German, started training in judo, and joined the Pioneers, a Soviet youth league for young teens, who were indoctrinated in the Soviet socialist ideology.[5]

Young Putin survived the rough streets of Leningrad at least in part because he developed an interest in sports. He first tried boxing and sambo, a Soviet combat sport that combines judo and wrestling. Having suffered a broken nose in boxing, Putin preferred sambo, and later switched with his trainer to judo, a martial art that relies more on mentally and physically manipulating the opponent than on brute force. While at the university, he earned the title of master black belt in sambo, and then two years later in judo, becoming the judo champion of Leningrad in 1976. "Judo is not just a sport....It's a philosophy. It's respect for your elders and your opponent. It's not for weaklings," Putin commented in his autobiography, «От Первого Лица» (*First Person*). The core of the book, published just two weeks before his 2000 presidential election, is a series of interviews of Putin by cooperative Russian journalists. Putin compared all other non-contact sports to ballet. Putin marvels at the "instructive aspect of everything in judo," the "ritual and the respect for one's opponent." He noted that instead of "jabbing him in the forehead, you bow to your opponent."[6] However, as we well know by now, the Russian strongman has no problem jabbing at his opponents, even to the point of murdering them.

Putin credits sports and judo for "dragging him off the streets." The sport shaped his character and worldview, giving him discipline, physical and mental agility, confidence, and a special perspective on how to deal with antagonists. This perspective would serve him well in his future roles as an intelligence operative and more recently as Russian president and a major player in international politics. "Judo teaches you to maintain control, to feel the sharpness of the moment, to see the strong and the weak sides of your opponent, to strive for the best outcome," he has said.[7]

Putin's reliance on the principles behind judo appears in some of his actions on the world stage. In 2014, displaying icy control and determination and "feeling the sharpness of the moment,"[8] he swiftly occupied Ukraine's Crimea without firing a shot. A year later, he bowed politely and then manipulated the United States and NATO in Syria, offering to help rid Syria of chemical weapons. This gained Russia entrée into the theater, which he used to launch air strikes on U.S.-backed opponents of Putin's ally, Syrian president Bashar al-Assad, to keep him in power. And in 2019, probing for strength or weakness in the United States' commitment to the Monroe Doctrine, he sent nuclear-capable Tu-160 Blackjack strategic bombers to Venezuela to deter the United States from ousting the Maduro regime, showing Washington that Russia can mess in America's backyard just as America does in Russia's. Putin's sense of opportunity and the right timing, as well as his ability to exploit the opponent's hesitation or temporary disorientation, is the result of his lifelong study of judo.

KGB Operative

Putin's career as a KGB operative is the third element that played a critical role in the formation of his outlook. The young Putin was fascinated with the profession of an intelligence officer; movies and novels fed his imagination. And, as most of us who went into the intelligence profession discovered, movies have nothing to do with the actual job of an intelligence officer. The real thing is far more fascinating and unbelievable.

The attraction for Putin was that a spy had the ability to manipulate thousands of people and control their fate—something that he has done skillfully and frighteningly well both domestically and internationally. Remarking on the prospect of becoming a KGB officer in his autobiography, Putin said, "What amazed me most of all was how one man's effort could achieve what whole armies could not."[9] Serving as part of—and indeed literally serving—the apparatus of oppression ran in the family: while his father was a member of the state's secret police, his grandfather was a cook for Lenin and Stalin.

Putin has occupied the Russian presidency longer than Brezhnev and nearly as long as Stalin. By the end of his fourth and (supposedly) final term, Putin will have kept control of the office for twenty years. His ability to outfox his Western counterparts in world politics is astounding.

As a ninth grader, Putin walked into the local KGB office to learn how he could become an officer. It was recommended he attend law school, so Putin later graduated from the competitive Leningrad State University (Leningradsky Gosudarstvenny Universitet, or LGU).[10]

After graduation, Putin's first assignment was in the Fourth Department of the First Chief Directorate (Pervoye Glavnoe Upravleniye) of the KGB, whose mission was foreign intelligence. The work would entail collecting and analyzing military, political, scientific, and technical information about foreign adversaries.[11] In other words, it meant stealing their secrets. U.S. intelligence has more diverse capabilities and gives preference to technical sources like high-resolution satellite photography of military installations, cyber hacking to snatch sensitive documents off computers, and listening in on phone calls. Soviet and now Russian intelligence favors HUMINT, which stands for "human intelligence." In Russian, it is known as *agenturnaya razvedka* (literally translated as "agent intelligence").

HUMINT is the riskiest form of intelligence work because the human source who provides secrets to his foreign handler—thus committing treason against his own country—risks his life if he gets caught. (I will be referring to spies by using only the masculine pronouns "he" and "his," simply because most spies, statistically, are men—go figure!) Soviet citizens who were human sources (spies) for U.S. intelligence and supplied Soviet government secrets to their American handlers were often executed if caught. The Russian government would also not hesitate to follow suit if it caught an ordinary Russian citizen providing sensitive information to the United States.

It is mission number one for American HUMINTers who recruit and handle foreign spies to protect their sources and those sources' family members, especially if they come from countries like Russia, China, Iran, North Korea, and some others where traitors will be killed, perhaps after a heavy dose of torture.

After 1977, Putin switched to counterintelligence, which focuses on protecting a country's secrets from foreign adversaries, and was posted to the Department of Investigations of the Leningrad KGB office.[12] Among the roles of counterintelligence (*kontr-razvedka*) officers is disrupting foreign intelligence operations aimed at recruiting spies within their country. Spies are typically government employees, members of the military, or defense contractors who have security clearances and access to classified information that foreign adversaries are eager to get their hands on. It takes years, tremendous government resources, and sophisticated tradecraft on the part of counterintelligence officers to catch a good spy.

Though the career path is a neglected stepchild in U.S. intelligence circles and often shunned by ambitious American intelligence officers, counterintelligence in Russia, as in the USSR, enjoys special status. Elevated in prestige since Bolshevik times, its tradecraft has been perfected into a vicious art form. *Kontr-razvedka* is, for ordinary Russians, the most feared and reviled branch of the government apparatus, because its primary mission is to spy on citizens. The state is relentless in its pursuit of uncovering and ending dissent. During my time in the USSR, Soviet citizens were afraid to speak with foreigners for fear of being summoned by the KGB for interrogations, being accused of being a spy, losing their job, getting thrown in jail, or being killed. After I left Russia and moved to the United States, my parents were harshly interrogated by the KGB several times. *Kontr-razvedka* was the Soviet and is now the Russian government's tool of state control over its citizens. When people disappear in the middle of the night, never heard from again, it is *kontr-razvedka* agents who have taken them.

This is the whole cloth from which Putin is made. "Traitors always end up badly,"[13] Putin said in 2010, referring in this case to a Russian colonel who allegedly worked as a double agent and gave up ten Russian "deep cover" spies living in the United States, posing as Americans. "We know who he is and where he is," said a senior Kremlin official of the Russian double agent. "Make no mistake; 'Mercader' has already been sent for him."[14] Ramon Mercader was a Spanish-born communist and agent of NKVD who in 1940, on Stalin's orders, assassinated Stalin's opponent Leon Trotsky in Mexico City with an ice axe to the head.

Putin later denied that Russian special services conduct assassinations of traitors abroad, even though they do. Instead, calling those who betray Russia "swine," he offered that "traitors will kick the bucket themselves."[15]

From 1985 to 1990, Putin was posted at the intelligence unit in Dresden, East Germany, and lived in the building that housed the German state security service, the Stasi. He was an operative (*operativnik*) collecting political intelligence, working under the cover of a director of the Dresden House of USSR-GDR Friendship. His primary targets were political figures and the plans of the main opponent, NATO. In *First Person*, he describes his work as looking for information on political parties and their current and future leaders' tendencies within these parties, along with policies on certain issues within foreign ministries in various countries. Part of the job was to estimate the targets' reaction during disarmament talks. Collected intelligence was analyzed and sent to Moscow.[16]

Another part of his work required the recruitment of foreign human sources,[17] a skill that requires an expert understanding of human psychology—an ability to size up individuals' personalities, weaknesses, strengths, and motivations. This experience would become particularly useful to him later as a Russian president adept at manipulating leaders of other nations, particularly our own. He seems almost able to hypnotize American presidents simply by looking into their eyes, making them believe that they are dealing with a soulful person who can magically "reset" the U.S.-Russian relationship.

We don't know how successful Putin was at his job, other than his claims of promotion and a medal for "outstanding services to the National People's Army of the GDR." In *First Person* he downplayed the insults of the infamous former head of East German intelligence, Marcus Wolf, who said that Putin could not have been important if he, Wolf, didn't know him. Putin told his interviewers that Wolf was correct, and that he didn't perceive his words as insulting. Later in the interview he casually mentioned that if East German counterintelligence knew everything about his intelligence unit's work in the GDR, their entire agent network of German sources would be ruined, implying that the Soviets protected their operatives' identities, activities, and human sources well.[18] Wolf admitted, moreover, that a good spy is able to convince people around him that he is mediocre.[19]

When it comes to American intelligence, it is true that the names of the best intelligence officers are publicly unknown. You will not find their picture on Facebook or Instagram. In fact, they don't have any digital footprint at all, because their effectiveness and their well-being, as well as the lives of their sources, depend on secrecy. When I was an active intelligence officer at DIA, only one of my friends outside the IC knew what my true job was. My own father, who is a naturalized American citizen living in New York, won't know that I worked as an intelligence officer until he reads this book. He only knew that I worked at the Pentagon as a contractor, a job that I held prior to joining the DIA. ███████████████ ████████████████████████ I periodically run into former colleagues who have a cover identity. When I introduce them to my husband, who is not in this business, I either introduce them using that cover or I let the friend introduce him or herself to my husband.

"Specialist in Human Relations"

Putin prides himself on his ability to "work and communicate with people" and to "work with information."[20] He views both these skills that he honed as a KGB operative as critical to his success as president. When his close friend asked him what his job as a KGB officer entailed, Putin responded that he was a "specialist in communicating with people," which can also be translated as "a specialist in human relations."[21] Working with people, as Putin explained during a press conference in 2001, entails the ability to communicate with a wide range of individuals, from journalists and scientists to politicians and rank-and-file citizens. "It is important to establish a dialogue and activate the best in your partner. You want to achieve results; you must respect your partner, acknowledge that he is better than you in some way. You must make him your ally…make him feel that there is something that unites you, that you have a common cause." This is exactly the approach that HUMINT officers use to target, assess, and recruit their sources. In other words, turn them into spies who are willing to betray their country, in service for a foreign land.

Fiona Hill is a former U.S. National Intelligence Officer for Russia and Eurasia, who in August 2019 stepped down from her position as senior advisor on Russia to President Trump at the National Security Council. In her book *Mr. Putin: Operative in the Kremlin,* she and co-author Clifford Gaddy concisely define the dual meaning in Russian security services parlance of the phrase "working with people." They explain that it can mean to study the psychology of your target to figure out how to recruit them as a source or use them for other purposes. And it can also mean to elicit information from citizens, in order to keep your pulse on the sentiment of the population at large.[22] There is a long tradition in Russia, dating back to czarist times, where secret police keep tabs on people by questioning anyone deemed suspicious or finding out about them through informants. The rulers look to assess the general mood of the population and take necessary measures to preempt discontent or revolt.

In the USSR, Joseph Stalin, who perfected these tactics, sent millions of Soviet people—based on the slightest suspicion of disloyalty—to be executed or to do hard labor in the GULAG labor camps. The end of Stalin's reign of terror did not end the practice of neighbors spying on neighbors and colleagues ratting on colleagues. This was a standard practice that many Soviet citizens used to gain favor with the domestic police (*militsiya*) in the hope that they would leave them alone. Growing up in the Brezhnev era, my parents—who strongly disliked the Soviet system—insisted on not trusting anyone and on not sharing what we talked about within our family. My mother and father taught me and my sister "to think for ourselves," rather than believe what we saw and heard on TV and in school, which channeled non-stop Soviet propaganda and misinformation. This constant fear of government authorities is still present in my eighty-four-year-old father. Despite the fact that he has been living in the United States for ten years, he never speaks on the phone about certain subjects, such as politics or money, invoking when necessary a Russian phrase "*Eto ne telephony razgovor.*" It means, "This is not a phone conversation," and typically signals the need to switch topics. Soviet people always assumed that their mail was read and phone conversations were listened to by the government. Anything that was sensitive, private, or likely interpreted by government *apparatchiki* as dissent had to be shared in person.

The practice of domestic security services pumping citizenry for "useful" information is alive and well in Putin's Russia. Putin proudly justified this practice in the interviews for his autobiography. "Collaboration with regular citizens is an important instrument in the functioning of the state," he said, adding that many people collaborated with security services. "Ninety percent of all intelligence information was obtained with the help of agent networks of Soviet citizens who acted in the interest of the state," he said matter-of-factly. Putin defended the state's use of these domestic spies, or *seksoty*—a shorthand for *secretny sotrudnik,* which means "secret collaborator" —by stating that there was a "difference between spying for money or out of betrayal of your country and doing it for ideological reasons."[23] That makes it sound like a noble purpose, but what it amounted to was having your own citizens snitch on one another to keep them living in fear and under the state's control. As a student of foreign languages at one of the leading universities in Moscow, my few trusted friends and I were always wary of the students suspected of being *seksoty.* You always had to watch what you said and did, especially when we were socializing with the British exchange students outside of the approved curriculum activities. If you had a *seksot* in your company, everything would get back to the authorities. And if you were thought unreliable, you could not go on a foreign student exchange program or work with foreigners—or perhaps you would suffer far worse.

Putin is also a master at working with and using information, another skill he obtained in the KGB, along with the ability to manipulate people. During his speeches, press conferences, and annual videoconferences with Russian citizens, he regurgitates from memory massive amounts of data to sell his policies to the Russian people. He has incredible command of information, including loads of specific numbers, which he presents on a wide variety of topics, from

economics and international affairs to history and military capabilities. In *First Person*, his elementary school teacher commented on
Putin's "very good memory" and "quick mind."[24] Having met with
Putin at the Valdai annual conferences, Dr. Angela Stent, another
former U.S. National Intelligence Officer for Russia and Eurasia and
currently a professor of Russian Studies at Georgetown University,
said this about him: "This is someone who is pretty well-informed
on issues...who is in command of the facts. He can reel off statistics."
She added that Putin can be direct and almost rude to people and
that he exudes self-confidence.[25]

Master Manipulator

Confident in his ability to work with people and information,
Putin doesn't trust others to communicate his message for him—he
chooses direct contact with the audience, without a middleman. This
is the case whether his audience is the Russian people or various
international audiences, including Americans. He conducts four or
more major, extensively analyzed speeches each year. The first one is
the so-called "Direct Line with the President" (Pryamaya Liniya s
Prezidentom), a televised question-answer session, which can last
four hours, during which he responds to people's phone calls and
email messages. The second is the speech to the Federal Assembly,
the Russian Parliament. The third is the end-of-year press conference,
and the fourth is the speech at the Valdai Discussion Club, an annual
gathering of foreign experts on Russia that provides insights into
Russian policies and promotes Russia's views on world politics. This
is in addition to numerous interviews Putin gives to major domestic
and international media outlets.

Putin does not shy away from giving interviews even to Western
journalists, who he knows would not go as easy on him as would the

Russian media, which are mostly state-controlled. He uses these interviews to promote his and Russia's positions and to denigrate American and Western foreign policies by redirecting the questions and manipulating his opponents. During a 2018 interview with Fox News, journalist Chris Wallace challenged Putin's long-standing denial of Russia's interference in the U.S. 2016 presidential election by stating that Special Prosecutor Robert Mueller had concluded, as a result of the investigation, that Russia was guilty and had charged twelve Russian military intelligence officers with the crime. In response, Putin emphasized that the most important information that he wanted to draw to American TV-viewers' attention was that there were voter manipulations within the Democratic Party favoring one of the candidates, based on the information obtained from the emails of a Democratic official by the hackers. Putin insisted that the information in the hacked emails was true, based on Democratic National Committee leadership resignations, which were evidence and admission of responsibility. Putin was referring to the leaked emails of then Hillary Clinton campaign chair John Podesta that revealed the Democratic Party headquarters' preference for Hillary Clinton over Bernie Sanders.[26]

Putin argued that the Russian company that Mr. Mueller charged is in the restaurant business and that it hired American defense attorneys to challenge in U.S. courts the accusation of meddling in the American election. He added that "the American court has found nothing yet; no interference on the part of this company."[27] Putin was referring to Yevgeniy Prigozhin, also known in the American media as "Putin's Chef," and his company Concord Management and Consulting. Mr. Prigozhin finances the Internet Research Agency (IRA), a Russian front company that was directly involved in the Putin-authorized intelligence operation to disrupt the 2016 election.[28] Putin denied that the hackers were affiliated with the Russian

government and recommended that the United States "stop manipulating the public's opinion, apologize to the voters, and quit looking
for someone else to blame."[29] He was demonstrating his deft use of
the KGB's art of diversion and counterattack.

Putin seized control of Chris Wallace's interview to pitch the
Kremlin's narrative, asking him to be patient when Wallace
attempted to steer Putin towards the question that he was actually
asked and threatening to simply stop talking and be quiet if Wallace
didn't like his responses. As a well-trained intel operative adept at
handling situations involving *kompromat* (compromising information), Putin refused to hold or even glance at Mueller's indictment
document that Wallace diligently kept trying to hand him. (As an
intel officer, you are supposed to ignore when the opposing side is
handing you something. This is done to avoid a situation that could
be interpreted by an outside observer, or through a picture, that
you took something from foreign intelligence that could be pay-
ment or something else, like a document.) When asked if Russia
has any compromising information on Donald Trump that may
have been obtained during Trump's visit to Russia, Putin at once
snatched the opportunity to belittle the U.S. president. "He was a
rich person, but there [are] plenty [of] rich persons in the United
States. He was in the construction business. He organized the
beauty pageants, but it never occurred to anyone that he would
think of running for president," Putin said.[30]

Putin used the entire interview with Fox News to promote the
Russian agenda and push "hot buttons" by raising issues that continue to divide Americans to this day. More than a year after Russia's
meddling in 2016 U.S. elections, Putin continued to sow discord
within American society by talking directly to the American people
on the network with the largest viewership in American cable news.
Putin was not looking to convince all Americans of Russia's

innocence. But he was able to plant the seeds of doubts in some of their minds and to amplify the effects of Russia's original intelligence operation by keeping Americans upset and divided: his mission was accomplished.

Putin took a similar approach during his interviews with Megyn Kelly of NBC in 2017 and 2018.[31] When Kelly pressed him about the U.S. Intelligence Community's unequivocal conclusion about Russia's interference in the 2016 U.S. election, Putin redirected the conversation to a variety of topics. He said that the complexity of attribution makes it impossible to determine conclusively the origin of cyber intrusions. Therefore, it could have been that American hackers breached DNC servers. He accused the United States of meddling in elections all over the world, and threw in, for good measure, comments about President Kennedy's assassination—as an example that assassinations happen in America as well as in Russia and other countries. Finally, he recommended that Americans change the Electoral College law to avoid a situation where the person who wins the popular vote can still lose the election.[32]

Ordinary Americans are not the only target of Putin's propaganda and misinformation. The Master Manipulator fooled at least two American presidents. George W. Bush famously said he "saw an honest man" when he looked into the Russian president's eyes. Barack Obama trusted Putin so much that he promised Putin's proxy, then president Dmitry Medvedev, "more flexibility" in American policy towards Russia, unaware that his conversation was captured by a microphone.[33] And the American media was so beguiled by the KGB operative in the Kremlin that Putin was chosen as "Person of the Year" by *Time* magazine in 2007[34] and four times in a row from 2013 to 2016 by *Forbes* magazine as the "World's Most Powerful Individual."[35]

Surviving the "Biggest Catastrophe"

The fourth factor that shaped Putin's thinking was the collapse of the Soviet Union and Putin's subsequent experience staring down a mob of angry protesters as a KGB officer in Dresden during the fall of the Berlin Wall. These two events left a profound imprint on Putin and influenced his strategic intentions regarding his motherland, Russia, and its chief enemy, the United States. Putin proclaimed in 2005 and has repeated since then that the collapse of the Soviet Union was the biggest catastrophe of the twentieth century. In December 2019, in response to a Russian journalist's question whether he would regret that military personnel from the former Soviet republics, including Georgia and Ukraine, would not be participating in a parade dedicated to the seventy-fifth anniversary of Russia's victory in World War II, Putin responded, "What I regret is that the Soviet Union no longer exists."[36]

Putin did not lament the defeat of communism, however. He bemoaned the loss of the strong state, embodied by the centralized, all-powerful government apparatus that the Russians refer to as the *vertical' vlasti* (power vertical). The idea of the strong state (*gosudarstvo*) is closely related to the idea of *derzhava* (great power) in Russian strategic thinking. Only the state can ensure that Russia is a great power and that it is viewed as such by other states. Therefore, Russian people throughout history have voluntarily surrendered primacy to the state and its interests while assuming a subordinate role. There is no such thing as the interests of the individual in Russian thinking, at least not in the way Americans view individual rights and freedoms. The interests of the collective (*kollektiv*) always come first, and the interests of the state are paramount.

In *First Person*, Putin described an incident that took place at the Russian Ministry of Security (MGB in the transliterated acronym of the Russian name) in Dresden, East Germany, on the day when the Berlin Wall came down in 1989. An angry crowd of German citizens broke into the MGB and surrounded the building, Putin's station as a KGB officer. The crowd got aggressive, presenting "a serious threat." In Putin's assessment, they were vengeful against the MGB, having endured years of invasive internal surveillance and persecution by the security services. Putin started protocols for destroying classified information, personally burning all sensitive materials: communications, lists of agent networks, names of sources, and the like. At one point, Putin went outside to explain to the protestors that they were on the premises of a Soviet military organization. When the suspicious crowd demanded to know why he spoke German so well if he was just an ordinary Soviet military officer, Putin lied and said he was a translator.[37]

Putin's request for armed backup forces was at first denied because "nothing could be done without orders from Moscow, and Moscow was silent." Though Soviet military personnel eventually arrived, and the crowd dispersed, the incident appears to have left a permanent mark on Putin. "Nobody lifted a finger to protect us," he recalls in *First Person*. "I got the feeling then that the country no longer existed. That it had disappeared. It was clear that the Union was ailing. And it had a terminal disease without a cure—a paralysis of power."[38]

The Soviet Union was officially dissolved on December 25, 1991. Elated Americans and Westerners watched the communist bulwark crumple like a house of cards, envisioning a free and democratic future Russia. The Russians saw a completely different picture. Almost overnight, the motherland plunged into chaos. The rushed economic reforms undertaken by Boris Yeltsin's new government, converting the economy from centrally planned to market driven, left ordinary Russians hungry and unable to make ends meet. Many lost their jobs due to privatization of government enterprises, and those still employed were not paid for months due to severe budget cuts.

I got a taste of the "damn nineties" (*proklyatye devyanostiye*), as the Russians refer to the Yeltsin era, when I had to take a trip to my hometown Ust-Kamenogorsk—which was technically in a different country than the USSR: Kazakhstan, where I was born and raised. I embarked on a transatlantic journey, on just a few hours' notice from my aunt, to visit my gravely-ill mother in 1993. At that time, I already had moved to the United States, become a permanent U.S. resident, and had lived there several years. Upon arrival, I found our old apartment devoid of any valuables, my father unemployed, and my mother dying in the hospital thanks to the USSR's horrendous socialist medical care. When I asked my father where all the books were from our extensive and cherished home library, the beautiful crystal from my mother's collection, and other sentimental things, my father revealed that he and my mother had had to sell everything. They needed the money to buy food and keep themselves afloat. My mother had lost her job in the food industry and my father had quit working as a taxicab driver because hardly anyone could afford riding taxis in our town, and he hadn't been paid for several months. As my father, sister, and I were getting ready to drive out to our *dacha* (summer cottage) for the night, my father unscrewed a light bulb from one of the rooms in our two-bedroom apartment to bring with us to the dacha, as he could not afford to buy an extra one, and they were not easily available anyway.

When we arrived, I noticed there were no locks on the door of our *dacha* and the furnishings consisted of two mattresses on the floor and a gas stove in the kitchen. As my father explained, this was intentional. The impoverished state of the newly independent Kazakhstan brought robberies, and he wanted the thieves to come in without having to break the door and creating a mess to see for themselves that there was nothing to steal. I listened to my father lamenting the good old USSR, with plenty of borsch and pirozhki to eat, as I struggled to grasp that my parents' lifetime savings, monetary and non-monetary, had vanished. We stayed overnight at the *dacha*, my father sleeping with his AK-47 under his mattress in case the thieves decided to visit us that night.

I was anxious to get back to the United States right after my mother's funeral, to return to my new job at the International Monetary Fund, the organization that was demanding accelerated economic reforms and austerity measures from Russia and the formerly Soviet Newly Independent States. I didn't tell my father that my job at the IMF entailed helping Western economists without Russian language skills chart a path for Russia to transition from central planning to a market economy. For my father, as for most Russians and Kazakhstanis, a market economy simply meant astronomical prices and becoming impoverished overnight.

When Putin assumed the reigns of Russia, his first order of business was to restore internal stability, reverse the economic crisis, and reassert state control of most, if not all, aspects of life in Russia. Putin won his first election as President based on the simple message: he would restore law and order domestically and rebuild respect towards Russia internationally. This message resonated strongly with the Russian people, whose impression of democracy and capitalism that arrived as a result of the USSR's demise was of chaos, rampant crime, high inflation, and the legal seizure of government assets by a small group of business-savvy individuals called the "oligarchs." Yesterday's ruling communists had transformed themselves overnight into today's monopoly capitalists. Ordinary Russian people, who never had a lot but could at least get by during communism, felt even poorer and less safe under capitalism.

Going Back to Imperial Roots

In addition to Eurasianist influence, Putin drew his ideology from the ideas espoused by two Russian thinkers who fiercely opposed the Bolshevik revolution and the Soviet system—Ivan Il'in and Lev Gumilev. Putin often quotes both philosophers, whose ideas are consistent with Eurasianism.[39]

An aristocrat and a Russian Orthodox Christian, Il'in (1882–1954), whose father was the godson of Emperor Nicholas II, never accepted the new Soviet worker-farmer government. Arrested several times for "anti-Soviet" activities while teaching at the Moscow State University, he was at one point sentenced to death by firing squad. In 1922, at the last minute, he was exiled for life and settled in Germany.[40]

Il'in believed that the survival instinct of a nation was found in national unity and that an individual was a "body part" of the state and therefore could not live or exist without it. He viewed Western-style democracy as one of "the greatest dangers" for Russia, because it assigned only a superficial role to the state, which in turn did not unite its citizens under it. Russia, therefore, was to chart its own independent path and assume its historical mandate of "the bulwark of European-Asian, and therefore the world's, balance and peace." Hostile forces in the West were "hatching a secret plot, backstage [*za kulisami*—a phrase that has been used several times by Putin] to dismember Russia, and that only the evisceration of this plot would make the West give up its intentions."[41] Advocating the importance of keeping all the lands of Imperial Russia together to ensure its self-defense, Il'in specified in his writings that an independent Ukraine would be an unthinkable "madness." Il'in died in Switzerland, but, in 2005, on Putin's orders and at the Russian president's own expense, Il'in's body was exhumed and reburied in the prestigious Donskoy

Monastery Cemetery in Moscow.[42] Putin pays his respects to Il'in by visiting his grave. While there he has also trekked to the graves of another Russian nationalist historian and novelist, Aleksandr Solzhenitsyn, and the "White Army" Officer in the Imperial Russian Army, Anton Denikin. Both Solzhenitsyn and Denikin lived in the United States. Putin had Denikin's body moved from the United States, where he had died, and reburied in Russia.

Lev Gumilev (1912–1992), an historian and anthropologist, was similarly a counterrevolutionary and a big critic of communism and Stalin. The son of revered Russian poet Anna Akhmatova, Gumilev published subversive writings during the Soviet period using Samizdat, an underground system of self-publishing dissident and censored literature. He spent years in labor camps until he was released by Khrushchev in 1956. Gumilev became an ethnographer and expert on the influence of Russian ethnic minorities. He had two big ideas: *passionarnost* and "super-ethnos." The former can be described as a combination of a large capacity for suffering, an irresistible inner urge for purposeful activity, and the capacity for heroic effort on behalf of a goal. The Russians, imbued with *passionarnost*, were not just a single ethnicity, but a "super-ethnos" encompassing influences of both Slavic people and the nomadic tribes from the eastern Eurasian steppe. Consistent with Eurasianism, Gumilev believed that Russia was its own civilization, a geopolitical and cultural phenomenon that is not European, but Eurasian.[43]

Gumilev and Il'in are not only quoted by Putin. Their ideas are part of Russia's foundational strategic-planning documents, such as its Foreign Policy Concept, National Security Strategy, and Military Doctrine, which codify Moscow's official policy and strategy. Various concepts that underlie these documents, including the Russian World—the idea that all Russians belong to Mother Russia regardless of where they live—the Eurasian Economic Union, Russia's "sovereign democracy," and the reintegration of Ukraine and other post-Soviet states into a Russian-led union—something that is viewed as a matter of survival— are all built on the ideas of Gumilev and Il'in. The roots of Putin's actions and policies—such as the annexation of Crimea, "fast-track" Russian citizenship for any former citizens of the USSR and Imperial Russia, the creation of a legal justification to defend, including militarily, the rights of Russians abroad regardless of where they live, destabilization operations in Western countries and the United States, and military power projection campaigns across the world—can be traced to Eurasianism and similar philosophies.

Man of the People

At sixty-eight, Putin is highly athletic and personifies strength. Acting as a benevolent patriarch, he often reminds Russians about the importance of eradicating alcoholism, drugs, and other vices and urges them to lead a healthy lifestyle. His 2018 reelection campaign's slogan was "Strong President—Strong Russia."[44] And Putin's message resonates with many Russians, who are used to sacrificing personal freedoms for security. With the exception of his plan to increase the retirement age, Putin's anti-democratic actions—such as suppression of the press and even alleged-assassinations of journalists, opposition leaders, and intelligence double agents—do not send the Russians into the streets. The Russians identify with Putin's survivalist attitude, cool-headed image, abrasive style, and sometimes crude language. Most families in Russia have direct experience with and not-so-distant memories of surviving the Great Patriotic War, post-war hunger, and shortages during Soviet socialist era. They find Putin's fighting spirit, even when he fights dirty, appealing. "Keep moving forward and only forward, even if you have to step on corpses," was my father's mantra to me when I was a child.

Putin often incorporates Russian street language and vulgarities, even in his official appearances, when he wants to get someone to back off by intimidating or insulting them. In 2006, during a press conference with news agencies from the G8 countries, responding to a question regarding potential sanctions against Iran, Putin shot back with a crude Russian saying: "If Grandma had certain gender attributes, she would be Grandpa. Politics doesn't tolerate subjunctive mood."[45] He tossed the question aside by suggesting it was useless to speculate.

In 2002, during a press conference in Brussels, a journalist from *Le Monde*, referring to the war in Chechnya, asked Putin about the Russian military's use of mines that could kill not only Islamic terrorists but also civilians. Angered, he stunned the translators and everyone in the room by responding: "If you would like to become an Islamic radical and are ready to go for a circumcision, I am inviting you to Moscow. We are a multi-confessional (multi-religious) country and we have good experts in this area. I will make a special recommendation and your surgery will be done in such a way that nothing would ever grow back."[46]

Just like terrorism, another hot button for Putin is his alleged romance with former Olympic gymnast Alina Kabayeva. Rumors about their relationship appeared in 2008, five years before Putin divorced his wife of thirty years, Lyudmila Shkrebneva, in 2013, with whom Putin has two daughters. When a Russian reporter asked Putin in 2008 about a rumored wedding with Kabayeva, Putin said, "I always disliked those obsessed with erotic fantasies who stick their flu-ridden noses in other people's lives."[47] Other examples of Putin's language that shocked foreigners were his wanting to hang former Georgian president Mikheil Saakashvili "by the balls" and instructing the Russian oligarchs to follow the law always and not just when the government grabs them by a "certain place."[48]

Some analysts believe Putin deliberately uses street language to create a populist image to contrast himself from the Russian establishment elite—which he is undoubtedly part of—and garner support from ordinary Russians. I disagree with this assessment. While Putin certainly is very scrupulous about cultivating and guarding a very specific image—one that incorporates strength to the point of ruthlessness, secrecy, mystery, and unpredictability—at his core, he really is a "street guy" of worker-peasant stock, rather than a charter member of the post-*nomenklatura* elite. Putin is also a KGB operative, not a librarian or a classical musician. Such colorful language would be quite normal for a Russian male with this kind of background.

Similarly, it is not uncommon for Russian men to walk around shirtless when it's hot doing "manly things" like hunting, fishing, or yard work at their dacha. This is not to deny that Putin seems quite vain and takes every opportunity he can to show off his fit physique in support of his "tough guy of the people" image. His own best PR agent, he eagerly takes part in photo-ops hunting tigers or wrestling bears—nearly always without a shirt. While Americans either chuckle or look perplexed at the sight of Putin's shirtless photos, Russians beam with pride for their "tough" president.

As for bears, it is not by chance that this clumsy, unpredictable, but powerful animal serves as Russia's symbol and therefore a sometime foil for Russians who want to prove themselves. I can understand, I suppose, why mixed martial-arts champion Khabib Nurmagomedov, from Russia's Dagestan, was prodded by his father to use a bear as his wrestling training partner when he was training as a nine-year-old. But I have no idea why my mother, as a young woman, would be wrestling a bear in the snow, as attested by an old black-and-white picture my sister has kept!

What Putin Wants

Shaped by two catastrophic events, World War II and the collapse of the Soviet Union, Putin has embarked on a personal mission never to allow another calamity to strike Russia again. His life experience has taught him that strength, physical and mental, is the key to survival and respect. "The stronger you are, the less likely people will be tempted to mess with you," is a maxim he applies to himself and to ruling his people and positioning Russia in the world. In 2011, as prime minister of Russia—when he temporarily released the presidency to Medvedev to follow the constitutional two-term limit, which he later changed—he explained why he thinks Russia must be strong. "Let's be candid," said Putin, speaking to the Duma, the lower house of the Russian parliament. "In the modern world, if you are weak, there will always be someone who will want to arrive or fly over to give you advice about which way you should go, which policy you should pursue, which path you should choose for your own country." Russia, Putin asserted, must become strong to avoid *diktat* from the outside—that is, from the United States.[49]

The strong state, a powerful military, and a tough, even ruthless ruler symbolize strength in the Russian mind. Putin has chosen the rebuilding of Russian *Derzhava,* or "Empire State," as the top national interest. It is not by chance that the current Russian Coat of Arms is a depiction of the two-headed Imperial Eagle, like the old Imperial Russia's Coat of Arms. To make Russia an empire again, it needs "little powers" to cluster around it, to serve as a security fence—in case another great power decides to invade Russia, as has happened throughout its history—and to legitimize in full this prestigious title. Organizing the post-Soviet countries in the Eurasian Economic Union (EEU), or just "The Union," is a Putin priority. The "little powers," such as Latvia, Estonia, Lithuania, Belarus, Moldova, Ukraine, and other former Soviet states—though Moscow continues to refer to them officially as the Commonwealth of Independent States (CIS)—are not really independent at all, in Putin's view. During my visit to Moscow after the USSR ceased to exist, I heard Russians joke about the phrase "Newly Independent States" by saying that these "new countries are independent because nothing depends on them."

During his 2019 annual "Direct Line Questions & Answers" videoconference, Putin asserted that before the collapse of the Soviet Union, 74 percent of the people voted to maintain the USSR, but Secretary General Mikhail Gorbachev and the Communist Party disbanded the Union anyway.[50] While it is hard to know whether this vote count is accurate, many Russians today regret the dissolution of the Soviet Union. While Putin realizes that resurrecting the USSR cannot occur, he believes that reconstituting "the Union" with Moscow as the dominant player is a security imperative for Russia.

In a January 2011 op-ed in *Izvestiya* announcing the creation of the EEU, Putin called it the "model for a powerful supra-national unification," whose creation is "dictated by the realities of modern times." Revealing its true purpose, Putin assured that the new entity would not be a USSR, but would serve as a "key power center in the world—akin to the European Union, the United States, and China—and a "starting point for further integration."[51] His goal is to expand Russia's influence throughout Eurasia—"from Lisbon to Vladivostok." Regaining economic and political control over the post-Soviet states would enable Moscow, over time, to turn the Union into a military alliance, helping counteract NATO and withstand the perceived threat of dismemberment by the West, in Putin's view. Russians often allege American and Western greed for Russia's vast natural resources, due to the world's growing population and diminishing resources, as one of the reasons the West would want to fragment and control Russia and Eurasia. Putin invoked his own post-Soviet and more aggressive "Monroe Doctrine" to dissuade America from encroaching on what he believes is Russia's turf.

Putin delivered on his promise to the Russians. Having ruled with an "iron hand"—a style that is viewed as a norm rather than exception in the land that produced Ivan the Terrible and Stalin—Putin has, overall, improved Russia's well-being as a country. Remember, it's not about the individual but the collective in the Russian way of thinking. He has restored domestic stability, improved the Russian economy, and modernized the military to the point where even the Pentagon must play catch up in certain areas. Putin's Russia is back on the map. Consistent with his declared wish for Russia to become a power "in geopolitical demand,"[52] few major international conflicts are adjudicated without Moscow now. He finds common language with dictators like China's Xi Jinping, Saudi Arabia's Mohammed bin Salman, Iran's Ayatollahs, Turkey's Recep Erdogan, and the Taliban. He also is getting along very well with Israel's Benjamin Netanyahu. Putin doesn't care to be liked; he wants to be feared. When he sends nuclear bombers to Caracas or near Alaska, he believes that he is giving Washington a taste of its own medicine for violating the Kremlin's "Monroe Doctrine."

Realizing that Washington will not allow him to fulfill his strategic agenda without a major fight, Putin has decided that he must remove this obstacle. So, he has designated Russia's second national interest, behind empire, as weakening, and, if need be, defeating, the United States—just as the Eurasianists envisioned.

The Kremlin's most recent strategic planning documents, approved by the Russian president, codify this agenda. Russia's 2016 Foreign Policy Concept designates as one of Moscow's primary goals the "strengthening of Russia's position as one of the most influential centers in the modern world" and the pursuit of its "unique, centuries-old mission" to serve as a "balancing factor" and "central coordinator in international affairs and world civilization." According to the document, Russia "will defend the rights of the Russian citizens living abroad," will "harshly respond...with mirror[ing] and asymmetric measures" to "America's unfriendly actions," and "will not allow military interventions into sovereign states conducted under the pretext of [the] responsibility to protect."[53] "Responsibility to protect"—sometimes referred to as R2P—is a human rights concept that the United States frequently invokes to remove tyrannical regimes when they commit atrocities against their own people. The Russians believe that state sovereignty supersedes R2P. Therefore, countries have no right to interfere in other states' affairs, no matter how despotic their governments are.

The Kremlin's most recent National Security Strategy from 2015 directly accuses the United States of pursuing a policy of containment against Russia, blames the United States and European Union for supporting an unconstitutional coup d'état in Ukraine, and identifies "regime change" by way of "color revolutions"—meaning popular uprisings such as the ones that took place in Georgia, Ukraine, and other countries—as a primary threat to Russia's security.[54] Both of these key documents were crafted by the Russian security establishment when implementation of Putin-directed interference by Russian intelligence services in the 2016 U.S. presidential election was underway.

As an intelligence briefer, I sometimes faced incredulous policymakers who asserted that the U.S. government also has policies, strategies, and plans but that they're not followed, suggesting that Russian ambitions reflected in these documents were simply "words" and "bravado." My usual response was that there aren't that many people in Russia who dare not to follow Putin-directed policies more than once.

How We Get Putin Wrong

As we are trying to solve the Russia riddle, it is undoubtedly important to understand who Putin is and who he is not. While he is a statist, Putin is not a communist, at least not anymore. Although he was a member of the Communist Party—a requirement for serving as a career KGB officer—Putin eventually became disillusioned with communism. In a newspaper article announcing his platform in the run up to his first presidential election, Putin blamed the efforts "to realize the communist doctrine for a quarter of a century," a "roadmap that turned out to lead to dead end," for Russia's economic, technological, and social backwardness.[55] In his interview with Oliver Stone in 2015, Putin admitted that he initially believed in what he thought seemed like a good idea but that it then became clear that the "economy and political system were stagnating" because "the system was not efficient." He blames the Communist Party of the Soviet Union for "pushing the system towards collapse" and for letting the USSR disintegrate.[56]

It is also worth mentioning that Putin is not an anti-Semite. After decades of hostile relations between the USSR and Israel, Vladimir Putin has drastically and greatly improved the Russian-Israeli relationship, becoming the first Kremlin leader to visit Israel in 2005. On his watch, in 2012, a massive $60 million Jewish Museum and Tolerance Center opened in Moscow, acknowledging Russia and the USSR's history of anti-Semitism, and recognizing the contributions of Jewish people to Soviet life. Putin donated a month's worth of his salary to the museum.[57] Similarly, Benjamin Netanyahu values his ties with Putin and Russia, as shown by his electoral campaign placing a special focus on Israel's Russian émigré population, estimated at 1.5 million. In hopes of getting Russian-Israelis' votes, Netanayhu placed ads and billboards in Russian highlighting his ties with Putin.

Most likely, Putin developed an amicable attitude toward Jewish people in response to the affection he received as a child from an old, religious Jewish couple with whom his family shared a communal apartment in St. Petersburg.[58] Aside from his tender childhood memories of Jews, the pragmatic side of Putin likely calculates that the 1.2 million Russian and former Soviet émigrés living in Israel represent a good pool of expatriates who could return to their own or their parents' motherland, adding some educated human capital to demographically struggling Russia.[59] Russia's population is projected to decline by 8 percent by 2050, according to the United Nations. Low birth rates, high mortality from unnatural causes, and emigration are the main causes of the decline.[60]

Whatever Putin's motivation, Jewish people are breathing much more easily in today's Russia than they did during my childhood. Anti-Semitism then was so ingrained and condoned—and even encouraged—by the Soviet government that people were unaware they were being anti-Semitic. The same applied for hatred of other ethnicities. When my sister and I had spats growing up, her biggest insult to me was Jewess (*Yevreyka*) and mine for her was *Kalbitka*, a derogatory term for a Kazakh. Although our family is ethnically Russian, my sister and father look distinctly Asian. But because of the rampant persecution of anyone who did not look Slavic, my parents, and probably my parents' parents, were strongly motivated to register their children as Russian in their passports—the main form of identification, even though only a few communist elite were permitted to travel.

Grounded in the personal rapport between realpolitik-minded Putin and the similarly practical Netanyahu, the Russian-Israeli relationship is based first on the shared belief that Islamic extremism is a common enemy with which there cannot be a compromise. Sharing the Russian view that there is no such thing as a "moderate Islamist," Israel did not criticize Moscow for its wars in Muslim Chechnya. Neither did it express any negative reaction to Putin's annexation of Crimea. This pragmatic relationship, viewed by Israelis as the best ever between the two peoples, was on display in May 2018 when

Netanyahu joined Putin on the Mausoleum stand along the Kremlin Wall on Moscow's Red Square for the Victory Day parade commemorating Russia's victory over Nazi Germany. During the visit, Netanyahu emphasized the importance of "security coordination between the Russian army and Israeli Defense Forces" in Syria.[61] Israel views Russia, with its new role as a power broker in the region, as critical to its ability to manage the threat from Iran. Russia also needs Israel, a traditional U.S. ally and friend, for its strategy of solidifying its foothold in the Middle East as a counterweight to U.S. dominance.

Putin may be a villain, but he is not a supervillain. He is ruthless with enemies, some of whom he has had killed, and he jealously holds power, squashes dissent, and has amassed a huge fortune for himself and his friends. But his character and role in Russian society is more complex than the portrayal often presented in the West. Viewed by Russians as a patriot, he is seen as fighting for what he views as Russia's vital interests. His approval ratings are usually between 60 and 80 percent and, as of July 2020, have not gone below 59 percent.[62]

That Putin places security and stability ahead of individual freedom can be a surprise only to someone who doesn't understand Russia, Russians, and the country's history. Unlike Joseph Stalin, Putin has not murdered, starved to death, or sent to the Gulag millions of Russians. His rule has been far less brutal than that of Vladimir Ilyich Lenin or even the czars. Alex Ovechkin is still the captain of the Washington Capitals, and he is allowed to score goals and win a championship for a foreign team, even while keeping his Russian citizenship. MMA champion Khabib Nurmagomedov trains in San Diego, California and is the American United Fighting Championship (UFC) lightweight champion, attracting record-setting numbers of pay-per-view American and international fans. Unlike Soviet citizens, Russians— except those under sanctions—can travel with relative freedom to other countries. As hard-nosed as Putin is, he is a moderate for a country that produced Ivan the Terrible and Stalin, one of whom killed his own son and the other of whom left his son to die in a concentration camp, having refused to exchange him for a German general.

Putin is not an anomaly or exception in Russian politics. He did not create the idea that the Russians must always think first about the needs of the collective whole and the state, rather than worrying about the desires of the individual. And he was not the first one to create the notion of a strong state as a prerequisite for survival and to stoke distrust of the West and America. These sentiments predate Putin by centuries. They stand for Russian mainstream thinking. There is an old belief that Russians chose collectivism instead of individualism because a Western-style individualist would not survive the severe Russian climate. Weather aside, a narrative that's deeply ingrained in the Russian psyche is that Russia is unique, entitled to defend an independent path that is legitimately *not democratic*.

It is misguided to think that if it were not for Putin, Russia would be a drastically different country. It is not by chance that the Russians elected Putin four times, with the number of votes favoring him ranging from 53 percent in the first election in 2000[63] to 76.7 percent in 2018.[64] Even though these numbers were certainly subject to some "adjustments" by the Russian government, if you want to imagine an alternative to Putin as ruler of Russia, consider the following: in each election that Putin won—2000, 2004, 2012, and 2018, and even in the 1996 election won by Yeltsin—the nearest rival was a communist candidate. Those who believe that Putin is difficult to deal with should look at YouTube videos of communist leader Gennadiy Zyuganov and ultra-nationalist Vladimir Zhirinovsky. These characters—who often spew anti-Semitic, xenophobic, and chauvinistic rants—are not atypical representatives of the Russian elite. Putin speaks favorably about both men.[65]

Pundits and analysts have debated whether Putin is a strategist, tactician, or mere opportunist. Reluctant to acknowledge any positive characteristics that the Russian strongman may have, many label him a thug and opportunist. There is no question that Putin is a skillful strategist and tactician with an excellent nose for opportunities to exploit. This hardcore KGB man, surrounded by equally crafty *siloviki* (powerful members of the security services), oversees a highly sophisticated "strategic planning" process that regularly turns out regimented plans for achieving and defending what they believe to be Mother Russia's vital goals and interests. Once the plan is ready, the Judo Man is constantly on the lookout for that momentary opportunity to attack his opponent. In the meantime, he tries to disorient the opponent and make him unbalanced with cyber strikes, propaganda shouts, and deception—all to reach specific goals that advance his plan.

It is easy to be blindly disgusted by Putin, the annoying apparatchik, who fights dirty and breaks all the rules rather than engage Russia. But wringing hands or reacting emotionally to his stunts and outrages will not make Putin abandon his plans or his efforts to achieve them. To develop a serious policy and a counterplan, we must first consider what is realistic when it comes to Russia and Putin.

CHAPTER 3

Russia Organizes for War

"If a fight is unavoidable, you must strike first."

—*Vladimir Putin*

T he FBI agent I met at the post–September 11 federal government's conference for the business community did come through on his word. He put me in touch with a colleague of his who was recruiting for a Russian crime intelligence analyst position. After a series of intense interviews at the FBI headquarters at the Hoover Building in Washington, D.C., I was elated to receive a job offer for a respected GS-14 analytical role, fighting Russian crime in the United States. This was not shabby, as these are highly coveted and rare "six-figure" jobs within the federal bureaucracy, and it appeared that, contrary to many of my friends' predictions, I didn't have to take a pay cut from my private sector salary. I couldn't believe my luck!

I filled out many pages, and then even more pages, of what is called an SF-86 form—paperwork that allows the feds to run a background check in order to grant you the top-secret security clearance needed for your national security job. Going back seven to ten years, and for some questions your entire life, the government verifies whether you are of an upstanding character and quizzes your neighbors, family, friends, and "associates" to decide whether to entrust you with the nation's secrets. I went to the local FBI field office in a tall, inconspicuous office building in Falls Church, Virginia, for a lie-detector test, a supremely unpleasant experience. But it was the least gruesome of more than half a dozen polygraphs I took throughout my job application process and career in the Intelligence Community. Although my FBI interrogator was very stern through a process we sometimes referred to jokingly as "the colonoscopy," he did not play the awful and dehumanizing games that some of his counterparts do in other agencies to elicit information.

My initial elation with the prospect of working at the FBI catching Russian criminals was premature, however. After about a year of the background investigation, I was informed by my would-be boss, a very professional and good-hearted fellow, that the investigators uncovered that "apparently" my father lived in Kazakhstan and that this may present an issue. "Yes," I confirmed, "I listed my father and his place of residence and nationality on my SF-86, so this should not have been a secret for anyone or required many months to uncover." He seemed eager to bring me on board and was kind enough to recommend that I write a letter to an FBI security official explaining why I should be given a clearance. I promptly penned a petition explaining that the chances of my father being placed under duress by the Kazakhstani or Russian government to coerce me to spill American secrets were almost nonexistent. My father was retired; he had absolutely no connection with any government, and I would not tell him about my new employer. And, I said, the Cold War was over, and Kazakhstan was not a U.S. adversary.

The FBI powers-that-be must have been unconvinced, because I received no response about my clearance, positive or negative. A few months went by and my no-longer-to-be boss indicated to me cryptically and apologetically that perhaps I wouldn't get to help him root out those terrible Russian mafia elements infesting our homeland after all.

Utterly devastated, after several weeks, I found my despair turning to resolve. Raised by my father never to give up and determined to become an intelligence officer no matter the wait or sacrifice, I sent several job applications to key American intel agencies. After a few more months of phone calls, interviews, and submitting writing samples, I received job offers from the Central Intelligence Agency (CIA), the National Security Agency (NSA), and the Department of the Treasury's Financial Crimes Enforcement Network (FinCEN), as well as eventually two different offers from the Defense Intelligence Agency. The same arduous process began anew of filling out papers and electronic SF-86s, being "hostilely interrogated" during polygraphs, and warning neighbors, friends, and employers that the feds may visit them again.

Years went by; my security clearance appeared to have sunk into a black hole. Neither accepted nor rejected, I was also provided with no explanation why my critical Russian knowledge and skills, which were praised during the interviews, became not so critical once the American security apparatchiks laid their hands on my clearance paperwork. As I suspected, the USSR was not the best birthplace to put on your SF-86 if you aspired to become a U.S. intel officer.

As time passed, I rose in rank in my private sector jobs, changed employers, gave birth to two children, and doubled my business sector salary from what the government intelligence positions offered. I even began a graduate program in intelligence at the Institute of World Politics (IWP) in Washington to get myself a head start in intelligence-analysis tradecraft. My recruitment officer at the CIA, with whom I stayed in regular contact over the phone, continued to say that she "had no new information" but that "someone was still working on my case."

In October 2007, six years after my September 11, 2001, decision to serve my adopted homeland, I reached out to my good friend and mentor, Gene P., a CIA veteran of four decades, a true American hero, and a kind soul. He explained to me that the more qualified you are to be an intelligence officer, when it comes to foreign languages and in-country experience, the more difficult it is to get recruited into the Intelligence Community. The government considers it too expensive to have to vet someone like me for a security clearance, who lived extensively, or was raised, overseas. The security clearance decision-makers are also too suspicious to hire candidates with foreign backgrounds for fear that foreign spies will infiltrate our government (never mind that most spies, such as Robert Hanssen, Aldridge Ames, Ana Montes, and scores of others, were American-born). And, of course, if that foreign-born person you cleared does turn out to be a spy, it's your butt that's on the line.

Nevertheless, having seen my passion for service in intelligence and patriotism for America, my mentor became determined to help me. Gene suggested a plan that would get me into the IC.

Planning for War

Convinced that America is working to bring about Russia's collapse and realizing that Washington will not permit him to implement his grand vision for Russia, Putin concluded, consistent with the precepts of Eurasianism, that war with America is inevitable.[1] Growing up on the rough streets of post–World War II Leningrad, the future KGB operative learned that if a fight was unavoidable, it paid to strike first. Similarly, Russian military strategists believe that attaining what they call "strategic initiative" over the adversary, especially "in the initial period of war"—in other words, being a step or two ahead of him by anticipating his moves—is essential for attaining victory on the battlefield.[2] This first strike does not have to be kinetic. It can be a cyberattack or covert-influence operation—such as the intervention in the 2016 election—designed to destabilize the opponent and delay, blunt, or even deter a response.

Putin often emphasizes the importance of outsmarting America rather than competing with its firepower.[3] The correlation of forces, at least in conventional arms, still favors the United States. Outsmarting your opponent requires thorough preparation and a deep understanding of how he thinks and fights. So, Putin tasked his generals with creating a strategy and a plan to execute it.

During their war-filled, turbulent history, the Russians learned the hard way the importance of a practical strategy tailored to a specific adversary. Russian war planning and the creation of a grand strategy is the result of a complex and deliberative interagency process called "strategic planning," directed and overseen by Putin himself.[4] The planning involves scrupulous work by the Russian government "interagency"—the Security Council, the military and intelligence services, and various domestic security and executive agencies, as well as specially created think tanks. The General Staff, the Security Council, and above all Putin, play the leading roles.[5] A roadmap is created for achieving Russia's national interests and for combating expected threats to security and regime stability. In general, this is how the Russian president crafts his grand strategy.[6]

As supreme commander in chief of the Russian armed forces, Putin has total authority over decisions regarding all things Russian: what Russia's core priorities should be, what relationship Moscow should have with the rest of the world, and when and where to go to war. This Russian concept of unilateral decision-making, called *yedinonachaliye,* envisions the commander having full responsibility for making strategic decisions based on his personal experience and knowledge.[7] Derived from *nachal'nik,* or chief, *yedinonachaliye* has no exact English translation. The closest in meaning is "unilateral," the opposite of "collegial," decision-making. It is George W. Bush's phrase "I am the decider," except on steroids.

The concept of *yedinonachaliye*, not uniquely Russian, was introduced in Russia, originally in military affairs, by Vladimir Lenin during the Bolshevik Revolution. He believed that *diktat* and iron discipline were necessary, and that "the will of thousands must be subservient to the will of one" for socialism to succeed. Lenin said that *yedinonachaliye* could still be democratic because "nothing prevented the subordinate collective from advis[ing] the commander."[8] But the commander was free to ignore their advice. Stalin expanded this concept into political affairs by gradually appropriating the authority to form political decisions along the lines of centralized military control.[9] For Putin, who was trained in the regimented, top-down KGB environment, a unilateral decision-making style, *yedinonachaliye*, is as natural as breathing.[10]

A trained attorney, Putin ensures that all his decisions are "legal." But when a Russian law is out of step with his thinking, rather than choosing an alternate solution to the problem, Putin swiftly changes the law. When he could not run for a third presidential term, Putin temporarily switched places with his Prime Minister Dmitry Medvedev, while de facto still holding the reins of power. In the meantime, the constitution was amended to allow for two six-year terms instead of four-year terms. It enabled Putin to run for a third and a fourth term, totaling another twelve years in office. By 2024, when his fourth term ends, Putin will have served twenty years as president of Russia and four as prime minister. In the summer of 2020, Putin again orchestrated an amendment to the Russian Constitution. This time, his prior terms as president were zeroed out altogether, allowing Putin to run for office again and potentially remain president till

2036. The amendment gained "overwhelming" support from the Russian people.

The wartime concept of *yedinonachaliye* has found acceptance with the Russian people even in civilian life. Associating weak governance with what they refer to as "the times of trouble," Russians have come to view absolute power as an antidote to chaos. Many believe a certain level of dictatorship preserves stability, while others tolerate dictatorship as a necessary evil. George Kennan, in his anonymous 1947 article in *Foreign Affairs*, referred to this tacit agreement by the Soviet government and the Russian people on the need for dictatorial power as being "canonized in Soviet philosophy" and "anchored in the Soviet structure of thought by bonds far greater than those of mere ideology."[11]

Russians like freedom, but they worry more about destruction and calamities brought by wars and revolutions. So, even when faced with a despot like Stalin, the Russians will often opt for acquiescence, passive resistance, or simply suffering. Suffering and sacrifice are signature traits of the Russian character, which Leo Tolstoy, Fyodor Dostoyevsky, Anna Akhmatova, and others eloquently described. In contrast, Americans avoid suffering. They work hard at their jobs to afford fun in life. The Russian language doesn't have a word for "fun." Russians believe that to live means to struggle and suffer.

The Kremlin leaders rely heavily on these traits of Russian character, knowing that when it comes to war, the Russians will out-suffer and out-sacrifice the enemy. The great Prussian military strategist Carl von Clausewitz had this to say about Russia's sacrifices in the 1812 war with France's Napoleon Bonaparte: "It was a great success; and it cost the Russians a price in blood and perils that for any other country would have been higher still, and which most could not have paid at all."[12]

Character traits matter if you want to devise a counterstrategy against an opponent. Such things don't make the president's daily intelligence briefing—they don't meet the inclusion threshold. The "touchy-feely" stuff, like the opponent's mindset and willingness to sacrifice, is not tangible; you cannot observe it through a spy satellite's lens or count it, and it doesn't go "boom!"

Preeminent British strategist Colin Gray called the American way of war "culturally ignorant," causing the U.S. military to suffer from "self-inflicted damage caused by a failure to understand the enemy of the day."[13] An example of this shortcoming is U.S. planners' arrogance and failure to anticipate how the insurgents in Afghanistan and Iraq might adapt, fight, and stymie the world's most sophisticated and technologically advanced military. Explosive Ordnance Disposal Officer LCDR Jason Shell, U.S. Navy, who has completed multiple deployments to Iraq and Afghanistan, believes, for example, that the insurgents' employment of improvised explosive devices (IEDs) enabled them, the weaker side, to "gain advantage" over U.S. forces. With a stress on *improvised*, IEDs—which were responsible for 60 percent of all American fatalities and half of American casualties in Afghanistan—mitigated U.S. advantages in resources, technology, and ground combat.[14]

Other observers blame the "series of perceived disasters in current conflicts" during the last two decades on U.S. inability to craft a serious strategy based on realistic goals and affordable costs and to understand the constraints involved.[15] A reality-based strategy would help guide our military "in and out of modern conflict." An essential element of a competent strategy is an understanding of how our rivals think and operate, "the kind of expertise that the United States does not currently enjoy," according to Andrew Krepinevich and Barry Watts, who worked at the Pentagon's Office of Net Assessment for three decades under the legendary American foreign-policy strategist

Andy Marshall.[16] (The Office of Net Assessment is the Pentagon's internal think tank that develops forecasts of foreign threats thirty years or so into the future, like what Russia's Military Academy of the General Staff, or *VAGSh*, does.) I believe the American way of war and strategy can be improved if we properly diagnose the opponent and set realistic goals rather than simply fixate on the adversary's order of battle and logistics or ensuring that our technological prowess overmatches theirs.

Russia's high tolerance for war casualties was as difficult for me to explain to policy officials, not attuned to foreign cultures and mindsets, as it was to answer the question of why the Russians keep voting Putin in as president. American society has grown so averse to war fatalities that it has come to expect its military to fight wars with little bloodshed. Consistent with U.S. culture that values the sanctity of life, whether it's American or foreign, the U.S. defense industry developed highly accurate weaponry called precision-guided munitions, or PGMs, which give accurate strikes that help avoid civilian deaths. Although the U.S. military works hard to minimize civilian casualties, occasionally mistakes do happen, and this often leads to intense media criticism.

In contrast, during the Syrian conflict Russia repeatedly bombed hospitals, for example, in addition to shooting down a civilian airliner over Ukraine in July 2014. On August 31, 2019, Russian airstrikes on a specialized hospital for women and children in Aleppo forced the evacuation of newborn babies—still in their incubators.[17] The Russians, shaped by their history and culture, view civilian suffering and fatalities as a natural part of war. Counterintuitively for an American and Western mentality, the Russian doctrine envisions infliction of civilian casualties as a way of de-escalating conflict. Russian military planners believe they can compel an adversary to sit down at the negotiating table by targeting civilians and concluding a cease-fire on terms favorable to Russia, because the Westerners cannot stand seeing imagery of human suffering on CNN. Similarly, Russia also believes that it can sustain higher losses than the United States or the West. U.S. war planners must consider this asymmetry before hostilities break out with Russia.

Another puzzle that continuously perplexes our incredulous policy "experts" is why economically weak Russia can field military hardware that rivals America's. The answer is simple: the Russians are fine with heavy spending on defense because they are afraid of war, fear their own government, and expect privation. They survived more than seven decades of Soviet socialist shortages, plus even more in the "capitalist" 1990s, when the oligarchs plundered the country.

Forecasting Future Wars and Warriors

Retired U.S. Navy vice admiral Arthur K. Cebrowski, who is considered the thought-leader behind the concept of network-centric warfare, made the following observation on the link between warfare and culture: "Nation-states, and even sub-state and transnational actors, wage war in ways consistent with their culture, values, and resources."[18] Russian strategists place a premium on understanding the adversary's culture and anticipating their way of warfighting. They also try to predict when and where future wars will occur. To achieve this goal, they spend considerable effort on what they call threat forecasting *(prognozirovaniye ugroz)*.

Forecasting future security is conducted by the Russian General Staff and Military Academy (VAGSh) with support from the Academy of Military Sciences (AVN) and various scientific research institutes operating under the auspices of the Ministry of Defense.[19] The General Staff is the main body of the Russian Armed Forces' command and control and is a rough equivalent of the U.S. Joint Chiefs of Staff. The chief of the Russian General Staff and the chairman of the Joint Chiefs of Staff are in regular contact.[20] Unlike politicians, the American and Russian militaries have maintained, for the most part, a regular and professional—albeit not exactly cooperative—relationship throughout the ongoing crisis in the U.S.-Russian relations. Fortuitously, both militaries possess the world's largest nuclear arsenals, mostly targeting each other. Thus, when operating in close proximity in Syria and other areas, for example, the silent treatment or name-calling, like politicians often use on both sides of the Atlantic, would be too risky.

Founded in Imperial Russia by Czar Nicolas I in 1832, the Military Academy of the General Staff (VAGSh), with its Center for Military-Strategic Research (TsVSI), is the brain trust of the Russian military and the main training center for senior officers who are groomed for leadership. It is primarily here that the Russian strategists and military theorists study war, in the attempt to forecast the "nature and character" of future conflicts.[21] The Russians prioritize monitoring and analyzing how the United States and NATO conduct their military operations to forecast how future wars in any theater will be fought.[22] Russian strategists and warfighters believe America has the most advanced technologies and weapon systems and the most effective tactics. They want to be able not only to defeat U.S. weaponry and warfighting strategy, but also to learn from it too.

They are well-versed in the works of world's leading military strategists like Von Clausewitz, China's Sun Tzu, Britain's Sir Basil Liddell Hart, and renowned Soviet military strategist Aleksandr Svechin, among others. The knowledge they obtain and secrets they steal about the new weaponry, technologies, doctrines, forces, tactics, and so forth, are processed in the context of these great thinkers and Russian history. They estimate the characteristics of future wars and develop the strategies, tactics, and weaponry they believe are needed to win.[23]

Another aspect of Russian military forecasting is the prediction of threats (*ugrozy*) or potential flashpoints in specific geographic locations. TsVSI, which was founded in 1985, conducts studies in support of large-scale, real-life wargames such as the one Russia staged jointly with China in the fall of 2019, the largest military exercise Moscow has held since the Cold War. TsVSI also develops operational concepts that are then tested in real combat conditions—for example, in Russian operations in Syria and Ukraine.[24]

Western analysts understand little about Russia's threat forecasting methods. Open sources focus mostly on the final product— descriptive assessments, rather than methodology. What is clear is that it involves continuous monitoring of the geopolitical environment, which Russia calls the "military-political" (or *VPO*) arena and includes software-based modeling. The algorithm incorporates a variety of inputs, such as a particular country's weapon systems, force posture, doctrine, military infrastructure, speed of mobilization, arms treaty information, frequency of going to war, and even the political statements made by a country's leaders with regard to Russia or its leaders.[25] Based on these inputs, the model assigns each analyzed country a level of conflict potential (*uroven' konfliktnosti*).[26] The assessment attempts to predict that country's probability of going to war with Russia and other countries.[27]

This threat prognostication method is in a way like the risk assessment methodology used by U.S. insurance companies to calculate premium rates for policyholders. Insurance underwriters use a software algorithm that computes the risk of a customer filing a claim against their policy.[28] The algorithm segments burly smokers with high blood pressure from cauliflower-devouring 10K runners in the case of a life insurance policy, and adolescent male drivers of red Mustangs from elderly housewives with beige Buicks in the case of an auto insurance policy. Just as insurers can be wrong before they sign you up about how likely you are to kick the bucket from lung cancer or crash your new sporty SUV, the Russian war prognosticators' assessments can be wrong too. It is a risky method, since Russians build the algorithms; that is, these algorithms can have the typically Russian "worst-case" bias and anti-American mindset baked in.

Russian planners view the American military as "ten feet tall." Their beliefs that U.S. ballistic missile defense is highly advanced and American leaders' intentions are much more sinister than in reality are all reflected in the General Staff's prognostications. The consequences of this could be that Russian weapon systems are designed to defeat a much more capable supervillain than America is or even wants to be. This, in turn, can prompt U.S. designers to supersede Russian weapons. As both countries' intelligence services are watching each other for threat indicators, war between Russia and America could become a self-fulfilling prophecy.

The Russians continuously adapt to new developments of American military capabilities and tactics by making changes to their doctrines and strategies every five years—or more frequently when needed, even every three to six months, depending on the level of hostilities. In recent years, they have elevated the role of cyber and special forces and non-military units, such as mercenaries and intelligence operatives, in achieving military and political goals. They believe in the accuracy and criticality of threat forecasting.

Putin himself places high priority on these forecasts, or *prognozirovaniye*, ordering his security and intelligence services to monitor foreign military activities closely, especially those of the United States.[29] In an op-ed he penned in *Rossiyskaya Gazeta* (*The Russian*

Gazette) describing his second presidential election platform, he stressed the importance of forecasting security threats thirty to fifty years in advance by "looking over the horizon." He urged the Russian military to create a "smart" military analysis and strategic planning system with credible algorithms for long-term forecasting, which would be able to turn out "ready-made" operational solutions for security agencies.[30]

The Russian threat assessment methodology is far more complex than anything I have seen as an intelligence officer used by our analysts to assess and plan for potential security threats to our country. As vice chairman of the Joint Chiefs General Paul Selva acknowledged in 2019, "We do little in terms of predictive analytics for the readiness of forces in terms of the future, rather than the past" to mitigate emerging risks.[31]

If we have any hope of winning or deterring a war, especially with Russia, we must establish a serious threat-forecasting capability. In addition, we must establish an analytic capability tasked with anticipating how a particular state or non-state entity—shaped by its history and culture—would go about warfighting against technologically superior (or, in the case of Russia and China, near-peer) American forces. Such in-depth prognoses would help us estimate if and how these actors could be deterred from war. Setting up such a capability would require an analytic cadre that is well-versed in foreign cultures and languages—or, as we say in the business, "capable of thinking and operating in the target's conceptual framework." In other words, a U.S. intelligence officer, in order to accurately assess threats from Russia or China, for example, and to explain or predict Moscow's or Beijing's behavior, must be able to think like a Russian or a Chinese would in a specific scenario—not like an American living in the United States. These, as we used to joke back in Russia, "are two big differences!"

Predicting Areas of Instability:
Where Russia and the U.S. Might Clash

Out of the various potential conflict scenarios forecast by the Russian General Staff, the one that gives the Kremlin the gravest concern is a conflict sparked along Russia's periphery with one of its post-Soviet neighbors—such as the one that Russia fought with Georgia in 2008—that draws in NATO and the United States. Russia would then be forced to fight the U.S. in a high-intensity conflict that could escalate into a broader war in Europe. After the end of the Cold War, Russian military-strategic forecasts assessed low probability for a direct war between Russia and the United States, instead predicting a local or regional conflict on its periphery. In the last two years there have been indicators that the Russians are now concerned about such an interstate "large-scale war." Potential flashpoints of concern include Russia's former Soviet satellites, sometimes termed "the Borderlands": the Baltics, Ukraine, Georgia, Moldova, Belarus, and Crimea, which Russia illegally annexed from Ukraine in 2014.

The Baltics—Estonia, Latvia, and Lithuania—are a special case due to their membership in NATO. Putin would think twice before intervening militarily against a NATO member, which would trigger Article 5 of Collective Defense. Despite military alignment with the United States, the Baltics are subject to intense influence campaigns by Moscow and efforts to ensure they are ruled by governments friendly or, at minimum, not hostile to Russia. The United States, having incorporated the Baltics into NATO, looks to peel off the other "Borderlands" from Russia's orbit. Steps taken include planning on EU and NATO membership for Ukraine, Georgia, and Moldova— moves that Russia vigorously opposes.

Each of these areas has unique circumstances: the ongoing conflict in Ukraine, a territorial dispute between Russia and Georgia, and Russian support for the breakaway republic of Transnistria from Moldova. But they are all vulnerable to escalation of hostilities and a U.S.-Russia military clash. Russia and the United States both regularly conduct military exercises in the region, with military close calls between the two becoming more frequent.

The threshold for Russia's intervention in the Baltics is higher than for the rest of the post-Soviet countries due to their NATO membership. But Russian military-strategic assessments include the Baltics as a potential conflict area, and Moscow doesn't rule them out as an area of future instability.

The General Staff's forecasting scenarios do not mention, at least in the unclassified military professional literature, a conflict involving the United States in Crimea. The Kremlin publicly dismisses Ukrainian and U.S. calls for Russia to return Crimea to Kiev. Reportedly, Putin stated that "the question regarding whom Crimea belongs to is closed once and for all."[32] A member of the Russian Parliament's Defense Committee compared demands to return Crimea to Ukraine with a call to return Texas to Mexico.[33] One of the main government-affiliated media outlets ruled out the possibility of forcible return of the peninsula to Ukraine because "no one wants to go to war with Russia," mocking joint U.S.-Ukrainian military drills in the region as presenting "as much of a threat to Russia's Crimea as black widow spiders," which are commonly found on the peninsula.[34]

These public dismissals aside, the Kremlin is concerned about the possibility of a Ukrainian attempt to take back Crimea with U.S. support. The United States continues to remind Russia that it doesn't recognize Crimea as a Russian territory. Ukrainian president Volodymyr Zelensky, during his meeting with President Trump in September 2019, asked for U.S. help in returning Donbass (where Russian-backed separatists occupied territory) and Crimea to Ukraine. In 2018, Ukraine and the United States conducted military drills that brought together

19 nations in the region and included "30 ships and other vessels, two dozen aircraft, and nearly 3,000 troops." An amphibious assault on an island in the Black Sea, 110 miles from the Crimean peninsula, was rehearsed against a fictitious enemy.[35]

Comforted by the erosion of NATO's military advantage in Europe since the end of the Cold War, Putin—who was confident that he could outplay President Obama—was concerned about the unpredictability of President Trump. The KGB man knew that for all Trump's sweet talk about making a deal with Russia, the real estate mogul—who released lethal weapons to Ukraine and authorized a deadly strike on Russian mercenaries in Syria—also carried a big stick. The Russians include Crimea in one of their security-threat scenarios, which raises the probability of its becoming a flashpoint.

While it is impossible to predict specific pathways to war between Russia and U.S.-led NATO, the following factors increase the probability of escalation: Russia's presupposition that sooner or later it will face a conflict with the United States; the Kremlin's hyper-sensitivity to security threats; the U.S. government's suspicions of Putin's intentions in the region; and the clashing interests of the two powers in Eurasia. General Gerasimov, in a 2013 article about the importance of strategic foresight and threat forecasting, quoted Aleksandr Svechin: "It is unusually difficult to foresee the circumstances of a war…as it requires an understanding of its own particular logic."[36] Nevertheless, Gerasimov wrote, "it is necessary to solve this task."[37] In 2019, Gerasimov wrote that Western policies compel Russia to "respond to a threat with a threat."[38]

While every war begins differently, following its own pathway and logic, Von Clausewitz taught that all of them have this in common: they suffer from an "uncertainty of all information." In other words, decisions are made by commanders in what he famously called the "fog of war." Here is what the great strategist wrote: "All action takes place…in a kind of twilight, which, like fog or moonlight, often tends to make things seem grotesque and larger than they really are."[39]

If all this sounds like alien stuff that happens "over there," as in the case of most U.S. wars, keep this chilling fact in mind: once a direct military confrontation between the United States and Russia has begun or is about to begin—although in an area that is geographically far from U.S. borders—Russian doctrine envisions the possibility of initiating strikes on the U.S. homeland.

Putin's Strategy to Defeat America—It Is Not Hybrid, It's Indirect

"Hence to fight and conquer in all your battles is not supreme excellence; supreme excellence consists in breaking the enemy resistance without fighting," wrote sixth-century BC Chinese strategist Sun Tzu.[40] In its nearly ten year war in Afghanistan (1979–1989), Russia experienced firsthand Sun Tzu's admonition that waging a war was devastating for the warfighters and stressful for the state. So, for the war against its "main enemy," America, Putin's generals are heeding the ancient Chinese general's wisdom that the smartest way to fight was by stratagem, a scheme used to outwit an opponent in order to achieve your ends.

On Putin's orders, the General Staff devised a strategy that would turn America's perceived weaknesses into Russia's strengths to win. Concerned that Russia—whose military strength diminished considerably after the collapse of the USSR—is outmatched by the United States technologically, the Russian generals first turned to an asymmetric strategy that is typically used by a weaker power against a superior opponent.[41] This strategy targeted America's reliance on technology and its open, democratic society. The former dominates all spheres of American life and is integral to the Pentagon's warfighting style, while the latter makes dissent and disagreements between political parties and various social groups commonplace. Russia perceives both of these aspects of American society as vulnerabilities to be exploited during both peacetime and war. Therefore, Moscow's strategy is to use these perceived weaknesses—which Americans consider strengths—to deter conflict or win it on terms favorable, or at least acceptable, to Russia. Later chapters tell exactly how Russia plans to go about it.

U.S. and Western analysts call Russian strategy "hybrid warfare" based on their analysis of the renowned February 2013 article by General Gerasimov penned in a Russian military journal.[42] These include a mix of various statecraft tools and forces—hence the name "hybrid"—such as regular armed forces, special forces, local militias, and such non-military means as cyber operations, disinformation, propaganda, economic pressure, and diplomatic maneuvers. Western observers interpreted Gerasimov's article as foreshadowing Russia's strategy during the Ukraine invasion, where these tools were used.

Calling Russian strategy and its way of war "hybrid warfare," however, completely misses the point how the General Staff thinks about warfare, its adversary, and the role of strategy versus tactics. Misidentifying Russian strategy leads to U.S. confusion about how Russia would fight a war. "Hybrid warfare"—conceptualized by former secretary of defense General Mattis—does not exist in Russian military doctrine.[43] Russian military officers only refer to it as a U.S. and Western concept. The crux of the Russian strategy and doctrine is not so much about the mechanics and tactics of warfighting as it is about the best ways to take advantage of the adversary. The strategy centers on a deep understanding of human behavior. The main target is the adversary's mind, not his military hardware. Everything else flows from there in a unified approach that is not "hybrid."

The official Russian strategy is called a "strategy of indirect action." The Russian generals borrowed heavily from the classic works of the British strategist, former army captain, and military correspondent for the *Times* of London Liddell Hart (1885–1970). Considered the father of the "strategy of indirect action," Hart pointed out that the United States' invention of the atomic bomb in 1945 and the hydrogen bomb in 1952 helped introduce a new guerilla-type warfare in the field of military strategy. Liddell Hart believed that "victory" in a "total war" was impossible due to the threat of annihilation by nuclear weapons. So, the menace of "mutual suicide" would prompt strategists to look for "indirect" ways of fighting the opponent, "hamstringing" him in a "limited war" rather than clashing with him directly in all-out, widespread aggression. "Indirect methods" as "the essence of strategy...endow warfare with intelligent properties that raise it above the brute application of force," Hart wrote in his classic book *Strategy*.[44]

Russia's version of "indirect action" is applicable to both war-time and peacetime—a false distinction to Russian strategists, in any case. The goal is always to change an opponent's calculus about fighting by waging psychological warfare on its population and armed forces. It envisions employment of non-military methods, such as economic coercion, diplomatic pressure, and subversive activities, as well as military tactics—from blockades to "scorched earth" and "sabotage." It also aims to isolate an opponent from his allies and prevent him from deploying forces.[45] All these measures are intended to weaken America's resistance and prevent it from mounting a successful defense against Russia should a conflict break out. During peacetime, this strategy is subversive. The Russians sometimes refer to this condition as "controlled instability."[46]

The Plan for Future Attacks on U.S. Homeland

In March 2019 at the General Staff's strategy conference, General Gerasimov unveiled Russia's updated strategy, which he justified as needed to respond to the "[United States'] and its allies' aggressive vector of foreign policy." The new strategy, which Western analysts dubbed Gerasimov 2.0, envisions employing armed forces in new types of wars and conflicts using both "classic and asymmetric measures."[47] Russia is in the second decade of a major military modernization, which began in the aftermath of the war with Georgia in 2008. It is developing and fielding advanced weaponry that rivals U.S. conventional arms. The Russian military has gained significant operational experience during its five-year campaign in Syria. These gains have earned Russia its designation as a "near-peer competitor" in the U.S. national security community and likely have boosted Putin's confidence of being able to prosecute, if he has to, a traditional military campaign against a technologically advanced opponent such as the United States or NATO.

Based on General Staff's military forecasts predicting that war between Russia and the United States is likely, Moscow has taken preemptive actions. On July 23, 2013, about seven months prior to his invasion of Crimea, Putin issued an "edict" for the General Staff. It had his approval for a series of military plans, including a Plan for the Defense of the Russian Federation, Plans for the Development and Employment of the Armed Forces, and a Mobilization Plan. Also among these plans was something that sounded unassuming but is actually menacing: a Plan for Strategic Containment and Conflict Prevention.[48] It is my professional assessment that this plan, which is not publicly available, is a top-secret (*sovershenno sekretno*) document and a critical piece of Russia's anti-American strategy containing publicly unknown operational concepts for future attacks on the U.S. homeland.

Chief of General Staff General Gerasimov confirmed in 2014 the existence of these military plans approved by President Putin's 2013 edict. He explained that these plans for a military attack are intended to "convince potential aggressors that any form of pressure on the Russian Federation or its allies will prove futile." In September 2014, Putin's former economic advisor Andrey Illarionov, during a conference in Lithuania, said that Putin had been working on a plan in preparation for a major war since 2003.[49]

Although we do not have the war plan itself (in actuality a series of plans), I offer my assessment of its contents based on a substantial body of open sources that describe Russia's strategic military thinking. These unclassified sources include Russia's declared doctrine, and threat perceptions, public statements by military and political leaders, force modernizations, and recent combat operations. In addition, writings in military professional journals by authoritative military theorists, including General Gerasimov, give us a good sense of Moscow's secret doctrine.

Putin's plan has a two-pronged approach to achieve Russia's goal of defeating America: a long-term, multistage prong and a contingency prong. The long-term prong aims to destabilize American society through ideological subversion over several years or decades (I discuss this later in the book). The contingency prong is designed to defeat the United States on the battlefield should an armed conflict break out. The second prong, by contrast, as described in the chapter on Putin's military option, covers Russia's ability to prosecute armed struggle throughout the entire conflict spectrum: from low-level confrontation and covert sabotage to high-intensity military operations. It will include Putin's nuclear strategy.

Destabilizing and Subverting America from Within

The long-term prong of Russia's war on America has already begun, as I mentioned in the first chapter. Russian strategists sometimes refer to this phase as "controlled chaos" or "controlled instability."[50] General Gerasimov—who, together with members of the General Staff's Military Academy, is the primary architect of Russia's broader "strategy of indirect action"—in his 2013 article pointed out that fomenting chaos in the target country can be achieved without a formal war declaration.[51] It can be done by exploiting the "population's protest potential," where one could "plunge the country in a vortex of chaos, humanitarian catastrophe, or even civil war"—all without its knowing that it has become a victim of foreign intervention. Russian military theorists believe that such potential for protest in democracies can be cultivated by enlisting unwitting members of the population and forming a so called "fifth column" within the enemy state.[52] Consistent with Liddell Hart's strategic guidance, the goal of this Russian strategic prong is to "weaken resistance" on the part of the opponent before "attempting to overcome it," by drawing him "out of his defenses." And you don't even need to put "boots on the ground" to defeat your adversary.

Russia works to create discord and national disunity here on U.S. soil, as it did during the 2016 election intervention, by undermining public trust in government leaders and institutions, fueling discontent, inciting political protests, and discrediting democracy itself as a system of governance.[53] These Russian activities continue today and present challenges to U.S. national security officials, especially with respect to the 2020 presidential elections.[54] "Although we cannot change the fundamentals of American strategy, we can disorganize it," proclaimed policy analysts in a prominent Russian think tank in its 2018 annual issue of an "International Threats" forecast.[55] The same report recommended the Russian government to stay away from "frontal confrontation" with the U.S. government in favor of using lobbying as a method of influencing U.S. policy and politics. It said that under U.S. law, foreign governments can lobby the federal government through agents, which is not considered interference in U.S. domestic politics. Using emotionally charged language, biblical themes, and arguments related to the defense of human rights and individual freedoms were recommended as narratives that would resonate with Washington's elites.[56]

Undermining the country from within by manipulating American elites is not a new Russian strategy. Soviet defector Yuri Bezmenov, who fled his KGB post in India in 1970 and was resettled by the CIA in Canada under the pseudonym of Tomas Shuman, revealed a similar Soviet anti-U.S. program.[57] Yuri Bezmenov, who worked as a propagandist for the KGB under the cover of a journalist for news agency *Novosti*, disclosed that this program was designed to transform the United States, over thirty-plus years, from a capitalist to a communist-socialist country through ideological subversion. The four-stage program, which was implemented by the vast network of KGB agents highly trained in psychological warfare, aimed to change the mindset and behavior of young Americans by exposing them to Marxist-Leninist ideas, such as equality of outcome, intolerance of dissent, and rejection of religion.

Intelligence operatives infiltrated academia, media, government institutions, labor unions, and Hollywood to portray socialist ideas as desirable and humane, and capitalism as evil and unjust. Spies, however, did not do all the work alone. They targeted left-leaning individuals, the so-called "useful idiots," and cultivated them as "agents of influence" who would educate the next generation of elites. In turn, these elites were supposed to assume senior roles eventually within government, business, culture, and other institutions—positions with the power to change or overturn the U.S. system. According to Bezmenov, the Soviets were pleased with the results of the subversion program in the United States.[58] The KGB found the first stage of the four-stage program completed by 1985 (I describe this program in greater detail in the chapter on "Active Measures," a Russian term for covert influence).

Putin's intelligence services have adopted and adapted key elements of the program revealed by Bezmenov to continue weakening the United States. Moscow has already started this strategic destabilization campaign against our homeland, using a variety of measures in "preparation of the battle space" by weakening the opponent. A low-intensity campaign is waged now, primarily through diplomatic posturing, cyber hacking, intelligence operations, and demonstrations of military force. But it will intensify if Russia perceives an increased threat from the United States to its security or national interests, especially in Eurasia. The following startling and highly revealing passage, from a senior analyst at a prominent think tank that serves the Russian president, describes the destabilization campaign: "Impose damage to the information and communication systems [and] critical infrastructure; conduct massive psychological influence on the population to alter countries' politics; confuse the opponent; disrupt his plans and policies; sabotage the political process; and create an internal opposition within an adversary state."[59]

Fomenting a crisis and bringing about the collapse of the U.S. government and democratic system are goals Putin is pursuing, beyond ideological subversion. According to the unclassified 2017 intelligence assessment, in the runup to the 2012 U.S. presidential election, the Russian government–sponsored, English-language channel RT News helped stir discontent by alleging election fraud, voting machine vulnerabilities, corruption of the U.S. "ruling class," lack of democracy in America, "corporate greed," and other inflammatory messages.[60] RT also advocated that Americans "take back" the government and change the U.S. system through a "revolution."[61] Russian strategists believe that "helping" Americans manufacture their own crisis is a low-cost way of keeping us distracted and focused internally rather than externally on what Putin does to achieve his strategic ambitions. Fearing superior U.S. forces, Russia's preferred way of "neutralizing the American threat" is without resorting to what we analysts euphemistically call the "kinetic" component—i.e., things that "go bang," such as missiles, tanks, jets, submarines, and all other traditional means of warfare.

As part of its covert intelligence operation to disrupt the 2016 elections, the Russians stirred up racial tensions, promoted police brutality narratives, and pitted pro-gun advocates against gun-control proponents and pro-immigration activists against anti-immigration activists. They did this by exploiting social media, which enabled the Russians to pose as Americans, and by sending Russian intelligence operatives to the United States to organize and participate in political protests.[62] Similar activities continue to this day. In 2017, Russian agents helped foment the deadly racial tensions during the "Unite the Right" rally in Charlottesville, Virginia, according to a Republican congressman from Virginia who was briefed by the FBI.[63] Having experienced multiple revolutions during its history, Russia knows firsthand the devastating effects of domestic instability, which is exactly why Russia believes internecine strife is the best weapon to turn America on itself.

Missing the Warning Signs

Intelligence officials often complain how difficult it is to assess foreign leaders' intentions as compared to their military capabilities, especially those of an unpredictable Vladimir Putin. But Putin has been remarkably open about his intentions, both with his statements and his actions. Could the problem be that our experts in the national security establishment have been ignoring the Russian threat because they were applying an American mentality when predicting the behavior of a country led by a former KGB agent? Did we dismiss Putin's declared threats and ambitions as inconceivable because they were senseless to the Western mind, thus missing countless indicators of an impending problem and opportunities to shore up defenses? The Russian government is much less secretive than the USSR when it comes to its goals and ambitions, strategy, and even military capabilities. All we need to do is listen very attentively to what Putin and his coterie of generals and diplomats have been saying and writing.

Russian senior military officers and strategists' views are published in unclassified professional military journals like *Voyennaya Mysl'* (*Military Thought*) or specialized newspapers like *Krasnaya Zvezda* (*Red Star*). *Red Star* is the "official newspaper of the Armed Forces of the Russian Federation," and *Military Thought* is the main publication of Russia's Ministry of Defense. General Gerasimov, chief of the Russian General Staff, and General Karakayev, head of Russia's strategic nuclear forces, are a mong the senior editing staff of *Military Thought*, making it one of the most authoritative sources of information on Russian strategic military analysis.

The breadth and depth of information available through unclassified but authoritative sources allows an experienced analyst to build a "big picture" composite of Russia's strategy and intentions, including those regarding the United States. Having knowledge of the Russian mindset and history is crucial, however. Without such knowledge and the willingness to employ it, you don't have the context for understanding what the Kremlin means by its broad and sometimes cryptic statements.

U.S. analysts are often dismissive of open sources, citing concerns about potential Russian deception, and therefore give preference to classified reporting. These concerns are exaggerated. While there is no question Russia is exceptionally skillful at deception and does it on a regular basis—targeting both domestic and foreign audiences— the Russian military does need a platform for propagating accurate views related to military theory in order to develop, educate, and train their own military cadre. Any influence attempts that do take place on the pages of open publications are more likely in English editions of Russian publications or can be spotted by an experienced analyst. A seasoned analyst who knows her target will spot the inconsistencies between open source and past clandestine reporting that show attempts at influence or deception.

There is remarkable consistency between what Russia says it is going to do, albeit often in indirect and obfuscated language, and what it does. Russia's foreign policy position and attitudes towards the United States and the West have remained largely the same— adversaries and opponents—never friends—regardless of who occupies the Kremlin. It was clear in the early 1990s, after the demise of the USSR, that Russia was not going to accept its Cold War defeat.

Just two years after the Cold War, under the leadership of buffoonish and frequently drunk Boris Yeltsin, Russia reminded the world that it will continue to play the role of a "superpower," providing the "balance of influence in the world," as stated in Yeltsin's 1993 Foreign Policy Concept. Consistent with this vision, three years later, Yeltsin's foreign minister and former head of the Russian Foreign Intelligence Service, Yevgeny Primakov, Putin's godfather to some Russians, articulated the concept of a "multi-polar world."

The Primakov doctrine envisioned Russia becoming a counterweight to U.S. global dominance by fostering the establishment of alternative power centers in key regions of the world. This was like the strategy that the USSR pursued against the United States during the Cold War. Moscow was to pursue closer ties with India, China, and Iran, and strengthen its position in the Middle East. Primakov looked to reduce U.S. influence in Eurasia and re-establish Russia's dominant role in the region.

In March 1999, in a clear act of defiance toward the United States, Primakov famously turned his airplane around mid-air over the Atlantic as he was heading to Washington to meet with President Clinton's vice president Al Gore.[64] Infuriated that the NATO bombing campaign against Yugoslavia, Russia's ally, was about to begin during the Kosovo War, Primakov cancelled the meeting, where he was supposed to discuss urgently-needed financial aid from the United States to Russia. In June of the same year, the Russians orchestrated what is known as the "Dash to Pristina." In a thoroughly-planned operation, two hundred Russian troops upstaged NATO peacekeeping forces by arriving earlier, unannounced, and occupying the airport in Kosovo's capital.

This dangerous move could have resulted in a broader confrontation between the Russians and NATO forces, as shown by the response from British general Michael Jackson to American general and Supreme Allied Commander Europe (SACEUR) General Wesley Clark. When Clark wanted to send paratroopers to prevent an advance of the Russian forces, Jackson responded, "I will not start a Third World War for you." Russia's willingness to take the risk of a military clash with NATO forces in Kosovo was an early sign of Moscow's deep anti-NATO sentiment and serious disagreement with its policies.

On becoming president, Putin continued what Primakov started an implementation of the "multi-polar world" in which Russia reasserts control of Eurasia and undermines American interests globally. In his first Foreign Policy Concept of 2000, Putin declared the "formation of the belt of good neighbors along the entire perimeter of the Russian border" as one of Russia's key priorities, and hinted at the "integration of the former Soviet states." He pronounced America's "economic and power dominance" as a threat to Russia's national interests. Putin's first Military Doctrine of 2000 chose "military blocs and alliances"— implying NATO—as one of the external threats. The doctrine also said that NATO countries close to Russia's borders resulted in an imbalance of forces threatening Moscow.[65] This did not deter George W. Bush, a year later, from embarking on a new "twenty-first century" relationship with Russia "based on friendship, cooperation, common values, trust, openness, and predictability."[66] Friendship? Common values? The FBI had just arrested its own agent Robert Hanssen, a 20-year spy for the KGB, in 2001. The most damaging spy in modern history, Hanssen sold some of the most sensitive U.S. secrets to the Russians, including our nuclear secrets, the existence of a secret, American-built tunnel under the Soviet Embassy in Washington, D.C., and the identities of Soviets who spied for America.[67]

Putin protégé Dmitry Medvedev, considered in the West a "modern, moderate" democrat by Russian standards, approved his version of Russia's foreign policy as president in 2008, the same year that Russia fought a five-day war with Georgia. His document unambiguously termed Russia "the biggest Eurasian superpower" and stated Putin's goal of integrating post-Soviet countries, called the Commonwealth of Independent States (CIS), into the Eurasian Economic Union (EEU), beginning with Kazakhstan and Belarus. Putin views the EEU as a counterweight to the European Union and wants to include as many former Soviet states as possible. Medvedev's document also accused the West of not abandoning the Cold War policy of "containment" against Russia. Without calling out the United States by name, the 2008 document accused America of "destabilizing" the world by using military force without the United Nation's approval, provoking an arms race, stoking nationalism and religious tensions, and fomenting conflicts in Russia's immediate vicinity. It was a written version of the anti-American statement that Putin made at the 2007 Munich conference, during which he figuratively called out the United States and the West to a duel by denouncing U.S. global leadership and values. Four years later, President Obama, seemingly oblivious to the threat, was heard on an open microphone promising Vladimir, through Dmitry, "more flexibility" once he was reelected in 2012.[68]

From that point through today, every Russian policy, strategy, and doctrinal document repeats and amplifies such anti-American and anti-Western sentiments and goals. Convinced, however, that Russia has no other choice but to embrace liberal democracy after the fall of the USSR, America has missed every warning sign that Moscow did not see eye-to-eye with Washington and was going to put up major resistance to our agenda, even by force. The U.S. security establishment was willfully unaware that a future conflict was afoot and missed many opportunities to head off Russian aggression. Putin, therefore, was able to present the West with a fait accompli in Georgia, Ukraine, and Crimea, along with the disastrous roiling of our democracy with the 2016 presidential election intervention.

Washington's naive and obtuse belief that liberal democracy is coveted by all has blinded our leaders, prompting them to reduce our intelligence and military resources targeting Russia. My question at a meeting during my initial days in the Intelligence Community about our inadequate satellite coverage over Russia was greeted with disbelief. I was viewed as a paranoid Russian when the real threat came from Middle-Eastern terrorism. At the time, Moscow was conducting a 2008 wargame in the North Caucasus. Another Russian defense analyst, Pavel Felgenhauer, was in Moscow, where he expressed his concerns to Radio Free Europe/Radio Liberty that the Russian wargame was providing cover for an impending invasion.[69] The West, however, was not paying the right attention. Frustration as a new intelligence officer was gradually growing in me when a couple weeks later Russia invaded Georgia.

While Washington was pursuing unending wars in various parts of the globe and misreading Putin—by judging him to be an "honest man" as President Bush did or a "bored kid in the back of the classroom," as President Obama called him—the Russian leader steadily and quietly crafted a deadly plan to undo America. The chapters that follow will describe the five main components of this plan: space warfare, cyberattacks, information warfare, sabotage by spies, and traditional military operations, including nuclear warfare.

The Playbook: Moscow's Five-Point Plan to Defeat America

Gene P. explained to me that although candidates like me are extremely valuable for the Intelligence Community, they have the most difficult time becoming IC employees. Our strength, that we speak the languages and understand the thinking of America's adversaries, is the very thing that IC security views as a vulnerability. Their thinking goes that if you speak a foreign language and have lived in a foreign country, you are subject to "foreign influence" and therefore are vulnerable to being recruited by foreign intelligence services as a spy.

This thinking is illogical. Most immigrants are American patriots who would not betray their country. They love America because it provides us rights, privileges, and even necessities we didn't have in out places of birth—freedom, economic opportunity, justice, safety, security, and other things that Americans born in this country don't even think about. Immigrants normally don't bite the hand that feeds them. We want to serve our country and repay America for what it has given us.

Most U.S. intel security apparatchiks don't understand this, or, as another mentor of mine, Ken D., put it, they "don't want to do their job" of vetting naturalized American citizens for security risks. It is very time-consuming doing a background check for someone who lived in a foreign country or traveled a lot internationally. Ken D., a very senior former Pentagon official who had also served in the Reagan White House, explained that security bureaucrats are the most illogical and unreasonable people he had met. They prefer to stall the clearance process for candidates with foreign backgrounds and experience in hopes that the candidate will eventually drop out, because they simply don't want to decide about clearing the candidate for intelligence work.

Gene P. said that the only thing that works to convince such bureaucrats to act is fear of involvement from their chain of command. Gene recommended that I write a letter to the Director of National Intelligence and the director of the Central Intelligence Agency about my case. So I did. I informed both heads of these agencies that after several years of trying to join the IC to serve my country, having actually received multiple job offers from several intelligence agencies, I had been neither granted nor denied a security clearance. I had also withdrawn from the CIA clearance process, because DIA had told me that they wouldn't continue to work on my clearance unless I terminated my processing with the CIA.

I never got any replies from the DNI or the CIA director. Several weeks later, however, I received my DIA clearance and the "Entry on Duty" date. The entire process of joining the Intelligence Community from November 2001 to July 21, 2008, took almost seven years. My husband, although proud of my American patriotism and perseverance, said that he knew of no other person who would dedicate seven years of his or her life to go through such a formidable process. He also warned me that as a free spirit, I was not built for a government bureaucracy. Elated that I could finally serve my adopted homeland,

I did not pay much attention to his words. Nor could I have possibly foreseen how prophetic they would be.

The Plan

Putin's playbook for his battle against the United States includes five instruments of war: space warfare, cyber-attacks and information warfare, spy craft, special activities known as "active measures," and traditional combat operations, including nuclear warfare. Putin routinely deploys these tools in his toolbox against America, except for the kinetic and nuclear options, which, however, he does often threaten to unleash.

It is critical that we understand Putin's way of war and the different conception of peace that Russia has. Technically, there is never peacetime, according to the Kremlin's doctrine. Russia views itself in a continuous state of struggle or confrontation with opponents, who are jockeying for a premium position in global geopolitics. And Putin is determined to grab one of the best spots.

To counter Russia's strategy and doctrine, first the United States must understand where Russia focuses its attention when challenging America. Russia is all about exploiting the opponent's vulnerabilities—which will vary from culture to culture—and indirectly influencing the adversary and his mind, rather than about the methods employed. The methods and level of conflict intensity will vary depending on the adversary and anticipated outcome.

In areas where Russia fights proxy wars with the United States, such as Ukraine and Syria, Putin eagerly shows off his military's prowess, new weaponry, and modern tactics. His intent is not only to prevent the United States from securing its influence in these areas, but also to showcase to Washington what kind of combat arsenal Moscow would bring to bear should kinetic warfare break out. Putin displays Russia's military preparedness to wage an all-out war with the United States if Washington crosses Moscow's security redlines. He believes America understands these redlines "telegraphed" in multiple Kremlin doctrinal papers but is willing to test his resolve, such as through NATO expansion.

Sanctions or not, Putin has shown during the past decade that he will invade or destabilize Russia's former republics—as he did in Ukraine and Georgia—rather than let them switch sides to NATO and the European Union. He will continue to unbalance America through cyber warfare and other tools in his playbook rather than let Washington democratize the former Soviet Eurasian countries. He understands well that he is playing a risky game that can lead to an escalation of tensions. But risk is something that Putin is accustomed to; it is a way of life for a former KGB officer. Bred as an intel operative, he plans for contingencies. Therefore, he has a plan in his playbook for an all-out war with America.

CHAPTER 4

Putin's Star Wars: Lasers, Jammers, and Satellite Killers

"Space operation will...precede air, sea, and land offensive operation.... The main task of this operation is to destroy the key elements of the adversary's space infrastructure and to disorganize his military's command and control.... This will enable [the Russian military] to achieve information superiority [over the U.S. military] by commanding and controlling the adversary's weapons and troops, reflexively.... Mass [space-enabled] missile strikes will target the key elements of the adversary's state and military command and control, critical infrastructure of the economy, and troops."

—Aerospace Defense *(a Russian professional military journal)*

On July 21, 2008, the day of my "Entry on Duty" (EOD), I walked through the Naval Research Laboratory (NRL) gate, located in what seemed to me a sketchy area of Washington. It was the beginning of my service at the Defense Intelligence Agency's Directorate of Analysis (or DI, as we referred to it), as a space threat intelligence analyst, to scrutinize and report on foreign threats to U.S. space systems.

The day I became a U.S. intelligence officer was one of the happiest days of my life. I was not deterred by an arduous process that had lasted close to seven years. Nor was I discouraged by mountains of paperwork, countless polygraphs, some of which included hostile interrogations and polygraphers testing me with accusations that I was a Russian spy, or my husband's warnings that I was not the type who can tolerate government bureaucracy.

Having recently given up a senior position at one of the prominent defense contractors that D.C.-area folks sarcastically refer to as "Beltway Bandits, and a nice, windowed corner office in Crystal City, I was quite unsettled by my tiny cubicle and the shabby looks of my new workspace at the Naval Research Lab, one exit on Route 295 away from DIA. I was surprised that well-paid senior professionals with specialized skills required to solve complex national security problems would work in conditions I had not seen since I left the Soviet Union. My initial disappointment was soon replaced by the excitement of receiving my new and shiny IC "blue badge," getting "read-in" to Top-Secret Sensitive Compartmented Information (TS/SCI) and signing non-disclosure agreements (NDAs), which allowed me to read the most secret intelligence reports, attend classified meetings, and carry highly sensitive documentation in a specially designed "courier" bag.

This special feeling of doing important national security work never left me, being privy to the nation's most sensitive secrets and being entrusted with information, some of which was obtained by people risking their lives. It helped me to get through long and busy days, deal with the exhausting government bureaucracy, and leave my crying small children at dawn. The little ones, often messing up my white, starchy shirt and black suit with their tiny hands, had trouble understanding why Pentagon generals, who needed to be briefed by mommy on an important issue, had made them get up so early before daycare.

Space Armageddon for America

Space will serve as the primary battlefield in Putin's war with America, should the conflict escalate into the kinetic realm. For such a contingency, Russia is developing and fielding weaponry to deliver a space Armageddon.[1] Russian military planners have watched American warfighters' tactics in conflict zones very closely across the globe for over twenty years. What the Russians have learned is that U.S. space capabilities were the primary reason for the American military's superior performance in Kosovo, Iraq, Afghanistan, Libya, and Syria. Of course, I am speaking about U.S. military victories in these conflicts, not the quagmires and disorder that followed. America's ability to put "iron on target" with speed and precision is unprecedented in the history of warfare, minimizing civilian loss of life. So is our intelligence services' ability to track down and help remove from the battlefield individual combatants and malignant actors like Saddam Hussein, Osama Bin Laden, and Qassem Soleimani. American intelligence can nearly always find the needle in a haystack, even if it takes us several years.

What makes America's science fiction–like way of war possible is the world's best and largest satellite constellation. This U.S. space arsenal is launched and operated by a combination of private industry and such military and intelligence entities as the Air Force and the National Reconnaissance Office (NRO), located in Chantilly, Virginia, the very existence of which was classified until 1992.[2] The non-profit organization Union of Concerned Scientists (UCS) estimates the number of American satellites at 1, 425 as of July 31, 2020, although the exact figure is classified and unknown to the public. By comparison, Russia's constellation, which is the third largest in the world, is assessed by UCS at 172, behind China's, which is estimated at 382.[3] These space birds provide critical military and civilian functions, including missile warning, communications, command and control, reconnaissance (imagery and signals intelligence), and weather data.

The Russians concluded that while superior space capability is the greatest force multiplier in America's way of war, it is also our greatest vulnerability, because of the U.S. military's near absolute dependence on it. This is just like in our civilian lives: before embarking on a long distance trip, we launch our favorite GPS-powered app (my husband and I often bicker about Waze, which is my preference, versus his Google Maps), instead of trekking to the nearest AAA office to obtain maps. Our troops rely on the same constellation of thirty-one GPS satellites for tasks like synchronizing operations, pinpointing targets, locating personnel, and doing myriad other things in a war zone. Even during wargame simulation exercises, I always had trouble finding physical maps to show moves by the United States' Red Team against the Blue Team, especially if the move involved a geographic area other than the conflict zone. I remember trying to get my hands on a world map at one of the war games conducted at a prominent U.S. military base to help a colleague, who must have slept through his geography classes, locate some places in Eastern Europe. Frustrated by not being able to find a map, I innocently tried to bring in my handbag, which contained a small paper map of the world—I usually carry one on me—into the wargame room during the break and was promptly stopped by a surly security guard who swiftly confiscated my alternative tools, insisting that these objects presented a security threat.

This is how former STRATCOM Commander General John Hyten described the American military's reliance on space when giving a public talk called "U.S. Strategic Command Perspectives on Deterrence and Assurance." Space, he said, "is fundamental to every single military operation that occurs on the planet today."

General Hyten admitted that every drone, fighter jet, bomber, ship, and soldier is "critically dependent" on space to conduct its operations.[4] He also revealed that Russia is building space weapons to threaten U.S. assets in the heavens and "create havoc for humanity" on earth.[5]

Having found American space superiority is also our Achilles' heel, Russian strategists set out to deafen and blind U.S. forces in a conflict.[6] By attacking American satellites, Russians will look to offset, if not negate, American superior conventional firepower. They also hope to paralyze U.S. forces psychologically by taking away what they perceive as the technological "crutch." Russian military theorists often write about the importance of targeting both the technical capabilities and the mind of an adversary, planning to disorganize his troops and weaken their will to fight. Crippling our satellites, in Russia's view, would enable them to disrupt the U.S. forces' "kill chain" and stymie the American way of war.

This is the essence of Putin's asymmetric warfare—that of a weaker opponent versus a stronger one, which is how Russia considers itself vis-à-vis the United States. He looks to defeat a stronger adversary by removing or degrading its strategic advantage and thus leveling the playing field. Moscow believes that in an all-out space war, America—whose entire society, from ATMs to gas pumps, is wired up through space—stands to lose more than Russia.

Even our ultimate deterrent, the nuclear forces and weapons operated by the Strategic Command, is reliant on space, because missile-warning satellites are an integral part of the nuclear command and control architecture (NC2).[7] America's missile warning constellation, called the space-based infrared system (SBIRS), is designed to detect and track incoming intercontinental ballistic missiles (ICBMs) and provide warning to U.S. leadership about an impending attack.[8]

An example of how our missile-warning satellites protect our forces occurred during the Iranian strike with sixteen short-range ballistic missiles on American military personnel stationed at two Iraqi bases on January 7, 2020. Iranian leaders ordered the strike in retaliation for the United States' elimination of prominent Iranian military commander Qassem Soleimani, who had a history of running operations that killed Americans. With one or two hours of warning time, provided by a combination of early-warning satellites and other intelligence, American forces were able to invoke dispersal protocols and take cover in bunkers that used to belong to Saddam Hussein's military. Some even contacted their loved ones in the United States, just in case.[9] President Trump announced the next day that one of the reasons that no Americans were killed by Iranian missiles was because "the early warning system worked very well."[10] Imagine if it hadn't worked well because the early warning satellites were messed with!

Built by Lockheed Martin and Northrop Grumman at a cost of around $1.7 billion a pop, American early-warning space birds present attractive sitting ducks for U.S. adversaries like Russia with advanced space and counter-space capabilities. Expressing his concern for the U.S. military's ability to protect these critical assets when he was STRATCOM commander, General Hyten described them in 2017 as "big, fat, juicy targets."[11] He advocated for a shift in the Pentagon's procurement strategy from acquiring large, costly space systems that are "exquisite" but "fragile and undefendable" to getting ones with smaller, cheaper, "more resilient and distributed capabilities."[12] Whether large or small, our satellites will be at risk in an armed conflict with Tier-1 adversaries like Russia and China. The American space industry must make newer satellites with built-in protections and have enough of them in inventory to be able to quickly reconstitute our mission-critical constellations in wartime.

Unfortunately, our space industry partners have not noticeably learned from Facebook and Twitter's sad experience of serving as launchpads for Russia's covert cyber influence operations. Two years ago at an industry event on Capitol Hill with commercial space operators, I asked a question about whether the space industry derived any "lessons learned" from the IT industry, which was caught off-guard by U.S. adversaries' advanced cyber capabilities and willingness to hack American IT networks, including those with critical missions. There was a collective shoulder shrug from the panel of space "experts" in response, indicating to me that it won't be long before we're unpleasantly "surprised" by satellite hacking and intrusions. American aerospace companies are naive if they think that Russia (or China for that matter) would not mess with their spacecraft, just like they did and continue to do every day with our IT companies.

Russia justifies its decision to wage space warfare on America by accusing the United States of militarizing space and undermining strategic stability.[13] Moscow believes that Washington has disrupted the balance of forces between Russia and the United States by developing advanced, space-enabled conventional precision-strike weapons that can be used for strategic purposes, such as the decapitation of an opponent state's regime—in other words, killing Putin and his advisors.[14] This mission, in the Russian General Staff's view, is reserved for nuclear weapons, earning them the title of "strategic." U.S. conventional superiority and precision gives us a notable advantage beyond that of nuclear weapons.

The threat of nuclear annihilation serves as a stabilizing force supporting what the Russians call "equal security."[15] The term "equal security" was coined by Russian propagandists who look to impose Russia's conception of international law on other countries to constrain the military advantage of major powers, especially the United

States and China. According to the concept of "equal security," no major power should develop military capabilities that overmatch other major powers' capabilities and fundamentally change the strategic balance of forces in the world.[16] Even so, Russia itself has always pursued the development of weaponry and strategies with the intention of beating the United States on the battlefield. In this sense, "equal security" is simply another Kremlin covert-influence trick, under the guise of strategic stability, to outsmart Washington.

The Russian General Staff's concern that the United States can now achieve strategic missions such as regime change with purely conventional arms, whether by targeting them directly, attacking them militarily, or backing insurgencies, animates its effort to defeat us in space. Just ask Slobodan Milosevic, Saddam Hussein, and Muammar Gaddafi about America's ability to dislodge a head of state. The Kremlin views the U.S. practice of removing unwanted leaders from power, even in the case of brutal dictators like Saddam Hussein, Bashar al-Assad, or the Iranian leadership, as a threat. It is one of the reasons why Russia has intervened in Syria, obstructing U.S. efforts to weaken Assad's hold on power. Driving Putin's paranoia of a U.S.-sponsored "color revolution" in Russia and his forcible removal from power is a fear, shared by other Russian elites too, that Washington seeks Russia's economic collapse and destruction.

Russian strategists believe that the United States has developed a new conventional forces triad, consisting of its Prompt Global Strike (PGS) capability, its ballistic missile defense (BMD), and so-called "space weapons."[17] PGS is a suite of weapons that will allow the United States to deliver a conventional precision-guide airstrike anywhere on earth in as little as an hour, in a manner close to that of an ICBM. Moscow believes Washington's new, nonnuclear strategic triad neutralizes Russia's nuclear deterrent and blunts its "second-strike capability," leaving Russia unable to respond to a U.S. first strike. This logic drives

Putin's desire to arm his military with hypersonic missiles capable of penetrating America's missile defenses. But while maligning U.S. BMD as "destabilizing," Russia is aggressively modernizing its own ballistic missile shield, "A-135." The Trump administration called out Putin's hypocrisy in the 2019 Missile Defense Review (MDR):

> Russia maintains and modernizes its longstanding silo-based strategic missile defense system deployed around Moscow, which includes 68 nuclear-armed interceptors, and has fielded multiple types of shorter-range, mobile missile defense systems throughout Russia. These include hundreds of S-300 and S-400 launch vehicles, each capable of firing four interceptor missiles. Russia is also developing the S-500 as an even more modern and technologically advanced air and missile defense system to augment the S-300 and S-400.[18]

This is a formidable capability that Putin wants Americans to ignore.

As for U.S. space superiority, Putin is pursuing counter-space weapons.[19] By counter-space weapons, the Russians mean anti-satellite (ASAT) capabilities, precision-guided munitions (PGMs), and what is called "command, control, communications, computers, intelligence, surveillance, and reconnaissance," or "C4ISR." Because of our highly advanced space assets, America has the world's most robust C4ISR systems, which underpin our entire network-centric warfighting capability.

At various space intelligence conferences, it is common to hear the adjective "exquisite" mocked by General Hyten, referring to American satellites. Unless you are a space and intel geek like me, you may wonder why such a beauty-related descriptor is used for a curious-looking, clunky piece of aluminum and kevlar (a material used for bulletproof vests and armor). Simply put, American space birds are "stuffed" with highly sophisticated sensor technologies and fly on incredibly complex missions for the Intelligence Community. From finding terrorist camps to targeting Osama Bin Laden and keeping an eye on missile launches and nuclear detonations, these are not your grandmother's satellites. No wonder the Russians want to clip these space birds' wings.

Putin is also developing anti-satellite or counter-space capabilities out of concern that Russia is falling further behind China and the United States. In January 2007, China conducted an ASAT test by destroying a weather spacecraft with a ballistic missile–based ASAT weapon. Due to excessive fragmentation of the satellite, the test resulted in almost one thousand pieces of orbital debris, posing significant risk to other operational satellites in low-earth orbit.[20]

Russia was blindsided by the Chinese test. Sharing a long border with China and a turbulent history, Russia views China as a latent threat. Moscow is especially suspicious about Beijing's long-term intentions in Eurasia, especially considering China's growing military power and more recent "Belt and Road" (formerly "One Belt One Road") initiative. I don't agree with the U.S. IC's 2019 assessment that the Russo-Chinese strategic partnership is solidifying. Putin, knowing the adversarial relationship between China and the United States, simply adheres to the philosophy that an "enemy of my enemy is my friend." As a former KGB officer, he also follows the rule of "holding his friends close and enemies even closer." He never criticizes President Trump or President Xi personally, but that doesn't mean he considers them friends either.

In February 2008, a little more than a year after the Chinese test, a highly complex operation code-named Operation Burnt Frost was authorized by President George W. Bush, where a U.S. Navy Aegis

BMD cruiser shot down a non-functioning American spy satellite with a Standard Missile-3.[21] A sea-based component of the U.S. Ballistic Missile System, Aegis BMD provides warships with the ability to destroy short- and medium-range ballistic missiles. There was a lot of excitement that day about this successful satellite intercept at the Missile Defense Agency (MDA), which develops and deploys U.S. BMD. At the MDA at the time, I was waiting for my DIA security clearance to become an intelligence officer. A BMD capability with proper modifications could act in an ASAT role and was a "big f**king deal," as now President Joe Biden might say. Knowing that Russia always felt that it had to match U.S. strategic military capabilities, I remember thinking that the Russians were now going to develop an ASAT capability of their own, now that China and the United States had it. I didn't need to read any intelligence reports to know this; it was common sense, knowing the Russian mindset. In July 2008, I joined the DIA Space Team that was created to track foreign space-intelligence threats, like ASAT.

Putin's security apparatus paid noticeable attention to this successful satellite intercept as well. In its 2010 Military Doctrine, the Kremlin codified BMD and "space weapons" as one of the principal threats to Russia's security.[22] The doctrine also implied that interference with Russia's missile-warning satellites was a redline, implying that a military response would be required.

Russia's Revolution in Military Affairs

Although Moscow often accuses the United States of weaponizing space, the Russians have always viewed space as a warfighting domain or a theater of military operations. In fact, in the early days of celestial exploration, the Russians were winning the space race. The USSR launched the first artificial satellite, Sputnik (which means

satellite in Russian) in 1957, sent the first cosmonaut into space in
1961, Yuri Gagarin, and sent the first female, Valentina Tereshkova,
in 1963. The Soviets were also the first to send an object—though not
a human—to the moon to conduct a spacewalk, to perform a two-
man spaceflight, and to establish a space station. Even the first dog
launched into space was Russian, a two-year-old mutt they found on
the streets of Moscow and named Laika.[23] (Purebred canines were
considered too spoiled and fragile for the harsh conditions of space
travel.) The Soviet head of state, Nikita Khrushchev, was so "drunk"
(pun intended) on the global triumph of Sputnik and so keen on
demonstrating the "superiority" of the Soviet socialist system vis-à-
vis American capitalism that every few months he pressed his space
engineers with the question, "What else are we going to surprise them
[i.e., the Americans] with?" He would demand they "launch something else" into space.[24]

Soviet leadership spared neither money nor animal and human
lives on the space program. Poor Laika, whose return to earth was
unplanned in the first place, died within six hours of flight due to
the capsule's overheating. In 1967, Soviet cosmonaut Vladimir Komarov was sent into space in a capsule unready to fly in order to
satisfy Soviet leader Leonid Brezhnev's desire to commemorate the
fiftieth anniversary of the 1917 Russian Revolution with another
celestial surprise for the West. The unsafe Soyuz 1 capsule crashed
into the earth at full speed, killing Komarov, who knew before the
flight that he was unlikely to live. He flew anyway, because he didn't
want his friend Yuri Gagarin, his designated alternate, to die
instead. U.S. intelligence was able to hear his final screams from a
listening post in Turkey. If you would like evidence of the Soviet
socialist system's "superiority," a Google search (a company
co-founded, by the way, by Sergey Brin, a Russian American who
has chosen the United States as his homeland) will serve up horrific

images of Komarov's molten corpse and the sound of his rage-filled last words.[25]

Although a pioneer in spaceflight, the USSR remained behind the United States in nuclear technology during the Cold War. The Soviets therefore used their space advantage and prioritized the development of long-range missile technology that could strike target U.S. forces in Western Europe and the American homeland.[26] In 1949, Stalin was putting pressure on his lead rocket scientist Sergey Korolev, who had previously been imprisoned in a Gulag labor camp for alleged subversion of military projects, to speed things up.

The Soviet leadership's paranoia over the U.S. atomic threat drove the USSR's development of strategic missiles, or ICBMs. Less than two months prior to the Soviet Union's placing Sputnik into orbit and shocking U.S. leaders and the American public, communist Russia had a different significant "first." In August 1957, the Soviets launched the world's first ICBM, three to four years earlier than predicted by the U.S. Intelligence Community, which didn't have good insights into Soviet missile and space technology developments at the time.[27] This liquid-fueled R-7, or Semyorka (a diminutive for "seven" in Russian), gave the Soviets a double-capability: a nuclear delivery system as well as a space launch capability.[28] Nikita Khrushchev reveled in Russia's early space dominance, boasting that the USSR could mass-produce ICBMs "like sausages," sending the American security establishment into a panic.[29]

From the very beginning, the Soviets understood the military implications of spaceflight. In the 1970s, there was a new breakthrough in Soviet strategic thought on space and warfare, thanks to Marshal Nikolai Ogarkov.[30] Chief of the Soviet General Staff for seven years and a combat veteran, Ogarkov predicted that space and missile technology would revolutionize the waging of war.[31] He was the thought leader of the concept of a revolution in military affairs

(RMA), which found appreciation with a prominent U.S. strategist and military theorist, Andrew Marshall, who headed up the Pentagon's Office of Net Assessment for several decades until 2015. According to the RMA concept, networks of space sensors and ground-based radar systems would enable automated command and control of troops and would allow weapons-targeting in real time. Ogarkov famously dubbed the emerging technologies as reconnaissance-strike complexes, predicting the emergence of nonnuclear, precision-guided munitions. He envisioned that intelligence data collected from the satellites would be instantly conveyed to the weapon systems' fire-control mechanism, shortening the warfighters' kill-chain.

A talented military strategist, Ogarkov was known for his willingness to disagree with the Kremlin, which eventually got him canned as chief of the General Staff and demoted. He opposed the Soviet invasion of Afghanistan and stubbornly advocated for a shift in Soviet warfighting strategy against NATO in Europe from nuclear to conventional. As part of his limited war doctrine, Ogarkov found targeting NATO forces with conventional precision weapons, rather than nuclear, would give advantages to Warsaw Pact forces, while avoiding turning Europe into nuclear wasteland. When in 1983 the Soviets accidentally shot down a Korean airliner, KAL-007, which strayed off course into Russian territory close to top-secret Soviet military installations, Ogarkov was the guy who held a press conference to justify the Soviet decision, which resulted in the deaths of 269 people, including many Americans and a Member of Congress.[32]

Previously top-secret and declassified U.S. National Intelligence Estimates (NIEs) from 1983 and 1985 reveal that, even back then, the Soviets viewed space as another warfighting domain, akin to land, air, and sea. The USSR was preparing for space warfare and was developing counter-space capabilities. Based on the findings of U.S. intelligence, the Soviets planned to "blind, dazzle, or otherwise interfere with American reconnaissance satellites." The Soviet "space warfare systems" were intended to deny U.S. access to space while preserving its own access in a crisis.[33] These intentions remain the same in Putin's Russia.

According to the 1985 NIE, Soviet anti-satellite systems included the following assets: a non-nuclear orbital interceptor, operational since the early 1970s; nuclear-armed Galosh ABM interceptors with a potential ASAT mission; two ground-based, high-energy lasers; and electronic warfare (EW) systems. As early as 1961 and 1962, the Soviets conducted four nuclear tests in space to advance their electromagnetic pulse (EMP) research and to determine the suitability of nuclear weapons to serve in an anti–ballistic missile (ABM) role.[34] In 1963, the USSR and the United States concluded a partial test-ban treaty that prohibited space nuclear tests. After the 1963 ban, the Soviets switched to conventional ASAT tests and conducted twenty ASAT tests from 1968 to 1982, demonstrating the capability to intercept spacecraft in low-earth orbit.[35]

Russia today has a very robust space program, which draws on the extensive technical knowledge and ability developed during Soviet times. Although the Russian space industry suffered degradation after the demise of the Soviet Union, it received increased funding, prioritization, and personal attention from Putin. He ensures that space and C4ISR technologies receive high priority in the Russian defense budget, behind only nuclear technologies, which are at the top of the list. Unlike its U.S. counterpart, the Russian space industry is controlled by the state, making prioritization of the Armed Forces' requirements versus civilian space needs a no-brainer.

Putin's Russia is a global leader in space launch and transport, enabling it to create notable U.S. dependencies on Russia. We rely on the Russian liquid-fueled rocket engine RD-180 to propel our Atlas V rocket and launch top-secret U.S. intelligence and military satellites since there is no American-made equivalent for it.[36] Its low price, reliability, and fuel efficiency attracted U.S. aerospace companies and drew praise from high-profile CEOs like SpaceX's Elon Musk. Until May 2020, when Musk developed an indigenous American alternative capability, the U.S. government relied on the Russian Soyuz rocket exclusively to chauffeur NASA astronauts to the International Space Station. Such dependencies can be fraught with negative ramifications during a time of deteriorating relations. It is not a good plan, in my view, to depend on your biggest geopolitical opponent for access to space, especially in an era when space warfare is a likely form of kinetic conflict between major powers such the United States, Russia, and China.

Russia has a formidable space order of battle, second only to that of the United States. Under Putin, the Russian Ministry of Defense reorganized its military space program, including the Space Forces, which Moscow created back in 2001.[37] The newly created Aerospace Forces combine Air Force and Aerospace Defense Troops with the mission to use the ballistic missile early-warning system, the satellite control network, and the space surveillance network, as well as to conduct military space launches. Conducting ASAT attacks on an adversary's satellites would fall into the Aerospace Force's list of missions. Russian defense minister Sergey Shoigu admitted in 2015 that the need to counter U.S. Prompt Global Strike doctrine forced change.[38]

Given that Russian military strategists have been thinking about space warfare since the dawn of space exploration, Moscow has a very mature space and counter-space doctrine. The Defense Intelligence Agency's 2019 unclassified report on foreign threats to U.S. space systems warns that Russian space and counter-space doctrine calls for attacks on adversary satellites for the purpose of blinding sensors, temporarily jamming them, or permanently destroying them. Supporting infrastructure, such as ground stations, is also on the target list. Russia has or is developing a range of air, ground, and space-based counter-space systems to attack or otherwise interfere with enemy satellites.[39] They practice some of these capabilities in military exercises. They successfully used electronic warfare capabilities in Syria, including the jamming of GPS.[40]

In any developing conflict, preemptive ASAT attacks could be authorized, because Russian military strategists believe that denying the United States use of satellites will de-escalate conflict because of American dependency on space. They believe that Russia can control escalation by targeting several types of U.S. satellites, either permanently or temporarily. The purpose of such selective targeting could be to signal Russia's resolve to take hostilities up a notch if the United States doesn't de-escalate. But Russia may very well be mistaken in its assessment of the U.S. response to limited actions, causing the conflict to escalate instead of de-escalating. No one knows what will happen once a conflict appears in the space domain, no matter how many times such scenarios are gamed out, because we have no baseline by which to judge such a conflict. It hasn't happened before. Even temporary disruptions of U.S. commercial satellites such as GPS would have disastrous consequences, given America's dependence on space.

An unclassified but little-known fact is that the GPS constellation carries nuclear detonation detection payloads (NUDET), which the United States installed to detect clandestine nuclear tests conducted anywhere in the world. GPS NUDET sensors are designed to measure physical outputs—light, gamma rays, x-rays, or neutrons—from a nuclear explosion. Should a nuclear explosion occur, "data from all of the satellites observing this event will be transmitted to ground terminals for processing."[41] This is one way we watch if the bad guys use a nuke. Should GPS NUDET be monkeyed with, it would be shocking news.

Briefing any senior U.S. military officer on whether Russia would interfere with a certain type of American satellite in a conflict is not easy. Not all satellites are equal. Certain satellites, in fact, are "more equal than others" because of the effects disruptions can produce—some can be temporary and only noticeable to a select group of users of space services; others can be disastrous. Russia understands this and is unlikely to do something highly irresponsible and super-escalatory—outside of a kinetic conflict, that is. But once we are in a space conflict, the gloves are off. Depending on the type of space attacks that Russia chooses to launch against our space birds, U.S. leaders may have no alternative but to respond forcefully to Russia's actions, provoking Moscow to escalate further. Of course, the severity of conflict depends on the leaders' war tolerance. Their personalities alone could determine what space actions and counteractions would occur. Russian leaders' tolerance for casualties can be high, as evidenced by the twenty million lives sacrificed in World War II. Stalin justified not evacuating Stalingrad because he thought soldiers would fight harder for a populous city. His assumption was correct. On the Soviet side, official Russian military historians estimate that there were 1,100,000 Red Army dead, wounded, missing, or captured in the campaign to defend the city. An estimated 40,000 civilians died as well.[42]

These are the issues that keep senior U.S. national security officials up at night. They kept me up many nights too, preparing for the next briefing or trying to resolve yet another intelligence puzzle. Truthfully, as unsettling as it could be, I miss the work.

Russia has been building its counter-space capabilities while advocating hollow, hypocritical, and cynical arms-control proposals for the "prevention of placement of weapons in outer space." According to the Defense Intelligence Agency and other authoritative

Western and Russian open sources, Russia's current counter-space capabilities include the following:

- Space Surveillance Awareness (SSA), which consists of telescopes, sensors, and radars that track and character-ize the missions of satellites in all orbits. A prerequisite for counter-space targeting, Russia's SSA is the best for-eign SSA, second only to our own.
- Electronic Warfare (EW) systems that consist of jam-mers capable of disrupting an adversary's command and control (C2), including GPS, tactical communications, satellite communications, and radars. Russia has showed its EW capabilities, including by countering U.S. GPS in Syria.
- Directed Energy Weapons are laser weapon systems intended to disrupt, degrade, or damage satellites and their sensors. Russia is developing an airborne laser weapon to disrupt space-based missile defense sensors.
- Orbital interceptors that cozy up to an adversary's satel-lites to inspect or attack them, causing temporary or permanent damage.
- A ground-based direct-ascent mobile ASAT missile called PL-19 Nudol, capable of destroying spacecraft in low-earth orbit.[43] It was most recently tested in Decem-ber 2020.[44]

These are very sinister space warfare systems that threaten our security and must be closely watched and countered. Unfortunately, the Pentagon's shift in strategy, aimed at countering unconventional threats, such as terrorism, in the aftermath of the September 11 ter-rorist attacks, has resulted in the United States' lagging behind

Russia in critical areas of space and missile technology, such as hypersonic missiles.

Not a Hypothetical Scenario

President Trump's secretary of defense, Mark Esper, addressing the Air Force Association's 2019 Air Space & Cyber Conference, said that the opening shots of a future war will be in space or cyber domains, America's "greatest near-term security challenge."[45] A few months earlier, his predecessor Patrick Shanahan told the annual Space Symposium in Colorado Springs, "Space is no longer a sanctuary—it is now a warfighting domain."[46] I have tracked foreign space-intelligence threats for DIA and immersed myself in highly sensitive intelligence on this issue. Esper and Shanahan are correct.

Pentagon leaders vow to move with urgency to find ways to deter conflict in space and respond decisively if deterrence fails, because the stakes are high. But we often fall into the usual trap of not paying enough attention early, either ignoring it or getting distracted fighting our little wars du jour. Isn't strategic intelligence—providing real-time warning to American leaders and the populace—a fundamental priority of intelligence? Indications and Warnings (I&W) and the importance of avoiding "strategic surprise" are what they teach in INTEL 101 classes.

Similar to missing the warning signs about Putin's intentions and Russia's refusal to accept Cold War defeat, we again ignored the I&W (indications and warnings) of Moscow's focus on space, counter-space, and its revolution in military affairs (RMA) conceptualized long ago by Marshal Ogarkov, saying, "It is just strategic targeting." We didn't have the imagination to extrapolate that once "space weapons" and BMD were designated as key security threats in major Russian doctrinal and policy documents, Moscow was going to move forward to counter this evolving threat. Moreover, as early as January 2001, the Rumsfeld Commission Report provided us with a warning on the possibility of a space Pearl Harbor and the need to "take seriously the possibility of an attack on [U.S.] space systems." The report observed: "The [United States] is more dependent on space than any other nation. Yet the threat to the [United States] and its allies in and from space does not command the attention it merits." The report specifically called out the Department of Defense and the Intelligence Community for "not being very well arranged to meet the national security space needs of the 21st century."

We were also aware of Russia's Revolution in Military Affairs (RMA) agenda and obsession with U.S. military tactics. Did we think that the old Russkis were doing it for fun? Remember from earlier chapters: there is no Russian word for fun! The Office of Net Assessment, then headed by the visionary Andrew Marshall, published a report in 1992 on its major study of the Russian RMA concept following the Gulf War. The report confirmed that RMA was indeed underway and that "we are probably in the initial stages of a transition to a new era of warfare." However, the 2001 terrorist attacks and Pentagon unease with the RMA concept itself pushed our focus to counterinsurgency, rather than pursuing strategies on countering near-peer competitors like Russia. In fact, the 2005 National Defense Strategy erroneously assumed that the United States "will have no global peer competitors and will remain unmatched in traditional military capability."

The 2005 *Quadrennial Defense Review* said that "irregular warfare was the dominant form of warfare confronting the United States." Consequently, the United States fell behind Russia in electronic warfare, or EW, and hypersonic weapons.[47] It also did not anticipate or fully appreciate Russia's intention to develop and operationalize anti-satellite capabilities and space warfare doctrine. Michael Griffin, who served as NASA administrator from 2005 to 2009, described the United States' lack of commitment to pursuing a technological edge in space as the United States' going "to sleep." As Griffin said, "We went on holiday for 25 years as far as investment in technological advancement, following the collapse of the USSR and Berlin Wall."[48] True, we don't need these "exquisite" capabilities to fight the Taliban. But they are not the only bad guys in town.

In a misguided move, Schriever Wargame, an important cross-agency simulation exercise which focuses on space threats to U.S. systems, was cancelled after the 2012 exercise, but it was later (wisely) renewed.[49] A senator, lecturing Air Force leaders at a budget hearing, mocked the idea of a Russian threat by saying: "Waves of Russian fighters will not be coming over the horizon any time soon."[50] Well, they did: in 2008 in Georgia; in 2014 in Ukraine's Crimea; in 2015 in Syria; and they will likely come again somewhere soon. The *Air Force Magazine* called this kind of approach to strategy "Counter-Revolution in Military Affairs."[51]

Wisely, former president Trump emphasized the Russian counter-space threat in the 2019 Ballistic Missile Review as a justification for America's investment in ballistic missile defense.[52] On his orders, the Pentagon also set up the U.S. Space Force, albeit eighteen years after the Russians founded theirs. This was an excellent start. Now President Biden needs to mandate that intelligence agencies get back to the business of strategic warning, prevention of strategic surprise, studying such nebulous things as the adversary's doctrines and strategies, not just their bright and shiny capabilities.

The Intelligence Community lacks such doctrinal experts, just as there is a shortage of linguists. Bureaucratic bean counters resist creating these positions because doctrine and strategic intelligence do not lend themselves to bean-counting. First, you will not be writing many Presidential Daily Briefs, or PDBs, if you are a doctrine and strategy person, because a PDB is an inherently short-term, tactical product, not strategic intelligence. A PDB warns the president about what just happened or is about to happen: Country X is launching Weapon Y, for example. Sometimes it will attempt to indicate Intention Z, but intentions are hard to assess when you don't understand the mindset and doctrine.

Doctrine and strategy aren't things that just happen, like events; nevertheless, they exist and need updating every five years or so. To develop doctrine and strategy expertise, an analyst must read hundreds of reports that are fifty to five hundred pages long, rather than a dozen five- to ten-page reports. There were only three intel analysts like me at my agency who deeply understood Putin's doctrine, strategy, and intentions. We had fluent Russian language capabilities (native in my case). We were working somewhat informally under the "top cover" of a senior officer, a highly competent former Russian Foreign Area Officer and Green Beret, whom I will call Charlie. Charlie didn't care about bean-counting or bureaucracy. He cared about the mission. The three of us briefed the highest levels of U.S. and allied governments and military leaders and received accolades for that work. But we were constantly brought down by bean counters who often didn't know what we were working on because they didn't have access to the most secretive intelligence. Eventually, the bureaucrats won; so, by 2017, none of us were analyzing Putin's doctrine and strategy, at least not for the DIA. One of us, another fluent Russian speaker, was transferred to a Latin American account. The bureaucrats decided that senior intelligence officers must broaden their experience, instead of deepening it in only one subject. They believe you can be a Russia analyst today and an expert on narco-traffickers tomorrow. Bodies, not experts, fill the billets—a common paper-pusher mentality.

Working for the U.S. government, I have learned that all governments have similarities, whether they are Soviet, Russian, or

American. Too often, the mission is not the most important thing to the apparatchiks in charge everywhere.

CHAPTER 5

Cyber Weapons: Waging War on U.S. Networks and American Minds

"By inserting disinformation in publications, advocating extremist ideas, inciting racist and xenophobic flashmobs, conducting interstate computer attacks on the critical infrastructure targets that are vital for the functioning of a society, it is possible to 'heat up' the situation in any country, all the way up to the point of social unrest."

—Major General Igor Dylevsky, deputy chief of the Main Operational Directorate
of the General Staff of the Armed Forces of the Russian Federation

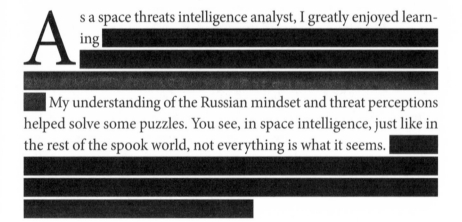

A s a space threats intelligence analyst, I greatly enjoyed learning ▮▮

▮ My understanding of the Russian mindset and threat perceptions helped solve some puzzles. You see, in space intelligence, just like in the rest of the spook world, not everything is what it seems. ▮▮▮▮

I loved every minute of my job. Well, except those minutes, which added up to hours, days, and weeks, when I had to deal with the bean counters and other types of bureaucrats. Everything you've heard about the government's being a giant, immovable, redundant bureaucracy is true. Regrettably, this also applies to the Intelligence Community, which should instead possess the flexibility and efficiency it needs to secure the country. This includes a rigid "General Schedule" (GS) ranking system that strictly regulates hiring rules, pay structure, and promotion practices for civilian employees. It often prevents the government from hiring and retaining the "best and the brightest" candidates because of its cumbersome, often illogical, and burdensome rules and requirements.

I found it odd and frustrating that senior analysts like me had to "pre-brief" our briefings intended for top generals and senior policy officials, not just once but several times. First, we briefed the chain of command, which consisted of GS-14s like me, and then GS-15s—those who occupied management positions, often for years and years. Coming from private industry, I thought that if the employer pays the employee $100,000 or more for their expertise, an organization doesn't need to waste time double-checking what the employee will say to their seniors. You should trust that they will do their job professionally and deliver what they were hired to deliver with excellence.

This was not about quality control though. This was about the bureaucrats' justifying their existence and "overseeing" the work of the Indians, as we called ourselves, some of whom knew their targets much better than the Chiefs. Some of the Chiefs were known for using the Indians' "pre-briefs" to learn the issue and then deliver the actual briefing to the senior customer themselves. The middle-management Chiefs resent the "face time" line analysts get with the senior customers—generals, policymakers, agency heads, and Allied governments. "It's a

jobs program," said one of my close colleagues, a very senior DIA officer, about the massive government bureaucracy.

Often, the bean counters would join analysts' briefings to high
senior officials, or "customers," to provide "top cover" from the chain
of command. My senior partner Charlie called them "straphangers."
Sometimes there would be so many "straphangers" hanging around
that we would have to negotiate room for the actual analyst-briefers
due to the constraints presented by the conference room sizes. Believe
it or not, the Pentagon and other government buildings have a significant shortage of conference rooms. By the middle of my tour in
the IC, DIA's bureaucracy had grown so much that the ratio of analysts to management was inverted. As a former director of analysis,
a burly but good-natured and competent gentleman, put it, "Imagine
me wearing a ballet tutu but being upside down." He was justifying
cuts of GS-14s and GS-15s from intel ranks, trying to get rid of the
bulge at the top.

Unfortunately, it is the senior analytic ranks that quite often
would be downsized instead of the bean-counter types, because the
management knew how to play the bureaucracy's game and hold on
to their jobs by their teeth—a unique skill that allowed them to
become the Chiefs in the first place. They know well how to weaponize the bureaucratic rules to push out any analyst whose personalities
or analytic conclusions they don't like.

Fortunately for DIA and the country, there are some managers
who care about the mission more than bureaucratic games. They also
know how to motivate intel officers to do their best based on understanding their expertise and personalities. Such managers understand that some analysts are not motivated by more money or higher
rank. Besides, most government civilian positions have little room
to grow, either salary- or rank-wise, because they are locked into the
GS structure. Therefore, smart managers reward intelligence officers

who excel at their craft by assigning them to more interesting and high-value projects. I was lucky to have a couple of managers like that at DIA. Thanks to them, I was able to excel at my job, contributing to America's security. It felt highly rewarding to help keep our country safe, to be called by senior officials a "national asset," to be recognized as someone who "possessed unique language skills" and "played a key role in one of the most highly visible special programs in the Intelligence Community."[1] It was gratifying to be "requested by name" to brief our most senior military commanders and national security leaders.

I am thankful to Mary S., who was my division chief when I was monitoring and analyzing ███████████████ I learned a lot from her. A former Navy officer, Mary was a highly competent ████ ███████████████████████████████████ ███████████████████████████████████ exper-tise essential for ███████████████████████ ████████████████ Mary understood how to reward me for my good work in a way that would be meaningful to me: by more work with a higher level of responsibility and impact. Having completed ███████████████████████████████████ ███ during which I served as DIA's representative for the entire Defense Intelligence Enterprise, I was supposed to turn over my work to Mary. ███████████████████ I had coordinated and negotiated the ████████████████████████████ ███████████████████████████████████ ███████████████████████████████████ ███████████████████████████████████ ███████████████████████████████████ ███████████████████████████████████ ███████████████████████████████████ ███████████████████████████████████

██

███████████████████

"You did the work, Rebekah. You go do the briefings for the big bosses," said Mary. She was confident enough in her own expertise and standing at DIA that she didn't need additional face time with her superiors. She also was confident in my expertise and ability to do my job well. But Mary also wanted to do what she thought was the right thing and reward her intel officer. Not only did she send me to ██

██

██

██

████████████████████████

I was both terrified and excited to perform this honorable role that is typically reserved for top-tier senior executive service only. As a "plus one," ██████████████████████████████████████

███████████████████████████████████—and sat right behind him during the official meeting, in case the approval process got beyond the pro forma and into the substance. In such an instance, I was prepared to pass him a note, whisper in his ear, or otherwise help answer a substantive question from anyone in the audience.

██

██████████████████████████████ another weapon was gaining prominence in Russia's military doctrine and strategy—cyber, or, as the Russians politely call it, "information confrontation."

Preparing the Battlefield

Russia has the most sophisticated and destructive arsenal of cyber weapons of any foreign nation. In the hands of President Vladimir Putin, who ultimately controls this cyber arsenal as part of what is called the State System of Information Confrontation,[2] these cyber weapons present a grave threat to America.[3] Having been in the offensive cyber business for the past three decades, Russia has developed a set of potent tools that are superior in stealth, programming power, speed of attack and penetration of the adversary's network, and creativity. The Russian president's toolbox rivals that of American cyber warriors, and Russia's highly innovative cyber doctrine has given Putin the ability to outplay the U.S. government and manipulate American citizens' attitudes and perceptions of reality. Comparing Russia's cyber hacking tradecraft with China's, another very capable cyber adversary of the United States, former CIA and NSA director General Michael Hayden said, "The Chinese have scale and the Russians have skill."[4] Former director of national intelligence James Clapper, referring to these countries' cyber tactics, called the Chinese "loud" and the Russians "stealthy."

Russia has a hugely different conception of cyberwarfare than the United States, rooted in its culture of secrecy, its conspiratorial mindset, and the state's drive to control its citizens' behavior and thinking. Conversely, U.S. cyber doctrine reflects American culture and values, such as freedom of speech, privacy, and the government's non-interference in individuals' lives. Regrettably, I must say, in recent years I have observed considerable erosion of these foundational American principles and their replacement with politically correct speech, "acceptable" opinions, feelings-based (rather than fact-based) conclusions, and behavior imposed by government on private businesses and religious organizations. It brings unwanted memories of my youth behind the Iron Curtain, where decades and even centuries of government censorship eventually led to individual citizens' self-censorship of free expression, the most sophisticated form of state oppression.

Based on their distinct cultures and values, Russia and the United States have approached the cyber issue from two different angles. The Americans, direct and straightforward in their thinking, have focused on the technical, "cyber" aspect—systems, networks, and data encoded in ones and zeros. The Russians, cunning in their thinking from having had to survive centuries of foreign invasions and domestic oppression, have focused on the "informational-psychological" aspect—actual information content, how information is perceived by human minds, and how it can influence and manipulate an adversary's thinking. In May 2017, DNI Clapper, commenting on Russia's techniques employed during their 2016 covert influence campaign, told NBC's Chuck Todd that the Russians are "almost genetically driven to co-opt, penetrate, gain favor."[5] Although I am ethnically Russian, as a strong opponent of political correctness and self-censorship, I wasn't offended by Clapper's comments, because I didn't interpret them literally as an intentional xenophobic attack on Russian ethnicity. I understood that his choice of words was intended simply as a colorful, albeit exaggerated, description of a cultural trait that is present in some Russians, just like their infamous propensity to consume large amounts of vodka.

While U.S. cyber doctrine centers on cyber per se and Russia's centers on information,[6] both doctrines emphasize having an information advantage over the adversary. But when American war planners speak about this advantage, calling it "information dominance," they mean having more information of intelligence value available to the warfighter, better access to information, better quality data, faster speed of delivery, preferably in real-time, and the like. Such "information dominance" would enable the warfighter to have better battlespace awareness and to achieve more precise targeting of the adversary, which would help win a conflict.

When Russian strategists talk about "information superiority," they mean all of the above, plus having control over an adversary's perception of the battlespace in wartime and his understanding of reality in peacetime. Such control is achieved by employment of military deception, called *maskirovka*, which means masking, and by disinformation in peacetime, which connotes distorted, untrue, or half-true information. The Russians believe, consistent with the teachings of Sun Tzu, that the surest way of winning the conflict is to dupe the adversary into abandoning his plans to fight or to defeat him by outfoxing him without a fight.

The essence of Russian cyber doctrine is captured by the term "information confrontation" (*informatsionnoye protivoborstvo*), or IPb, a doctrine defined as "intense confrontation in the information sphere aimed at achieving informational, psychological, and ideological superiority, imposing damage to the information systems, processes, resources, critically important structures, and means of communication, and also sabotaging the political and social system and [wielding] massive psychological influence on the troops and population."[7] As I wrote in previous chapters, there is a presupposition of conflict in the Russian mindset based on its turbulent history. In addition, based on Russia's perception of U.S. policies, warfighting campaigns in the last two decades, military exercises, weapons development, support of NATO expansion to include former Eastern Bloc countries, and democracy promotion in Russia's perceived sphere of influence, Moscow has concluded that sooner or later it will face Washington in an all-out kinetic war. Putin's war planners believe that the best way to get ready for such an eventuality is, during peacetime, to do what we call in the military intelligence business "preparing the battlespace." Information confrontation is one of the several methods that Russia employs to achieve this mission.

We had heated debates over the proper English translation with CIA analysts, who insisted on "information warfare" as a more appropriate English equivalent. But *informatsionnoye protivoborstvo* literally means "information counter-struggle," which more accurately reflects the Russian mindset of being besieged by enemies and having to fend off enemy attacks, though the phrase is awkward in English. "Counter-struggle" also has the connotation of defensive action, which Russia views as important for the perceptions of domestic and foreign audiences. Russian leaders believe that their citizens are more likely to fight harder if they think that they are defending the motherland in a struggle against a foreign enemy than if they think that they are acting as an aggressor, even in the information sphere. They also believe it is to their advantage to portray to foreign audiences that their military doctrine is defensive, and therefore they have moral superiority over the adversary.

The Russian government wordsmiths don't provide the benefit of the doubt to their opponents, though. During arms control negotiations they insist that there is no difference between offensive and defensive weapons because defensive capabilities can be used in an offensive role. For example, Moscow insists that Washington's Ballistic Missile Defense is a destabilizing offensive capability because it blunts Russia's role as a nuclear deterrent via a second-strike, thus upsetting the existing strategic balance of military power between Russia and the United States.

As a linguist, I believe it is vitally important to understand and accurately convey the meaning of your intelligence target's terminology, because that meaning captures the target's thinking on the issue and is reflected in the actual doctrine. If you don't understand the target's lexicon, you don't understand the doctrine and how the adversary will fight. If you don't understand the doctrine, you cannot assist your warfighting colleagues in developing a counterstrategy to defeat the adversary. Not having such an understanding is how, even as a superior opponent equipped with cutting-edge weaponry, you lose or are perceived to have lost a conflict to an enemy dressed in rags instead of military uniform and armed with IEDs and rusty AK-47s. As the *Washington Post's Afghanistan Papers* reveal, the U.S. military didn't have the faintest idea about the culture, mindset, and warfighting style of its adversary before invading Afghanistan, in the aftermath of the September 11 terrorist attacks.[9] It is unfortunate that the bean counters at DIA also do not see the value in having █████ ███ ███

The concept of "information confrontation" is reflected in several Russian strategic-planning documents, which are developed by the General Staff and the Security Council, with the assistance of the intelligence services. These doctrinal materials include the Military Doctrine, the National Security Strategy, and the Foreign Policy Concept. They are approved by President Putin.[10] The 2016 Doctrine of Information Security of the Russian Federation, signed by President Putin on December 5, 2016, officially codifies "information confrontation forces and methods" as one of the key methods of ensuring Russia's information security.[11]

When the Russians talk about information security, they mean not just security of the software and hardware, but security of the actual content from external influence, especially Western. The Russian government believes that the concept of a nation's sovereignty extends to the information domain. Russia has even coined a term for the Russian internet—RUNET. Putin wants to keep Western ideology out of the Russian information space because it is harmful to Russia. The Russians continue to view democracy as chaotic and unstable based on their experiences of the societal breakdown in the 1990s, in the aftermath of the Soviet Union's collapse and the disastrous Yeltsin years. The Russian government's leaders believe democracy and individual freedoms threaten the country's stability because they foster an antagonistic relationship between the state and its citizens, between individuals and the collective.

The Kremlin has always believed that to retain power and regime continuity, it must keep a firm hold on its population, both in what they think and how they behave. Having control of the information flow that goes in and out of the country has always been a priority. During Soviet times, censorship was especially strict. Those who did not have the "correct opinion" were persecuted, even jailed. There is a word in Russian, the noun *inakomyslyashchiye,* which means "those who think differently." Thinking differently was not allowed when I was growing up in the USSR. If you were one of the *inakomyslyashchiye,* you made sure that no one except your close family and one or two real friends knew what you thought. People kept their opinions to themselves and always maintained the "party line" in conversations with strangers.

Regrettably, I am seeing similar alarming tendencies emerging in America. Today, the ideas and values that used to serve as the cornerstone of American democracy, such as diversity of thought and freedom of expression, are no longer cherished by many Americans. There are emerging a different "correct" way and "incorrect" way of thinking about such issues as patriotism, racial equality, ethnic and cultural differences, freedom of religion, immigration, the mission of police, how much government involvement in people's lives is appropriate in a democracy, and even capitalism. Those who think incorrectly (i.e., who practice "wrongthink")—American *inakomyslyashchiye*—can lose their jobs, be banned from social media platforms, mocked, and ostracized by friends, colleagues, and family. Putin and his cyberwar squad are acutely aware about this "new normal" in American society, and they are "cyber-gaming" and exploiting it for all its worth to weaken and defeat us. One of Russia's most recent covert intelligence operations, which followed the Putin-ordered intervention in the 2020 U.S. presidential elections, is the spreading of the QAnon conspiracy theory, amplified by Russian cyber spies. As part of Putin's playbook, Russian intelligence services are always on the lookout for clever ways to incite social unrest in America.[12]

Russia's preparation of the battlespace for a conflict with America involves three types of cyber operations, or rather "information operations," in Russian doctrinal parlance, as elucidated by several unclassified threat assessments by the Intelligence Community and open testimonies by intelligence leaders. The first category of operations is focused on collection of intelligence, in support of the Russian government's policy and operational requirements, such as negotiations, meetings, and phone calls with U.S. political and military leaders. Central to winning any conflict, these include U.S. plans and intentions on policy issues, such as arms control, U.S. economic sanctions against Russia, and ongoing conflicts where Russian and U.S. interests are at odds, such as in Ukraine and Syria. In other words, this is traditional espionage by cyber means.

The second category is strategic reconnaissance for future targeting, which involves mapping out computer access to facilities and other targets that the Russians would want to strike during wartime. And the third is focused on cyber-enabled influence operations designed to change how Americans think about its government and one another and to influence U.S. policy towards Russia in the Kremlin's favor.[13]

A 2017 Joint Statement for the Record by former DNI Clapper, former director of the NSA and head of U.S. Cyber Command Admiral Michael Rogers, and USDI (Under Secretary of Defense for Intelligence) Marcel Lettre characterized Russia as a "highly advanced and aggressive cyber actor who will continue to target the United States, including our vital systems, in order to collect intelligence, conduct influence operations to support Russian military and political objectives, and to prepare the cyber environment for future contingencies."[14]

A 2017 unclassified DIA intelligence report entitled *Russia Military Power* characterizes information confrontation as a "holistic concept for ensuring information superiority during peacetime, crisis, and wartime."[15] Information confrontation envisions the weaponization of information to neutralize an adversary's actions by achieving two measures of influence: an information-technical effect and an information-psychological effect. "Information-technical effect" refers to cyber operations, such as computer network defense, exploitation, and attack. Examples include the Russian government's hackers' breaching DNC servers and exfiltrating internal DNC communications as part of the Kremlin's attempt to disrupt the 2016 election. The technical effect was thus achieved by Russians' compromising of the DNC computers. "Information-psychological effect" refers to the change of the target's perceptions, beliefs, or behavior in favor of the Russian government's objectives. Such an influence can be achieved by publicly revealing false, distorted, unfavorable, or embarrassing information. Information confrontation is an instrument of Russia's statecraft that Moscow employs against its adversaries—especially against its "main enemy" the United States—at all times.

During its 2016 cyber-enabled influence operation, Russia achieved the psychological effect when its intelligence agents released the stolen DNC communications through WikiLeaks. This information revealed that the DNC was taking actions to improve Hillary Clinton's chances of winning the Democratic Party's presidential nomination and to decrease Bernie Sanders's chances. The hacking of the DNC emails led pro-Clinton U.S. intelligence officials to the erroneous conclusion that Russia was trying to help President Trump win the election. This led to charges that the Trump campaign and Russia "colluded" in the effort, which tied the country up for more than three years in congressional probes and a special counsel office's investigation. The adversarial process set up to investigate the "collusion" arguably led to a president's impeachment. Putin had struck gold. I'll have more details about the election intrusion in an upcoming chapter.

The psychological effect on Americans that Putin wanted to achieve was the perception that the U.S. electoral process is not fair and honest, as Americans believe and as the U.S. government portrays to the rest of the world. Putin's goal was, among other things, to discredit American democracy and send a message to U.S. leaders that they have no business lecturing Russia about the unfairness of its elections. He succeeded in that and much more, paralyzing the entire U.S. governing system immediately after Trump assumed office.

The "Code War": Nuclear Effect without a Mushroom Cloud

If the space domain would be the primary battlefield in a kinetic conflict with Russia, cyberspace would be the place where such kinetic conflict would originate. As discussed in the first chapter, Russia and America are already engaged in a conflict that is largely non-kinetic in nature but that has the potential to escalate into a real war. The higher the tensions, the more likelihood for misunderstanding or miscalculation given the fundamental differences in the cultures, values, and worldview between Russia and America. Fighting two proxy wars in Ukraine and Syria and a shadow war in the U.S. homeland, which the Russians seek to tear apart with racial, ethnic, religious, and political divisions, there is plenty of opportunity for the conflict to go hot between nuclear-armed Moscow and Washington.

Cyber, just like space, makes such an escalation into hostilities even more likely because, unlike in conventional warfare, which is governed by the Laws of Armed Conflict, or the so-called Geneva Conventions, there are no established rules for the cyber game. Striking or otherwise interfering with an intended target in a cyber operation, such as nuclear command and control or other critical infrastructure, can lead to the "unthinkable." As we saw in the case of Stuxnet, a U.S.-Israeli computer worm that was covertly deployed to a uranium enrichment facility in Iran to sabotage and slow down the Iranian nuclear program, even a carefully planned covert cyber operation can get out of control and spill over into unintended targets, wreaking havoc in global cyberspace.[16] Although Stuxnet achieved its mission of destroying numerous centrifuges in Iran's Natanz uranium enrichment facility by causing them to burn themselves out, the virus mutated and spread to other "supervisory control and data acquisition" (SCADA) systems installed in similar power plants, infecting other energy-producing facilities and wreaking havoc all over the world.[17] As the first known computer virus that actually crippled hardware, Stuxnet was a "game changer" in cyber warfare, earning respect from cybersecurity researchers and instilling fear in governments, including the Kremlin.

Russia's war planners do indeed view cyber weapons as a strategic capability that is comparable to nuclear weapons with regard to the destructive effect they can produce on the adversary's military, economy, vital support structures such as hospitals, and popular psyche. Cyber has a major advantage over nuclear weapons, however, in the Russian strategists' view: a cyberattack doesn't produce a nuclear cloud that kills millions of the adversary's people, devastates its land, and could annihilate an entire country. A mass cyber strike on the enemy's critical infrastructure can cause a mass energy black-out of the sort that the Russians orchestrated in Ukraine in the mid-dle of freezing winter. Such a cyberattack could potentially, though not necessarily, result in catastrophic consequences if it hits nuclear plants, chemical facilities, or biological research labs.

Alternatively, a moderate but still damaging cyber intrusion in government computer systems, such as the ones that Russia con-ducted on the Pentagon in 2015, could simply send a message to the adversary that the opponent is rummaging through your defense-related systems and make you wonder what else he has com-promised: Your top secret intelligence data? Your weapons systems? Such an intrusion would cause you to lose confidence in the integrity of the data on which you rely and tie up resources needed to kick the adversary out of your networks, which is quite a formidable task, as the State Department learned when it was hit by the Russians in 2015.

U.S. officials, including former secretary of defense Ashton Carter, acknowledged that in July 2015, Russia, in a "sophisticated cyberattack," shut down the unclassified computer network of the Pentagon, including of the Joint Chiefs of Staff.[18] This was not a run-of-the-mill espionage cyber intrusion designed merely to steal con-fidential data, but a full-on attack—affecting four thousand military officers and civilians—designed to damage systems.[19] When the State Department got hit in 2014 with the "worst ever" cyber intrusion, it took them months to kick the Russians out of their computer net-works, after the Russians had snuck into the agency's unclassified email system.[20] In 2008, with the help of a thumb drive, the Russians penetrated the Pentagon's classified computer network, which is "air-gapped"—i.e. separated from the public internet.[21] Even in the middle of the 2020 coronavirus pandemic, the Russians were hacking various health organizations, universities, businesses, and government agencies associated with the development of COVID-19 vaccine and governments' response to the pandemic.[22]

There is virtually no entity that Russia's hackers do not target—government agencies, military organizations, private businesses, banks, email providers, high-profile individuals—you name it. If you have a computer or a smartphone you are vulnerable. In 2016, Russian military intelligence hacked the World Anti-Doping Agency, leaking the private medical information of tennis stars the Williams sisters and of Gold Medal Olympic gymnast Simone Biles.[23] Russia's 2014 Yahoo breach affected 500 million users.[24] You never know when you can be in need of specific sensitive data or some *kompromat* (compromising information), the Russian cyber spies reckon. Ever wonder what kind of dirt Putin has on you?

Even a "mild" cyber intrusion, in which you don't need to wrack your brain to figure out someone's password (apparently the password for Hillary Clinton campaign chairman John Podesta's email, which the Russians hacked, was "password"—although this is disputed), when integrated into a carefully planned intelligence operation, could send the entire nation into a political tailspin, as Americans learned in 2016.

The General Staff views the cyber and information domain as a place for conducting military operations, escalating conflicts, and achieving military objectives. Cyberspace is a theater of military operations in Russian doctrinal parlance, akin to land, sea, air, and, recently, space. As Americans have witnessed already, based on Putin's doctrine, Russia is not only infecting U.S. computers with the software viruses and hacking them; it is also infecting American's brains with a different virus. This "weaponized information" virus seeks to distort Americans' perception of reality so that they turn their attention away from Russia and inward, fighting one another, dismantling their government institutions such as police, and attacking their president.

Putin is stirring up chaos and disorder in America to save himself from a regime overthrow that he believes Washington seeks. Putin believes that destabilizing America by amplifying internal strife through social media and covert interference will help prevent an all-out war, which he would be ready to fight with the U.S. under certain scenarios. As the United States continues to try to peel off Ukraine from Russia's orbit, it may be prudent to make a thorough intelligence assessment as to whether Putin would invade Ukraine if Washington pushes too hard. Before we consider such a move for Moscow "highly unlikely," it is worth remembering that Putin understands how Americans think but doesn't think like them. He thinks like a Russian and a former KGB operative. While it may have seemed irrational to American national security experts that Putin took over Ukraine's Crimea, for the Russian president, the long-term risk of not having Crimea as part of Russia outweighed the short-term risk of invading it.

The Russian government was back at it four years after the 2016 election, fanning the flames of the civil unrest that gripped America in June 2020. The strife originated with protests on account of a white police officer who employed excessive use of force against a black criminal suspect, George Floyd, resulting in Floyd's tragic death. Infamous for its egregious abuse of the rights protected by the U.S. constitution, Russia expressed "concern over human rights violations in America" through Putin's press secretary Dmitry Peskov's CNBC comments on the protests and civil unrest. Peskov's comments followed those of the Russian foreign ministry, which alleged that the United States "has certainly accumulated systemic human rights problems: race, ethnic and religious discrimination, police brutality, bias of justice, crowded prisons, and uncontrolled use of firearms and self-defense weapons by individuals, to name a few."[25] This was meant to help stir the pot through "information confrontation."

Six months after Russia's 2016 cyber-enabled influence operation targeting the U.S. election, deputy chief of the Russian General Staff's Main Operational Directorate, Major General Igor Dylevsky spoke at the Sixth Moscow Conference on International Security about information technology's ability to "detonate and unleash an inter-state military conflict."[26] He said, "By inserting disinformation in publications, advocating extremist ideas, inciting racist and xeno-phobic flash mobs, [and] conducting interstate computer attacks on the critical infrastructure targets that are vital for the functioning of a society, it is possible to 'heat up' the situation in any country, all the way up to the point of a social unrest." He commented on the unique nature of information weapons because they are "bloodless" and "don't destroy the environment" and yet are able to deliver a blow to the adversary through such peaceful channels as the internet, tele-communications networks, and mass media.[27]

Dylevsky ominously warned that no country, "the most devel-oped" or the most "backwards," can consider itself safe from infor-mation weapons. An aggressor can "destabilize any society and dismantle any government," simply by employing information tech-nology in combination with activities that incite racial, nationalist, and extremist sentiments and animosity.[28] In typical Russian style, Putin's cyberwar general used intentional ambiguity when he described the potency of cyber when used as an "information weapon." His language could be interpreted in either or both of two ways: he could have been implying that U.S. uses cyber to create a phenomenon called a "color revolution" by supporting opposition to the foreign government in power, such as the so-called Arab Spring. Or, he could be talking about Russia's attempted interven-tion in the 2016 election.

American four-star U.S. Air Force general Michael Hayden, speaking at the National Academy of Sciences about the future of U.S. elections and voting, called Russia's intervention in the 2016 election a form of "honorable international espionage" that was "dramatically weaponized."[29] If you can forget that it is our own country that was attacked by Russia in such a spectacular way, you can respect the ingenuity of Russian intelligence tradecraft, especially if you have an intel background. Just like Russian military officers and cyber operatives have respect for the American way of war, which is based on technology like that of precision-guided weapons and the Stuxnet computer worm, U.S. intel officers may have an appreciation for Russia's 2016 covert influence campaign. General Hayden admitted that U.S. intelligence attempted similar cyber tactics as the ones used by Putin's operatives in 2016, but that "they'[d] never been this successful." "This was incredibly well done," he said. "Stolen data was pushed back into the American information space in an impressive operation."[30]

Let's learn from our mistakes. It is up to the U.S. government to understand Russia's game plan and develop a counterstrategy to keep Americans safe. We have a joke in the intel and security circles that the Russians play chess, the Chinese play Go, and the Americans play checkers.

It is time for us to conceptualize our own game and force our opponents to play on our terms, just like they have been compelling us to play on theirs.

Unacceptable Damage

The most dangerous cyber operations that Putin has up his sleeve are attacks on American critical infrastructure. Such cyberwar activities can result in catastrophic effects, including severe damage to various industries and military facilities, and loss of life.

The 2019 Intelligence Community Annual Threat Assessment warned about Russia's capabilities to conduct cyberattacks against U.S. critical infrastructure that "can disrupt electrical distribution networks for at least a few hours." Moscow has already demonstrated similar cyberattacks on vital infrastructure facilities in Ukraine in 2015 and 2016. The same report alerted Americans about Russia's actively "mapping out our critical infrastructure with the long-term goal of being able to cause substantial damage."[31] Russian doctrinal experts view the ability to hold U.S. critical infrastructure targets at risk as highly valuable leverage to deter the United States from military action against Russia, control conflict escalation, or negotiate an end to hostilities. It is another reason why cyber is considered by Russian war planners a strategic capability comparable to nuclear. The ability to launch a mass cyberattack on U.S. vital facilities provides Russia with an option to threaten the United States with a non-nuclear version of "mutually assured destruction." Such a contingency option could be used in the event Moscow fails to compel Washington to refrain from launching a kinetic strike against Russia, or to de-escalate a rapidly developing threat before it escalates into military hostilities.

Fortunately, former president Trump, who had been widely accused of being a "softie" on Putin and Russia, smartly granted special legal authorities to U.S. cyber warriors to conduct offensive cyber operations against our adversaries. With newly untied hands, American cyber forces, which were constrained in their ability to respond to or deter Russian cyberattacks during the Obama Administration, are now ramping up cyber operations against Russia's power grid, according to former and current government officials.[32]

Like other Russian offensive actions, cyber strikes on U.S. critical infrastructure are conceived, counterintuitively to a non-Russian mindset, as a de-escalatory move. The Russian doctrine envisions such strikes as part of an integrated warfighting concept called Strategic Operation to Defeat Critical Infrastructure Targets of the Adversary, (SOPPKVOP, in Russian). Developed by the Russian General Staff, this warfighting concept was revealed by retired General Colonel Viktor Barynkin during a 2010 conference of the Military Academy of the General Staff.[33] Barynkin explained that in modern warfare, conditions dictated that Russia change its targeting strategy. Russian war planners no longer seek the destruction of the adversary per se, but rather the defeat of the adversary's key infrastructure.

The Russian planners view SOPPKVOP as part of Russia's strategic non-nuclear deterrence framework, which seeks to impose costs on the aggressor against Russia by delivering a damaging blow to his vital infrastructure.[34] The size of the damage must be sufficient (and likely to grow) to convince the adversary that achieving victory is costly, prohibitive, or unachievable, compelling adversaries to abandon their intentions of unleashing hostilities against Russia. The Russian planners believe that each adversary has a certain threshold beyond which it cannot sustain economic, human, and military losses. The Russians termed this threshold "unacceptable damage," and they estimate this number for each adversary based on the algorithms developed by operational research experts.[35] The Russian planners believe that the Americans have significantly lower tolerance for sustaining losses in war, making Russia more likely to be able to withstand protracted or high-intensity conflict. They are surprised that despite the relatively low casualty rate in the recent conflicts in Afghanistan and Iraq, thanks to the United States' superior command of precision warfare, the American people are still very critical of the U.S. military and political leaders for allowing loss of life of their soldiers and occasionally of foreign civilians. Russia's high tolerance for casualties was evident in World War II when they lost twenty million lives.

The Russian government's cyber hackers have been laying the groundwork to operationalize their Strategic Operation to Defeat Critical Infrastructure of the Adversary so they can hold U.S. vital systems at risk in the event of war. According to the 2015 IC Worldwide Threat Assessment, Russian cyber actors were developing cyber tools to access industrial control systems (ICS) remotely. ICS systems "manage critical infrastructure, [including] electric power grids, urban mass-transit systems, air-traffic control, and oil and gas distribution networks." Russian hackers "successfully compromised the product supply chains of three ICS vendors." These compromises resulted in "customers' downloading exploitative malware directly from the vendors' websites along with routine software updates."[36]

Since at least March 2016, Russian cyberthreat actors targeted the computer systems of several U.S. critical sectors with malware. Six out of the sixteen sectors designated by the DHS (Department of Homeland Security) as critical were penetrated by the Russians, including energy, water, aviation, commercial facilities, critical manufacturing, and nuclear facilities. The Russians employed a five-step process within the cyber kill-chain framework, which includes reconnaissance, weaponization, delivery of malware, and installation. The Russians "staged malware, conducted spear phishing, and gained remote access to energy sector networks. After obtaining access, they conducted network reconnaissance, moved laterally, and collected information pertaining to [i]ndustrial [c]ontrol [s]ystems."[37] The rest of the critical sectors designated by the DHS are chemical, the defense industrial base, emergency services, financial services, food and agriculture, government facilities, the information technology

sector, healthcare and public health, and the newly designated election systems.

American computer-systems defenders don't have much reaction
time to detect and contain Russian cyber operatives before they
wreak havoc on their victims' networks. The Russians have the fast-
est "breakout time" among foreign cyber actors—twenty minutes,
according to Crowdstrike, a U.S. computer security company.[38] That
is, twenty minutes is all it takes Putin's cyber squad attackers from
"gaining initial access to a victim's computer to moving laterally
through its network." This includes the time the hacker spends "scan-
ning the local network and deploying exploits in order to escalate his
access to other nearby computers."[39]

Russian hackers, which Crowdstrike internally calls "Bears," were
the most prolific and efficient hacker groups in 2019, with an average
breakout time of eighteen minutes and forty-nine seconds. They're
followed by North Korean groups, with a breakout time of two hours
and twenty minutes, the Chinese with a time of four hours, Iranians
with a time of five hours, and cybercrime gangs, or "Spiders," with a
time of roughly nine hours and forty-two minutes.[40]

Not an Act of War

Russian war planners view cyber as an effective instrument to
weaken or defeat America because they believe the United States'
advanced technological edge is a vulnerability to be exploited.
American reliance on information technology in all aspects of life—
healthcare, education, manufacturing, banking, transportation, and
aviation, to name a few—provides an excellent opportunity to hit
America where it hurts should a conflict between Russia and the
United States unfold or become imminent. The thinking goes that if
Americans are precluded, even temporarily, from withdrawing

money from ATMs, filling their cars with gas, receiving treatment in the hospital, flying to a coveted vacation spot, or even watching cable TV, they may change their minds about helping stage Putin's removal from power, returning Crimea to Ukraine, or otherwise engaging in a high-stakes conflict with Moscow. The Russians think that Americans have low tolerance for surviving without their usual creature comforts and would eagerly place pressure on their government to stand down from a planned military action against Russia, should Moscow telegraph with a cyber strike its resolve to escalate conflict to the next level.

And if the Americans don't get the message and proceed with combat action against Russia, Putin's war planners count on exploiting the U.S. military's dependence on both cyber capabilities and space by degrading or destroying some American satellites, computer systems, command and control (C2), or weapon systems. The Russians believe that by carefully calibrating their cyber strikes on the U.S. homeland they can keep the conflict with Washington simmering just below the threshold of a military response from America.

Prior to unleashing Putin's 2016 covert influence operation targeting the U.S. election, Russian cyber legal experts thoroughly studied the U.S. legal framework to ensure they wouldn't cross the line and provoke a military response from Washington. Russia's brazen intervention in the 2016 U.S. election was not an act of war based on the legal principles codified in the *Tallinn Manual 2.0*, which serves as a reference for attorneys whose job is to apply international law to cyber.[41] It turns out that hacking the DNC and releasing the emails into the U.S. public domain through WikiLeaks did not violate the UN Charter's prohibition of the use of force. It did not constitute an initiation of armed conflict and therefore and did not merit a U.S. military response in self-defense, according to a British law professor who led the team that developed the *Tallinn Manual*.[42] It pays to understand your opponent—even his legal framework.

Russia evidently was studying the U.S. legal framework and how it is applied to cyber for several years. This was apparent from an observation that the Russians made of their American counterparts during a bilateral meeting on cyber issues. The Russians wanted to know what exactly is meant by the word cyber and why the Americans use this word "cyber" in official government documents if none of the related legal documents contained this word. Americans similarly have an issue with the phrase "information weapon" that the Russians want to insert in the official discourse on cybersecurity, and even to the extent of proposing a treaty that would ban "information weapons." The problem is that Russians could interpret any information content that is critical of Russia, Putin, or Russia's policies or information which promotes issues disapproved by the Russian government, such as LGBT issues or same-sex marriage, as an "information weapon."

The 2019 Intelligence Community Annual Threat Assessment characterizes Russia as a "highly capable and effective" cyber actor, which poses a "significant cyber influence threat."[43] It called out Russia's cyber actions targeting election infrastructure in 2016 and 2018 elections. The threat assessment also warned that U.S. adversaries "may seek to use cyber means to directly manipulate or disrupt election systems—such as by tampering with voter registration or disrupting the vote tallying process—either to alter data or to call into question our voting process."[44]

Russia is waging aggressive information warfare, an effort which Moscow benignly terms "information confrontation." Every day, countless American industries, companies, think tanks, and government organizations are bombarded by Russian cyber intrusions that our cybersecurity defenders give cute names like "Cozy Bear," "Fancy

Bear," "Energetic Bear," "The Duke," "Not Petya," and so on. But there is nothing cute about it when your most dangerous adversary—which the U.S. government innocently terms its "strategic competitor"— hacks the Pentagon, the State Department, and the White House. The Russians were even reading President Obama's unclassified emails![45]

CHAPTER 6

Spies and Disruptors: Infiltrating America

*"It is necessary to inculcate in the psyche of intelligence
agents who conduct clandestine operations the belief that
morals and social norms mean absolutely nothing for
intelligence work."*

—from the section on the "Qualities of an Intelligence Agent" of the Russian Manual on Operational Tradecraft and Clandestine Activities of Special Services

There was no day when I didn't want to get up and go to work in the morning. I got to DIA headquarters at the Bolling Air Force Base around 7:00 a.m. Driving in on Interstates 495 and then 295 while sipping my coffee and listening to the news on the radio, I couldn't wait to log in to my antiquated government computer and read the morning "intel traffic" on JWICS, which stands for the Joint Worldwide Intelligence Community System. JWICS is a "top-secret, sensitive, compartmented-information" network operated by my agency, the DIA, for the entire military and defense Intelligence Community. Getting on the road early was important to stay ahead of another kind of traffic, the horrendous Washington-area car congestion that doesn't seem to abate except at night. An equally strong motivation to arrive at Bolling early was to be able to find a parking spot within walking distance of the DIA building. If you got there much past 8:00 a.m., you were out of luck and had to drive around the entire base in search of a legal parking spot, sometimes for twenty to thirty minutes. The Intelligence Community had grown so much in the post-9/11 world that parking was in extremely short supply at many intel agencies, and certainly at the DIA, the CIA, and the Pentagon, the places where I spent my work days.

Upon arrival at the DIAC (this is what we called the DIA headquarters, the Defense Intelligence Analysis Center), I would often grab my second cup of coffee at the little coffee shop that we called "Fake Starbucks." Unlike the CIA, which has a real Starbucks at headquarters, DIA's coffee shop served coffee in Starbucks cups, but it was not operated by Starbucks. The contrast is emblematic of that between the DIA and the CIA, where intelligence officers consider their Defense Department counterparts a slightly lesser breed of animal. The shop is called "Midway," a double-entendre riffing on the famous naval battle in the Pacific Theater of World War II, in which the U.S. Navy spectacularly defeated the Japanese Imperial Navy six months after the Japanese attack on Pearl Harbor, and the fact that the cafe was located midway between the DIA's old building and the new addition that was built after September 11, 2001. We did have a Dunkin Donuts, though, where long lines of sweets-craving intel officers queued up for their coffee and sugar fixes.

One morning, Charlie called me into his office and announced that we had been summoned to Brussels to brief NATO's Military Committee (MC) and the North Atlantic Council (NAC). The NAC is the principal political decision-making body within NATO and the primary authority on all political, military, and security issues affecting the whole Alliance. The MC is the senior military authority, consisting of three-star generals and admirals, and the primary source of military advice to the NAC and the Nuclear Planning Group. The MC gives direction to the two strategic commanders, Supreme Allied Commander Europe (SACEUR), and Supreme Allied Commander Transformation (SACT). SACEUR, a dual-hatted position that coincides with that of the Commander of the European Command (EUCOM), has always been held by a U.S. military officer, a four-star general. SACEUR is the one who would be commanding U.S. and NATO forces if conflict with Russia broke out in Europe. SACT is responsible for the transformation of NATO's military structures, forces, capabilities, and doctrines to improve the military effectiveness of the Alliance.

Having received ███████████████████████████████████ ███ ████████████████ the Pentagon's Assistant Secretary of Defense for Global Strategic Affairs and Deputy Assistant Secretary of Defense for Nuclear and Missile Defense Policy thought that it was very important to ████████████████████████████████████ Charlie and I strategized how to ██████████████████████ ███ ███ ███ ███ ███ ███ ███ ███ ███ ██████████████████████████████████ intro, and I would drill it down in detail ████████████████████████████ It worked very well. But first, we endured an exhaustive "murder board," a kind of a ritual rehearsal during which the person selected to brief a high-level official or group delivers a pre-briefing to the chain of command management and then is peppered with questions, some out of left field, to make sure that the briefer is well prepared for anything, including questions.

Policy officials sometimes ask random questions because their portfolio includes multiple countries. A briefer should be able to cover her topic comprehensively without drifting outside of her proverbial "lane" and to artfully and politely punt random questions if the "customer goes off the reservation." Senator McCain, outraged by Putin's continuous attempts to sabotage U.S. policy, asked one of my colleagues during a briefing to Congress "why the heck" India was buying Russian missiles. My colleague had to politely explain that he was not in the position to answer the senator's question because his intelligence target was Russia and not India.

On September 11, 2013, a few days before Charlie and I were supposed to fly out to Brussels, the *New York Times* published an op-ed by Putin.[1] The op-ed, titled "What Putin Has to Say to Americans about Syria," was another one of Putin's tricks to dissuade Barack Obama from following through on his earlier warning that Syria's Bashar al-Assad crossed the "red line" when he targeted his own citizens with a chemical strike. The intel folks were witnessing Russian "information confrontation" doctrine targeting the psychology of the American people and the decision-making of the U.S. president himself. Although not as multi-faceted as Russia's eventual 2016 covert-influence operation, this was consistent with what appeared to be a covert-influence op aimed at preventing the United States from striking Syria.

The adjective "covert" may seem like a misnomer here to non-intel experts, given that the effort was openly displayed in a newspaper. But this is the difference between covert intelligence operations and clandestine. Covert ops take place in plain sight. Everyone, including the target of this operation, can witness the activities orchestrated by the opposing intelligence service, but no one understands what is going on or why. Russia's 2016 intel op targeting the U.S. election was covert. Anyone could see social media posts that praised or disparaged both presidential candidates and anyone could see rallies supporting or opposing Trump and Clinton. But no one, except the Russian intelligence services and authorized actors, knew that Moscow was behind those activities. Clandestine intelligence operations are usually hidden from sight. No one, except those who authorized and are conducting the op, and especially not the foreign target, knows that it is happening. The 1980s intelligence operation in which the Russians bugged the U.S. Embassy in Moscow, turning it into a giant microphone so they could listen in on the American governments' secret communications, was clandestine.[2] The U.S. government, which naively used Russian construction workers and materials, had no idea that it was happening until the project, costing U.S. taxpayers $23 million, was almost complete.

In his op-ed, Putin, who deems himself an "expert on human relations," appealed "directly to the American people and their leaders," exhorting them to refrain from striking Syria.[3] A trained intel operative, Putin understands how his target thinks. Or, as the Russians like to say, *doktor znayet svoikh patsiyentov* ("the doctor understands his patients"). Ordinary Americans don't like war and want to go about their lives, as life is generally good. Americans are more comfortable being friends rather than adversaries with other nations. I routinely notice that the word "friend" is used in a context where Russians would normally employ a Russian equivalent of the word "acquaintance"—a word used less often in American English. If U.S. leaders seek to launch military action against a foreign state, the American people want proof that there exists a just cause making such a military action absolutely necessary and that it will not cause significant loss of human life.

So, in his appeal, Putin made sure to hit all the "hot buttons" for the American people to cause them to refuse to support Obama's potential action against Assad. He reminded Americans that Russia and the United States, despite the fact that they "stood against each other during the Cold War," were also "allies once and defeated the Nazis together."4 Putin invoked the images of "innocent victims," "inevitable civilian casualties, including the elderly and children," "escalation, potentially spreading the conflict far beyond Syria's border," "unleashing terrorism," and "further destabilizing the Middle East and North Africa." He tried to sow doubt that Assad was responsible for gassing his own people by putting the blame on opposition forces, knowing that, unlike in Russia, Americans believe that you are innocent until proven guilty (until recently, that is, in Washington, D.C.). Appealing directly to Obama's vanity, Putin characterized his relationship with the U.S. president as "working and personal, marked by "growing trust." He admonished Americans that major political and religious leaders, including the pope himself, opposed a U.S. strike on Syria. For good measure, the former intel operative disputed America's claim to being exceptional, stating, "When we ask for the Lord's blessings, we must not forget that God created us equal."

This was an ingenious practical application and display of the Russian doctrine of weaponizing information to achieve a psychological effect on Obama and the American people and prevent enforcement of the "red line" and to undermine support for punishing Assad—all courtesy of our own national newspaper, the *New York Times*. A few days later, Russian foreign minister Sergey Lavrov convinced his counterpart John Kerry that Russia would remove the chemical weapons arsenal from Syria, so there was no need for a punishing strike. And so, there was none. It was exasperating to watch.

I made sure to bring a copy of the *New York Times* with me to Brussels. It was an excellent case study that I wanted to use when ██

Although Putin's maneuver allowed the American president to save face while claiming a diplomatic victory, four years later weapons-grade chemicals were either returned or had remained in Syria, because Assad was still gassing his people. On April 7, 2017, President Trump enforced Obama's 2012 "red line" by launching fifty-nine Tomahawk cruise missiles at the Shayrat airbase in Homs, from which a sarin gas attack had been launched on April 4, 2017, killing more than eighty Syrians. A year later, after another suspected chemical attack by Assad on the opposition, Trump enforced the U.S. "red line" again, more than doubling the number of missiles launched.

I could understand Obama's initial desire to establish a working relationship with Russia in the beginning of his term, even after Russia's incursion into Georgia, considering it was the Georgians who technically started the conflict in 2008. Every president since Franklin Roosevelt, both Democrat and Republican, has tried to be friends with Russia. Americans want a productive relationship even with authoritarians and totalitarians, and they believe that helping solve human rights issues in dictatorships is the right thing to do. But in the second year of Obama's second term, after having tried for five years and failed, it was naive at best. Continuing to look into Putin's eyes and fail to see that he was not going to miraculously abandon Russia's centuries-old suspicion of the West or to compromise national interests in favor of "reset" games with its "main enemy," was mistaken and foolish.

My trip to Brussels was successful. It was an unforgettable experience to sit next to the deputy secretary general at the huge, round conference table with twenty-eight country flags in the iconic NATO headquarters conference room, a view you normally would see on CNN. Briefing NATO's highest levels—twenty-eight three-star generals and admirals, as well as political leaders—and watching them listen to your every word and then hearing them ask for more intel during the question and answer period was an honor that most intelligence officers don't experience in their entire career. I will always remember the feeling of awe and honor, mixed with a few butterflies in my stomach. Charlie and I also got to brief General Breedlove, Supreme Allied Commander Europe (SACEUR) and head of U.S. European Command, the position that would be commanding U.S. and Allied forces should a kinetic conflict between Russia and NATO break out in the European theater.

My senior partner and I apparently knocked it out of the ballpark. The DIA leadership received an email from our ███████████████ ██ ██ ████████████████████ Charlie and I made our agency proud.

On my return to the United States, it was time for the annual DIA performance evaluation. After receiving accolades from the big bosses, my immediate supervisor called me into his office. I was expecting to hear more praise for earning "platinum standard" for DIA from NATO's most senior leaders. To my astonishment, my supervisor said: "Rebekah, you are working too hard, and it creates a problem." I looked at him, bewildered. "You are making it impossible for other analysts to compete with you. And it makes it difficult for me to rate their performance." You see, a senior analyst of my level was supposed to deliver four to five briefings per quarter to earn an "outstanding" rating on a performance evaluation. I was doing more than fifty briefings per year, plus writing finished intelligence analysis reports, and doing other projects. My heavy briefing schedule was driven by many "by-name requests" from the customers needing to be briefed. This was because military and public policy officials found it valuable to hear an explanation of the mindset that drives Russian doctrine and strategy from someone who has direct experience with this mindset and can think in these terms herself. Charlie knew that by selecting me as his co-briefer for high-level briefings, we would fulfill the mission of serving our senior customers and make DIA shine To accomplish our mission, we stayed late and came in on weekends to prepare for high-level assignments, unlike so many other government employees, something we apparently should *not* have done.

I didn't know how to respond to my DIA supervisor who, I could tell, was sharing his conundrum with me rather than expressing his displeasure. I could not possibly imagine that my success, which was ultimately DIA's success, would breed resentment from certain analysts and invite bureaucratic shenanigans from other managers. Some folks in the government are much more adept at weaponizing bureaucratic games and buzzwords, like "favoritism" and "fairness," rather than working hard to fulfill the intelligence mission and honing their skills in the target's language, culture, capabilities, and intentions. This is what an intelligence officer's job is: to assess the foreign adversary's capabilities and intent to hurt America, so that our warfighters and policy officials can devise counterstrategies.

I told my supervisor that I needed to go prepare for another project. Charlie already had another assignment for me. This time it was an ███ ██ ████████████████████████████████ Being involved in this project allowed me to get a taste of operational work, which is different from intelligence analysis. It was the highlight of my career.

A Brutal, World-Class Espionage Machine

"A KGB case officer was a combination of a priest, a therapist, a best friend, and also a mortal enemy. He was somebody who was trying to get you to do things that would ultimately destroy you, whether professionally or personally."
—from KGB archives, The Intercept

The most critical and potent instrument in Putin's playbook is the work of intelligence operatives and the spies they recruit. Intelligence operations conducted by Russia's agents and secrets obtained from foreign spies who betray America make the entire playbook work. Collectively, Putin's intelligence apparatus enables all the tools of Russia's statecraft: space operations, cyber intrusions, active measures—including sabotage and assassinations—and military campaigns. Intelligence operatives collect and process data from satellites to enable space warfare, hack American networks to disrupt elections, chase and murder those who can't keep Russia's secrets and who criticize Putin, help identify and characterize military targets, and, most importantly, assist military commanders in developing strategies, doctrines, and plans to defeat the adversary. Following Sun Tzu's teachings, Russian intelligence employs intricate tradecraft to provide "foreknowledge" to their commander, a spymaster himself.

Sun Tzu warned that "foreknowledge cannot be elicited from spirits; it cannot be obtained inductively from experience, nor by any deductive calculation. Knowledge of the enemy's disposition can only be obtained from other men."[5] One of the key differences between the Russian and U.S. approaches to intelligence is how much priority they place on human intelligence, or HUMINT, versus technical intelligence, such as obtaining photographic images through spy satellites, intercepting phone calls, hacking emails, collecting weapon systems signatures, and so on. Culturally, American intelligence is predisposed to technical collection, which they view as more accurate and trustworthy, because technology doesn't lie. The Russians, on the other hand, are infatuated with HUMINT, which can provide human-informed context and a bigger picture about what is going on.

With technical intelligence, we may not know what happened before and after the phone call, or even why it took place. An intercepted phone conversation, for instance, or a satellite picture of a deployed weapon system are snapshots of information of intelligence value at a point in time. Likewise, we may see the deployed weapon system or deployed forces, but from the image alone we do not know why they were deployed, what the commander's intent is, or what to expect next.

██
██
███████████████████████████████ You may even be able to debrief him not once, but several times, based on questions that the analysts, knowledgeable on certain intel issues, help develop. HUMINT usually can help answer the question "why?" while technical intelligence cannot. Therefore, the Russians put a lot of stock in HUMINT. A secondary reason is that the Russians don't have the financial resources that U.S. intelligence has to build highly sophisticated reconnaissance systems, though their technical collection means can be advanced.

Russia has one of the world's most preeminent—and ruthless—intelligence services. Putin's top three intel agencies are the Foreign Intelligence Service (Sluzhba Vneshney Razvedki, or SVR), the Main Intelligence Directorate of the General Staff, or military intelligence (Glavnoye Razvedovatel'noye Upravleniye, or GRU), and the Federal Security Service, or domestic intelligence (Federal'naya

Sluzhba Bezopasnosti, or FSB). These agencies are only rough counterparts to the U.S. Central Intelligence Agency (CIA), the Defense
Intelligence Agency (DIA), and the Federal Bureau of Investigation
(FBI). Their combined Soviet predecessor, Committee on State
Security (Komitet Gosudarstvennoy Bezopasnosti, or KGB), Putin's
alma mater, traced its origins to the All-Russian Extraordinary
Commission, or Cheka (based on the Russian acronym ChK),
which Vladimir Lenin established shortly after the Bolshevik Revolution of 1917.

Cheka's initial mission was primarily domestic, to ensure the
"dictatorship of the proletariat" of the young Soviet State by rooting
out the "enemies of the people" who were supposedly plotting a
"counter-revolution." Violence and executions were Cheka's main
instruments, advocated not only as justifiable but necessary by the
chief of Cheka, Polish-born revolutionary Felix Dzerzhinsky, Lenin,
and his successor Joseph Stalin. Cheka operatives called themselves
Chekists *(Chekisty)*, the term that came to refer to Soviet intelligence
services in general, including the KGB, invoking the terrifying images
of the Red Terror. The Chekists carried out the repressions by arrest-
ing people suspected of political subversion and sending them to
labor camps or executing them without trial. They usually took their
victims in the middle of the night without explanation. The families
never heard from their loved ones again.

Nowadays, the Russian security and intelligence services—
including their former members, who predominantly occupy key
positions in Putin's government as well as in strategic industries like
oil and gas—are referred to as *siloviki* ("men of force and power").
Siloviki have largely inherited Chekists' operational methods but
have refined the "special tradecraft" of eliminating the opposition.
Instead of executions by a shot in the back of the head, they use a less
messy method: poisonings.

The ruthless legacy of the Cheka is illustrated in an admonition for intelligence officers from a Russian intelligence tradecraft manual: "It is necessary to inculcate in the psyche of intelligence agents who conduct clandestine operations the belief that morals and social norms mean absolutely nothing for intelligence work."[6]

The Soviet Cheka, in turn, operated on the same principles as the czarist Okhrana (The Guard), or secret police, who used provocations and penetrations of various groups to uncover various plots to overthrow or assassinate the czar. Professional revolutionaries therefore conducted their activities "underground," using false identities or pseudonyms. For example, Lenin's real name was Vladimir Il'yich Ul'yanov, and Stalin's was Joseph Vissarionovich Dzhugashvili. A combination of secrecy and deception captured by the Russian term *konspiratsiya* were essential components of the operational security that the Chekists practiced. Soviet and later Russian intelligence services demanded strict adherence to the rules of *konspiratsiya* from its operatives and placed a high priority on the security of its secrets and operations, making it very difficult to identify and break into. A 2006 intelligence tradecraft manual describes one of the missions of *konspiratsiya* as creating "a false impression with the adversary about an operation conducted by an opposing intelligence service."[7] This is achieved by "influencing the adversary's mindset and psychology through *dezinformatsiya*." This can be possible only by thoroughly studying the adversary and the doctrine of its intelligence and counterintelligence services in advance. In other words, one must "feel the adversary."[8]

Since 1917, Soviet and Russian intelligence have attempted some audacious operations against the "main enemy," the United States, craftily employing secrecy, deception, and ingenuity and understanding the enemy's mindset to steal secrets and penetrate various U.S. government agencies.

A startling example of Moscow's spy-craft trickery and Washington's gullibility was the construction of a new U.S. Embassy in Moscow in the 1980s. The Soviets had finally agreed to let the Americans move from the run-down pre-Bolshevik embassy, which they had constantly bombarded with electronic attacks, to a new building. The Soviet government managed to convince Americans to let them "help" build the new building, using Soviet construction workers and Soviet-made construction materials. Despite being warned by a Soviet defector soon after the construction began that the new embassy building would be riddled with listening devices, U.S. government experts arrogantly thought that there was nothing that the Soviets would implant in the building that American technicians could not disable.[9] Years and millions of dollars later, it became clear that they were disastrously wrong.

After the Soviet bugging of the new U.S. Embassy became public in 1986, followed by a series of congressional investigations, President Reagan in 1988 ordered the building torn down.[10] My former intel professor, a dear friend and mentor, was a senior intelligence official at the time who was dispatched to Moscow to tell the U.S. ambassador to Russia about the plan to throw out the Russian construction workers on Reagan's orders. Having arrived at the embassy, my friend was stunned to see Russian janitors and equipment installers wandering around what was technically U.S. territory, mopping the floors and stringing cables around the building as though they were in a Soviet ministry. Looking for a secure space to speak privately, without the Soviets eavesdropping, he and a couple of senior embassy officials climbed up on top of the roof, away from the Soviet spymasters' ears. Along the splendid view of Moscow skyline on a bright sunny day were the towering golden domes of a nearby church that American Embassy staff named "Our Lady of Electron" because they suspected that it housed some of the electronic hardware used by the

Russians to eavesdrop on Americans. My friend, whose mission was also to survey how the Soviets were able to listen in on U.S. communications, could discern a large antenna concealed behind an opaque covering in one of the church's windows. He explained that the Soviets were beaming microwaves toward the embassy in order activate listening devices inside the building.[11]

It turned out to be impossible to "debug" the embassy because the Soviets embedded the sensors in the very structure of the building. Columns, beams, and rods made from "specially" pre-cast concrete formed a giant antenna. Stunned by the sophistication of the construction, which housed a power source that purportedly could last a hundred years, the American technicians didn't completely understand either the technology or the design used for the interception of U.S. Embassy communications. According to the same defector— ███ ███— this surveillance system included numerous features. In addition to the technology embedded in the structure of the building, underground tunnels ran to the foundation walls, and microphones were installed within the furniture and office equipment, which would allow the Russians to have both audio and video of everything that was going on inside the American Embassy.[12] The Russians, who are culturally predisposed to expect things to go wrong, are known to place a premium on redundancy. If one part of the systems goes down or doesn't provide the visibility of U.S. secrets that Moscow wants, another part fills in the gaps. They use the same approach when building their own communication systems, which they expect the Americans to work hard at attempting to breach.

The U.S. government ended up removing the top four floors that contained the SCIFs (sensitive compartmented information rooms), where the most sensitive areas of the embassy would be located, ████

███████████████ and replacing it with the new four floors built out of American construction materials by hiring private contractors and using American Navy personnel.[13] In 1987, a Senate committee described the Soviet spy-craft as "the most massive, sophisticated, and skillfully executed bugging operation in history."[14]

This was not the first time that U.S. government was fooled by microphones provided by Soviet intelligence. In 1952, U.S. technical security personnel uncovered a listening device that was hidden in the wooden replica of the Great Seal of the United States.[15] The Seal was hanging right over renowned U.S. Ambassador George Kennan's desk at his office in the embassy. It was gifted by the Soviets to U.S. government officials at the end of World War II and was transmitting secrets to the Kremlin until it was discovered years later during an electronic "sweep." In the 1960s, in several intelligence operations, the Soviets daringly tried and sometimes succeeded in planting microphones in Congress.[16]

Evidently, the U.S. government is slow to learn from its mistake of employing Soviet and Russian personnel in U.S. Embassy offices in Russia. As recently as January 2017, a female Russian national was fired from the U.S. Embassy in Moscow based on suspicion of espionage. Recruited by the U.S. Secret Service, she worked at the embassy for ten years and had access to highly confidential electronic communications, including the schedules of the U.S. president and vice president. The woman regularly met with an agent from FSB, Russia's main domestic security and intelligence agency.[17]

Russia uses its own embassies in the United States as the base of intelligence operations against America and Americans. Russian intelligence operatives under official cover work out of the embassy-based residency *(Rezidentura)*, posing as diplomats. They collect political, military, economic, and scientific intelligence, spot and recruit Americans who would spy for Russia, and run technical collection operations.

The chief of the *Rezidentura* is called the "Resident," the equivalent of the American chief of station at a U.S. Embassy. The Russian Embassy compound in Washington, D.C., and consulates in New York and San Francisco are all located at high points of elevation to enable interception of U.S. communications by arrays of antennae and other electronic equipment perched on the rooftops.[18]

On orders from the Trump administration, the San Francisco Consulate and the trade missions in New York and Washington were closed in the fall of 2017 in response to Moscow's cutting the number of U.S. diplomats in Russia. A day before the embassy closure, clouds of smoke could be spotted coming out of the embassy rooftop chimney, an indicator that the Russian spymasters were hastily burning classified documents before departing. Putin with his own hands fed volumes of sensitive intelligence into the furnace in the Soviet intelligence mission in Dresden, when angry Germans surrounded the building in the run up to the fall of the Berlin Wall. "We burnt so much stuff that the furnace burst," he recalled in his autobiography *First Person*.[19]

The closure of several of the Russian government facilities in the United States is just one example of the significant tension in U.S.-Russian relations that began to spiral in the aftermath of Putin's annexation of Ukraine's Crimea. Having finally recognized the failure of the "reset" policy with the Kremlin, the Obama administration imposed economic sanctions on select Russian entities and individuals, which resulted in a chain reaction between Washington and Moscow of reducing one another's "diplomatic" presence at embassies and consulates. Sanctions and fewer "diplomats," undoubtedly justified and necessary, also undermined both countries' intelligence collection capabilities during geopolitically precarious times. This included ramifications for ongoing conflicts and military activities in Ukraine, Syria, and Afghanistan, among other places.

Fake Americans or Russian "Illegals"

In *The Art of War*, Sun Tzu taught that the most effective way to defeat the adversary is to "attack by stratagem"—that is, "to avoid what is strong and strike what is weak."[20] War by stratagem rather than brute force requires a nuanced understanding of the adversary. The iconic ancient Chinese strategist admonished, "If you know the enemy and know yourself, you need not fear the result of a hundred battles." Relying on Sun Tzu tenets and the judo principles of using the opponent's own force against him to throw him off balance, Putin's strategy against America hinges on Russia's ability to develop a deep understanding of the strengths and weaknesses of American society to identify vulnerabilities to exploit.

To help gain detailed knowledge and understanding of how American society functions, how we think, and what makes us tick, the Russian intelligence services employ a HUMINT tradecraft that is—with minor exceptions, such as Israeli intelligence—quite unique to Russia, and earlier the USSR. The Russians insert what are called "illegals" *(nelegaly)*, or deep-cover intelligence officers, within the adversary's society who pose as the citizens of that country or a different country, but not Russia. Unlike their "official cover" counterparts, the illegals don't have the benefit of diplomatic immunity, which would protect them in the event of being exposed. They know that if their cover is blown and they get arrested by the law enforcement of their adopted "homeland" they will go to prison.

Illegals spend years and even decades in the target country, including the United States, living like normal Americans or other nationals of the host country. They obtain jobs, go to universities, build relationships with people who could be valuable to Russian intelligence, and sometimes even raise children who have no idea that their parents are not who they think they are. These deep cover officers take orders from Moscow, using clandestine communications devices and covert Russian intelligence agents. The illegals build and reinforce their cover—sometimes for many years without being tasked with any operational assignments—to fit in well in the American culture, while learning about the nation's psyche. Their ultimate purpose is to help their true homeland take on, destabilize, and defeat "the main adversary" by stratagem.

The most recent case of Russian "illegal" intel officers living in the United States became public in 2010. In a multi-prong counter-intelligence operation titled Ghost Stories, the FBI arrested a spy ring of ten illegals who operated in several U.S. cities, including Washington, New York, and Boston. It took the FBI ten years to identify and surveil the suspects, gain evidence of a crime, and build adequate legal cases to arrest the Russians— a formidable task. This suggests that the illegals infiltrated American society well.

In his 2000 acceptance speech after he was elected president, Putin noted that the Russian intel agencies were "continuing to do their work well." After the FBI arrested the illegals in 2010, I wondered whether in his words of praise in 2000, Putin was also giving credit to the spy ring members operating in America. Regardless, in 2010, Putin, who was temporarily serving as Dmitry Medvedev's prime minister, displayed his high regard for the work of the expelled intel operatives by hosting them and singing old Russian patriotic songs from the Soviet movies about deep-cover Soviet intelligence agents operating in Nazi Germany. In an interview with journalists, Putin reminded everyone what a difficult life the ten agents led in America. "Just imagine: first, you must master the [foreign] language to the native level, then think in it, speak it, while fulfilling the tasks of the mission given, in the interest of the Motherland, for many, many years, without relying on diplomatic cover," he said.[21]

Putin also mentioned that Russia already knew who betrayed the ten deep cover operatives but refused to say what punishment these alleged traitors would be given. He said, "Such matters are not decided during a press conference." He added that, usually, such people "end up dead because of drunkenness or drugs, under a fence."[22] Around the same time, a senior official in the Kremlin was quoted by the Russian newspaper *Argumenty I Fakty* (*Arguments and Facts*) saying that "Mercader [Leon Trotsky's assassin] has already been sent" for the person who gave up the ten Russian agents to U.S. law enforcement. The Russian government sometimes "leaks" useful information to the media to send a message to its target audience. In this case, the strategic message would be aimed at potential Russian "turncoats" who may be considering switching sides and betraying Russia. Putin wants such candidates to know they will be tracked down and eliminated no matter where they escape to.

The Russian intelligence tradecraft sending deep cover officers "behind the enemy lines" dates to the Cheka. The newly established Soviet state was initially not recognized diplomatically by the West, including the United States, leaving Soviet intelligence without the traditional option of operating out of embassies and consulates. To overcome this obstacle, the Soviets trained vast networks of illegals and sent them first throughout Europe, and then, eventually, the United States. Initially, the Russian-born revolutionary and communist Ludwig Karlovich Martens and Arthur Adams, the first known Soviet intelligence officer, teamed up to start a covert operation in the United States in 1919 out of an "unofficial" embassy facility and trade mission called "Amtorg," which is an abbreviation of the Russian for "American Trade."[23] The program was designed to steal American technological and economic secrets by enticing U.S. companies with promises of business opportunities. By the time the negotiations were complete and the Soviets had syphoned out of Americans the information that the government needed, the Soviet representatives refused to sign a contract. After Martens and Adams were deported in 1920 on charges of being affiliated with the Communist Party, which advocated the overthrow of the U.S. government, the Soviets deployed the first illegal officers to operate in America under false identities.

These spy ringleaders worked closely with the Communist Party USA (CPUSA) in penetrating the federal government bureaucracy, such as the Departments of State and War. The Soviet illegal officers who posed as Americans set up spy networks of American citizens who were ideologically enamored with communism as, in their view, a progressive form of government. They were tragically beguiled into thinking that communism would save the world's problems of inequality and capitalist "oppression," without realizing the repressive and violent nature of communism, and its predecessor, socialism. I often observe similar naiveté, a lack of historical knowledge, and absence of critical thinking among today's American elite, including some government leaders and even former presidential candidates who openly advocate socialism in America.

The spy networks run by Soviet illegals in America included dozens, even hundreds, of members who performed various functions.[24] There were talent-spotters who assessed potential spy candidates, recruited (*verbovka,* from *verbovat'*) candidates to become spies, and couriers who hand-carried U.S. secrets obtained by spy ring members who worked in U.S. government agencies. The Soviet intelligence program was so successful in the United States and throughout the world in the 1930s that historians called this period the era of "Great Illegals." In Britain, Arnold Deutsch, one of the most prominent and effective Soviet illegals, was responsible for the recruitment of the "Magnificent Five," a group of Cambridge graduates who infiltrated high levels of British government while working for the Soviets. Also called the "Cambridge Five," its most prominent member, Kim Philby, worked at the British Embassy in Washington, D.C., and provided critical intelligence to the Soviets during the Second World War.

In the United States, beginning in late 1941, the Soviet illegal officer Iskhak Akhmerov (codenames YUNG and ALBERT) ran successful spy networks in New York and later Baltimore, handling Washington-based agents. His wife Helen Lowry (codenames MADLEN and ADA) was the niece of the head of CPUSA, Earl Browder (codename RULEVOY, or "Helmsman" in Russian), illustrating the close relationship between Russian intelligence and American communists. Moscow allowed, and in some instances even encouraged, Russo-American "cross-pollination." The NKVD, one of Cheka's successors, penetrated "all the most sensitive sections of the Roosevelt Administration," according to the Soviet defector to Britain and former KGB archivist Vassily Mitrokhin.[25] Among Soviet penetrations of U.S. government were unwitting "useful idiots" such as Harry Hopkins, who mistakenly aligned ideologically with the Soviets. Hopkins was the closest wartime advisor of President Roosevelt. He called the brutal Soviet dictator Stalin "Uncle Joe," kissing up to the Soviets, in an attempt to join forces with them to defeat the Nazis. While Hopkins was not an official spy, he viewed the Soviets as a benevolent partner in the United States' fight against Nazi Germany and fed confidential information to the Soviet ambassador, while using Iskhak Akhmerov as a back channel to the Kremlin.[26]

Hopkins's information was so valuable to the Soviets that the KGB later dubbed him a "Soviet agent," [27] according to Mitrokhin. The Russians have a separate category and name for these types of intelligence assets, calling them *agenty vliyaniya*, or "agents of influence." This is another difference between the Russian and American intel tradecraft and missions: American intelligence seeks to collect foreign secrets to assess the capabilities and intentions of foreign adversaries as accurately as possible and without bias. Russian intelligence, in addition to stealing secrets from its perceived adversaries, also seeks to influence the perceptions of the U.S. intelligence and national security apparatus toward Russian capabilities and intentions and to steer the United States' Russia policy in a direction favorable to Moscow.

This misunderstanding of the ultimate mission and goals of Russian intelligence contributed to the Obama administration's desire to downplay the significance of the Russian illegals network, which the FBI dismantled. Their view was apparently that if the Russians didn't steal any American secrets, they didn't cause any damage to U.S. security. The narrative, summarized in the sarcastic statement by one of the defense attorneys for the Russian spies that their only success was infiltrating American "neighborhoods, cocktail parties, and the PTA," was very convenient for the Obama White House. Busy trying hard to make friends with Russia in 2010, as they viewed Medvedev as a moderate compared to Putin, the Obama administration took the attitude of "move along, nothing to see here." The overall U.S. reaction was similarly indifferent to the exposure and arrest of one of the most damaging Soviet spies, the FBI senior counterintelligence officer Robert Hanssen, in February 2001, during George W. Bush's administration. At some point, one begins to wonder whether the naiveté of our government leaders about foreign mindsets and intentions borders on willful and liable reluctance to learn lessons from history.

The Obama White House was so invested in its misguided "reset policy" with Moscow that it almost jeopardized, albeit inadvertently, the entire FBI operation to round up the Russian illegals.[28] The FBI was not allowed to arrest the Russian spy-ring members until former Russian president Medvedev, who was visiting the United States at the time, returned to Moscow. The success of the "Ghost Stories" operation depended on the FBI counterintelligence agents' ability to arrest all the members of the spy network simultaneously in various cities in the United States. In one instance, the FBI officers were waiting on the clock for the right time to move in on their suspects, concerned that they would miss the window of opportunity if the illegals escaped to Russia. As the operation progressed, at least one of the Russian deep cover officers, red-headed Anna Chapman, sensed that something was not right after she met with an undercover U.S. counterintelligence officer who was posing as a Russian Embassy official. His job was to elicit an action from Chapman that would allow the United States to charge her with a crime.

Throughout the years Russia has invested significant resources into the illegals program. The Russian intelligence services believe that through deep cover officers they can obtain insights about their foreign targets that they cannot collect through traditional espionage methods used by Western intelligence. Evidence of this commitment to the success of the program is the extremely high level of training that the Russian foreign intelligence agency SVR provides to these officers. The illegals are trained for at least four and on occasion up to seven years. Foreign language training to the "native level," as Putin noted, is just one aspect of the training. They learn to behave, speak, and think like Americans, Canadians, English, French, or whatever nationality they assume. The training is provided in a one-on-one setting by an intelligence officer who spent a long time in the target country. Every minor detail is accounted for—from the clothing you wear, where you carry your wallet, and what you keep in it or in your pockets (for males) to how you hold a cigarette and how you clap and count. (Americans usually stick their fingers outward as they count, while Russians press them in toward their hands.)

Another subtle difference between Russians and Americans is in our facial expressions. Many Americans smile frequently—or at least they don't frown. When they smile, they show their teeth. Life in America is exceptionally good compared to Russia and most other places in the world. Russians rarely smile, and if they do, they don't show their teeth. Smiling often is considered a sign of foolishness in Russian culture. Because life is generally hard, there are few reasons to smile, and therefore Russians tend to view those who smile as odd. Although I have been Americanized in many ways, my normal resting facial expression must have remained Russian, because my daughter frequently asks me, "Mom, what's wrong?" When I deny anything worrisome is happening, she asks me, "Why are you frowning then?" One of the female Russian illegals—who operated in the United States under deep cover while posing for more than twenty years as an ordinary Canadian residing in the United States—noted that the hardest thing for her to get used to was to be able to "project a happy, worry-free American personality."

Before inserting illegals into the target country, the Sluzhba Vneshney Razvedki (SVR) Directorate Line N, which runs the illegals, builds what is called a "legend" (*legenda*) for each officer. It includes a new name and a completely new identity and biography, including the place of birth, where they went to school, who their parents were, and so on. To obtain a false identity, Russian intelligence officers scout cemeteries in foreign countries in search of graves belonging to children who died young. They then try to illegally obtain a birth certificate for the dead child through bribery or trickery. A new person is "born" in a graveyard, hence the FBI's name of "Ghost Stories" for the operation to arrest the Russian illegals.

As part of reinforcing and building the cover, the illegal travels to his or her place of birth, schooling, and other locations that are part of his or her cover story, called in Russian intelligence tradecraft the legend (*legenda*). Frequently, the illegals are deployed as married couples to make it easier to maintain the life of isolation that is typical of them, and also to avoid an illegal having an intimate relationship with a local person and blowing his or her cover. Several of the ten Russian illegals were couples.[29] Tracey Foley and Donald Heathfield, who posed as a Canadian couple who had moved to the United States, were Russian and originally Soviet intelligence officers Andrey Bezrukov and Elena Vavilova. They had two sons who were born in Canada and who didn't know the truth about their parents. The two boys, who didn't speak any Russian, were deported together with their parents to Russia after their parents were released from U.S. prison and sent to Russia as part of a spy swap. In exchange for the ten Russian illegal officers, Russia released to the United States and Great Britain four Russian citizens who were working for the U.S. and British intelligence services. One of the sons of Foley and Heathfield (Vavilova and Bezrukov) filed a legal appeal and received permission from the Canadian government to retain Canadian citizenship and return to Canada.[30]

The following are some of the instructions from the section on the "Qualities of an Intelligence Agent" from the Russian *Manual on Operational Tradecraft and Clandestine Activities of Special Services*. They explain some of the training requirements for the illegal officers.[31]

> An illegal agent must know the history of his target country very well…especially its moral, political, psychological, cultural, and historical values.[32]
>
> …An illegal officer must know his new legend-based biography better than his real one. He can forget the name of his real aunt's cousin or the date of his college diploma, but he does not have a right to forget any fact, detail, event, or date related to his second biography.[33]

The manual also instructs on the importance for any intelligence agent to prioritize the mission above everything else.

> It is necessary to inculcate in the psyche of intelligence agents who conduct clandestine operations the belief that morals and social norms mean absolutely nothing for intelligence work. The intelligence agent [*razvedchik*] in his work cannot constrain himself by any ethics. Purely practical factors play a decisive role in clandestine operations: Is this needed? Is this achievable? Can this operation be kept secret?[34]

Coming with a Knife to a Gun Fight

While American counterintelligence (CI) works hard to mitigate the threat of Putin's spies, we are not well-postured even to minimize, let alone root out, the problem. My friend, a former senior intelligence official who served in high-level counterintelligence positions in the U.S. government described our counterintelligence posture vis-à-vis the Russian (and Chinese, for that matter) espionage threat as carrying knives to a gun fight. He identified two key problems that we have not been able to solve for years: lack of foreign language and culture expertise and unwillingness or inability to do what is called "offensive counterintelligence" operations.[35]

██

██

██████████████████████████████████████ Such understanding is especially important because American and Russian intelligence are founded on two vastly different philosophies and are influenced by different historical experiences. Even though the United States, being a nation of immigrants, has a large reservoir of candidates with native or near-native foreign language capabilities, the U.S. IC has not been able to bring them on board in meaningful numbers. As I wrote in previous chapters, the federal government's hiring bureaucracy tends to screen out applicants with foreign backgrounds. It is much easier and less expensive for the bureaucrats to vet American-born candidates with no foreign travel history than naturalized or even first-generation Americans.

The second problem of American counterintelligence is what my friend and former senior counterintelligence official described as "stylistic."[36] Unlike the Russians, who make it extremely painful and even dangerous for American intelligence officers to steal Russian secrets, especially inside Russia, ███████████████████████████ ███████████████████████ And we are even less aggressive in trying to find out what the Russian intelligence services are up to. In other words, we are waiting for a counterintelligence case to surface to start an investigation rather than working earlier to find out the GRU and SVR plans that target America.[37] Such a strategy would entail taking the fight to the adversary and going on offense by running provocations and false-flag operations. Such "offensive CI" operations entail sending "dangles," or intel operatives who pose as double agents and seeking to switch sides and work for the Russians. Once the Russians debrief a "dangled" officer, he can inform U.S. IC about Russian intelligence requirements, debriefing tactics, and other issues. Gaining such insights on the opponent would help us protect our own sensitive information and collect theirs. Such offensive CI operations are risky and sometimes even dangerous for our officers, but they can be very fruitful.

In 2019, the Intelligence Community wisely warned Americans about the threat posed by Russian intelligence and security services.[38] The unclassified Annual Threat Assessment presented by the DNI to the Senate Select Committee on Intelligence called out Russia for its "cyber espionage, influence, and attack threat to the United States and our allies." It characterized Moscow as a "highly capable and effective adversary" who "will continue targeting [U.S.] information systems, as well as the networks"…"for technical information, military plans, and insight into our governments' policies."[39] But the public statements of the director of the National Counterintelligence and Security Center (NCSC), Bill Evanina, in 2019 and 2020 reveal that the IC may be again underestimating the Russian spy threat.[40] Evanina mentioned the threat of espionage, influence, and election interference coming from Russia (and China), warning that "Putin will want to ensure the [U.S.] election is as chaotic as possible."[41] However, when comparing the Russian and Chinese espionage operations conducted against the United States, he identified China as a much more formidable threat to the United States because of the extent of Chinese espionage. Evanina said Russians are "more tactical" and that they "spend their time and effort" on recruiting "strategically placed" human spies "onesie-twosie."[42]

I disagree with the NCSC director that quantity is a good metric to assess the counterintelligence threat. I argue that one or two strategically placed spies, such as Robert Hanssen and Aldridge Ames, who spied for the Russians for years, can do a lot more damage than dozens or hundreds of agents who lack good access to secrets sought by the foreign adversary. FBI's Hanssen and CIA's Ames were arguably the most effective Russian spies in U.S. history. Between the two, they are responsible for selling extremely sensitive information to the Russians—including strategic nuclear intelligence—and for the execution of several Soviet intelligence officers who were U.S. assets.[43]

CHAPTER 7

Active Measures: Subversion, Election Sabotage, and Assassinations

"All warfare is based primarily on
deception of an enemy. Fighting on
a battlefield is the most primitive way
of making war. There is no art higher
than to destroy your enemy without
a fight—by subverting anything
of value in the enemy's country."

—Sun Tzu, Chinese general and philosopher, 500 BC

[redacted]

Proud of my ability to contribute in unique ways and to be selected for such an honor, I was receiving accolades from people [redacted]

[redacted] The bean counters did not care that I was doing critical work for the entire Intelligence Community or the country. They cared about the PDBs, or Presidential Daily Briefs, and other intel reports that we weren't writing while we did other things. I needed to avoid getting a bad or mediocre performance evaluation even while doing critical work for the country and making DIA shine. So, Mike H., the defense intelligence officer for Russia/Eurasia, the most senior Russia position in the entire Defense Intelligence Enterprise, wrote a "Performance Appraisal Input Letter for Rebekah Koffler" to the chief of the Europe/Eurasia Regional Center—that is, the chief bean counter.

The letter characterized me as an "outstanding performer and invaluable member" of DIA's Russia strategic intelligence analysis team and commended me on the [redacted]

██████████ It also reminded the bean counters that the impact of my work "could not be captured in conventional performance metrics like the number of PDBs produced." In this letter, Mike H. expressed confidence in my ability, as "a top intelligence officer who makes DIA shine, to advance to positions of leadership at DIA."

Mike and Charlie, who ███████████████████████████ did their best to protect my two other DIA colleagues and me (Charlie collectively called us "the troika") from the bureaucrats. Old-time partners, they served together in a sensitive HUMINT unit in Potsdam, Germany, from the 1980s until well after the collapse of the USSR. As retired U.S. Army officers—and a special operations officer (SOF) in Charlie's case—who risked their lives running HUMINT operations behind the adversary's lines, these gentlemen understood what mattered. They were not about to let the bureaucratic process impede the mission. Eventually, Mike's commitment to the mission and desire for DIA's clandestine shop to outshine the CIA's came in direct conflict with the DIA apparatchiks' religious devotion to "process" and their unwillingness to change. The apparatchiks won. Mike was soon gone from DIA and the IC.

In the meantime, in February 2014, Putin's "little green men," as Ukrainians called them—soldiers in green uniform but without any identifying military insignia—seized control of Ukraine's Crimea.[1] Consistent with Putin's information-warfare doctrine, several days prior to the invasion, Russian intelligence services hacked into YouTube and Twitter and leaked a private telephone call between Assistant Secretary of State for Russian and European Affairs Victoria Nuland and U.S. Ambassador to Ukraine Geoffrey Pyatt.[2] The two U.S. diplomats in the intercepted phone call discussed who would be the best candidate among the top opposition figures, to replace the ousted pro-Russia president of Ukraine, Viktor Yanukovich, who had fled amid violent protests in Kiev. They coordinated phone calls with each other in which they would support the candidate whom they favored because of his prior government experience. They planned to call another candidate, a former professional boxer, and talk him out of joining the new Ukrainian government, because he would be more valuable on the outside in the diplomats' view. Russia seized the opportunity to unmask what Moscow views as U.S. interference in Ukrainian politics in pursuit of Washington's "regime change" policy in the countries that Russia considers part of its strategic security perimeter.

Things were heating up in DIA's Russia shop. It was time for the ███ ███ ███ ████████████████████ I had my marching orders to get ready for what we call in government "TDY," or temporary duty travel.

Diligently, I was sifting through numerous intelligence reports to make sure that Charlie and I had the most up-to-date information for the ██████████████ I stayed in late and came in on a weekend, at the risk of management's calling me out again for "unfairly" outcompeting my less driven government coworkers. As I was building my briefing one morning, an Army Major colleague named Bill came up to me and somewhat uncomfortably asked if I could help him put together a ██████████████████████████████████ ████████ "I've got this," I replied to Bill, "No worries." I told him that Charlie and I had it under control and that I would be ready for the "murder board" in a couple days. I was stunned when Bill somewhat sheepishly announced that the ██████████████████████████ ███ ███ ███████████

I am all for teamwork and will gladly help my colleagues prepare for high-level engagements. But it didn't make sense to me that Bill would be selected for this extremely important project. Although competent in his own right, Bill was neither ███████████████ ██████████████████████ And this was a "by-name request"—the "name" being mine. ███████████████ clearly wanted the same DIA briefers who delivered "platinum standard" the year before. I went straight to Charlie's office, confident that this was a misunderstanding that he would promptly correct. Charlie, the top Russia person on the analytic side, outranked most of our Europe/Eurasia chain of command, and he always did what was best for the mission. I also knew that he had previously explained to the management that he couldn't bring just any analyst to brief the highest levels of the U.S. and Allied governments and risk embarrassing the agency in the interest of "fairness" and "equality." It had to be a senior analyst who knows the target and the intel issue at hand, inside and out, and who also is an experienced briefer.

When I had made it down the hall to Charlie's teeny-tiny but comfortable office and asked what was going on, he gave me a strange look and said that Bill was correct and that he was taking him as co-briefer to Brussels. Charlie seemed like he wanted to explain more, and he knew that I was eager to hear an explanation, but he paused right there. In an unusual act of defiance, I snapped, "If Bill is going to be your co-briefer, then Bill should build the briefing." As I walked out of Charlie's office, mumbling that I had other projects to work on, he said, "Rebekah," with a disconsolate look in his eyes that was so unlike him, "I cannot get into this now, but I do need you to build the briefing. And I need you to help Bill prepare to deliver it to NATO. Please do it." I knew at that moment that something was going on that distressed Charlie. And when your senior intel partner asks you to do something, you do it.

What Charlie could not tell me, and what I found out much later, was that he was under investigation for allegations of "favoritism." Someone, a malicious slanderer, filed a complaint that Charlie and I were having an intimate relationship and that he was assigning good projects to me in return, at the expense of other analysts. "Favoritism" is a buzzword that incompetent government workers like to throw around to justify their failures. Malicious complaints are weapons that some government apparatchiks deploy against their opponents, with whom they disagree. They are very adept at using Russian-style "asymmetric" strategies to unseat those they are unable to compete against based on merit.

These allegations were completely unfounded and irresponsible, considering we were in the middle of a national security crisis. Charlie and I had a strictly professional relationship. We were—and are—both married, and our spouses know and like each other. The four of us have spent time together recreationally. But Charlie and I were close professional partners. Our work required us to spend time together, travel together, stay after regular office hours—if such a thing can exist in the intel world—and occasionally come in on weekends. Sometimes, when we were leaving the office late, Charlie would give me a ride to my car. As a high-ranking officer, he was permitted to park his car close to the DIA building, while I had to leave mine further away, in the area for regular folk. After Charlie gave me a ride to my car, we would occasionally spend a few minutes strategizing or going through a checklist of things we had to do the next day. Can you imagine the frustration of the "investigators," who probably expected some "hanky-panky" going on in the car or some emails coordinating a secret rendezvous? They didn't find anything, of course.

This was a hoax perpetrated against two dedicated senior intelligence officers who were simply doing their job: trying to keep America safe. This hoax reveals the malicious informant's mindset.

My slanderer either couldn't imagine that a female intel officer could be selected for top assignments because she was the best fit for the job—rather than because she was sleeping her way to the top—or they wanted to level the playing field by leaving out someone who was "working too hard." Or both. Even with no evidence, an apparatchik nevertheless opened an investigation.

I didn't know any of this at the time. I trusted Charlie's judgement. Without any further questions, I helped Bill with the briefing. Charlie and Bill accomplished the mission in Brussels. But DIA did not receive a "platinum standard" award this time.

I didn't have to wait long to get another exciting assignment. The non-kinetic cyber conflict was brewing, and I was called on to participate in an ███████████████████████████████████████ which took place at a contractor's facility in Northern Virginia. Sponsored by the National Intelligence Council (NIC), which is part of the Office of the Director of National Intelligence, this high-profile ██ ███████████████████████████████ opponent. When I returned to DIA at the conclusion of the ████████ Charlie told me that the ███████████████████████████████████████ who was presiding over this whole event, called him personally to thank DIA ███████ ██████████████████████████ for my excellent work.

A few months later, the Deputy NIO for Cyber position opened at the NIC/DNI. This was a rotational position that was filled by senior analysts from various agencies in the IC as part of the Joint Duty Assignment program (JDA).[3] This program was established to correct the deficiencies found by the September 11 Commission, one of which was a lack of cross-communication among various agencies and lack of opportunities for intelligence officers to serve at other IC agencies. The commission concluded that this shortcoming had led to the IC's failure to "connect the dots" and miss what we call "indications and warnings" about the threat that Al-Qaeda would strike U.S. homeland. In the post-September 11 IC, completing a two-year JDA rotational assignment at another IC agency became a requirement for senior analysts to be eligible for a promotion. My ultimate professional goal was to become the top Russia intel officer in the DIA and then in the IC. As a steppingstone, I applied for the NIC/DNI assignment. In a highly competitive interview process, I won the rotational position as Deputy National Intelligence Officer for Cyber. This is a particularly important and highly prestigious position in the IC.

I learned about my big professional victory the day before Christmas in 2014. I was elated. This was going to be my dream job! Cyber is probably the most cerebral element of Russian doctrine and strategy, a puzzle that I was eager to help the IC solve to keep our country secure. I had a lot of respect for my future boss, the National Intelligence Officer for Cyber, a highly intelligent attorney and veteran CIA officer who had spent a decade at CIA's Information Operations Center.[4] Since the position was located at "the Agency," he and I agreed that, time permitting, I could run a couple floors down and continue to work on the ████████████████████████████ ████████████████████████████ I planned to put in whatever hours were needed to continue to be part of this critical project, because I knew that much of what the IC did against the Russia target depended on how well my team members and I did on it. I was determined to make it work. I knew my husband, who bore the lion's share of family responsibilities while I was serving as a DIA intelligence officer, would understand—and the kids would too, eventually.

After DNI Clapper approved my candidacy for this JDA, the DIA and the DNI signed a Memorandum of Understanding authorizing me to serve as Deputy NIO for Cyber for two years, with an option to stay an additional year. I was about to become the "number two" person for Cyber in the U.S. Intelligence Community. I was on cloud nine. My late mother, who had always hoped I would go to the United States and be successful at whatever I did, would have been proud.

Duping the Enemy into Doing Your Will

"Politicians from foreign lands blame Russia for interfering in elections and referendums of all kinds across the word. In reality, things are even more serious—Russia has interfered with their minds, and they don't know what to do with their new consciousness."
—Vladislav Surkov, Putin's Goebbels

Aktivnyye meropriyatiya, or "active measures," are perhaps the most misunderstood technique in Putin's playbook and Russia's state-craft. A uniquely Russian—and before that, Soviet—intelligence tradecraft, active measures are designed to unbalance, subvert, discredit, or neutralize the adversary in order to advance the Kremlin's strategic goals and disrupt the opponent's.[5] Typically offensive in nature, these counterintelligence operations incorporate deception (*maskirovka*), disinformation (*dezinformatsiya*), forgeries (*fal'shivka*), blackmail via compromising information (*kompromat*), provocation (*provokatsiya*), intimidation, and even assassinations.[6] To conduct active measures, Russia uses, both in the United States and globally, specially trained intelligence operatives, front companies or organizations under the Russian government's control, and so-called "agents of influence."[7] Agents of influence can be Russian citizens who covertly work for the intelligence services, posing as diplomats, trade representatives, consultants, academics, journalists, and even religious leaders. They establish contacts with Americans in relevant professional fields to gain assistance in advancing Russian government–directed policy goals on specific issues. U.S. citizens can unwittingly become involved in Russian influence operations, serving as agents of influence who are unaware that their professional or business contact is working for Russian intelligence. The term for such American agents of influence is "useful idiots" or "fellow travelers."

A "trusted contact" is another type of agent of influence used by the Russians to dupe Americans into doing Moscow's bidding. Manipulated by Russian intelligence operatives on the basis of their professional interests, political views, or business goals, these Americans unknowingly further the agenda of the Russian government. Russian intelligence aggressively pursues such contacts within the U.S. government, business community, and think tank circles to influence the U.S. leadership's decision-making in the direction the Russian government desires and to predispose American elites favorably toward Russia. Unwitting agents of influence are not recruited by Russian intelligence and are not tasked with specific orders. They are targeted by Moscow because of their ideology, which aligns with Russia's, rather than because of their ability to steal American secrets.

While they are not compensated for their "assistance" in the same way that recruited spies get paid for providing U.S. secrets to the Russian state, the Russians ensure that trusted contacts, fellow travelers, and useful idiots receive some sort of reward for themselves or their families in order to keep the relationship going. Regardless, Russians believe that the value a well-placed agent of influence can bring through his or her position in the U.S. government or other areas, justifies the resources invested in the cultivation of such assets.

One of the most highly-placed agents of influence who was of remarkable value to the Soviets during World War II was Harry Hopkins, a trusted confidant and wartime advisor to President Franklin D. Roosevelt.[8] Hopkins had tremendous influence on FDR, who brought him to all the major wartime conferences, including the one at Yalta with Stalin and Churchill. Hopkins sought to establish friendly relations between the United States and the Soviet Union because he saw the USSR as playing a decisive role in defeating Nazi Germany. According to a prominent KGB defector, Oleg Gordievsky, Stalin's success in obtaining concessions from his British and American negotiators—such as regaining territorial control over the Baltics, Moldova, and eastern Poland, which the USSR had obtained as a result of the pact with Hitler—was undoubtedly helped by Stalin's "knowledge of the cards in Roosevelt's hand."[9] This foreknowledge was a direct result of Soviet intelligence's infiltration of the Roosevelt administration with the likes of Harry Hopkins, who appears to have been both a traditional spy and an agent of influence who helped the Soviets spot "useful idiots" among Americans.[10]

A more recent example of a Russian agent of influence is Maria Butina. While studying at American University in Washington, D.C., Butina, a gun-rights activist, befriended scores of Americans in various elite Washington circles, including the National Rifle Association. At the direction of a senior Russian government official, she cultivated these relationships for the purpose of influencing American politics and advancing Russia's foreign policy goals. The FBI arrested Butina on July 15, 2018. She was charged with "conspiracy to act as an agent of the Russian Federation within the United States without prior notification of the attorney general."[11]

Political influence operations are a more sophisticated type of active measures program. Covert political influence was one of the missions of the ten Russian sleeper agents who were deported out of the United States in 2010.[12] The reason the FBI wrapped up its ten-year counterintelligence operation "Ghost Stories" in 2010, rounding up these Russian operatives who posed as Americans and acted as agents of influence, was because some of the agents were getting close to high-level U.S. government officials, including a "cabinet member" of the Obama administration. Hillary Clinton, who headed up the State Department, is believed to have been the target of the Russian covert-influence operations.

According to a declassified CIA document, in the 1980s Soviet intelligence operatives trained in active measures established "valuable contacts" in the Arms Control and Disarmament Agency, the Congressional Research Service, the Library of Congress, and the Brookings Institution, a left-leaning think tank in Washington, D.C., among other organizations.[13] The following are some examples of the active measures operations these KGB operatives stationed in the United States ran:

1. Influence of U.S. government policies by creating a large, vocal, and influential body of public opinion that has been formed by Soviet disinformation[14]

2. Influence of U.S. religious leaders and groups to oppose U.S. military spending for new weapon systems[15]

3. Creation of anti-nuclear coalitions and encouragement of bilateral peace programs[16] like the Sister Cities program, such as the one that Vermont senator and presidential candidate Bernie Sanders was participating in when he was mayor of Burlington, Vermont. Sanders established a sister-city relationship with the Soviet city of Yaroslavl' in 1988.[17]

4. Influence of U.S. and world opinion against President Ronald Reagan's Strategic Defense Initiative (SDI) program; creation of opposition within the think tank and policy community against SDI to eventually "disrupt or halt the entire SDI research program"[18]

5. Division of the United States and NATO using their disagreements over SDI[19]

President Reagan was the target of aggressive Soviet disinformation and broader active-measure operations. He was portrayed by the Soviets as warmonger, eager to unleash a nuclear war between the USSR and the United States. The Soviets also targeted American religious organizations and the Christian community with active measures, using the Moscow Patriarchate of the Russian Orthodox Church and other Soviet religious organizations that were heavily infiltrated by the KGB. The goal was to manipulate American churches into helping shape U.S. public opinion in favor of the "peaceful" Soviet program and against "aggressive" U.S. policies. Putin's Russia continues to target the American religious community by promulgating a narrative that Russia is a bulwark of conservative and traditional values that is mounting a decisive effort to combat decadent liberal Western values. Unfortunately, religious Americans who feel increasingly marginalized and even threatened by liberal trends in a society that rejects the notions of traditional marriage and family, and even gender, can be ripe targets for being unwittingly duped by the Kremlin's propaganda.

I was once astonished by pro-Putin sentiment expressed to me by a devout American when I was giving a briefing on Russian doctrine and strategy at a faith-based academic institution. "Look, Rebekah," she said, "as Christians, we feel under attack in our own country."[20] She stated that President Putin's efforts to promote traditional conservative values in his country and abroad and defend religious freedoms are refreshing and appealing to Americans of faith. She truly believed that Putin is a man of faith and solid principles who wants friendly relations with the United States. It was painful for me to acknowledge that an intelligent, educated, and honorable—albeit naive—American like her was blinded by Russian disinformation and propaganda. I was even more disturbed by the realization that the country that was founded on the principle of religious freedom now pressures its devout citizens to perform, support, and

condone acts and behaviors—such as gay marriage and abortion—
that are fundamentally incongruent with their religious convictions.[21]
And if these Americans refuse to do so, they are accused of bigotry
and homophobia, smeared, ostracized, and even driven out of businesses on which their livelihoods depend. There is something Putinesque, if not Stalinesque, about these atrocious acts of enforced con-
formity. Sadly, my children's America is no longer the same land of
freedom that my mom idealized and sent me to more than thirty
years ago. And unlike me, my children and other God-loving Americans will have nowhere to flee. There is no other country now that
provides refuge to persecuted religious worshipers the way that our
grandfathers' America used to.

Consisting of overt and covert activities, active measures can be
a single operation with a short-term goal or a series of operations
(*kombinatsiya*) that amount to a multi-year intelligence campaign.
Short-term active-measure operations can be aimed at specific goals
such as discrediting a government official or organization or "liqui-
dating" an opposition member. In the 1970s, the Soviets ran a multi-
part series of articles in its propaganda outlet *New Times* that implicated the CIA in the killing of President John F. Kennedy and accused
the Agency of conducting subversion operations and political assassinations.[22] In the 1980s, the Soviets launched a disinformation operation, code-named Infektion, which spread the falsehood that the
HIV virus was an experimental biological weapon developed by the
U.S. military.[23] The typical tactic for this type of active-measure operation was to place an article containing an anti-American accusation
in an obscure foreign newspaper, usually in a third world country
where the Soviets had news organizations controlled by the KGB.[24]
The Western press would pick up the article containing a false claim,
and it would eventually find its way to a major U.S. publication. Official newspapers and news agencies of the Soviet government, such

as *Pravda, Izvestiya, Novosti,* and TASS, which served as the state's propaganda instruments, would further circulate and amplify the false anti-American narratives. A Soviet KGB defector who tried in vain to warn Americans in the 1980s that their country was already "at war" with the USSR referred to the official Soviet media apparatus as the "communist equivalent of George Orwell's Ministry of Truth."[25]

Today, the Russian government's propaganda machine includes *Sputnik, RT* (formerly *Russia Today*), *Pravda,* and *Izvestiya,* among other outlets. Unlike Cold War times, when it took days and weeks to spread disinformation and forgeries carefully masterminded by Soviet intelligence, today, with the omnipresence of the internet, Russian "fake news" can reach any corner of the globe within seconds. Ironically, our own U.S. technology giants, like Facebook, Twitter, Instagram, and the like, can now power Russian active measures. Today's themes are not that much different, however, from those Moscow spread during the Cold War: "The United States creates chaos in the world by invading sovereign countries";[26] "Washington is to blame for the spread of coronavirus";[27] "U.S. ballistic missile defense is destabilizing";[28] "Turkeys bought at Walmart cause food poisoning";[29] and so on and so forth.

At the heart of Russian active-measure tradecraft is the concept of reflexive control, developed in the early 1960s by Soviet psychologist-mathematician Vladimir Lefebvre.[30] This philosophical concept of "reflexion" is focused on predicting and influencing choices by single individuals or groups, such as "political parties, military units, states, and even civilizations." Using his mathematical skills, Lefebvre developed an algorithmic model based on the so called "anti-selfishness principle" that determined how an individual perceived his or her interests and made choices within the context of the group that he or she belonged to. Eventually, he designed a special formal apparatus for modeling cognition-based human choice as part of a reflexive game theory. It is a Russian counterpart to the classical game theory used by Western social scientists and military planners.[31] Unlike classical game theory, which studies the behavior and the strategic interactions between rationally-minded decision makers, Russian reflexive-control theory seeks to control or narrow the choices. Detailed knowledge of the subject's psychology, his "inner world," and his "images of the self" is a critical piece of the Russian model, which builds the "mental mechanism of choice." This mental mechanism can be manipulated by employing against the target a combination of deception, disinformation, forgeries, pressure, intimidation, and other techniques. Once conveyed to the target, he will interpret this "special information" according to his psychological mindset, leading him voluntarily to make the decision that is predetermined by the manipulator. This is the essence of reflexive control.

Although Lefebvre emigrated to the United States, where he continued his research until his death in April 2020, the Russian government continued to use reflexive-control theory for military planning and intelligence operations. The Russian General Staff, which continues to teach the concept to its military officers, is attracted to the idea that a person's thinking can be manipulated and exploited based on one's psychology and existing biases.[32] Why simply try to "guesstimate" an enemy commander's future course of action when you can influence their decision-making calculus by distorting the perception of reality?

Here is how former CIA director James Jesus Angleton—famously known for his paranoia over the U.S. government's being penetrated and deceived by Soviet intelligence—described his theory of perfect deception, the cornerstone of Russian active-measure tradecraft, which is rooted in the idea of reflexive control.

Imagine a wife, attempting to deceive her husband, who has bribed his psychiatrist into telling her how her husband interpreted all the lies and misleading clues she furnished him. Based on the husband's reaction, she would tailor her lies, elaborating on some, changing others, and ceasing some. Through trial and error, eventually, the wife and psychiatrist would feed the husband with a story that perfectly aligns with his beliefs.[33]

According to Angleton, "The deceived then becomes his own deceiver."[34] In this story, the wife is the Russian intelligence services, the husband is U.S. government officials and members of the elite, and the psychiatrists are the various Russian intelligence operatives, including the sleeper agents who have burrowed into American society to develop a deep understanding of its collective mindset, internal dynamics, and issues that dominate our national discourse. It is Russia's understanding of our hot buttons that makes it possible for the Kremlin to conduct tailored intelligence operations designed to influence U.S. domestic politics, incite disorder, and undermine faith in the democratic process, including the electoral process. It is high time for Americans and the U.S. government to understand how Russian disinformation works so we don't become our own deceivers, the way that the FBI and some U.S. intelligence agencies did during Moscow's intervention in the 2016 election. Perpetuating the officially disproven "Russia-Trump collusion" falsehood, like some American media figures, government officials, and public opinion leaders continue to do, is doing Putin's bidding and adhering to Moscow's will.[35] There is little that would bring more satisfaction to the Russian master spy than concluding that he duped half of an entire country of "useful idiots" into believing that he had placed his own puppet into his "main enemy's" presidential seat.

Strategic Ideological Subversion of the Enemy

"KGB subversion may be painless, but its long-term result is more devastating than a nuclear explosion."
  —Yuri Bezmenov (a.k.a. Tomas Schuman), Soviet defector and expert on active measures

"We can see that all elements of the socialist ideal—the abolition of private property, family, hierarchies; the hostility toward religion—could be regarded as a manifestation of one basic principle: the suppression of individuality."
  —Soviet dissident Igor Shafarevich, *The Socialist Phenomenon*

Russian military planners have forecast that kinetic war with the United States is only a matter of time. To better position itself for victory, or even to win the conflict without a fight as part of its strategy of "indirect action," Russia works to weaken America systematically over time by forcing it, through constant active-measure operations, to battle with itself. This is just the type of Sun Tzu–style "strategic judo" that appeals to Putin, an old intelligence operative and avid judo practitioner. Conflict is the natural state of things, and peace per se doesn't exist, according to the Russian worldview. This "presupposition of conflict"[36] has been formed throughout centuries of strife, instability, and repression—beginning with the czarist era, continuing with the bloody revolutions of 1905 and 1917 through Stalin's Red Terror purges and the Communist Party rule until 1991, and finally going from the chaotic 1990s in the aftermath of the USSR's collapse right through to the rule of Putin.

The Marxist-Leninist doctrine practiced by the Russian revolutionaries and other socialist movements in Europe in the early 1900s explained the concept of the permanence of conflict in the following way: Fueled by naturally existing differences, tensions, and contradictions, struggle among societal classes is permanent and periodically erupts into war. Conflict is the normal order of things, not only within a single society, but also among differing social systems, such as capitalism and communism, as well as socialism, the steppingstone–stage between the two.

To win in this conflict, communists believed it was imperative to engage in a permanent struggle of ideas, or political warfare. Soviet leaders, who believed that the young Soviet socialist state was under threat of attack by Western capitalist countries, adopted political warfare as an integral part of its overall statecraft. They believed it must always be conducted against the adversary. Since conflict and war are "normal," according to Soviet communist doctrine, then political warfare in peacetime is simply a continuation of war. This view stands on its head Von Clausewitz's classic doctrine that war is a continuation of politics by other means. The bottom line: politics is war and war is politics, according to the Russian/Soviet view.

Communists who took over Russia after the violent Bolshevik Revolution in 1917 and established the first socialist state in 1921, the Union of Soviet Socialist Republics (USSR), conceptualized the idea of "active measures" as a way of waging constant warfare against the adversary. Lenin, who disdainfully referred to Western and American elites as "deaf mutes" who are "incapable of understanding the real state of relative power," advocated the employment of "special maneuvers" that "can speed up our victory over capitalist countries."[37] He instructed his Soviet People's Commissar for Foreign Affairs, Georgy Chicherin, to declare the "fictitious separation" of the Soviet government from the Communist Party and the Politburo, "and especially the Comintern," the Communist International organization, "to pacify the deaf mutes."[38] These directives were intended to deceive

the Western leaders and elites that the Soviet government was separate from communism, whereas in fact they were unified. Lenin justified deception as a way of making the capitalist governments "shut
their eyes" and become not only "deaf mutes" but also "blind" to
Moscow's strategic goal of replacing capitalist economies with a
"world system of communism."[39]

Lenin accurately foresaw the gullible nature of Western elites. He
was convinced that deceptive tactics like *dezinformatsiya* deployed
against Americans, the British, and other Westerners would enable
the Soviets to fool the Western world about its true communist intentions, which were to dominate the world. "The deaf mutes will believe
us. They will even be delighted and will open their doors wide to us,"
Lenin said. "Through this door," Lenin directed the Kremlin to send
intelligence operatives under the guise of diplomatic, cultural, and
trade representatives "to conduct destabilizing activities in the West
and the United States."[40] "They will open up credits for us, which will
serve us for the purpose of supporting communist parties in their
countries. They will supply us with the materials and technology,
which we lack, and will restore our military industry, which we need
for our future victorious attacks upon our suppliers." Lenin summarized, "In other words, they will work hard, in order to prepare
their own suicide."[41]

Indeed, Americans and other Westerners did work hard supplying the Soviet Union with technology, financial credits, and "know-
how," as part the New Economic Policy (NEP). This was the Soviet
tactic of making a temporary pause to the doctrinaire principles of
socialist central planning and a studied "return" to private ownership
in the agriculture, retail, and light and heavy industries. Run by the
USSR from 1921 to 1928, NEP was also a massive active-measure
campaign of strategic deception called "strategic disinformation"
(*strategicheskaya dezinformatsiya*). Scores of profit-driven, naive

Western technicians, whom the Soviets cynically called "assistants of socialism," flocked to the Soviet Union to help build factories, including for heavy industry, such as aviation and tank production. The West effectively helped industrialize the new communist state.[42]

The "strategic disinformation" operation of NEP confirmed to the Soviets that the Western countries could be fooled into taking action that is favorable for the Soviets and damaging to themselves.[43] It demonstrated that a series of active measures could be strung together into an elaborate, multi-level "strategic disinformation" operation with a long-term anti-Western goal. In 1958, "strategic disinformation" was launched as an official, though highly secret, policy targeting the West, including the United States, as revealed by Soviet KGB defector Anatoly Mikhailovich Golitsyn.[44] Golitsyn, who defected to the United States in 1961, provided valuable strategic-level intelligence to the CIA and had an outsized influence on James Jesus Angleton, CIA's counterintelligence chief for twenty years (1954–74).[45]

Golitsyn disclosed in his debriefings to the CIA that under the leadership of KGB chairman Alexander Shelepin the Soviets developed a long-term "strategic disinformation" policy that the CIA later dubbed the "master plan" to deceive and destabilize "the main enemy," the Unites States, and its NATO and Japanese allies, while weakening the ties between them.[46] To achieve this goal, Shelepin created an elaborate and extensive disinformation apparatus within the Communist Party and Soviet government, including Department D (for *dezinformatsiya*) in the Soviet Military Intelligence Service, and two "activist methods" departments and an active measures department within the KGB. According to Golitsyn, "strategic political disinformation operations" constituted a "systematic effort to disseminate false information and to distort or withhold information…in order to "confuse, deceive, and influence the noncommunist world…jeopardize its politics, and…induce Western adversaries to contribute unwittingly to the achievement of communist objectives." Strategic disinformation and active measures were to be conducted through secret channels, such as "secret agents at home and abroad, penetrations of Western embassies and governments, [and] technical and other secret means," including provocations, "border incidents, and protest demonstrations."[47]

From his defection in 1961 until 1965, coupled with his consulting work for the CIA providing analysis of the KGB influence operations against the West, Golitsyn warned U.S. intelligence about the threat of Soviet strategic active-measure operations.[48] The goal of these operations was to push the political systems of the West "closer to the communist model." In 1984, amplifying his warnings to the U.S. government, he revealed to the American public his grave concerns about the Soviet threat to the survival of the West in a book, *New World for Old*.[49]

Golitsyn's stark warning was echoed the same year by a different Soviet defector and KGB-trained expert in active measures, Yuri Bezmenov. Bezmenov warned Americans about the Soviet strategic ideological-subversion program that targeted America. He warned that the Soviet plan—like the "master plan" Golitsyn warned of— would transform American society into one with a fundamentally different power structure, value system, and culture in a four-step process. As part of this process, the Soviets, with the assistance of agents of influence and useful idiots, were to reorient the thinking and behavior of the entire U.S. population.[50] While it is not clear whether Golitsyn and Bezmenov referred to the same plan or not, the Soviets almost certainly had a national-level program of strategic influence targeting the West, including the United States.

At great risk to his life, in 1970 Bezmenov escaped his KGB posting in New Delhi, India, by disguising himself as a hippie and making his way to the U.S. Embassy. Disillusioned with the communist system and disgusted by the brutal tactics of the Soviet government, he wanted to defect to America. Initially resettled by U.S. intelligence in Canada under a new identity and pseudonym, Tomas Schuman, Bezmenov came to love America and embrace the capitalist system. He tried to alert Americans to the threat of Soviet plans to subvert the United States from within. He described the four phases of the Soviet long-range ideological subversion strategy in his 46-page manifesto *Love Letter to America*[51] and in his lectures, public speeches, and television interviews, recordings of which are available on YouTube.

The first phase of subversion, called "demoralization," takes fifteen to twenty years, the minimum length of time that the Soviets believed was needed to brainwash a single generation. During this phase, the Soviets, by manipulating the media and academia, sought to influence young people's mentality in order to make them question existing capitalist values and embrace new socialist ideas. Skilled at propaganda, disinformation, and reflexive-control tactics, the Soviet active-measure operatives worked to distort the younger generation's perception of reality to make them unable to see and unwilling to look for the truth. Even faced with the facts, younger Americans would choose the position that was ideologically aligned with new doctrines such as Marxism and Leninism rather than free-market capitalism. The Soviet propagandists and their agents of influence appealed to the young people's sense of self-preservation: "Would you rather live in a 'cruel, polluted, profit-oriented capitalist society'? or in a 'scientifically planned, rational, pollution-free, kind society with just re-distribution of wealth'?"[52]

The second phase, termed "destabilization," was to take two to five years and focused on transitioning every aspect of American society— the economy, foreign relations, defense industry—according to the new socialist principles. This phase would be marked by massive expansion of the government, which would gradually assume control over more aspects of individuals' lives. To make such a transition appealing and more palatable to citizens, the "benevolent dictators" would promise "free goodies" and various entitlements.[53]

The third phase, called the "crisis," would entail a change of government, including by violent means, which in turn would replace an economic system based on the free-market competition with a new, socialist-style system controlled by the "Big Brother government in Washington, D.C."[54]

The fourth and final phase is called "normalization" and would last indefinitely. It would mark the completion of the convergence of capitalism with socialism and communism, where capitalism would be "renovated" to look more like socialism. Social progress, collaboration, and peaceful co-existence with the socialist and communist world would take hold.[55]

Yuri Bezmenov claimed in 1985 that the first two phases of America's transformation were completed and "over-fulfilled" faster than the Soviets had anticipated.[56] Bezmenov blamed American "leftist" professors, Hollywood, and "sixties peace activists" for helping carry out the Soviets' master plan to destabilize America.[57] "Most of it is done to Americans by Americans," he lamented. He was frustrated that his warnings fell on deaf ears. As most defectors, he envisioned that the U.S. government would find his expertise valuable and use it to develop counterstrategies to protect America from the Soviet strategic-subversion campaign. To his exasperation, he struggled to find a meaningful career in the United States. The *New York Times* and the CIA rejected him for employment. "We have no need for someone with your experience," the CIA politely replied to his offers to work for the Agency.[58] Seriously? U.S. intelligence desperately needs active-measures experts now, and I am sure it needed them back in the 1970s.

At one point, in a dumb move, U.S. government apparatchiks barred Bezmenov from entering the United States from Canada, with the idiotic and surreal justification that he had been born in the USSR and was formerly a member of the Communist Party.[59] Well, duh! This is precisely why he was an expert on Soviet deception and active measures. Bezmenov found it ironic that "the hostility and inertia of the bureaucracy" in the United States is "the same as in the Soviet Union."[60] Having experienced first-hand during my intelligence career the stupidity and maliciousness of some government bureaucrats, I share this sense of irony with Yuri.

The Soviets' plan was to brainwash three generations of Americans to the point where, despite the abundance of information, "no one could come to sensible conclusions." Ironically, while the Soviets were able to fool scores of naive American souls, many Russians understood very well which system was better, despite all the government's propaganda. I remember during my student years in Moscow the faculty leadership preparing my class for the upcoming visit of British exchange students. We were drilled for the *politboy* (political battle) with the Brits on how to disparage the Western capitalist system, praise the Soviet socialist system, and present arguments on the merits of socialism versus capitalism to the British. After the dress rehearsal, some of us were joking how "capitalism may be rotting, but it smells very nice" and how we would love to go live in the West and be "exploited" by capitalists. Although we didn't talk about this openly, some of us were planning to escape to Britain, the United States, or another Western country. To prevent student defections, the university had a very stringent selection process for the exchange programs. Only the "trustworthy" (i.e., true believers) were chosen to go abroad. Not being a communist activist, I was surprised and elated to learn I was unexpectedly chosen to go on an exchange program to Surrey University in England in my fourth year. After my experiences on that trip, I needed no explanation of which system, socialist vs. capitalist, was superior.

Russia's strategy of "indirect action," which includes the tactic of "controlled instability," is a modern version of the Soviet master plan to destabilize the United States. In 2013, around the same time Russians began taking steps to intervene in the 2016 election, a senior analyst from the Russian Institute of Strategic Studies (*RISI* in Russian), a think tank that provides analysis for Putin's administration, described a four-phase strategy to destabilize and subvert an adversary in a book called, *Geopolitics of the Third Wave: Transformation of the World in the Post-Modern Epoch.*[61] The strategy outlines how to covertly disrupt and transform the foundation of the enemy's system of governance while avoiding a direct kinetic confrontation. In a four-step process, the aggressor-country destabilizes the victim-country to the point of "controlled chaos," creates opposition that can assume power in a new system, transforms the existing system of governance into a new one, and solidifies the new government institutions based on new principles.

Like the Soviet master plan, the new plan envisions the complete reprogramming of the entire population's view of the victim-country by influencing its mass media, educational institutions, and religious, philanthropic, and cultural organizations. The author justified this strategy as low-cost, with "optimal profit-risk ratio" and minimal human losses. He didn't specify what countries played the roles of the aggressor and victim, but he accused the United States of pursuing this approach to create chaos in various parts of the world. Russians often engage in projection, where they believe the United States does something that they do or envision doing themselves. In the same year, the chief of the Russian General Staff also described a multi-step strategy of controlled chaos to defeat an adversary state.

Lenin's words about Americans and Westerners "preparing their own suicide" and Khruschev's "We will bury you!" sound particularly ominous this year. The defectors' warnings about the threat of Soviet strategic ideological subversion to our country carry a special meaning, as Americans are preparing to cast their votes in the 2020 election at the time of this writing. This is perhaps the most consequential choice about the direction of this country in years, made amid Moscow's strategic long-range effort to remake America.

Having endured the effects of Putin's 2016 covert influence and destabilization operation—marked by three years of partisan investigations that culminated in the impeachment of the previous president—Americans are dangerously close to falling into a trap presented by Putin's playbook. Once again, Americans' anger and frustration are directed inward, at each other, blinding us to real security threats and economic challenges, and distracting us from a substantive and dispassionate debate. Such a serious conversation is needed this time, about which system—capitalist or socialist and, ultimately, communist—will ensure the freedom, economic prosperity, and longevity of the American nation. Giving Putin another strategic win by electing a U.S. president who has begun taking our country down a radical path to socialist destruction is a tragic mistake. The Kremlin's spymaster, whose country has been irreversibly damaged by socialism and who desperately wishes to permanently handicap Russia's "main enemy," has welcomed such a turn of events with open arms.

We are living through the scenario Yuri Bezmenov described, no matter whether the current situation is a result of old Soviet-style active measures and strategic ideological subversion or we did it to ourselves—or probably both. The threat of the progressive movement to fundamentally remake America is real. Socialist senator Bernie Sanders revealed the left's true agenda to move the country leftward in "as progressive a way as we possibly can."[62] Single-payer health care, gun control, and defunding the police are just a few of the misguided steps planned by some of our leaders, who are eager to "renovate" capitalism and create a "workers' paradise on earth." Many of us immigrants from socialist countries have been through this horror movie before. We do not want the sequel.

Americans have gotten a preview of how socialism works when, in the beginning of the coronavirus pandemic, governor of New York Andrew Cuomo gave special access for COVID testing to his family members and friends.[63] Clearly, Cuomo thought he was justified in treating ordinary New Yorkers like Orwell's animals, who were "more equal" than others.

The problems facing America during the coronavirus pandemic illustrate the need for maintaining a domestically based capitalist system. The supply of pandemic response products cannot keep up with demand because the government apparatchiks, in a typical failure of centralized planning, neglected their duty to stockpile strategic reserves of essentials. Meanwhile, businesses irresponsibly outsourced the production of essentials like vaccines, medicine, and protective equipment to China, another sworn enemy of America, which U.S. government officials failed to monitor closely and stop. Well into the coronavirus nightmare, we were still scandalously unable to buy hand sanitizer, paper towels, and protective facial masks. Does anyone really believe that once the government is in charge of most aspects of our lives, as the logic of socialism dictates, and benevolent dictators start handing out "free stuff" that there will be enough for everyone? I can tell you, I don't want my daughter's or my son's teeth drilled without Novocain, a traumatic experience I had to endure. Believe me, the dentist will want her family to get the first dibs on Novocain when their teeth need to be fixed. And then it will be the dentist's mother, brother, sister, friends, and all their families. All of them ahead of my family and yours. The workers in charge of toilet paper will also do the same. I guarantee, the list of scarce goods and services will be long.

Destabilizing the Enemy through Election Interference

"The Russian government interfered in the 2016 presidential election in sweeping and systematic fashion."
—the Mueller Report

"The investigation did not establish that members of the Trump Campaign conspired or coordinated with the Russian government in its election interference activities....As soon as news broke that Trump had been elected President, Russian government officials and prominent Russian businessmen began trying to make inroads into the new Administration. They appeared not to have preexisting contacts and struggled to connect with senior officials around the President-Elect."
—the Mueller Report

"I'll tell you a secret. Yes, we'll definitely intervene [in the 2020 election]."
—Vladimir Putin

As unsettling as Russia's election intervention in 2016 was for Americans, I hope that the reader realizes by now that messing with our elections is not the most devastating or the only tool in the Kremlin's toolbox. It is only one page in Putin's playbook, designed to keep America off-balance. Sabotaging U.S. elections serves Russia's broader purpose of subverting, destabilizing, and, if necessary, defeating our military. Russian planners believe it will help them achieve the Kremlin's desired strategic outcome of a weakened United States immersed in political dysfunction, struggling economically, bogged down in external conflicts, alienated from its allies, and torn by racial, religious, ethnic, and other social tensions. A distracted America is far less likely to interfere with Putin's strategic ambitions. Sun Tzu wrote: "Hence the general is skillful in attack whose opponent does not know what to defend; and he is skillful in defense whose opponent does not know what to attack."[64]

Embroiled in dysfunction, clashing with one another as to whether we should call a biological male a "she," to take only one example, we are unable to see clearly the real threats. No matter how many warnings we are given, when presented with facts of a violent mob burning our cities, destroying historical properties, looting businesses, and murdering police officers, we are unable to come to a sensible conclusion. The media has called this chaos "peaceful protests." Did Russian brainwashing really work that well? Putin has been celebrating for the past four years.

Russia's intervention in the 2016 election is not the first time that Moscow meddled in America's domestic affairs. A CIA document declassified in 2013 reveals that the Soviets conducted active-measure operations against U.S. elections as far back as the 1984 and 1988 elections.[65] Fearing Ronald Reagan's policies aimed at containing the USSR—and socialism and communism—the Soviet government launched a covert influence operation to harm Reagan's re-election chances. In January 1984, the FBI denounced a forgery created by Soviet intelligence. Dated 1947, the forgery purported that Reagan was working in collusion with the FBI and the House Committee on un-American Activities concerning communist infiltration into the Hollywood film industry. Invocations of "McCarthyism" in the run up to the presidential election were aimed at discrediting President Reagan.[66]

It is worth noting that the "collusion" disinformation spread by the Soviets in 1984—a hoax, in Trumpian parlance—used a similar narrative that the Russians used in the 2016 covert-influence operation to dupe the FBI and U.S. intelligence into believing, in some cases willfully, that Trump's presidential campaign was compromised by Russian government operatives. As a linguist, I would observe that the word "collusion" is not part of American everyday language, nor is it used in the U.S. jurisprudential lexicon. But "collusion" is very much an English translation of the Russian word *sgovor*, which reflects the connotations of conspiracy, secrecy, and illegal machinations that are very much part of the Russian cultural and historical legacy. It is my judgement that the dramatic and absurd Steele dossier was likely based on Russian disinformation. In fact, according to declassified materials, the FBI itself had strong suspicions expressed in January and February 2018 that that the Steele dossier was based, in part, on "Russian disinformation" due to the RIS [Russian Intelligence Services] infiltrat[ing] a source into the network" of sources that contributed to the dossier.[67]

Consistent with reflexive-control game theory, the Russians in significant measure rely on Americans—brainwashed by Moscow's disinformation and ideological subversion—to help Russia defeat America. A stunning example of attempted "collusion" by an American with the Russians to influence U.S. elections was discovered in 1991 when the Soviets opened KGB archives. A highly sensitive memorandum from KGB chairman V. Chebrikov to the Soviet Communist Party and the USSR government chief Yuri Andropov revealed an offer from the iconic U.S. senator Edward "Ted" Kennedy to help the Soviets "influence public opinion and political circles" in the runup to the 1984 election. Kennedy, through his "close friend and trusted person" John Tunney, using "confidential contacts," proposed a series of steps intended to soften the image of the Soviet Union, its leaders, and its policies among American voters and to "counter Reagan's militaristic policy."[68]

The proposed measures outlined in the four-and-a-half page memo included Kennedy's traveling to Moscow—together with

Republican senator Mark Hatfield—to meet with General Secretary Andropov and "Kennedy and his friends" arranging interviews for Andropov with the largest TV companies in America. Andropov and some Soviet political and military officials would have a chance to interview with "Walter Cronkite and Barbara Walters" and explain to Americans Soviet "peace initiatives and the real balance of forces between the USSR and [United States]," which was being "egregiously distorted by Reagan's Administration." Seeking to "improve...Soviet-American relations," and to "eliminate the threat of nuclear war," Kennedy believed hearing from the Soviet leaders directly was important for U.S. voters because "it is difficult for Americans to get the essence of such complex issues" as "most Americans don't read serious newspapers and journals."[69]

I have little doubt that Senator Kennedy was genuinely concerned about the tensions between the USSR and the United States because of the possibility they could lead to a nuclear conflict. But it was inexcusable for Kennedy to seek the adversary's assistance in swaying his own fellow citizens' voting preferences, even though he may have been blinded by his misguided ideology and the belief that the Russians think like Americans. They don't.

Russia's 2016 election intervention and the reaction it prompted, which many intelligence practitioners viewed as an act of advanced covert intelligence tradecraft, was a watershed moment in the lives of all Americans. Just like the terrorist acts of September 11, 2001, which removed our long-held sense of security, Russia's 2016 election sabotage operation has forever changed Americans' sense of confidence in the integrity of the U.S. presidential election process. I don't find it persuasive that the Russians changed the outcome of 2016 election, for reasons I will explain later in this chapter. Former director of national Intelligence James Clapper acknowledged in his classified testimony, declassified by President Trump's DNI Richard

Grenell, that he is "not aware of any evidence that the outcome of 2016 presidential election was manipulated through cyber means."[70]

To understand the psychology behind Moscow's 2016 operation, it is helpful to review a Russian political deception operation that is considered the inspiration and prototype of future strategic-level active-measure operations run by Soviet and now Russian intelligence. Codenamed *Trest* ("trust," as in a syndicate), this complex, multi-year operation was designed by Soviet intelligence to "liquidate" opposition to the communist regime in Russia domestically and abroad and trick Westerners into unwittingly helping the communist government "consolidate its power throughout Russia."[71]

In August 1921, Soviet intelligence set up a fictitious organization, the Trust, which was headquartered in an office building in downtown Moscow called the Municipal Credit Association Building, out of which the operation was run.[72] Felix Dzerzhinsky, Lenin's head of intelligence, ran the operation, overseeing a top Trust official, Edward Opperput. The Trust dispatched to the West agents-provocateurs who posed as dissidents and members of the Monarchist Association of Central Russia (MOTsR), a real organization whose mission was to restore the czarist regime to Russia. These agents traveled abroad to establish contact with Russian émigrés, who had fled Russia after the Bolshevik Revolution and the civil war between the Red and White Armies and resettled in major cities in Europe. Trust operatives posed as dissidents spreading the disinformation that communism in Russia did not take hold, that the country was in shambles, and that the Trust was looking for émigré and Western support to stage a counter-revolution to reinstate the monarchy.[73]

Trust agents were able to infiltrate the anti-Soviet organizations in the West and identify key members of the opposition movement. To prove their bona fides and pretend that the Trust was a powerful organization, the operatives provided false passports and other secret documents to the Russian dissidents. They believed their families needed to travel to Russia so they could stage a counter-revolution. They smuggled these dissidents into Russia, took them to Trust head-quarters and other facilities, and delivered arms and explosives to "fellow partisans." They staged sabotage missions and assassinations, including blowing up police stations and breaking prisoners out of jail. The Trust arranged tours of the fake "underground" dissident writers movement for the émigré writers, taking them to meetings with "editors" of "dissident" journals.[74]

Trust operatives were able to convince even at-first skeptical anti-Soviet movement leaders and Western governments that the communist experiment was on its last leg in Russia, that it was absolutely not a threat to the West, and that when the situation was ripe, the Soviet government would be overthrown and the White Russian exiles could return to their homeland. All they needed was Western financial support and leaders capable of governing Russia. A high-ranking Soviet official and clandestine Trust operative, Aleksandr Yakushev, even succeeded in securing a meeting in Paris, which lasted three hours, with Grand Duke Nikolai Nikolayevich Romanov, who was working to unite all anti-communist monar-chist émigrés abroad. The pretext that Yakushev used for the meet-ing was the message that the Grand Duke was the only person capable of uniting the exiled Russians and reestablishing Imperial Monarchist Russia.[75]

The Trust was able to fool the West again, just as the Soviets did when they tricked it into helping them industrialize and even mili-tarize the Soviet economy with a temporary, phony initiative mas-querading as a turn to capitalism called the New Economic Policy (NEP). As during the NEP deception operation, when the United States and Europe provided technology and financial credits to the USSR, Westerners provided assistance to the fake anti-communist movement, including money, which the Trust used to finance the very deception operation targeted against them.[76]

Western intelligence services were eager to cooperate with the fake "dissidents" and grew dependent on the fake intelligence provided by Trust agents. Once Trust operatives identified all the key leaders in the exile circles, they lured them into the USSR on fictitious missions to "topple the Communist regime," arrested them, and then, after fake show trials, executed them one by one. Those who could not be tricked into traveling to Russia were kidnapped or vanished, among them a Russian-born secret agent of the British Intelligence Service, Sidney Reilley (a.k.a. Sigmund Rosenblum) and Russian counter-revolutionary and litterateur Boris Savinkov (a.k.a. V. Ropshin).

In a stunning finale of the mysterious Trust Operation, in 1927, Edward Opperput, the top Trust official who had choreographed the scheme, defected to Finland. In his debriefings to Western intelligence, he disclosed in rich detail that the Trust was both a Soviet deception operation and the name of a cover organization, and that he himself was a Soviet state security operative. Western intelligence services were dumbfounded that they could have been manipulated for seven years by the Soviets. The anti-communist movement of the Russian émigrés was demoralized, having its members' dreams about Russia's return to monarchy and their return to their homeland shattered and their leaders murdered.[77]

Having shocked the West with the revelation of the ingenious Trust deception operation, Opperput then re-defected to his secret intelligence work in Russia, stunning Western governments even further. The Russians wanted Western powers to know that they had been duped. Opperput was a dangle, a "dispatched" defector, and his "defection" to the West was a false-flag operation. Having reached their strategic objectives of industrializing and even militarizing the

USSR with Western money through the NEP and having decapitated the leadership of the anti-communist movement abroad, the Soviets decided to wrap up the operation. Soviet intelligence demonstrated to its Western counterparts that it was capable of carrying out world-class covert-influence operations and that it had become "a force to be reckoned with" globally.[78]

A dedicated Chekist (Cheka was a predecessor of the KGB), President Putin was schooled in the principles of Soviet intelligence tradecraft started by his brutal predecessors Lenin, Dzerzhinsky, and Stalin and continued by others during the seventy-year rule of the Soviet Communist Party. On his orders, Russian intelligence operatives launched an active-measure covert-influence operation called "Project Translator," targeting the 2016 U.S. presidential election.[79] Three years before the election, around July 2013, a cover organization, the Internet Research Agency (IRA; Agenstvo Internet Issledo-vaniy), was registered as a Russian corporate entity. Funded by a Russian oligarch, Yevgeny Prigozhin, who is a close associate of President Putin, the IRA opened an office at 55 Savushkina Street in St. Petersburg. The strategic goal of the covert-influence operation, which was conducted under a broader program of "political and electoral interference" called "Project Lakhta," was to "conduct information warfare against the United States of America," to "sow division and discord in the U.S. political system, including by creating social and political polarization, undermining faith in democratic institutions, and influencing U.S. elections, including the upcoming 2018 midterm election."[80]

Project Lakhta was a large-scale operation which continues to this day and includes a management group and several departments for finance, IT, design and graphics, analysis, and search-engine optimization.[81] Around September 2016, Project Lakhta's monthly budget submitted to parent company Concord exceeded 73 million rubles, or more than $1.25 million. (In their doctrinal writings, Russians often talk about cyber-enabled intelligence operations' being a cost-effective and bloodless way of conducting non-contact warfare with the adversary.) In 2014, two female intelligence operatives, Anna Bogacheva and Aleksandra Krylova, were dispatched to the United States on a reconnaissance operation in support of the mission to "spread distrust towards candidates for political office and the political system in general." They and other IRA operatives traveled through the United States, stopping in Nevada, California, New Mexico, Colorado, Illinois, Michigan, Louisiana, Texas, New York, and Georgia. The operatives posed as Americans to collect intelligence from U.S. political and social activists.[82]

In 2014, IRA intelligence analysts began to "track and study various U.S. groups on social media sites dedicated to U.S. politics and social issues."[83] As is typical to ensure the success of an active-measure operation, a high level of granularity about the target's behavior and psychology is critical—the target being the American population and its various demographic, social, religious, and ethnic, groups. IRA operatives on the ground in America used stolen identities of real U.S. persons, including their dates of birth and social security numbers. By around mid-2016, the Russian operatives started their interference campaign in the U.S. election.

The following is a gist of the Russian operation. The description is based on declassified documents authored by the FBI, DNI, and the Justice Department, the Mueller Report, investigations conducted by the House Permanent Select Committee on Intelligence and its Senate counterpart, as well as other Russian and Western open sources, and my professional expertise in Russian doctrine, including active-measures tradecraft.[84] The Russians tried to hack both the DNC and RNC networks, fishing for information of value on the candidates' platforms. They had better luck with the DNC, as the RNC purportedly had better security "locks" on their computer systems.

In March 2016, Russian military intelligence GRU cyber units Military Unit 26165 and Military Unit 74455 hacked the computers and email accounts of various members of the Clinton campaign, including its chairman and manager, John Podesta. GRU breached the computer systems and exfiltrated hundreds of thousands of documents from the DNC and the Democratic Congressional Campaign Committee and from hundreds of email accounts of Clinton Campaign officials. Always on the lookout for dirt that could be weaponized to discredit the candidates and their campaigns, the Russian spies were pleased to find in the emails of John Podesta something they knew would enrage part of the extreme left-leaning members of the American electorate and amplify existing societal conflict. Using WikiLeaks and fake cyber personas DCLeaks and Gussifer 2.0, created by Russian spy operatives as cutouts, the Russians released the stolen information into U.S. mainstream media channels. These strategically timed, intentional "leaks" exposed the secret preference of Democratic leadership toward Hillary Clinton, at the expense of the self-proclaimed democratic socialist Bernie Sanders. (The designation is an oxymoron, by the way, because there is nothing democratic about socialism.) This embarrassing information, which laid bare the corruption within the Democratic Party, led to the resignation of the DNC chairwoman Debbie Wasserman Schultz.

In parallel, the Russians launched a multi-pronged social media campaign on Facebook, Twitter, and Instagram, targeting Trump, Clinton, Sanders, Ted Cruz, and Marco Rubio, as well as the various demographic groups of Americans. The Russian spies bought $100,000 worth of Facebook ads that promoted the Russian Internet Research Agency (IRA) groups—posing as American organizations—on various newsfeeds. Appearing to be American activists, they were able to fool real Americans, including U.S. political figures, into retweeting derogatory, inflammatory, and divisive disinformation and creating negative commentary. Digital bots automated the spread of "fakes" with the speed of a click, and human trolls kept the discourse nasty, inflaming anti-American passions. It is estimated that 126 million persons viewed IRA Russian spy-created content on Facebook, and 1.4 million people were reached by Russian intelligence–controlled Twitter accounts.

On the ground, Russian intelligence operatives, masquerading as American protestors, staged rallies and counter-rallies across America that both favored and discredited Trump and Clinton. Russians focused their agitation tactics on purple states, as they understand the importance of those areas in the U.S. electoral process. The Russian agents-provocateurs, who had been secretly deployed to U.S. soil, were pleased with their success. They were having fun. At one point, they fooled a female American into being paraded in a pro-Trump rally in a metal cage, posing as Hillary Clinton wearing an orange prison suit. They also tricked an American activist into staging the presentation of a birthday gift to their boss back in Russia, IRA chief Yevgeny Prigozhin, which the Russian could watch on TV. At a political rally in front of the White House, the American fellow, at the Russian spies' direction, held a sign "Happy 55th Birthday, Boss!" This was a signal to Prigozhin that the Russian active-measure campaign to blow up the 2016 election was proceeding spectacularly well.

Russian nationals affiliated with the Russian government targeted various Americans in and out of the U.S. government, including people associated with the Trump campaign, as part of a broader strategy.

While social media content created by Russian spies to deceive Americans as well as their other covert and overt activities generally appeared to support Donald Trump and Bernie Sanders, and hurt

Hillary Clinton, Russia's primary intent was to agitate, deepen conflict, and spur social unrest, as the Russians knew that Mrs. Clinton
was expected to win the nomination and the presidency. Moscow
pursued a strategy that it thought would ensure the deepest divisions
within American society, even though Putin may have developed a
preference for Trump simply because he knew Clinton would continue President Obama's Russia policy, which became tougher after
the failed "reset." Putin also most likely expected Trump to be softer
than Clinton on Russia. But on this one, he miscalculated.

An election's outcome is traditionally not the main goal of Russian active-measure operations. Nor does Moscow typically have a
specific political preference—it doesn't vote Democrat or Republican,
it votes "anti-American." While the Kremlin normally prefers a presidential candidate who would pursue a friendly foreign policy
towards Russia, the Russians are not unrealistically optimistic about
their own capability to sway the U.S. vote in a specific direction.
Instead, they use election interference to damage the reputation of
the candidates, create dissent within American society on important
issues, undermine Americans' faith in the integrity of the electoral
process, diminish U.S. defense policy planners' ability to augment
America's military might, and to pursue other similar objectives.
Discrediting in American eyes a future U.S. president, whoever it
eventually becomes, helps degrade his or her ability to govern and
pursue their agenda. In this sense, election interference tactics serve
Russia's broader agenda and strategic goal: to weaken, destabilize,
and ultimately defeat the United States. Americans' choice to elect
an extreme-left president who would put the country on a socialist
footing, even if this president is not a fan of Russia, is a development
that Putin and the Russian state only welcome. Having worked on
subverting America and sending it on a path toward self-destruction

for decades, getting a radical socialist U.S. president is the Kremlin's dream come true.

Having pressed the right hot buttons, Russia's strategy to agitate American voters into a frenzy worked. Deeply divided over social, racial, religious, immigration-related, and other issues, American society was plunged into chaos and instability. This is exactly what the Russian strategists, including chief of the Russian General Staff General Gerasimov and the senior analyst of the Kremlin's in-house think tank, the Russian Institute of Strategic Research (RISI in Russian abbreviation), V. Karyakin, planned in their doctrinal writings about Russia's strategy of indirect action and asymmetric tactics to be practiced.[85] It is also what Russian defectors had been warning U.S. intelligence and the American people about.

The Russians, however, were just as stunned as Americans that Donald Trump won the presidency on November 8, 2016. In addition to orchestrating an unprecedented upheaval in America, having in the White House a president who expressed interest repairing relations with Moscow was an unexpected, albeit welcome, outcome. Immediately after Trump's victory–continuing their vicious campaign to tear America apart–Russian agents, using false U.S. personas, began to stage simultaneous rallies both in support of president-elect Trump and in protest of his election. "Show your support for president-elect Trump" was a slogan in one Russian intelligence–controlled rally, while "Trump is *not* my president" was the theme of another, both in New York. In North Carolina, Russian spies held a rally, "Charlotte Against Trump." Despite the "Trump-Russia collusion" narrative that emerged during the Russian 2016 disinformation operation and continues to be promulgated by the American media and by people who dislike Trump, Putin and Russia are not pro-Trump. They are against America and Americans.

The Mueller Report could not find a single American, within or outside of the Trump campaign, who knowingly cooperated with the Russians to interfere in the 2016 election.[86] The report also debunked the myth that Putin had a direct link to Trump or his circle in the run up to the 2016 election. "As soon as news broke that Trump had been elected President, Russian government officials and prominent Russian businessmen began trying to make inroads into the new Administration. They appeared *not to have preexisting contacts* [italics are the author's] and struggled to connect with senior officials around the president-elect," reads the Mueller Report.[87] After an almost two-year, $32 million dollar (!) investigation, Mueller produced nothing on the Putin-Trump "collusion." Putin was laughing: "The mountain gave birth to a mole," the master spy quipped.[88]

As with any other successful active-measure operation, Russia's 2016 covert-influence campaign relied on active participation of the victim of the disinformation and deception. And in this case, what the Russians were able to achieve pales in comparison with what U.S. intelligence and federal law enforcement communities have done in the period after Trump's election, ripping the already severely polarized country apart. The Russians did not change any single vote tally, according the investigation by the Senate Select Committee on Intelligence (SSCI).[89] No evidence was uncovered of actual voting machines' being compromised to prevent voting or disrupt the ability to count the votes. This was never the Russian intent. They are not interested in trying to change your voting preferences because they know they cannot. They know they don't have that power. But they want you to think that they have it. The Russian spymasters are seeking to "hack" your mind, remember? They want to "infiltrate ideas into your mind," as Yuri Bezmenov put it.[90] This is how the Russians believe they can distort your reality, lead you to make an erroneous decision, and change your thinking and behavior. It is extremely unlikely that they swayed even by accident too many American voters in any direction. How many of your friends or family on the opposite side of the political spectrum have you converted recently? None? Me neither. We are so determined in our convictions today that families break up based on political disagreements. Although global elites refuse to acknowledge it, the American people, not the Russians, elected Donald Trump president in 2016. For millions of voters, they made this choice because they had lost confidence in the Washington establishment's commitment to serve the people's interests rather than their own.

The Washington establishment fell into the trap of a Russian deception operation because of their incompetence and inability to discern and counter Russian active measures. The Russians accurately assessed how polarized American society was on issues like race, religion, and immigration. They were able to manipulate these societal divisions and whip up upheaval on U.S. soil. The Russian active-measure masterminds also had a good grasp of the level of antipathy that existed among American elites toward candidate Trump and his personality. They exploited this animus by amplifying and likely feeding the bogus Steele dossier narrative into the information stream of U.S. intelligence. As absurd as the infamous "Golden Showers" fairy tale of Donald's escapades in Moscow sounds, it has all the markers of a classic Soviet-style *kompromat*.

Washington bureaucrats did a big disservice to the American people. Once they uncovered traces of Russian deception, U.S. intelligence and law enforcement, rather than giving a counterintelligence briefing to the Trump campaign members and warning them about the dangers of the Russian trickery, assumed that some campaign members and Trump himself were in cahoots with the Kremlin. After the election, the FBI launched an unprecedented counterintelligence investigation into the president of the United States! That is Stalinesque.

On President Obama's orders, the DNI orchestrated an Intelligence Community Assessment (ICA) on Russian election interference, which itself reads like a Russian disinformation paper. It is based on true facts and contains mostly reasonable analysis, creating the illusion of complete credibility, but it has untruths burrowed deeply within it to misdirect the victim of deception—in this case the American people.

There are several key problems with the ICA document issued by the DNI on January 6, 2017, titled "Assessing Russian Activities and Intentions in Recent U.S. Elections," which discussed Russian cyber-enabled intelligence operations targeting the 2016 election.[91]

First, the releasing of an unclassified version of a premier and highly sensitive intelligence product by the Intelligence Community is extraordinary. In my experience, it was virtually impossible to even pronounce the words "Russia" and "cyber" in the same sentence without the classification level's going into the stratosphere, let alone to release that into the public domain, which all U.S. adversaries, including Russia, monitor for open-source intelligence.

Second, the ICA was produced in thirty calendar days, over the holiday season, starting on December 6, 2016, when President Obama ordered it—a notoriously difficult time to get anything done in Washington, D.C. Conducting research and analysis, doing production at three separate classification levels, coordinating within the IC, and declassifying a super-sensitive, highly consequential document like this normally take months, not three to four weeks. And, as I said, nothing happens in the government in the last two weeks of December. The Intelligence Community is after all a government bureaucracy.

Third, an Intelligence Community Assessment, just like its much longer and more in-depth counterpart, a National Intelligence Estimate (NIE), an authoritative, flagship IC product, is supposed to be coordinated by the seventeen intelligence agencies. This is why it is called a community wide "assessment." The January 6, 2017, product was hurriedly written and coordinated by only three agencies—CIA, NSA, and FBI—and overseen by the DNI.

Fourth, it was either intentionally politicized or drafted based on limited sources (a strong possibility given the very short timeframe), or perhaps authored by analysts who don't have a background in Russian doctrine and strategy. I believe it was all three of these things, to varying degrees. "We assess with high confidence that Russian president Vladimir Putin ordered an influence campaign in 2016 aimed at the U.S. presidential election, the consistent goals of which were to undermine public faith in the U.S. democratic process," the assessment stated.[92] So far so good. I concur with this judgement. But the analysts also assert "with high confidence" that "Putin and the Russian government" sought to "denigrate Secretary Clinton and harm her electability and potential presidency" and "help president-elect Trump's election chances when possible by discrediting Secretary Clinton and publicly contrasting her unfavorably to him." I do not concur with this conclusion.

Assessing leadership intentions is extremely difficult—much more difficult than the adversary's military capabilities, which are concrete and can been seen on a satellite-produced photo or read about in a stolen design document or operational manual. Intelligence bureaucrats often complain about how hard it is to read foreign adversary's mind and tend to avoid or evade giving straight answers, often to the annoyance of generals and members of Congress. It is especially hard to estimate the intentions of someone like Putin, who is a trained intelligence operative highly adept at deception, misdirecting his opponent, and keeping his goals and plans secret—unless he wants you to know about them. To make a judgement like that with high confidence would require multiple remarkably reliable sources of information, including from technical collection. Putin does not use email, and his trusted circle is extremely small. He has already demonstrated multiple times what happens to those who betray the Russian state. Ask Sergey Skripal, a former GRU officer and a double agent for British intelligence, whom Russian operatives poisoned in 2018 in England.

Fifth, there was a 180-degree turn in the intelligence assessment as to whether Russia had a preference for a specific candidate in 2016. In July 2017, Obama administration DNI Clapper told the House Permanent Select Committee on Intelligence (HPSCI) that there was none, while the National Intelligence Officer (NIO) for Russia and Eurasia (a top analytic position in the IC for Russia) told HPSCI on December 5, 2016, a day before President Obama ordered the ICA, that there was none. In her briefing, which was declassified since, she stated, "In terms of favoring one candidate over another the evidence is a little bit unclear....It is unclear to us that the Kremlin had a particular...favorite or they wanted to see a particular outcome. This is what the reporting shows."[93]

Thirty days later, the three agencies, which apparently represented the entire IC of seventeen organizations, unanimously agreed that the Russians preferred Trump to Clinton. "All three agencies agree with this judgement," stated the ICA. "CIA and FBI have high confidence with the judgement, while NSA has moderate confidence."[94] That is, the analysts appear to disagree on the reliability of intelligence underpinning their conclusions, but, nevertheless, the three agencies signed on to the opposite analytic line from December 5, 2016. From an uncertain testimony to HPSCI whether the Russians had a favorite candidate or a particular outcome, the ICA authors switched to "high confidence" for the CIA and FBI and "medium confidence for the NSA" that Putin wanted to help Trump and hurt Clinton in the matter of four weeks during the 2016 holiday season.

Clapper explained this discrepancy, saying he received "this very, very sensitive information," which the National Intelligence Officer for Russia and Eurasia "and many others in the community were not aware of."[95] Hmm. Only Clapper received this information? Well, let me be clear: unless Clapper or ICA spies talked to Putin himself and got him drunk or slipped a truth drug into his tea, the confidence level on this point should have remained low regardless of one man's—Clapper's—"very, very sensitive information." This sudden change of the key analytic line in what is supposed to be the most authoritative intelligence product on a strategic-level issue suggests that the analysts were, willingly or unwillingly, under extreme, compromising pressure to produce a politicized intelligence report. Disturbing anti-Trump public statements the directors of the FBI, CIA, and DNI made on their leaving the government and their insinuations or outright accusations of Trump's being a Russian agent strongly support this judgement.[96] "He is wholly in the pocket of Putin," announced CIA director Brennan.[97] Making such unfounded accusations about a sitting U.S. president without a shred of evidence when you have access to the most sensitive secrets of our nation is a gross abuse of power. That is Putinesque.

This would not have been the first time that intelligence leaders during Barack Obama's administration politicized intelligence. Fifty intelligence analysts, including from the Defense Intelligence Agency, officially complained to the Pentagon's inspector general that their leadership at Central Combatant Command (CENTCOM) had softened up their intelligence assessments on ISIS to make them more palatable to and in line with Obama's claim about progress made by U.S. forces to eradicate ISIS.[98]

Nowhere in the ICA, however, was discussion of Russia's long-range strategic goal of destabilizing America by sowing discord and inflaming societal divisions and conflict. This reflected the authors' lack of broad-based knowledge of Russian perceptions of the U.S. "threat" and intentions to counter it, as codified in multiple Russian doctrinal and strategic planning documents. The ICA read like a politicized current-intelligence product rather than an unbiased strategic-intelligence report of high consequence.

No big surprise there. Deep research and long-term study, which involves reading volumes and volumes of doctrinal and military writings, is discouraged in the IC. It doesn't produce "clicks," doesn't get your analysis into a Presidential Daily Brief. Besides, the IC capability on Russia has been decimated in the aftermath of the end of the Cold War and the so-called "peace dividend." Serious experts on Russia have been "retired," forced out of the intel community, or reassigned to other jobs.

The faulty ICA was probably among the milder forms of government incompetence and abuse of power during the 2016 election. According to declassified materials, the FBI knew, or at minimum suspected, in January and February 2017, that the infamous anti-Trump Steele dossier was a product of Russian disinformation.[99] Christopher Steele's "primary sub-source" was a D.C.-based Ukrainian-born and Russian-trained attorney, Igor Danchenko, a suspected Russian intelligence asset. In 2009, the Bureau launched a counterintelligence probe into Danchenko as a potential "threat to national security" because he was offering to the research fellow of a prominent foreign policy advisor in the Obama administration and a co-worker an opportunity to "make a little extra money" by selling classified information.[100] Nevertheless, the FBI continued to use, four times, the bogus Steele dossier—which Danchenko confessed was largely based on bar talk he had had with his Russian drinking buddies—in support of the FISA application to obtain authority to surveil Carter Page, a Trump campaign aide.[101] The FBI effectively spied on a Trump campaign official, a U.S. citizen, and people he communicated with, as authorized by a warrant the Bureau had fraudulently obtained from the secret Foreign Intelligence Surveillance Court based on a request that centered on Russia-fabricated gossip.

How does a Russian national and intelligence asset burrow himself into the heart of Washington policy circles and wield such an outsized influence on American domestic politics? Danchenko was employed as a "researcher" by the liberal-leaning Brookings Institution headed by former Clinton-administration senior official Strobe Talbott. This is not the first time that Russian intelligence targeted and possibly infiltrated the U.S. foreign policy community, including Brookings. Based on declassified CIA records, as early as the 1980s, Russian intelligence officers, posing as "scholars," cultivated "well placed individuals" "not only in U.S. government but in such places as the Arms Control and Disarmament Agency…the Library of Congress…and [yes,] the Brookings Institution."[102]

Talbott, was considered by Russian intelligence "a special, unofficial contact," according to Sergey Olegovich Tretyakov, a Russian defector to the United States who, as Deputy *Rezident* in New York (i.e., Deputy Chief of Station in U.S. intelligence parlance) of Russia's foreign intelligence SVR, oversaw Russia's covert operations against the United States at the United Nations. The term "special unofficial contact" refers to the identity of the most secret, highly placed intelligence sources. Mr. Talbott has denied Tretyakov's claim.[103]

The FBI committed multiple errors in submitting its application to the secret FISA court requesting permission to spy on Page.[104] The most egregious was not an unintentional error, but rather a deliberate falsification of the official government document. An FBI attorney illegally altered a document to state that Page was not a U.S. government source, when he was in fact a CIA asset who reported to the Agency on his meetings with Russian intelligence in the course of his private consulting business.[105]

Finally, multiple Obama administration officials inappropriately unmasked the identity of President Trump's national security advisor and former DIA director—and my boss—General Flynn in highly classified intelligence reports that contained his conversations with Russia's U.S. ambassador Sergey Kislyak.[106] Various Obama administration officials jumped to the unfounded and irresponsible conclusion that this thirty-year military officer who had risked his life in combat zones was a Russian agent. The FBI entrapped him into making a false statement regarding his communication with the Russian ambassador and then charged him with the felony of lying to federal officers. Senior FBI officials strategized on how to entrap Flynn, according to the declassified notes of FBI agents who went to interview Flynn at the White House. One of the agents posed the question, "What is our goal? Truth/Admission or to get him to lie, so we can prosecute him or get him fired?" according to declassified written notes.[107]

Declassified transcripts of Flynn and Kislyak's conversation revealed that there were no inappropriate or illegal quid pro quo dealings with the Russians, only a typical diplomatic effort to ratchet down the tensions with the nuclear-armed Kremlin.[108]

The FBI and intelligence apparatchiks' actions against General Flynn appear to me to be in retaliation for his stated goals of reforming the Intelligence Community in order to make it more responsive to the needs of warfighters and policymakers.

Rogue elements within U.S. intelligence and law enforcement added fuel to the fire during the 2016 presidential election. Leaks of classified information by government and intelligence officials from the FBI counterintelligence probe of the Trump campaign served to delegitimize Trump when he was a candidate. After becoming president, anti-Trump officials painted him as Putin's puppet during television interviews. However, as we now know from the testimonies to the Senate and House Intelligence Committees—declassified by the Office of the Director of National Intelligence—senior IC officials acknowledged that they had not seen any evidence of conspiracy between Trump or his staff and the Russian government. Nevertheless, this false narrative helped prompt those Americans who were unhappy with the election results to launch the resistance movement against a democratically elected president.

The American people were victims of two covert-influence operations—one by the Russians and another by the Washington establishment's security services. This was Orwellian.

Trump was left presiding over a country polarized to the point where civil discourse between Americans on opposite sides of the spectrum was impossible. He was operating with roughly half the population doubting his legitimacy and some even working to unseat him. This was a gift to Putin: a distracted America, the "main enemy," cut up by its own windmills, is a good America for the Kremlin.

The Russians soon realized, however, that while they had managed to paralyze U.S. domestic politics for three years, the election "bonus" of having an alleged pro-Russia Trump did not work out in their favor. During his presidency, Trump executed the most aggressive policy toward Moscow since Reagan, while stringing Putin along with friendly promises of bettering relations. Like Putin, Trump is a pragmatist, something that he learned as a business executive. He did, quite sensibly, want to rachet down diplomatic hostilities with Moscow and even establish a working relationship with the only other nuclear superpower. But Trump wanted to do it on his terms, not on Putin's.

Russia's intervention to sabotage the 2016 election and disrupt U.S. politics has strategic implications. By targeting our country with an active-measure operation in 2016, Putin has already interfered in the 2020 elections, the 2024, and probably in every election going forward. After 2016, when both the Russians and the Washington establishment tried to subvert American democracy, will Americans ever feel confident in the integrity of our elections? Or will we wonder whether "the Russians are coming" during every U.S. election?

During the 2020 election campaign, U.S. intelligence warned that Putin had already delivered on his promise to interfere again. "I'll tell you a secret. Yes, we'll definitely intervene," Putin had said. He made the ostensibly tongue-in-cheek promise in response to a reporter's question whether Russia would meddle again in U.S. politics in 2020. But he really meant it, and he was signaling as much to keep us off-balance. In the run up to the 2020 presidential election, NSA and the FBI provided a rare warning about a highly sophisticated Russian cyber intrusion software called Drovorub ("Log cutter"). Drovorub was being deployed by the 85th Main Special Service Center (GTsSS), military unit 26165 of Russia's military intelligence GRU, which was involved in the hacking of the DNC, as part of Moscow's covert-influence operation to disrupt the 2016 election. The warning called out Drovorub as a threat to national security systems, the Department of Defense, and the defense-industrial base.[109]

This time the Russian agents-provocateurs were "supporting" Bernie Sanders and President Trump and trying to "denigrate" now president Biden, according to intelligence officials.[110] But don't let intelligence "experts" and the media fool you.[111] By "favoring" Trump—whom they had aimed to discredit in 2016 through the fabricated, salacious Steele dossier—the Russians were also supporting Biden, because Putin's reflexive-control gamers understood that the "Russia-Trump" issue remained a "hot button" for the American electorate. The Kremlin kept pushing this button to continue driving the wedge between Americans deeper, until now, when we have been completely split apart.

Whom, do you think, Russia was rooting for in 2020 as the next occupant of the White House? A presidential candidate who is an ailing and confused former vice president with the most liberal track record in the Senate? Or a hard-nosed, "America-First" businessman who ordered the bombing of three hundred Russian mercenaries in Syria, authorized cyber strikes on Russia's agency that did the hacking of 2016 elections, and set up American Space Forces to fight "star wars" with Moscow? "Helping" Americans choose the presidential ticket that was bound to place the United States firmly on the radical path of socialism would be just the right move towards advancing the Kremlin's long-held strategic goal of ideological subversion of America. Just like in 2016, Putin was hoping to win regardless of who was to become the U.S. president. If Trump and Pence had won, Russia would have continued to push our hot buttons and foment disorder. If Biden and Harris had won (as in fact happened), the United States would march toward "the workers' paradise" of socialism, as it is now.

The art of Soviet intelligence tradecraft displayed in Operation Trust, the 2016 "Translator Project," and 2020 covert-influence active measures hinges on the deceiver's ability to access and read the mind of the victim, to understand the victim's psychology. It is only by entering the victim's mindset and understanding his likes and dislikes, his biases and dreams, that the aggressor can manipulate the victim, step by step, into misperceiving reality, coming to wrong conclusions, and taking steps—predetermined and desired by the aggressor—toward his own destruction. It's all about psychology.

The Russian exiles who were duped by the Soviet Trust operatives were living in the West in squalid conditions, without jobs or hope of improving their futures. The émigrés fell into the Soviet agents-provocateurs' trap because they were told something they wanted to hear—a promise, a sign of hope, and a "way out of their wretched existence."[112] In 2016, U.S. intelligence and law enforcement communities were duped into believing that the absurdities written in the Steele dossier were authentic and that candidate Trump "colluded" with the Russians because they either were either incompetent in Russian intelligence tradecraft, had anti-Trump biases, were corrupt and wanted to prevent a Trump presidency, or (highly likely) all of the above. They jumped to wrong conclusions without any shred of evidence. The Russians with their various actions painted a picture, which looked plausible to certain U.S. intelligence officials, that Russians had infiltrated the Trump campaign.

And the Russians also knew it was what they wanted to believe. Americans who were put off by Trump's unconventional communication and leadership style and disliked his personality and behavior—sometimes understandably so—assumed that he could be a Russian agent. Together, the rogue government apparatchiks and anti-Trump–leaning elements started a resistance campaign that culminated in the president's impeachment, dragging the country into "controlled instability" sought by the Kremlin. Wittingly or unwittingly, yet again, some of us were fooled into doing Moscow's bidding. Remember what Yuri Bezmenov said: "It's what Americans do to Americans" that Russian active measures rely on for their success.

James Jesus Angleton described the psychology behind the art of perfect deception by using a firefly and beetle analogy. Female fireflies signal their "availability to mate" by flickering their lights. "The assassination beetle, the natural predator, has learned over time to imitate those signals," he wrote. The "male firefly, responding to the mating call, instead of finding a mate…is devoured by the beetle."[113]

From Russia with "Wet Affairs"

"Treason is the biggest crime on earth, and traitors must be punished."
   —Vladimir Putin

"If there is a person, there is a problem. If there is no person, there is no problem."
   —attributed to Joseph Stalin

The *KGB Counterintelligence Dictionary* from 1972 defines active measures as "counterintelligence activities designed to penetrate the adversary's decision-making and plans and impede or disrupt his unwanted actions before they take place."[114] Active measures differ from defensive counterintelligence—such as measures to protect state and military secrets—in that they are offensive in nature, enabling to uncover hostile acts by the adversary at the earliest stage of their conception.[115] They are designed to confuse the adversary, make him unmask his cover, and compel him to take action in unfavorable conditions in the direction desired by KGB counterintelligence. Active measures also include activities to "establish agent networks within the adversary's territory in order to collect intelligence, conduct covert operational games with the adversary, subvert, misdirect, and find *kompromat* [i.e., compromising information that could be used for blackmail]. They also include actions to secretly lure, into the territory of the USSR, persons of operational interest, and so on."[116]

What this definition omits (or perhaps it falls under "so on") is that active measures, now called benignly "assistance measures"[117] after the USSR's collapse also include "wet affairs" (*mokryye dela*). "Wet affairs" are targeted assassinations, bearing a codename that refers to the spilling of blood. They include killings, kidnappings, poisonings, "forced suicides," and other acts of intimidation and murder.[118]

Dating back to the early days of the USSR, wet affairs were practiced as statecraft, ordered at the highest levels of the Soviet government. It was Lenin's, and especially Stalin's, favorite tool—deployed by the Cheka and its successors the GRU, NKVD, and KGB—to "eliminate" (*likvidirovat'*) persons perceived as a threat to the regime. Soviet secret police labeled the targets of "wet affairs" as "enemies of the people," a disinformation technique designed to conceal the true purpose of the killings, which is to eliminate opposition to the regime. "Wet affairs" took place within the USSR's borders and abroad against all enemies of the Soviet state regardless of nationality.[119]

Leon Trotsky's assassination ranks as the most high-profile "wet affair" the Soviet secret police conducted. Trotsky, a Bolshevik and Red Army hero, was Stalin's archrival. Paranoid that Trotsky was planning from exile in Europe and Mexico to overthrow the Soviet regime and eliminate Stalin himself, the Soviet dictator acted. "Uncle Joe," as American "fellow travelers" and President Roosevelt charitably called him, gave the order to kill Trotsky in 1939. The operative in charge was Pavel Anatolyevich Sudoplatov, who, as deputy head of Soviet foreign intelligence, oversaw the administration of "Special Tasks," where targeted assassinations and other types of "wet affairs" were planned. Sudoplatov, together with a seasoned and ruthless Soviet intelligence operative, an "illegal" sleeper agent named Nahum Eitington, masterminded Operation Utka ("Duck") to track down Trotsky and "liquidate" him.[120]

Operation Utka had twin parts, involving separate teams of operatives codenamed "Horse" and "Mother." Neither team was aware of the other's existence. Much of the plot was operationalized in Greenwich Village, New York City, which housed the offices of the U.S. Communist Party (CPUSA). New York was the home base for many

Trotskyite organizations and was crawling with spy networks of Russian "illegal" intelligence operatives and American spies working for the Soviets. These spy rings were run by Jacob Golos (né Yakov Naumovich Reizen), a Ukrainian-born revolutionary who worked as a covert agent for Soviet intelligence and was naturalized as a U.S. citizen in 1915. Golos, a zealous Stalinist and the deputy of Earl Browder, the chief of CPUSA, assisted the Soviet secret police in infiltrating Trotskyite circles by providing key contacts.[121]

In August 1940—a few months after Trotsky had miraculously survived Operation Horse, an armed assault on his villa in Mexico—Operation Mother succeeded. Spanish communist and Soviet intelligence agent Eustacia Maria Caridad del Rio Hernandez, codenamed "Mother"—as she was a mother of four children—and her son Ramon Mercader, codenamed "Raymond," carried out the murder under the supervision of their handler Eitington. Mercader had been introduced to Trotsky by his girlfriend, New Yorker Sylvia Ageloff, who was devoted to Trotsky. He had been ordered by Stalin's agents to befriend and seduce the single Ageloff. Through his successful romance with her, Mercader had visited Trotsky's villa several times, had tea, and became trusted. On August 20, 1940, during one of his visits, Mercader mortally wounded Trotsky with an ice axe that he hid under his overcoat. Caridad and Eitington, who were waiting in a car for Mercader outside the villa, drove away once they realized that he had been captured and beaten by Trotsky's bodyguards and detained by the Mexican police.[122]

Another notorious example of a "wet affair" took place in May 1981, most likely on the orders of Soviet intelligence. Pope John Paul II, who, in addition to being pontiff, was a Polish anti-communist, was gravely wounded by a Turkish assassin in St. Peter's Square in Rome while riding in an open car. The assassin later admitted that he was carrying out a plot by Bulgarian intelligence, shocking millions of Catholics around the world. In March 2006, an Italian investigative commission concluded the Soviet leadership, and probably Soviet military intelligence, the GRU, was behind the pope's attempted assassination.[123]

Putin's Russia has renewed the practice of "wet affairs," also termed "special tasks." A federal law, "On Countering Extreme Activity," which Putin approved in 2002, two and a half years after he assumed the presidency, and updated in 2006, authorizes targeted assassinations.[124] The law "On Countering Extreme Activity" defines extremist activity very broadly, giving the Kremlin flexibility in its application. Below are some examples of "extremist activities":

- "Carrying out of mass disorder, hooligan acts, [and] acts of vandalism motivated by ideological, racial, national, and religious hatred or enmity, and equally motivated by hatred or enmity with regard to a specific social group"
- "Publicly expressed slander or false accusation of persons who hold Russian government positions or perform the duties of the state of the Russian Federation"
- "Diminishing national dignity"

The law further designates as a crime the organization of and preparations for such activities, as well as inciting someone to carry them out. Also included in extreme activity financing and any other type of support.[125]

Scores of Russian journalists and numerous political opposition leaders have been victims of "wet affairs" because they criticized Putin or the Russian regime or exposed the corruption and other misdeeds of the Russian government. Among such modern-day, high-profile murders are the killing of Anna Politkovskaya and Boris

Nemtsov. A Russian journalist and Putin critic, Politkovskaya reported on the atrocities of Russian forces during the Second Chechen War (1999–2009) and was shot and killed in her apartment elevator on Putin's birthday in October 2006. Boris Nemtsov, a former Russian deputy prime minister and opposition leader and Putin's ardent critic, was shot on a bridge near the Kremlin in February 2015.

"Wet affairs" have been carried out in various ways. Crudely, through shootings, stabbings (with the sharp pick-end of an ice axe in Trotsky's case), and staging car accidents or suicides like throwing a victim out of a window. However, "wet affairs" have also been more creative. In 1938, Pavel Sudoplatov, who was behind the plot to assassinate Trotsky, killed a Ukrainian nationalist on Stalin's orders. The murder weapon was a box of chocolates containing a bomb.[126] Ratcheting up the sophistication, death by poisoning is Russia's all-time favorite, dating back to the founding of the USSR. Although it requires special technical skills, precise dosing, and careful selection of a suitable type of poison, the Russians are attracted to this type of "special tasks" method because it can be executed clandestinely, without the noisy drama that comes with a handgun or an ice axe. The Russians perfected their various poison-derived murder weapons so that the symptoms often mirror natural human ailments—such as heart attack or gastritis—and it appears that the person died from "natural causes." Often it is difficult or impossible to find traces of the poisonous substance in the victim's body.

The first poisoning laboratory was established in 1921 on the orders of Lenin (who himself survived an unsuccessful poisoning attack in 1918 by curare from tropical plants). Known as the "Special Room," it was a top-secret facility that later was replaced by "Laboratory No. 1," or the *Kamera* ("Chamber"). To determine their effectiveness, poisons were tested on prisoners.[127] One of the most infamous poisonings was masterminded by Soviet intelligence at the request of their Bulgarian counterparts. The victim of the poison attack was Bulgarian journalist Georgy Markov, who had defected to England and was working for the BBC and Radio Free Europe. Extremely critical of the Bulgarian regime, Markov became the target for elimination by the communist dictator Todor Zhivkov. On September 7, 1978, while walking along Waterloo Bridge in London, an assassin poked Markov in the leg with an umbrella, which shot a ricin-laced pellet into the wound. While he barely felt the prick, he developed fever, nausea, and vomiting, and died four days later.[128]

Several Russian dissidents and opposition leaders have experienced fatal or near-fatal poisonings, including Anna Politkovskaya, before she was shot dead, and Vladimir Kara-Murza, a friend and close associate of the murdered former deputy prime minister Boris Nemtsov. Kara-Murza, a long-time critic of the Kremlin, was poisoned twice and put on life support both times, yet he survived. He is a Russian citizen and a legal U.S. resident. At the time of this writing, another Russian opposition leader and Putin critic, Alexey Navalny, is struggling for his life in a Russian prison.[129] Navalny fell ill on a flight from Siberia to Moscow after he drank some tea at the airport. After the Russian doctors said they could not find the cause of his condition and did not identify any poison in his body, Navalny was medically evacuated to Germany, where the doctors announced that he had indeed been poisoned with a military-grade nerve agent called Novichok.[130] Upon his return from Germany, Navalny was jailed by Russian authorities.

According to a 1993 CIA document, Soviet intelligence used various types of poison, including arsenic, potassium cyanide, scopolamine, and thallium. Other likely substances are atropine, barbiturates, chloral hydrate, paraldehyde, and warfarin. Diagnosis and tracing is complicated when two or more substances are used.[131]

In addition to eliminating journalists and political opponents at home, Putin's Russia, just like the Soviet Union, also carries out extrajudicial assassinations abroad. In a most brutal case of a "wet affair," two Russian GRU operatives murdered a former FSB officer, Aleksandr Litvinenko, who had defected to England and did contract work for British intelligence. Litvinenko was an ardent critic of Putin, whom he implicated in having directed apartment bombings in Moscow to justify his second war on Chechnya. Litvinenko also publicly accused Putin of being a pedophile; such criticism of a "Russian government official" is a criminal offense under the law on extremist activities. The murder weapon that killed Litvinenko was a cup of tea laced with the radioactive agent "polonium," which Aleksandr drank with his assassins during a business meeting in a luxury hotel in London.[132]

Russian GRU agents in Salisbury, England, in 2018 conducted a more recent attempted murder by poisoning. The victims of this attack on UK soil were former GRU officer Sergey Skripal and his daughter Yulia, who were visiting from Moscow. A Russian double-agent working for MI6, Britain's Secret Intelligence Service, Skripal was part of a Cold War–style swap for ten Russian "illegal" officers in 2010. The GRU operatives, who were dispatched by Moscow to Salisbury, used a military-grade nerve agent called Novichok. Skripal and his daughter miraculously survived after being quickly taken to a nearby hospital from a bench where they sat slumped over, incapacitated, frothing at the mouth. Novichok is a chemical agent originally produced in the Soviet Union during the Cold War. It causes death by invoking contraction of all muscles and leading to cardiac arrest and asphyxiation.[133]

Not so lucky was British national Dawn Sturgiss. A mother of three, she was fatally exposed in Salisbury to the chemical weapon deployed by Skripals' GRU assassins. She died after using a counterfeit "Nina Ricci's Premier Jour" perfume bottle containing Novichok found in the trash by her partner, Charlie Rowley (who claims it was boxed and sealed). The discarded bottle with a spray application was most likely used in the poisoning of the Skripals. The Novichok-laced bottle was inconspicuously smuggled into the United Kingdom by the Russian military intelligence agents.[134] British intelligence services concluded that the attempted murder of the Skripals was indeed a Russian intelligence operation, which was "almost certainly also approved outside the [GRU] at a senior level of the Russian state."[135] The two "wet affairs" operations Russian intelligence has carried out in Britain—the murder of Aleksandr Litvinenko in 2006 by hard-to-detect radioactive agent Polonium-210 and the attempted murder of Sergey and Yulia Skripal with a military-grade nerve agent Novichok in 2018—effectively amount to two attacks with weapons of mass destruction (nuclear and chemical) by Putin's Russia on the British soil.

A much less inconspicuous extrajudicial assassination Russia executed was in Germany in August 2019. A man riding a bicycle gunned down a Georgian of Chechen descent, Zelimkhan "Tornike" Khangoshvili, in Berlin Park. The man placed two shots in Khangoshvili's head in broad daylight. The German government has concluded that Russia was behind the "state-sanctioned" assassination of Khangoshvili, who was living in exile in Germany, having served as a mid-level commander leading Chechen separatists in combat against the Russian forces during the Second Chechen War.[136] While the Kremlin officially denied responsibility, later that year in December 2019, Putin, during a press conference with German *Der Spiegel*, called Khangoshvili "an absolute blood-thirsty killer" who "eliminated 98 people in [the] Caucasus alone." Putin stated that Russian intelligence was negotiating with its German counterparts to extradite Khangoshvili without success and accused Germany of letting "bandits stroll around on the streets of Berlin."[137] Putin's non-denial denial is a similar tactic that he used to "deny" Moscow's responsibility for the intervention in the 2016 U.S. election. While denying that Russian operatives hacked the DNC servers, Putin said that it doesn't matter who did it because true information about the corruption within the Democratic Party was exposed to the American people. He recently employed the same intentional ambiguity when he shared the "secret" with journalists that Russia would "intervene" in the 2020 election. Unbalancing your opponent by confusing, misdirecting, and deceiving him is a classic tool of disinformation and active measures, of which Putin is a grand master.

When it comes to Russia's conducting "special tasks" on U.S. soil, there have been a handful of unconfirmed cases. In November 2015, Mikhail Lesin, a former Russian media executive and Putin advisor who was residing in the United States was found dead in a Washington, D.C., hotel. In October 2016, his death was deemed "accidental" by the U.S. Attorney's Office for Washington and the Metropolitan Police Department. It was reportedly "caused or contributed to by blunt-force injuries to the head, neck, torso, and upper and lower extremities 'which were induced by falls.' Acute ethanol intoxication was cited as a factor." But while the investigation did not officially find evidence of foul play in Lesin's death, an official from the Office of the Chief Medical Examiner revealed that Lesin's neck bone was fractured in a way that is "commonly associated with hanging or manual strangulation."[138]

Russian special services focus on leaving no trail that would indicate foul play. According to a 1993 CIA document, "[e]ven in cases where the Soviet hand is obvious, investigation often produces only fragmentary information, due to the KGB ability to camouflage its trail." The same document warned that many "incidents" staged by Soviet intelligence "never become officially recognized as executive action" (i.e., "wet affairs"), resulting in assassinations' being "recorded as accidents, suicides, or natural deaths."[139]

In July 2004, the New York–born Russian-American journalist and the chief editor of the Russian edition of *Forbes* magazine Paul

Khlebnikov was gunned down with nine bullets on the streets of Moscow late at night. This was likely a politically motivated, targeted assassination of an American citizen who was exposing the corruption of the Russian oligarchs through his work. His wife and three children survived him. Iconic Russian dissident writer Aleksandr Solzhenitsyn, mourning Khlebnikov's death, wrote, "He died for the Truth and for Russia."[140]

In March 2007, former CIA officer and staffer for the U.S. Senate Select Committee on Intelligence Paul Joyal survived a brutal attack near his home in Maryland.[141] The attackers shot Joyal in the groin four days after he implied during a Dateline NBC broadcast that Putin and the Kremlin were responsible for Aleksandr Litvinenko's death. Although the FBI was originally involved in the case, five years after this highly likely murder attempt, the criminals had not been found. Paul, with whom I spoke briefly about the "incident" at an invitation-only gathering for security professionals a couple of years after it took place, was convinced that the "incident" was the work of Russians.

There is certainly a higher threshold for Russian intelligence to perform most "wet affairs" on U.S. citizens living in America, higher than in Europe, including the United Kingdom. This threshold is predictably lower for Russian émigrés who became naturalized U.S. citizens, like me, and even lower for Russian citizens living as U.S. legal residents, like Kara-Murza or Lesin. However, intimidation, such as showing up at your house under false pretenses, approaching you at public events, or other mild forms of harassment, is fair game for the Russians when it comes to intelligence officers here in the United States. After my departure from the DIA, my husband and I decided to report to the FBI's Washington, D.C., field office a few bizarre visits to our house. The FBI agents, who were trained counterintelligence officers with expertise in Russian tradecraft, were quite sober in their guidance to us. In Russia itself, U.S. intelligence officers experience harsh harassment. They are under constant surveillance by the FSB, the domestic security and counterintelligence agency. Their temporary houses in Russia get searched. Sometimes toilets are left unflushed to signal that they were there, in your house. In some more extreme cases, your pets get poisoned. The more tense U.S.-Russian relations are, the more hostile the FSB is towards U.S. intelligence officers in Russia.[142]

Russia's employment of "wet affairs" and other "special tasks" will continue under Putin's rule, which may last as long as 2036. The old KGB operative is unambiguous in his view that certain acts, such as Russian intelligence agents' switching sides to spy for foreign countries, deserve severe punishment. In an interview with the *Financial Times* in June 2019, Putin said that "treason is the biggest crime on earth, and traitors must be punished."[143] He added, "I am not saying that it's necessary to punish in [the] way that was done in Salisbury, not at all. But, nevertheless, traitors must be punished." In 2010, responding to a question as to whether he had ever had to sign an order "to liquidate enemies of the motherland abroad," Putin said, "Traitors will kick the bucket on their own—whatever they got in exchange for it—those 30 pieces of silver they were given, they will choke on them."[144] A "senior Kremlin official" echoed Putin's sentiment, when commenting on the Russian officer who gave up the Russian spy ring of ten sleeper agents in the United States rounded up by the FBI in 2010. "Make no mistake," he said, "A Mercader has already been sent" for the "traitor," referring to Trotsky's assassin.[145]

The spymaster also said, "It is not at all a fact that one must kill a person."[146] Was he implying that intimidation by brutal means—such as a shot in the groin or a prick of poison intended to make you suffer but not die—works just fine? If you switch sides, the idea is to make you fear that, if Putin sends one or not, a Ramon Mercader–like assassin with the modern equivalent of a crude ice axe can find you anywhere on the globe.

CHAPTER 8

Putin's Military Option: Things That Go Bang

"If you don't want to feed your own army, you will be feeding someone else's."

—*Vladimir Putin during his 2019 annual "Direct Line with the President" press conference*

"Politeness and weapons can accomplish much more than politeness alone."

—*President Putin*

I was working to wrap up my Defense Intelligence (DIA) projects so I could start my two-year rotation at the National Intelligence Council (NIC) as Deputy National Intelligence Officer (NIO) for Cyber. The Russia briefing circuit for my "troika" colleagues and me, as Charlie called us, intensified as the Obama administration's policy officials finally began realizing that they had been outplayed by the Kremlin all along. Resets, the Ray's Hell Burger "summit" with Medvedev, and promises for "more flexibility" after the 2012 reelection notwithstanding, Putin was motivated exclusively by the national interests of Mother Russia, not by the prospect of being

America's friend. Moscow continued to destabilize Ukraine by providing covert military support to the opposition forces, thwarted U.S. attempts to end the civil war in Syria and the reign of the murderous Assad regime, and intensified the hacking of American companies, banks, and government agencies. An elaborate disinformation campaign was underway to conceal Russia's responsibility for shooting down in error a civilian airliner, Malaysia Airlines (MH) flight 17, a few months earlier, killing 283 passengers. Eighty children were among them.

My "troika" colleagues worked hard to develop as accurate an understanding of our target as possible. The better we understood it, the higher confidence level we could give in our assessments when briefing senior officials. ████████████████████████████████
██
██
██
██
██
██
██
██
██████████████████████ This was always a sobering reminder to me of the business that we were in.

During one of my designated days working on the ████████
████████ the NIO for Cyber, my soon-to-be boss, invited me to the farewell party of the outgoing Deputy NIO for Cyber, who happened to be my former DIA colleague from my earlier days on the Space and Command & Control account. The two of them introduced me to the National Intelligence Council team, including the chairman. It seemed like an awesome group of folks to work with, and I couldn't

wait to start. Since I was already working at the Agency once or twice a week, transferring from DIA to the NIC seemed a no-brainer, so my boss-to-be NIO let me move some of my things in the new office, identified some intel to read, and told me my parking space number at the NIC/DNI. I knew that I had reached a serious level in the IC, even if it was temporary, for two years; very few people, unless you are senior executive service, a highly senior government rank, get assigned parking in the IC!

As my start date of February 8, 2015, was approaching, I was cleaning out my cubicle at the DIA. I sarcastically termed it the "call center," because the desks were aligned in rows so close to one another that it reminded me of the customer service call centers at Worldcom and UUNET, where I had been an executive during my earlier career in the information technology industry. Analysts, working to solve intelligence puzzles, prefer quiet isolation to a noisy "collaboration" environment, which the management thinks we want. My desk cleanup was interrupted by a phone call on my secure line from the DIA's Joint Duty Office asking me to come up and see them. I rushed in anticipation upstairs, prepared to hear that everything was ready and that I should be moving over to Langley, Virginia (where the CIA is located). Instead, the JDA program officer, a nice lady, handed to me an email from the human resources department of the Office of the Director of National Intelligence (ODNI), which cryptically said that "Ms. Rebekah Koffler" could not "assume her JDA position as Deputy NIO for Cyber at the NIC/DNI" due to some unspecified security-clearance issue. It didn't make any sense, because, as a DIA intel officer, I had a "blue badge," which meant that I already had top-secret/SCI clearance that provided clearance and facilities access throughout the entire Intelligence Community—at least it had up until that point. Certain that it was a mistake of some sort, since the memorandum of understanding (MOU) had already been signed at the highest levels of the DIA and DNI, I told the JDA lady that I would sort it out and let her know.

For the next several weeks, I banged my fists against the worst closed doors of the government bureaucracy. I was bumped around from one bureaucrat to another—DIA security, CIA security, Europe/ Eurasia management, and DNI human resources, as well as my would-be boss, the NIO for Cyber. Charlie and my other colleagues were puzzled, as no other DIA detailee who served at the NIC/DNI had had to go through a separate clearance process, including Charlie when he was a Deputy NIO for Russia during the 2008 Russia-Georgia crisis. There was a regulation on reciprocity that mandated that top-secret security clearances granted by one IC agency must be accepted by any other IC agency. Frustrated by not being able to have a deputy on an extremely busy account, the NIO for Cyber asked the deputy chairman of the NIC to get involved, and he promised me that he would keep the position open until the ███████████

███████████████████████████████████████

███████████████████████████████████████

███████████████████████ required a much higher-level access than the one I needed for the JDA as his deputy.

A couple of weeks later, the NIO for Cyber forwarded me an email that he received from the DNI human resources stating that "Ms. Koffler [had withdrawn] her application for Deputy NIO for Cyber" and asked me if this was true. I was stunned—some government apparatchik had told a blatant lie. I responded to the NIO that it was "absolutely not true" and stated in the email, copying DNI human resources, my commitment to get to the bottom of whatever was going on. I continued to keep trying to get answers, but to no avail. In another couple of weeks, I received an email from what appeared to be CIA security, which serves as the Executive Agent of DNI Security, and processes candidates for the NIC/DNI positions.

The email informed me that I would "not be onboarding to my JDA as Deputy NIO for Cyber" and that I should not be contacting them again as they didn't have any additional information for me. The email also stated that the decision did not affect my DIA clearances and that I should continue my DIA career.

Exasperated, I reached out to DIA's Equal Employment Opportunity (EEO) office and to the DIA's inspector general's office for a consultation. I also continued to go to the ███████████████████ ████████████████████ I figured that if there was really a security concern of some sort, my "blue badge" accesses to the building at Langley, the SCIF, and to the computer network would not work there. To the contrary, everything worked just fine, and my CIA boss Frank T. was happy to see me continue coming in to work on the project. None of this made any sense to me.

In my pursuit to regain the position that was unfairly and unjustly taken away from me, I wrote an official complaint to my Europe/Eurasia management, highlighting that while CIA security was blocking me from starting my joint duty assignment, the Deputy NIO for Cyber position had remained unfilled for almost two months and needed my expertise in Russia and Cyber. I also approached CIA director John Brennan after a public event where he was giving a speech and explained that one side of his agency was blocking my hard-won rotational assignment, which was in great need of my critical skills, based on a mysterious security issue, while another side was successfully utilizing my critical skills in an even more sensitive project. I respectfully asked for his support to resolve this nonsensical conundrum. Brennan promptly brushed me off, stating that he could not get involved in such matters. A couple of days later my DIA chain of command informed me that they knew that I had approached the CIA director, that I had indeed been "wronged," and that they would help me remedy the situation.

The next day, one of my chain of command bosses, the same one who complained earlier that I was "working too hard," called me into his office. He told me that I was "spending too much energy" on this Deputy NIO for Cyber rotation issue and that it was "wearing me down." He warned that if I didn't drop it, I "could lose my security clearance all together." Bewildered, I asked why I would lose my security clearance. I hadn't done anything wrong. He didn't respond. I felt trapped, the way I felt many times when I was living in the USSR. As an individual, you are completely powerless in Russia. The all-powerful state apparatus crushes you at every turn.

That evening, I got from a colleague whom I trusted the name of a prominent Washington attorney who specializes in national security and security clearance issues. I called the attorney, and, upon hearing my story, he recommended that I "lie low" for the time being while he tried to gently inquire through his contacts at the CIA what was going on. He also shared that he had another client, also an immigrant from Russia, who was abruptly terminated from the DHS Immigration and Customs Enforcement (ICE) agency without explanation. I heeded the attorney's advice.

I tried to immerse myself in work and have faith that things would eventually straighten out. I was delighted when Charlie summoned me to travel to St. Louis to brief ██████████████ ██████████████ TRANSCOM stands for Transportation Command, one of the functional combatant commands, which is responsible for providing logistics for American warfighters in conflict zones. General Selva was getting prepared for his Senate confirmation hearings to become the next vice chairman of the Joint Chiefs of Staff (VCJS).

On the day of my flight to brief the incoming VCJS, I had to stop at the Agency early in the morning to attend a highly important meeting. My CIA boss Frank T. selected a small subset of our

interagency team ███████████████████████████
██████ He limited participation to one person per agency. As typical for high-level engagements, this was a common way to ensure that only analysts with a substantive speaking role were included in high-level meetings to avoid a bunch of management "straphangers" tagging along in search of valuable facetime with the big shots. Frank had handpicked me to provide some details on this ███████████████████on DIA's behalf. Charlie concurred that I should be the one to ████████████████████████
██
██

██████ When my turn came to speak, Frank introduced me to Brennan and praised my unique contribution to the project. I was looking directly into Brennan's eyes as I was briefing him. I couldn't tell, though, if he remembered me from before, when I had asked him to intervene with his CIA security staff. Frank was pleased with my remarks and with how the whole meeting went. I drove home from the CIA, left my car in my driveway, and took a cab to the airport to fly to TRANSCOM.

The briefing to███████████████████████████
██
██████████████████████████████████Charlie, another colleague who was part of the "troika," and I did an excellent job, according to feedback from TRANSCOM and Stewart. Content with our work, the three of us headed out to the airport the next day to spend the upcoming weekend home with our families and to celebrate America's Independence Day. What happened on the flight back to Washington the next morning would change my career trajectory forever. And because my career as an intelligence officer is an intrinsic part of my life and my identity, it would change my perception of who I was.

New Doctrine More Dangerous Than the Cold War's

*"In our [war]games, when we fight Russia or China, blue
[the United States] has its ass handed to it."*
    —analyst from RAND Corporation, a U.S. govern-
    ment–affiliated think tank

Putin's playbook does not leave much to chance. A brilliant tactician and a skillful strategist, Putin has ensured that Russia has a
fallback option in his five-point master plan to defeat America. In
the event that Moscow's strategic nonmilitary destabilization campaign against America is insufficient to counter what Putin views as
Washington's long-term effort to impair Russia's economy through
sanctions and erode Moscow's sphere of influence in Eurasia, the
Russian General Staff, on Putin's orders, has developed a more traditional statecraft instrument—the military option.[1] It includes a
brand new doctrine,[2] innovative warfighting concepts,[3] modern
weaponry, command and control systems, and of course, the nuclear
Armageddon scenario.[4]

Upon occupying the top seat in the Kremlin, from which multiple generations of czars ruled Russia, President Putin adopted a
new Military Doctrine in April 2000.[5] It was updated twice: in 2010[6]
and in 2014,[7] based on Moscow's interpretation of the global strategic security environment and the General Staff's forecasts of security threats to Russia and the Kremlin. At the time of this writing,
the next iteration of the Russian military plan is due, which will
most certainly factor in Moscow's increased threat perceptions
associated with the dissolution of the Intermediate-Range Nuclear
Forces (INF) treaty, expiring Strategic Arms Reduction Treaty
(START), Washington's posture aimed at democratizing Ukraine
and Belarus, and former president Trump's forceful policy toward

the Kremlin. The new doctrine will likely be even more aggressive in addressing and preempting the perceived threats. Remember, Russians structure their security posture based on what they think, not on what we think. And those are "two big differences," as the Russian saying goes.

While Kremlin propaganda says its actions are only defensive in nature, Putin's new military doctrine is aggressive. It is even more dangerous than the one which the Soviet Union followed during the Cold War. It claims to be asymmetric, but in reality it is both asymmetric and symmetric. It is asymmetric because it relies on nontraditional methods that fall below the threshold of provoking a military response and because it targets perceived U.S. vulnerabilities—such as reliance on space and cyber technology and aversion to casualties. But it is also symmetric because it positions Russia to fight a conventional kinetic conflict with modern weaponry, such as precision-guided munitions (PGMs).[8] It is more dangerous because of the special role reserved for nuclear weapons.[9] Unlike during the Cold War, when the Soviets were preparing for a "bolt-out-of-the-blue-sky" nuclear strike from the United States, with the eventual symmetrical goal of Washington's decapitation and total annihilation, today's doctrine is more grounded in "reality"—Russian reality, that is. Putin's doctrine is focused on Russia's preparedness to fight a limited war—including with nuclear weapons—with the narrow objective of "defending" what Moscow views as its strategic perimeter. In other words, the nuclear option is not a theoretical doctrine. It has battlefield utility.

The 2014 military doctrine reveals that Russia continues to view the United States and NATO as the "main enemy,"[10] although it obfuscates this view with a traditional disinformation tactic—calling out NATO as a "military danger" to Russian security that will, under certain conditions, become a military threat. Semantics aside,

Putin's new doctrine is more than a deterrence doctrine. It is a warfighting doctrine.

The new doctrine designates several "key dangers," Moscow's standard set of grievances against the United States, including "NATO expansion to Russia's borders," the "strategic missile defense system," the "Global Precision Strike concept," "space weapons," and the deployment of strategic nonnuclear precision-guided munitions (PGM) systems.[11] The new Moscow doctrine places the responsibility on Russia's armed forces to address these threats. In the process of "mitigating" these perceived threats, Russia has developed and continues to develop military capabilities that can be used offensively against the United States. Russia is now what the Pentagon calls "a near-peer competitor" to the United States from a military standpoint.

In a conflict, Russia plans to contest the United States in all domains: air, sea, land, space, and cyber. Recognizing U.S. technological superiority, the Russian doctrine envisions degrading or disrupting the U.S. forces' "kill chain" by the targeting the C4ISR (command, control, communications, computers, intelligence, surveillance, and reconnaissance) and space systems on which America's forces critically depend for its defense intelligence and warfighting operations. ("Kill chain" is a U.S. Airforce concept of a six-stage target cycle—find, fix, track, target, engage, and assess, also known as F2T2EA.)[12] Just like our smartphones, U.S. PGMs, or "smart weapons" are guided to a large extent by GPS satellites, unlike the previous generation's, which are now called "unguided" or "dumb" bombs. To impede or thwart U.S. military operations, Russia has developed formidable counter-space (anti-satellite) and cyber capabilities to create what the Pentagon calls an anti-access/area denial (A2AD) environment. Russia's will use A2AD-type capabilities[13] to deny, or at minimum impede, U.S. forces' access to the conflict zone, so it can "seize strategic initiative" during the initial period of war, as the doctrine dictates, interdict U.S. forces' reinforcement, and fight the conflict with the balance of forces favoring Russia.[14] Russia believes that its new doctrine, with weapons to match it, enables Moscow to inflict "unacceptable damage" on the U.S. and/or the Allied military, economy, and population and end the conflict on terms favorable or at minimum acceptable to the Kremlin.

Russian military strategists envision a small local conflict within its "strategic buffer zone"—Ukraine, Georgia, Belarus, the Baltics, and the North Caucasus—as a potential pathway to war between the U.S. and Russia. They believe that unless squashed by Russia, such a conflict may escalate into a regional battle and even a large-scale war because of the United States' "responsibility-to-protect" doctrine, NATO obligations, and aspirations to absorb some of Russia's former Soviet protectees into the European Union, NATO, and the overall Western sphere of influence. It is for this reason that the Russian doctrine calls for a rapid force-deployment into the zone of simmering conflict, overwhelming the adversary with force and squashing the conflict, thus presenting the United States and NATO with a fait accompli.[15] Preemptive action is included in the doctrine to gain strategic initiative quickly during the initial period, but this is not widely publicized by the Russians.[16] General Gerasimov, the chief of the Russian General Staff, invoked "covert inception" in his 2013 doctrinal article, "The Value of Science is Its Forecasting."[17] The Russian strategists justify such action as preemptive defense, using similar arguments as President George W. Bush did when he authorized the U.S. invasion of Iraq in response to fear the country might deploy biological weapons. Realizing that once started a conflict between the United States and Russia would be hard to contain, the Russian planners place much emphasis on managing conflict escalation.

To dominate conflict by maintaining "strategic initiative," a Russian doctrinal principle, the General Staff has developed an approach to achieve what's called "escalation dominance." "Escalation dominance" was conceptualized by the iconic American thought leader on nuclear warfare Herman Kahn as a way to compel the adversary to concede in a conflict by demonstrating a superior position over him so that the adversary would perceive any further escalation as a losing bet.[18] Through "escalation dominance," the Russian General Staff targets America's will to initiate, engage in, or continue to fight with Russia. An example of the effect of Russia's escalation dominance posture on U.S. leadership's decision-making was Barack Obama's failure to prevent or forcefully respond to Moscow's cyber intrusions into the U.S. government and military systems, including the Kremlin's covert-influence operation to blow up the U.S. 2016 presidential election. There was a concern that Putin would launch a destructive cyberattack on the United States—which is much more dependent than Russia on technology for daily existence—crippling the U.S. economy and daily activities.[19]

Russia believes that it can "out-escalate" the United States in a conflict because it is less reliant on technology, has a higher tolerance for losses, and has a population more used to experiencing hardships. In other words, Russians can "out-suffer" Americans, which would enable the Kremlin to up the ante in a war with the United States. A hypothetical example would be if Russia were to deploy military forces into Belarus to "assist" the "Union State" (i.e., the Union State of Russia and Belarus) member in response to the Lukashenko regime's collapse. Russia would view the collapse as U.S.- and NATO-assisted and react if one or both declared a "no-fly" zone over Belarus (like in Libya)—something that Russia would interpret as a precursor to a kinetic conflict. In response, Russia might retaliate and paralyze U.S. hospitals in a massive cyberattack—not unlike in 2017 when some U.S. healthcare systems were shut down as a result of Russia's broader cyber attack NotPetya.[20] Moscow's highly escalatory move would be intended to signal that if the U.S. and NATO do not stand down from "meddling" in the "Union State," then Russia would break through the "no-fly" zone and invade Belarus and establish control. In this situation, Moscow relies on its assumption that Washington would find it hard to respond to Russia's action proportionately without triggering another even more escalatory act by the Kremlin.

Although I have skipped a few "rungs" on Herman Kahn's famous 44-step conflict "escalation ladder," nevertheless, this scenario is entirely illustrative, since I am not in a position to write about the scenarios based on actual wargames that I participated in. All I can say is that my experience is similar to that of RAND Corporation analyst David Ochmanek, who has participated in RAND wargames sponsored by the Pentagon and former deputy secretary of defense (DEPSECDEF) Robert Work. "In our games, when we fight Russia and China, blue [the U.S. military] gets its ass handed to it," Ochmanek disclosed to the publication *Breaking Defense*.[21] Former DEPSECDEF Work echoed Ochmanek's commentary: "The simulated enemy forces tend to shut down [U.S.] networks so effectively that nothing works." Worst of all, both former DEPSECDEF and the RAND analyst said, "The [United States] doesn't just take body blows, it takes a hard hit in the head as well.... Its communications satellites, wireless networks, and other command-and-control systems suffer such heavy hacking and jamming that they are suppressed, if not shattered."[22] And then, according to Work, when "'the red force really destroys our command and control, we stop the exercise,'...instead of figuring out how to keep fighting when your command post gives you nothing but blank screens and radio static."[23] This is exactly what the Russian doctrine envisions and counts on—breaking the U.S. forces' will to fight by taking away their technological advantages and crutches.

Putin's New "Uber" Weapons

Although conventionally Russia is not a direct match to the U.S. military globally, Moscow is top dog in its region when it comes to its military and weaponry. Should a kinetic conflict break out between Moscow and Washington, the U.S. military will be forced to fight a fundamentally different war than those it has fought in the last several decades. Russia's robust, modern precision-strike missiles, air-defense systems, electronic warfare capabilities, and ability to disrupt undersea cables that carry communications,[24] among many other capabilities, will present a very tough operating environment for U.S. forces. Power projection and freedom of maneuver that the U.S. military has grown to take for granted will be significantly hindered in a conflict with Moscow.

Today's Russian military is far superior to its Cold War forces and especially so compared to the years just after the Soviet Union's collapse.[25] Putin has transformed Russia's military into a force to be reckoned with. This is largely the result of an unprecedented military modernization program that Putin launched in the aftermath of the Russia-Georgia war in 2008. Although Russia won the five-day war, squashing Georgian forces before the United States could make the decision to assist Georgia, which is not a NATO member (speed of action is what the NATO doctrine calls for), Moscow was not pleased with its performance. Russian commanders openly criticized Russia's lack of modern command-and-control systems and ability to strike targets on the move, as opposed only to stationary targets. Putin's generals realized that if Moscow were ever to face off with Washington, it would need to come up with a creative doctrine and upgrade its arms.

Putin has always increased the defense budget within overall Russian government spending, even when it was experiencing an economic downturn exacerbated by U.S. sanctions or lacking the benefit of high oil prices. The Russians are typically much more easily convinced to make sacrifices to militarize the country than Americans. Having been preparing to fight the "main enemy" for generations, they are quite used to tightening their belts so that Mother Russia can be armed with robust weaponry. "If you don't want to feed your own army, you will be feeding someone else's," Putin said during one of his annual press conferences, called "Direct Line with the President."

During his March 1, 2018, annual address to the Russian parliament, Putin announced an entirely different class of weapons, which have no analogues in the world, designed to target the United States and NATO.[26] As usual, he justified the development of these weapons as a necessary counter to the U.S. ballistic missile defense (BMD) capability, which threatens Russia's retaliatory nuclear-strike ability in Moscow's view. The Kremlin believes that by shielding the United States and its Allies with a BMD umbrella, the United States removes its own vulnerability to a Russian nuclear strike, which in turn tempts Washington to attack Russia or its interests in its strategic buffer zone. Despite assurances that USBMD is not intended or scaled for such a mission, Moscow believes it must plan for a worst-case scenario if future technological breakthroughs by the United States provoke Washington's leadership to act "recklessly" toward Moscow.

Putin introduced six new weapons and demonstrated video animations of these systems targeting the United States. "It is not a bluff," warned Putin, fully aware that U.S. and Western intelligence would be dissecting the address's every word.[27]

The first one is a heavy ICBM, "Sarmat" (RS-28), dubbed by Western analysts "Satan-2," as it is replacing the Voevoda complex,

Satan-1. Putin emphasized that Sarmat will be difficult to intercept by U.S. BMD systems because, though weighing more than 200 tons, it has a short active-boost flight path. It will be equipped with a wide range of capabilities to include decoys and will have a range of 11,000 km. More importantly, Putin warned, it will be able to sneak up on the United States and attack from the South Pole as well as the North, just like traditional ICBMs, confusing America's missile defenses.[28]

The rest of Putin's devastating new mega-weapon systems, some of which didn't have a name yet, are below.

- The Avangard (designated by NATO the "SS-19 Stilleto mod. 4") hypersonic glide vehicle, capable of delivering nuclear or conventional payloads on an ICBM while traveling twenty times the speed of sound and avoiding U.S. missile defenses.[29] The U.S. was able to observe Avangard in November 2019, as part of the START Treaty inspection.[30]
- The Kinzhal (Dagger) air-launched ballistic missile.[31]
- The Burevestnik (Thunderbird) nuclear-powered and nuclear-armed cruise missile.[32]
- The Poseidon (codename "Status-6," a.k.a. Kanyon) unmanned nuclear-powered and nuclear-armed underwater drone or "autonomous torpedo." According to the Jamestown Foundation's assessment, Poseidon's speed and depth will enable it to "penetrate U.S. anti-submarine defenses." If detonated close to the U.S. Atlantic or Pacific coasts, "the blast would create a gigantic, highly radioactive tsunami, destroying and contaminating large stretches of densely populated U.S. territory, like New York, Washington, Boston, and Los Angeles."[33]

- The Peresvet laser combat system, designed to blind American satellites, to disrupt U.S. intelligence collection in wartime.[34]
- A small-size, super-powerful nuclear reactor integrated into a cruise missile, such as the Russian KH-101 or U.S. Tomahawk.[35] It would make the missile able to fly a virtually unlimited distance and in a trajectory unpredictable to an enemy, making it invulnerable to U.S. missile defenses.

In early 2017, Russia deployed, in violation of the Intermediate-Range Nuclear Forces Treaty, a land-based cruise missile designated SSC-X-8.[36] (The INF Treaty, signed between the USSR and the United States, banned all of the two nations' land-based ballistic missiles, cruise missiles, and missile launchers with ranges of 500–1,000 km and 1,000–5,500 km.) Former vice chairman of the Joint Chiefs (VCJS) General Paul Selva warned that this missile "presents a risk to most of our [U.S.] facilities in Europe" and is "part of a wider deployment by Russia of sea-, air-, and ground-launched nuclear-capable missiles."[37]

Russia has used the conflicts in Ukraine and Syria as testing grounds for some of its new weapon systems and warfighting concepts. Russian forces have also been gaining valuable combat experience. In September 2015, when Putin deployed forces to prop up the Assad regime, ██

██

██

██

██

██

With its modernized weapons arsenal, Russia is capable of mounting significant combat power while degrading U.S. warfighting capability by employing novel electronic warfare, anti-satellite, and cyber capabilities against U.S. forces.[39] Meanwhile, the U.S. military experienced deep cuts and atrophy of some asymmetric capabilities, such as electronic warfare, during the Obama administration and before. In April 2016, Lieutenant General H. R. McMaster, who later became President Trump's national security advisor, warned the Senate that in the next war, U.S. forces may be "outgunned and outmanned" unless the United States stops "shrinking the Army before it's too late."[40] Any advantage that Putin may perceive is more likely to provoke his aggression within Eurasia rather than decrease his appetite for restoring the losses that Russia has incurred in the aftermath of the collapse of the USSR.

The "Unthinkable" Thinkable: Armaggedon

Putin's new military doctrine reserves a special role for Russia's nuclear forces in wartime. Unlike the Cold War, when nuclear weapons were primarily a psychological weapon intended for deterrence, today Russia tests and plans to use nuclear weapons to achieve military victory.

Russia has the largest nuclear arsenal among the nuclear states, and Putin has ensured that it is kept in good shape. Moscow systematically invests in the modernization of its nuclear arsenal and training of its nuclear personnel, the Strategic Rocket Forces. Although live nuclear testing is not permitted under the Comprehensive Nuclear Test Ban Treaty, Russia has been found by the U.S. Intelligence Community to violate the accord. According to former director of the Defense Intelligence Agency Lieutenant General Robert Ashley, Russia was "likely violating the treaty by secretly carrying out nuclear tests with very low explosive power...creating nuclear yield."[41]

Russia periodically deploys strategic bombers on overflight missions close to U.S. borders to practice and to test U.S. responses to its breeching the U.S. air-defense identification zone (ADIZ). Moscow also has conducted nuclear mock-attacks on the U.S. homeland. As part of an "Open Skies" mission, the Russians conducted overflight over a U.S. nuclear lab to conduct reconnaissance.[42] (The Open Skies Treaty permits each state party to conduct short-notice, unarmed reconnaissance flights over the others' entire territories to collect data on military forces and activities. It is intended as a confidence-building measure, but the Russians have been using it to collect intelligence to enable its offensive doctrine against the United States.)

The Russians regularly practice nuclear launches in simulation exercises, with Putin "pressing the button" with the defense minister and the chief of General Staff at his side.[43] The Russians believe that regular practice of authorizing a nuclear-weapon release keeps their leader psychologically prepared for this action. They learned an important lesson during the Soviet era about keeping their leader ready. According to declassified debriefings of the Soviet General Staff officers, General Secretary Leonid Brezhnev "trembled" when he was asked to push a button in a hypothetical war with the United States, during a 1972 command-post exercise. According to the scenario, a "U.S. attack would kill 80 million Soviet citizens and destroy

85 percent of the country's industrial capacity." Brezhnev kept asking Soviet defense minister Grechko, was this "definitely an exercise?"[44]

The Russian president has the ultimate authority to authorize a nuclear strike, which is done through the Cheget, Russia's "nuclear football." However, the defense minister and chief of the General Staff can also authorize a nuclear weapons release. The nuclear command-and-control system (NC2) obtains authorization from the Russian president or the other two designees in about ten minutes, launching nuclear strikes that can be delivered to their targets from land, sea, and air.

Russia is the only country that possesses the capability to devastate the U.S. homeland by destroying numerous targets. However, Moscow has no plans to launch a surprise nuclear attack on America, nor does it expect one from Washington. Instead, the Kremlin anticipates that a local or regional conflict may escalate into a nuclear scenario should it perceive that its regime or vital interests are threatened.

The 2014 Military Doctrine declares the conditions that would trigger Russia's nuclear use. It spells out that Russia "reserves the right to employ nuclear weapons in response to nuclear or other WMD use against Russia or its allies, and also in the event of aggression against Russia with conventional weapons if the very existence of the state is at stake."[45] By "state," the Kremlin means its regime. What is not mentioned in this open document is Russia's undeclared nuclear policy called "escalate-to-deescalate."[46] While Russia denies its existence, multiple doctrinal writings by Russian military and nuclear strategists advocate this concept.[47] The idea is that Russia can employ non-strategic (tactical) nuclear weapons with short ranges to compel its opponent to terminate conflict on Russia's terms. It is for this reason that Russia has developed the SS-X-8 GLCM (ground-launched cruise missile) in violation of the Intermediate-Range Nuclear Forces Treaty (INF) Treaty. The

Kremlin wants to be able to use or threaten to use this nuclear missile against targets in Europe if conflict erupts on its periphery—for example, involving the Baltics, Ukraine, and Belarus.

On June 2, 2020, Russia also adopted a new nuclear policy, "Principles of State Policy of the Russian Federation in the Sphere of Nuclear Deterrence."[48] The document, while consistent with the 2014 Military Doctrine, outlines the Kremlin's specific red lines, which, if crossed, would trigger Moscow's nuclear response. Among the four conditions that would call for a Russian nuclear strike is "the adversary's influence on and disruption of the critical infrastructure facilities belonging to the Russian government or military."[49] What is notable is that the "influence and disruption" of Russian critical infrastructure does not have to be with nuclear means to trigger a nuclear response. Moscow likely includes cyber attacks on these facilities as possible triggers for a nuclear response, given that the Russian doctrine is typically effect-based—meaning it cares about the impact of the attack rather than the type of weapon or whether non-military means are used for an attack. Strategic-level effects typically call for a strategic-level response, hence the possibility of a nuclear response.

The bottom line is that Russia reserves the right for "first use" of its nuclear weapons, which could unleash a nuclear war that would be difficult to control. Even though Russian planners believe they have figured out the tolerance levels of the U.S. leadership and population for various Russian actions, including nuclear use in a conflict, Moscow is capable of error. Given that an exchange of nuclear weapons between two nuclear-armed powers has never occurred, no one really knows how anyone, especially the American people, would respond. President Trump called out Russia on this misguided "escalate-to-deescalate" doctrine in his 2018 Nuclear Posture Review, having authorized, wisely, the development of a small-yield nuclear weapon to counter Russia's doctrine.

Russian strategists have done much thinking about nuclear warfare and how the nuclear conflict would play out between Moscow and Washington. And while the Russians have an advanced thinking and nuanced doctrine that draws on an extensive body of knowledge, both Western and Russian, there is always the risk of things' not going according to plan. For example, Russia may be underestimating the willingness of Americans to tolerate mass casualties, given the hundreds of thousands of COVID-19 deaths it has absorbed.

There are two examples of how simple errors and malfunctions brought the United States and Russia to the brink of Armageddon. In 1995, then president Boris Yeltsin's "nuclear football" was accidentally activated because of a malfunction in the Russian missile warning system intended to detect nuclear launches. The early warning missile system misidentified a Norwegian scientific rocket as a submarine-launched U.S. missile that was heading in the direction of Moscow. Chaos ensued among Russian authorities when the world came dangerously close to its destruction.[50]

In another incident that happened in September 1983, during a very tense period in U.S.-Soviet relations, the Russian missile warning system registered U.S. nuclear missiles heading toward Russia, which required the duty officer to launch a counterattack. Coincidently, NATO was conducting a military exercise. A single individual, Colonel Stanislav Petrov, a Soviet Air Defense Forces officer who was on duty monitoring the Soviet early warning system, decided that it was a mistake.[51] Contrary to the Soviet understanding of the U.S. doctrine of mass, not limited, nuclear strike, the Russian system "detected" only a few "U.S. missiles" that were heading toward Russia. This knowledge of the U.S. doctrine helped Petrov make the decision not to alert any of his superiors, taking the heroic risk of being wrong. He suspected that the Russian missile warning system was broken and so avoided a retaliatory response and nuclear catastrophe. It certainly pays to know your adversary's doctrine. Russians are not the only ones whose missile warning systems are not foolproof. In the 1950s, a flock of Canadian geese confused the North American distant early warning–line radar system, which mistook the birds for a Soviet nuclear attack.[52]

There is no question that Russia is preparing for a nuclear conflict with the United States and NATO. Will this conflict be deterred or fought? If this existential threat to the U.S. homeland and civilization is to be deterred, U.S. intelligence and national security need to understand the mindset of their strategic opponent: Vladimir Putin.

On a Wartime Footing: Mobilizing Mother Russia for War

In 2013, Putin initiated steps to move Russia in the direction of a wartime footing. He would not be caught asleep at the wheel ignoring his General Staff's forecasts of a war with Russia's archrival, the United States, the way Stalin did with Hitler. Despite eighty-seven separate, credible intelligence warnings the Soviet dictator received during 1940–41 about Germany's possible plans, Russia was utterly unprepared when Hitler launched "Operation Barbarossa" against the USSR on June 22, 1941. It was the most violent and devastating military invasion in history.[53]

A committed realpolitiker and student of history, Putin undoubtedly assessed that, even if his General Staff had said nothing, given its prominent geostrategic position, Russia is always in danger of being attacked by another great power such as the United States. Russia, after all, has been at war for two thirds of its existence. Preparing for war is always a prudent step for someone of the Russian strategic mindset, which holds—standing the famous phrase by Carl von Clausewitz on its head—that politics is only a continuation of war.

In July 2013, Putin issued a presidential edict, "On the Questions of the General Staff of the Russian Federation," which authorized the Mobilization Plan of the Russian Federation.[54] It was updated on January 7, 2014. On January 14, 2014, Vice Premier Dmitry Rogozin announced via his Twitter and Facebook feeds that, in accordance with the "decision of the president and as adopted by the government of Russia and the military-industrial commission," a "new mobilization plan of the state economy went into effect beginning in 2014."[55] The plan was intended to direct the "defense industry, including approximately 800 companies, to gear up for a sudden increase in capacity, instead of conserving its capacity." This action was being taken to prepare for the possibility of declaring an *osobyj period* ("special period").[56] A "special period" is a legal regime that enables the Russian government to take certain emergency measures aimed at the intensive preparation of the country, the armed forces, and the state security forces for war.[57]

The announcements resulted in action. Since early 2014, Putin's Russia has been in the process of active mobilization, moving to a wartime footing.[58] "Mobilization" entails a state-wide coordination effort across the military, economy, state administration, and, indeed, across the entire Russian society, to ensure the country's readiness for war.[59] The "special period" is when the Russian government can dictate whatever emergency measures it believes are necessary to prepare the country and its population for war. This "special period" legal regime can last months or years. There is no indication at the time of this writing that the "special period" regime is over. If anything, it is possible that Putin's Russia continues to operate in a state of constant preparation for war.

In December 2014, the National Center for State Defense was established.[60] It is a wartime structure similar to Stavka VGK (Stavka Verkhovnogo Glavnokommandovaniya), the Soviet command and control center from which Comrade Stalin commanded the armed forces of the USSR during World War II. Putin's Stavka coordinates the activities across all Russian armed forces to ensure permanent combat readiness. It also includes a 24/7 watch center, which monitors the security environment for intelligence indicators to identify potential hot spots. Based on intelligence data provided by Russian military intelligence, the GRU, the chief of General Staff General Valery Gerasimov receives intelligence briefings several times a day. The center is equipped with a system that forecasts intelligence threats and offers potential options for the commanders' decision-making.[61]

The Russian General Staff, which conducts annual strategic-level military exercises, has been conducting so-called "snap" exercises to audit combat readiness of the Russian Armed Forces.[62] Russia has previously used military exercises to mask real-life military operations, such as the invasion of Crimea in 2014, from detection by U.S. and Western intelligence.[63]

Putin's invoking of the "special period" is a troubling development. Being in a continuous state of mind of expecting an adversary's attack carries substantial risks. You are likely to see things that you expect to see, even if they are not there. For Russia, whose strategic culture is already predisposed for the expectation of conflict, once you declare a preparation for war, the risk of overreacting to some policy or activity of its "main enemy," the United States, is much higher, becoming a self-fulfilling prophecy.

The high risk of such a worst-case scenario mindset is demonstrated in the following real-life examples from a period of high tension in Soviet-American relations in 1983.

A declassified NSA document, Serial: 2/19/2515-84 Spot Report, dated August 15, 1984, with the subject line: "Bogus Notification of War Between Soviet Union and United States of America," included a report on an incident that occurred the year before. I have marked the blacked-out portions with XXX. Prior to declassification, the report was classified at TOP SECRET//COMINT-UMBRA/TALENT KEYHOLE//X1, one of the highest of the possible classifications used for communications intercepts.[64]

> (SC) AT XXX ON 15 AUGUST 1984, XXX INFORMED A SOVIET PACIFIC FLEET, AND PROBABLY A STRATE-GIC MILITARY AUDIENCE THAT "WAR HAS BEGUN WITH THE UNITED STATES OF AMERICA." (SC) THE STATEMENT WAS CANCELLED BY XXX.[65]

It is not clear why the NSA report and the summary are dated 1984, reporting on the activity from 1983. There are heavy redactions on the first page. The clue may be in the redacted portions.

The declassified report includes this communications intercept:

> 18:19:02 I am closing on the target.
> 18:20:08 Fiddlesticks. I am going, that is, my Z.G. [indicator] is lit [missile warheads are already locked on].
> 18:30:30 I am turning lock-on off and I'm approaching the target.
> 18:20:49 I have broken off lock-on. I am firing cannon bursts.
> 18:21:34 Yes, I am approaching the target, I am going in closer.
> 18:21:35 The target's [strobe] light is blinking, I have already approached the target to a distance of about two kilometers.
> 18:21:40 The target is at 10,000 [meters].

And four minutes and six seconds later:

> 18:25:46 Z.G. [missile warheads locked on]
> 18:26:20 I have executed the launch.

18:26:22 The target is destroyed.[66]

The target in this report is a "passenger Korean Airlines flight (KAL) 007, which had taken off from Anchorage, Alaska, in September 1983 on its way to Seoul. It was programmed to fly commercial track R20, which skirted Soviet Airspace along Kamchatka." It had 269 people aboard, including U.S. Congressman Larry MacDonald, a Georgia Democrat.[67]

The transcript is "the cold voice of an experienced pilot performing a maneuver he had practiced many times." He was a Soviet fighter pilot who was following the order to destroy a "hostile intruder" who had "crossed into the Soviet airspace" and into a "Soviet radar zone, over Sakhalin." It appears that KAL-007 was shot down as it was exiting the Soviet airspace or even after it exited.[68]

KAL-007 got tragically off course but didn't know it. It was shot down, killing everyone on board, because the Soviets perceived it as a "spy plane." This tragic accident was a result of the "Soviet concern for border security['s] escalating to paranoid intensity by August 1983." The accident happened within the context of deteriorating U.S.-Soviet relations. "Soviet tempers boiled over in April of 1983 as a result of a U.S. naval exercise in the Sea of Okhotsk. By Soviet accounts, the U.S. Navy flew bombing runs on April 4 that penetrated deeply into Soviet airspace in the militarily sensitive Kuril Chain area and led to an Andropov-issued shoot-to-kill order."[69]

What is revealing is that at no time did the Soviets try to identify the aircraft they had shot down. Having been sensitized to the possibility of a U.S. attack, they assumed that any intrusion was deliberate rather than a mistake. NSA analysts and linguists, "going through the tapes…heard nothing about either aircraft identification or warning. Ground controllers variously identified the raid as either an RC-135 [a U.S. reconnaissance aircraft that the Russians were tracking earlier that morning and in pursuit of which had scrambled two fighters] or an unidentified intruder. The pilot was not asked to iden-tify or warn."[70]

What is equally alarming is that the NSA analysts at Elmendorf, Alaska, who intercepted the Soviet tracking of KAL-007, may have had the opportunity to preempt the tragedy. They didn't do so because they assumed the Soviets were "practice tracking." Although one analyst was convinced that it was "actually valid tracking" and not a practice, he was overruled by a "Group Senior Coordinator," so the incident wasn't reported up the chain. When ███████████ ███ ███████████████████████ a civilian airliner had disappeared and issued a CRITIC███████████████████████ ███████████████████████████ CRITIC is the highest level of urgency report from the NSA director (DIRNSA) about a possible threat—such as an impending attack on the United States or its Allies—that is so significant that it requires immediate attention by the president and the NSC. It is only after the "iron-clad confirmation provided by another intercept, in which the Soviet SAM controllers were discussing a Soviet pilot having shot down the civilian aircraft, that the second CRITIC report was issued and the matter was ele-vated all the way to President Reagan and his advisors.

What we have here is an illustration of two diametrically opposed mindsets—the Soviet "worst-case scenario" and the American "best-case scenario"—both contributing to the misinterpretation of the situation, leading to a tragedy that could have been averted.

After the KAL-007 incident, tensions rose even higher, with Reagan calling the Soviet action a "terrorist act" and "crime against humanity." Gravely concerned that the United States would launch a nuclear attack on the USSR, the Soviets placed their entire nuclear arsenal on maximum alert following the malfunctioning of their early-warning system. The system mistakenly interpreted the sun's reflections on a cloud in the American Midwest as a sign that missiles had been launched. The Soviet missiles were deployed. Aircraft, submarines, and mobile launchers were put on standby, ready for commanders to give the order to launch.

Coincidentally, on November 9, 1983, NATO was getting ready to practice a nuclear launch in a military exercise, Able Archer 83. "In the original scenario (which was later modified), the 1983 exercise was to involve high-level officials, including the secretary of defense and the chairman of the Joint Chiefs of Staff in major roles, with cameo appearances by the president and the vice president.[71] The Kremlin, having received the intelligence stream about NATO's nuclear simulation, went into convulsions, assuming that it was the real thing rather than a practice drill. By the time the Soviets learned about Able Archer 83, the KGB and GRU were on high alert for two years, having been tasked in 1981 by KGB chairman Yuri Andropov and the general secretary of the Soviet Communist Party, Leonid Brezhnev, himself to look for indications of U.S. intentions to launch a nuclear strike on the USSR. The Kremlin's obsessive fear of a surprise nuclear attack by Washington stemmed from the KGB's issuing a computer-generated intelligence estimate, which indicated that the "correlation of world forces" favored dramatically the United States, therefore concluding that the USSR was losing the Cold War. It is in this context that Soviet intelligence—who had initiated a massive clandestine collection program codenamed RYAN (*Raketno-Yadernoe Napadeniye*; "nuclear missile attack" in Russian) to find signposts of U.S. preparations for war with the USSR—saw in the U.S. posture exactly what it had been looking for for a long time. A full-scale simulated release of nuclear weapons by the NATO forces could only mean one thing to the paranoid Soviets—the beginning of nuclear war.

A mass Soviet nuclear attack awaited only an order from Andropov. There was no communication between Moscow and Washington throughout the crisis to clear up the situation. Fortunately, no order was given, and at the conclusion of the NATO exercise on November 11, the threat indicators went down, easing the tension.[72]

War with Russia, including a nuclear one, is no longer a theoretical discussion. A small handful of U.S. military commanders and intelligence analysts within the U.S. national security community understand it. President Trump was certainly concerned enough, judging by his withdrawal from the Intermediate-Range Nuclear Forces Treaty, which Russia has violated. With the treaty scrapped, he authorized the development of U.S. small yield nuclear options to counter Russia's escalate-to-deescalate doctrine.[73] On May 21, 2020, Trump's State Department issued a notice to withdraw the United States from the Open Skies Treaty, which Moscow has been misusing to gain valuable intelligence in preparation for waging war with America.[74] Russia exploited "Open Skies" imagery in support of an aggressive new Russian doctrine of targeting critical infrastructure in the United States and Europe with precision-guided conventional munitions.[75]

Current tensions between Moscow and Washington are not unlike those in 1983. There has been little improvement in each side's understanding of one another's intentions. Russia ascribes the worst possible motives to U.S. leaders, while Washington traditionally dismisses the Kremlin's mindset because it simply doesn't fit into standard North American thinking and culture. We can never rely on the chance of cooler heads' prevailing should a crisis unfold between Russia and the United States. We were often lucky in the past. But luck isn't a strategic concept—only a random set of events. I hope that *Putin's Playbook* has illustrated what such a crisis can lead to, given Russia's prevailing expectation of war with the United States.

To avoid a catastrophe, it is imperative that we understand our strategic opponents. Even if we don't plan on going to war with them, we must remember that war may choose us. Tragically, there is inadequate understanding within the Intelligence Community of how seriously Putin's Russia thinks about and prepares for a kinetic conflict with the United States. This lack of understanding stems directly from the IC's glaring gaps in expertise in Russian doctrine, strategy, and mindset, which in turn is due to an irresponsible absence of the critical skills needed to read, understand, and think in Russian, the way the Russians operate with us. If we are not capable of thinking like the adversary, we will not be able to disrupt his plans and protect the United States. Putin is counting on our ignorance to win.

Epilogue

"I think that if I were to single out one specific group of men, one type, one category, as being the most suspicious, unbelieving, unreasonable, petty, inhuman, sadistic, double-crossing set of bastards in any language, I would say, without any hesitation: 'the people who run counter-espionage departments.' With them, it is no use, having just one story; and especially, not a true story; they automatically disbelieve that. What you must have is a series of stories, so that when they knock the first one down you can bring out the second, and then, when they scrub that out, come up with a third. That way, they think, they are making progress and keep their hands off you, while you gradually find out the story they really want you to tell."

—Eric Ambler, The Light of Day

It was early on a sunny July morning when the three of us—Charlie, one of my "troika" colleagues, and I—boarded an airplane returning from St. Louis back to Washington, D.C. A couple of days before, the government had issued an ███████████████

██

████████████████████████████ Happy to be returning home for
the July 4 weekend to spend time with my husband and kids, I was
anticipating a relaxing flight.

The flight turned out to be completely full, so the three of us were
separated. I was in the aisle seat of the penultimate row. Having followed the stewardess's instructions to everyone to buckle our seat
belts and turn off electronics, I opened up my *Voyennaya Mysl* (*Military Thought*), a professional journal in Russian that I subscribe to
through a cut-out third party company in New York. It is not an easy
read for non-native Russian speakers, and although available to the
public, it contains much information of intelligence value. I enjoyed
reading it in my spare time.

As I was flipping through the articles, reading in Russian, it didn't
occur to me how the image of red stars, photos of men in Soviet military uniforms, and Cyrillic letters on the magazine's cover may or may
not be perceived by my fellow passengers. America is a land of immigrants, and living in the Washington, D.C., area, I often see people
reading newspapers in Chinese, Spanish, and other foreign languages
on the Metro and in other public places. In my daily life, I don't think
about having an accent when I speak English, though I have one. It is
slight, with a touch of British overtones, but no trace of harsh Russian
consonants that many native Russian speakers have. My American-
born children didn't even realize that I had one at all until my daughter's friends asked her, "Why does your Mom have an accent?"

As the airliner began to gain altitude, a male passenger sitting
across the aisle from me in a single seat asked me if I wanted to switch
seats with him. "Sure," I said. I was in a two-seat row, next to someone. I didn't speculate about why someone would prefer sitting with
someone else instead of alone. But I was content with the possibility
of sitting all by myself instead of potentially having to make small

talk with my neighbor. Since we were still climbing altitude, I told the fellow that we had to wait until we were allowed out of our seats before switching.

I noticed that the fellow began fumbling with something in his duffel bag that he had on his lap, even though the flight attendant made the rounds earlier checking if everyone had their carry-on bags safely stowed under the seats. He then took out his mobile phone and, in quick successive moves, took several pictures of the inside of the airplane and of the wings out of both windows. The fellow then turned to me and asked me if I was afraid to fly. I shook my head and said "no." I certainly have done my fair share of flying both for work and on vacation, including across the Atlantic.

He informed me that not only was he unafraid of flying, but he was "excited to fly." He was so excited that he was going to "jump right out of the airplane." I closed my *Military Thought* magazine, looked at him quizzically, and asked, "Why?" He leaned as close as he could, without having to unbuckle his seatbelt, towards me and responded, "Because I am crazy." He took off the dark shades I had just noticed he was wearing, and his eyes directly met mine.

They didn't look right. He did indeed look kind of crazy. A thought crossed my mind: "On drugs?" I then took a good look at the fellow. He seemed tall and athletic; a white man maybe in his early twenties. He wore an all-black, tactical-style, heavy-duty jacket, pants and Gore-Tex boots. He continued to fumble with some gadgets, and perhaps cords, in his dark duffel bag.

Realizing that something was off, I said to him, "Today is not a good day to jump out of the airplane." Confined in a crowded plane and cognizant, particularly as an intelligence officer, of the terror alert, I started to get nervous. Strange behavior on an ascending airplane just after takeoff would alarm anyone, let alone someone like me who was immersed in the threats that confront our country. I looked to see if I could wave to the flight attendant and noticed that she was making her way through the aisle from the front of the airplane towards the back. As she was getting closer, his fumbling with gadgets intensified. He didn't open the bag and take whatever he had in it out to do whatever he wanted to do. He then started strangely touching and pressing the back of the seat in front of him in a specific spot. My mind began to race as I tried to figure out what the fellow could be planning to do.

One thing that was clear is that in order to jump out of the moving airplane, he had to create an opening or a hole in it first. But how? Explosion? Get the door open somehow? Was he going to conduct a cyber intrusion of some sort? Was he planning to somehow commandeer the airplane? I knew that researchers had recently demonstrated the ability to hack into an airplane's electronics and take control over it. My analytic brain began churning out various potential scenarios of what he could do. Then, rather than wracking my brain, I decided simply to take him at his word. He said he wanted to jump out of the airplane. He was busy with something. He must have devised a method to do it. "See something—say something," the government's July 4 admonition flashed through my mind. Time might be of the essence.

I tried to motion the flight attendant and whisper to her, without the guy overhearing me, that there was a problem and that I needed her to move me away so I could tell her what the problem is. She dismissed me, responding that there were no available seats. I tried to indicate that the guy next to me was threatening to jump out of the airplane and may have a way of doing it. But she looked like she was going to walk away. Unsure what he intended to pull off or what he had brought on the airplane, I wanted to get out of his immediate area. I tried to get up and see for myself where I could possibly move and if I could find someone else more astute and cooperative, possibly another flight attendant in the front of the airplane, to alert about a potential problem. The stewardess then shoved me back into my seat and sternly ordered me not to get up. Not understanding, she no doubt perceived me as uncooperative.

When she left, the fellow was continuing to fumble with the duffle bag. I noticed a red light among what looked like gadgets and cords, peaking through the opening. Whatever he was doing, he was trying to look surreptitious about it. Realizing that I couldn't rely on the flight crew's help, I decided to distract the fellow by engaging him in a conversation. I expressed interest in where he was from and what he did for a living. He shoved his driver's license into my face, volunteering that he was forty-one years old, although he looked half that age. He said that he was a truck driver who delivered hazardous materials that could "blow up entire cities." His eyes were burning with glee and madness. He began to recite scores of names of various chemicals he ferried with his truck, most of which I had never heard of. In response to my request, he gave me his email address, which I tried to pass to the stewardess on her next round, hoping to ask if she could possibly check out the fellow's social media to see if he had posted any threats. Not wanting to alert him that I was worried about his intentions and possibly create a disturbance in the air, and not exactly sure of what to do, I quietly inserted the piece of paper with his email written on it in one of my magazines, possibly the Russian-language *Military Thought*, whose cover was filled with Soviet military images, and handed it to her.

Finally, the flight attendant came back and said that she was ready to move me to the front of the airplane. As she was escorting me up front, I asked her if she was taking care of the problem. Certainly, the guy's comments demonstrating his proficiency with "hazardous materials that can wipe out entire cities" were disturbing. For goodness sake, who talks like that on a moving airplane? The flight attendant glanced at me with a vacuous look. I realized that she might be thinking that I am a lunatic. She responded that she was taking care of the problem and left.

In a few minutes, I felt the airplane starting to descend and saw that the flight attendant took her seat in the serving area. I gave a sigh of relief, smiled at her, and mouthed "thank you." I was grateful that she understood me and was indeed taking care of the problem. The airplane was making an emergency landing at the nearest airport.

Little did I know at the time. The flight attendant had concluded that I was a problem too.

If this doesn't sound like a bizarre thriller to you, what transpired next was straight out of Stephen King. And, apparently, I was the main character, a villain. As we were descending, I noticed several police and security vehicles through the window. I pictured how the police officers were going to drag the crazy dude with his duffle bag out of the airplane.

Instead, the minute after we touched the ground and came to a halt, a big, burly, middle-aged police officer appeared in front of me and tersely said, "Let's go." He walked me out of the airplane and men in hazmat suits immediately swarmed around me. I was ordered to take everything out of my pockets and show them my hands. I didn't have anything on me. They searched me and handcuffed me, and then the older police officer put me in the back of a dark SUV. I tried to explain that I was the "good guy" and the "bad guy" was still on the airplane, but he slammed the door and left. I sat there for what seemed like hours, trying to process what had just happened. I was freezing because of the blasting AC and desperately wanted to pee. The handcuffs were hurting my wrists and hands. My hands are small, so I started wiggling my way out the handcuffs so I could knock on the window and tell them that I needed a bathroom break. It then occurred to me that getting myself out of the handcuffs may not be such a good idea, as it could be misinterpreted. Although, who could possibly view me as a threat? I am a slender, 5'2", 101-pound female. But then again, this whole thing was surreal. I wiggled my hands back into the handcuffs. At some point, the older police officer came back. He seemed nicer and asked me to tell him my side of the story.

After I explained what happened, he took the handcuffs off, turned off the AC, and brought in a female officer to escort me to the restroom. She returned me to the police car. My initial shock began to subside and I started playing back the events in my head to see how exactly things got so off track. Sometime later, another officer showed up and introduced himself as a member of the local FBI's counterterrorism task force. He asked, with an air of surprise, what I was doing in the police car. I explained that I was a "blue badge" DIA intelligence officer, and that the flight attendant misidentified me as a threat. The FBI officer told me that the flight attendant had said that I was disruptive on the airplane, causing her to request an emergency landing. He also said that Charlie tried to correct the misunderstanding by telling the police and FBI officers that I was "one of ours." It turned out Charlie had no idea that something abnormal was happening on the airplane until he saw me escorted by police off the airplane. That's how "disruptive" I appeared.

Eventually, the FBI took a statement from me, concluded that I was not the threat that the flight attendant said I was, and told me I was free to go and get on the next flight home. Having searched my carry-on bag and two of my magazines, *Foreign Affairs* in English and *Military Thought* in Russian, the FBI officer returned them. The police officers who were present during the FBI's questioning of the crazy guy said they agreed that he appeared "odd." Although they could not be certain he would not pull off some other threatening act in the future, they had to release him because the FBI counterterrorism taskforce did not find any explosives or any other materials of concern on him or in his luggage. I asked if anyone was planning to do a cyber forensic analysis to see if the airliner's electronics were breached at any point during the flight. I was told "no." The FBI officer apologized for the misunderstanding and what had happened to me, and wished me good luck.

Following DIA protocol, Charlie and I called DIA security and my chain of command and reported the incident. DIA security instructed me to report to their office on Monday morning instead of going to my normal place of duty. On Monday and Tuesday, I was first interviewed by a male special agent at DIA security and a female psychologist about the airplane incident. They both were very nice. They said that they understood what had happened—I was trying to alert the flight crew about a potential threat on the airplane presented by a male passenger. The special agent assured me that everything was going to be resolved quickly, based on his initial assessment, but that I needed to take a psychological test that afternoon. The online test was long, and I guess, given that it was a psychological test, some of the questions were strange. In several instances I had no idea what was being asked. I understood all the words but could not understand the meaning of the question. The psychologist said that I should just pick an answer and not think about it too much.

When I finished the test, she turned the computer screen around, away from me, to check the results. She made a remark indicating that there was something not quite normal on my test results. I didn't worry about it, because this is what often happens after examiners in the Intelligence Community give you a polygraph. The polygrapher tells you that there is an issue of one kind or another that you are reacting to and sends you home "to think about it." Then it turns out that you actually did pass the test. Sometimes, they call you in for a second time, with a different person. And then you pass it with that person—usually, that is. A former colleague was forced out of DIA because he couldn't "pass" a polygraph six times. He was as honest as they come, so I'm not sure what "not passing" means.

Occasionally, you get a real jerk of a polygrapher who accuses you of doing "mental gymnastics" and "employing counter-measures." And you have no idea what they are talking about. So, I asked the psychologist to explain what she meant. She repeated what sounded like some psych-lingo gibberish to me. I said, "okay," not attributing too much importance to it. The agent came in and said that he and the psychologist would complete their report and that I could go back to work.

Thinking that the nightmare thriller events of the past weekend were behind me, I plunged back into my work. I shared with two of my colleagues the bizarre incident on the airplane. Both of them said that it was clear that the flight attendant was reacting to my slight but noticeable accent and the military magazine I was reading in a foreign language that she couldn't understand. Perhaps, I now reflect, it seemed extremely odd to her that someone was handing her a strange foreign magazine with military equipment on the cover and an email address inside it. Still, she had never bothered to talk to me in any detail before deciding to have the pilots land the plane.

After a few days, I was sent to a four-week Russian language course in the unclassified area of the military base where DIA headquarters is located. Out of all the analysts who could use Russian language training, the bureaucrats selected me. As a native speaker of Russian, it wasn't obvious to me why I needed to brush up on my language skills! Another episode straight of out Joseph Heller's *Catch-22*.

Towards the end of the program, I was called out by my division's staff officer, who said that I should collect all my things because I was not going back to class. She teared up as she told me that she had some bad news for me. My security clearance was being pulled and my "blue badge" was being deactivated. She shared that she went through something similar when her security clearance was yanked and she was placed on an extended administrative leave after she couldn't pass several polygraphs. She was smoking nervously. It seemed that her unexpected duty to escort me out of the building brought back some bad memories. She also shared that she was compelled by the DIA to take numerous psychological counseling sessions in order to pass her polygraph. She eventually did pass it, though, and her clearance was restored.

She brought me into the office of the head of DIA security. He was the same guy that my managers were bugging regarding the purported "security-clearance issue" after the CIA lied that I had withdrawn my application to be Deputy NIO for Cyber on the National Intelligence Council at the Office of the Director of National Intelligence. The head of security told me that he was suspending my clearance and sending me on administrative leave.

Several weeks later, I received a notification that my clearance was being revoked based on absurd allegations. The most outrageous charges were that I had a "psychological condition" that could interfere with my work, and that I was under foreign influence and had leanings toward communism. I was stunned.

I initially refused to believe that something this Orwellian could happen in the United States, the country of justice and freedom, in contrast to where I grew up, the USSR. The mental illness accusations sounded so Sovietesque. The Soviets used to round up dissidents and others who didn't agree with socialist and communist ideology and incarcerate them in mental hospitals. The thinking went that if you didn't agree with socialism, you must be a lunatic. Sane people were supposed to be on board with the party line. And if you were not, you must be insane.

Right away, I called the same attorney with whom I consulted when the CIA lied and blocked me from assuming my Deputy NIO for Cyber rotational position at the DNI. The attorney said that he couldn't promise anything, but that he had dealt with many similar clearance issues and that he was going to try to help—for a hefty fee, of course. He was supposed to be the best in the security clearance field. My husband and I are a family of modest means, but we decided that it was very much worth it to spend what we had to in order to restore my job, my income, and most importantly, my career. You see, without a security clearance, I was going to lose my job at DIA, and I could not get an outside job in my field of expertise. And once a clearance is revoked, it is extremely hard, and in many cases impossible, to restore it. It becomes a chicken-and-egg problem: you need a security clearance to get hired in your field, but you need someone to hire you in order to try and restore your clearance. Besides, my job as an intelligence officer was my calling. I wasn't about to let the apparatchiks take it away from me. So, I hired the purported best attorney in the field to join me in my fight for justice.

In order to regain my DIA position and restore some dignity, my husband and I ended up spending tens of thousands of dollars both in legal fees and to obtain independent psychological evaluations of me, which the attorney recommended. After an extensive evaluation, two prominent and highly experienced psychiatrists refuted the dubious assertions against me by the junior DIA psychologist, who was not a clinician. One of these psychiatrists was also a retired U.S. Air Force officer who had evaluated nuclear missiliers at U.S. Strategic Air Command, STRATCOM's predecessor, before they went on duty to guard U.S. nuclear weapons. This unassailable witness was appalled at what he saw as DIA's abuse of power and attempt to weaponize the security clearance and psychological evaluation process.

Eleven of my senior DIA colleagues stood up for me by writing character witness testimonies to DIA security. I learned in these letters just how much my colleagues valued me. Four of my supervisors directly disputed the reckless allegations of DIA's Soviet-style apparatchiks. I almost teared up when I read the following testimony from one of my intel partners:

> Based on my observations and experience of working with her over many years, I firmly believe that Ms. Koffler is a loyal, trustworthy American with high moral standards and outstanding character. The basis for her actions and her outlook on life lies in her solid faith in God, her love of family, and her steadfast belief in the United States of America as the best—and most honorable—nation on earth. Ms. Koffler has always taken her oath of office seriously and has proven repeatedly that she is the type of person who is worthy of the highest trust that this nation can bestow. In my sincere opinion, it is in the best interest of the United States of America that she retains her access to classified information and that she continues to serve as an intelligence analyst in the Defense Intelligence Agency.

I had an outpouring of personal support from my colleagues. They invited me to team lunches, birthday parties, and retirement parties. They did the same thing for me as we did to support the DIO for Russia, Michael, whom DIA threw out the previous year based on unsubstantiated allegations of being in cahoots with the Russians. Charlie gathered us then and told us that, as someone who had served with Mike for many years running the risky HUMINT operations in Potsdam, he could assure us that Mike didn't do the things that DIA was alleging he did. Charlie liked to say that "we don't leave the wounded on the battlefield."

I fought with everything I had to get my job back, hoping that "cooler heads" would prevail at the DIA, as one of my colleagues put it—to no avail. The airplane incident involving the stewardess mistakenly identifying me as a threat seemed to be only a pretext for the DIA apparatchiks to get rid of me. Eventually, DIA dismissed the foreign influence allegation—there was nothing they could grab onto that could stick. But DIA security would not turn over to my attorney the results of the psychological test, which supposedly indicated that I was a lunatic. It was clear that DIA apparatchiks did not want an independent professional evaluation of their bogus test results. So, DIA refused to restore my security clearance and my job. My attorney found out that there was one person on the panel of "deciders" who absolutely couldn't stand the idea of my returning to DIA.

I hired another attorney, who, after also trying to get my clearance reinstated, said that the administrative process had been exhausted and that if I wanted him to litigate it would cost a minimum of $60,000. Other attorneys were telling me that the government knows that an ordinary American has a limited amount of financial resources, and the bureaucrats deliberately draw out the process, simply waiting until you run out of money. It's a strategy of attrition warfare. During a consultation with yet another attorney, who had won an EEO discrimination case for a pregnant DIA intel officer, she expressed her indignation with the DIA and DIA's inspector general. She said to me, "Not a day goes by when I don't receive a call from a DIA employee who feels discriminated against." She said that many DIA employees feel helpless because the DIA inspector general's office is not as independent as it is supposed to be. In most cases, the IG sides with DIA management. This was quite a revelation.

When our family retirement accounts were wiped out, my husband asked me to give up the fight. It was not only destroying our finances but also our family. He and my best friend told me that, as a free thinker and person of action, I was never meant to be a government employee, as painful as it was for me to lose the job I loved so dearly and thought of as my true calling.

It took me years to recover and get firmly on my feet again. I found it deeply ironic that having fled the oppressive Soviet Union, I now faced in my new homeland—which prides itself on being the land of freedom and justice—the same type of government abuse of the power by American "commissars."

Writing *Putin's Playbook* has been part of my transition to a new life, a process of getting used to my new identity as an author and intelligence expert in Russian doctrine and strategy, as opposed to an intelligence officer. It is similar to my former role, except instead of digging through and making sense of secrets, I now mine vast amounts of open source information of intelligence value in order to make independent analytic judgments. I will always be an intelligence officer at heart, though.

I hope that, despite the significant redactions from the Defense Intelligence Agency, readers of this book have enjoyed and learned from the first independent analytic product I've written in my new role as an author. Despite my strong nonconcurrence with the redactions, which I expressed to the DIA reviewers, who asserted that the material contained "classified information," I had no choice but to accept the censorship if I wanted U.S. government approval to publish *Putin's Playbook*. The lengthy prepublication review, which took more than twice as long as the promised sixty days, had already jeopardized the publication of my book and resulted in a six-month delay. So, I felt pressured to comply with the government's orders. I have preserved DIA's excisions so the readers can see for themselves that the heavy-handed censorship displayed here is more consistent with Putin's playbook than with the norms of a democratic society.

How Washington Can Mitigate Falling Prey to Putin's Manipulations and Reduce the Possibility of a Nuclear Dogfight with Russia

"He, thinking that I was about to kill him in self-defense, was about to kill me in self-defense, so I had to kill him in self-defense."
—Thomas C. Schelling, *The Strategy of Conflict*

On November 2, 2019, President Trump attended an unorthodox mixed martial arts (MMA) bout at the Madison Square Garden in New York City. The foul-mouthed, pot-smoking, vegan Californian Nate Diaz was clashing with Floridian Jorge "Gamebred" Masvidal, who had emulated Al Pacino's character in *Scarface* by wearing a custom-made mobster-style white suit and red shirt at the UFC 244 press conference prior. The two gangsters were preparing to fight for the newly created "BMF" belt, an acronym for an offensive phrase. The Miami "gangsta" bloodied the Californian cannabis-lover to the point that the cage-side doctor called a stoppage in the fourth round, prompting harassment and even death threats from frustrated fans.

I confess to a great interest in MMA, just like former President Trump, whom Jorge Masvidal publicly praised at UFC 244 for being the "baddest MFer"—a compliment.

Why does MMA attract me? Chiefly because it epitomizes the nexus of intelligence, warfare, and strategy. Attaining victory in an MMA fight requires a deep understanding of your opponent. The bout, which can last anywhere from a few seconds to fifteen minutes (twenty-five minutes for championship fights), is a culmination of months and years of extreme physical and mental training, scrupulous study, analysis of your rival's technique, and careful development of your own strategy. Brute force is not a guarantee of victory in mixed martial arts. You must understand how your strengths and weaknesses stack up against your opponent's.

Is he a striker, wrestler, or grappler? Orthodox or south-paw stance? How does he win his fights? By "finishing" his opponents or by the judges' decision? Does he finish his opponents by a knock-out or submission? Does he possess endurance? What was his disposition during the stare-downs? Is he intimidated psychologically? Determining answers to these and related questions helps the fighter assess his opponent, estimate how his opponent will fight, and develop a strategy to beat him. Without proper reconnaissance, you cannot understand your rival, diminishing your chances of winning. Our intelligence professionals and foreign policy decision-makers engage in (or should be engaged in) a remarkably similar process to prevail over America's adversaries, competitors, and even transactional partners.

In December 2019, the *Washington Post* published the so-called *Afghanistan Papers*. These are confidential government documents generated because of the U.S. government's effort to understand the causes of its failed eighteen-year war in Afghanistan. Two thousand pages of impressions by four hundred direct participants in the war, ranging from generals to diplomats, lay bare the stark contrast between the real situation on the ground and the mischaracterizations and outright lies presented by government officials to Americans for almost two decades. Candid admissions by these insiders revealed that the simple reasons for Washington's abysmal performance in Afghanistan was its complete lack of understanding of the region and absence of knowledge of Afghan culture and history. "We were devoid of a fundamental understanding of Afghanistan—we didn't know what we were doing," Douglas Lute, a three-star Army general, who served as the White House's Afghan war czar during the Bush and Obama administrations, told government interviewers in 2015, "What are we trying to do here? We didn't have the foggiest notion of what we were undertaking."[1]

Sadly, this unvarnished evaluation of the Washington establishment's foreign affairs "expertise" by Ambassador Lute, whom I had an opportunity to brief on Russia in 2013 as he was assuming his Brussels-based posting as the U.S. permanent representative to NATO, doesn't apply solely to Afghanistan. Our Russia policy and national security communities are similarly full of uninformed, albeit sometimes well-meaning, bureaucrats and ideologues. Anyone who dares to challenge their long-standing groupthink analytic line or policy prescription is a threat to their self-appointed "expert" title and cushy nine-to-five government job with "extra" benefits. Sitting agreeably at your desk on your way to retirement so you can draw another paycheck in your post-government career—in addition to a pension from Uncle Sam—is a much safer choice than rocking the boat by crafting or approving an intelligence warning that runs counter to your boss's or policy "customer's" preconceived notions about your intelligence target. Washington think tanks and "Beltway bandit" consulting firms are bursting at the seams with "experts" who mucked things up for America by pursuing "pie-in-the-sky" policy ambitions and implementing wrongheaded warfighting strategies. Few, if any, of these "professionals," as they like to call themselves, are held accountable for creating crisis after crisis across the globe, including Washington's dangerously hostile relationship with Moscow. Our policy elites' incompetence poses the risk of plunging the United States into all kinds of versions of hell with Russia, including nuclear Armageddon.

It is time to step back and take stock of the post–Cold War relationship between the United States and Russia. How much have we learned from our policies of continuous "resets" with the Kremlin? How much have we improved our understanding of the drivers for

Putin's behavior, the motivations behind Moscow's international posture, and the "otherness" of the Russian mindset? These are core intelligence questions needing an answer beyond simply dismissing Putin as a shallow megalomaniac driven by schadenfreude. Without answers to these questions, intelligence analysts cannot accurately assess why Russia is building the weapons and non-kinetic capabilities or conducting the military maneuvers that it is. The policy community cannot devise strategies on how to deter or respond to the Kremlin's unwanted behavior. And Pentagon planners cannot craft warfighting strategies and defense policies to deter or win a conflict with Russia.

Labeling Putin irrational, reckless, or delusional may be satisfying intellectually for some, but it will not bring Crimea back to Ukraine, return Abkhazia and South Ossetia to Georgia, or reverse the effects of Russia-backed Bashar al-Assad's chemical attacks in Syria. As I wrote in April 2021 for an opinion piece in *The Hill*, "Calling [him] a 'killer' will not scare Russia's master spy, whelped in a fear-equals-respect culture. If anything, the name-calling will help Putin maintain his unpredictable, mysterious, and ruthless image, which is part of his attraction for Russians, who don't think like Americans." As *Putin's Playbook* has shown, "we are dealing with a nation with a bloody historic experience of violent intimidation, poisonings, ice-axe attacks, and war-torn devastation. Having a strong, if brutal, leader who can stand up to the West is viewed by many Russians as an asset."[2] Let's be honest for a change. Russia could have militarily crushed both Ukraine in 2014 and Georgia in 2008 if it wanted to. It could have sent Estonia into complete darkness when it launched a twenty-two-day long cyber-attack in 2007 targeting commercial and government networks, including such vital services as online banking, to express its displeasure with the relocation of a Soviet-era monument in Tallinn. Moscow's covert-influence operation during the 2016 presidential elections could have included devastating cyberattacks on U.S. networks, rather than merely cyber intrusions and social media manipulations. But Russia did none of that. While Putin does take risks, these risks are highly calculated and based on deep studies of Russia's opponents. He measures how far he can go; he is strategic, not suicidal.

Although many in the Washington establishment are angry because they falsely believe the Russians elected the (wrong) U.S. president in 2016, America's leadership class must find a productive, or at least nondestructive, way of dealing with the former KGB operative. Putinism is here to stay beyond 2024, when Putin's last fourth term expires (probably until 2036). Although Russia's uber-presidential governmental model and authoritarianism, or *yedinonachaliye*, vests significant executive power in one person, Putin alone could not have orchestrated the constitutional machinations bolstering his power over the years. It is only possible with the enablement of the extensive web of plutocrats from the power ministries, oligarchs from quasi-state industry conglomerates such as GazProm and Rosneft, and the *siloviki* ("securocrats") from the intelligence services.

This highly personalized "power vertical," considered dictatorial and corrupt by the West, has for centuries been the Russian model of governing, largely with the tacit consent of the Russian people. Even Yeltsin's Russia, for example, which starry-eyed Westerners saw as the promised land of a budding democracy, was ruled by a tight group of influential advisors ranging from close family members to business tycoons who hovered around Yeltsin's daughter, Tatyana Dyachenko. They were a circle of insiders referred to by the mafia-like name, "the Family." Let us be reminded of the famous quote by French philosopher and counterrevolutionary Joseph de Maistre, who advocated absolute rule by the sovereign, aided by a public executioner to cure social chaos: "Every nation gets the government it deserves."

Saving Russians from themselves by engineering democratic structures is foolish and naive in a country whose entire history demonstrates preoccupation with state control over its citizens combined with an intractable fear of foreign invasion and interference. It is a dangerous experiment that has brought us into a non-kinetic war, or Cold War part two, with the Kremlin that has the potential, at any moment, to escalate into a military and nuclear conflict. Not only did these ignorant policies not turn Russia into a land of liberty, they made America less safe and brought disorder to our internal politics and domestic life.

We are not learning from these failures or putting America's security first. Instead, we are trying to ensure the well-being of distant Eurasian peoples, only repeating our mistakes. In Ukraine, we are pumping in foreign aid to one of the most corrupt countries in the world in a misguided attempt to turn another oligarchic system into a beacon of liberty and symbol of prosperity. We are even sending highly sophisticated anti-tank Javelin missiles to Ukrainian forces, risking further escalation with Russia—policies that please our consciences but will not stem Russian aggression or lower hostilities. Members of Congress are even willing to go so far as to impeach, try, and remove our president from office over Ukraine—a president whose only sin was a patriotic desire to prevent American taxpayers' hard-earned dollars from falling into the corrupt hands of Ukrainian apparatchiks and oligarchs bred in the same 1990s tradition of pillaging Russian oligarchs. We have seen this Russian movie before. Do Americans really need another decade-long sequel in Kiev?

The same establishment "experts" who ignored the festering Russian threat until Moscow's annexation of Crimea and Putin's intervention in the 2016 elections are now trying to sell us the snake oil that Ukraine is part of American vital security interests. Is America's safety, security, territorial integrity, and long-term survivability even remotely reliant on Ukraine? Either the "experts" are ignorant themselves, or they think that Americans are ignorant or easily manipulable into another foreign policy fiasco by the do-gooders, who seem to be concerned more about Ukraine's sovereignty than our own. These same well-wishers have created an illegal immigrant crisis on our southern border, threatening fellow Americans' safety and security. No, I'll say it: Ukraine is not a vital security interest of the United States. Stability in Eurasia and Russia, which has the world's largest nuclear arsenal outside of America, is though.

Call me a selfish American chauvinist, but I care less about divided, corrupt Ukrainian officials and more about the security and stability of our homeland and the lives of our military's sons and daughters. I do care passionately about freedom because I lived without it. But I have also learned that freedom can only come from within a nation, wanted and accepted, along with all its responsibilities and downsides, by most of the citizens. People must want freedom more than they want stability or bread. The agony of having to make this choice as well as the true nature of the enigmatic Russian mindset was revealed by Fyodor Dostoyevsky, revered in Russia, in *The Brothers Karamazov*:

> There is no knowledge that could supply them with bread as long as they remain free. So, in the end, they will lay their freedom at our feet and say to us: "Enslave us, but feed us!" And they will finally understand that freedom and the assurance of daily bread for everyone are two incompatible notions that could never coexist! They will also discover that men can never be free because they are weak, corrupt, worthless, and restless.

In the aftermath of the 2020 election, few Americans realize that stepping on the path to socialism eventually means having to make a choice between bread and freedom. Furthermore, socialism is not only about giving bread to everyone; it is perforce the state's controlling everyone's desires, thus eliminating any sense of freedom.

In *Putin's Playbook*, I have provided a warning to the American people that Russia is preparing for war with America, which Moscow believes is inevitable. I also describe Putin's war plan and toolbox of statecraft instruments, which he believes will assure Russia's victory in a kinetic war or in a prolonged strategic destabilization campaign against America. This warning was not provided to American citizens, despite the U.S. government's knowledge of the escalating Russian threat. This failure to warn left Americans exposed to covert psychological manipulations by the Kremlin to distort our beliefs about who the real adversary is. Having lost trust in their government, Americans have turned the fight inward, blaming the capitalist system, their fellow Americans, and their former president for the devastating domestic disorder and dysfunction that have beset our country. This is the classic outcome of Russia's reflexive-control theory outlined in the playbook—distort the enemy's perception of reality, leading him to self-destruction.

The strategic deception and ideological subversion strategy that Soviet defector Yuri Bezmenov warned us about in the 1980s took root in America. We are fighting each other too much rather than Russia (or China); trying to uproot our own system and unseat our democratically elected leaders and adopt the socialist model that led to the destruction of the USSR. We are voting for radical leftists whom Marx and Lenin would have endorsed as candidates or useful idiots.

In the meantime, the same type of American apparatchiks who banned Bezmenov—despite his prescient warnings—from entering the United States from Canada after helping him defect from his intelligence posting in India, destroyed my career in American intelligence. The deep-state "experts" even used similar tactics on me as they did on Bezmenov forty-five years ago, as well as on other analysts whose views didn't align with their groupthink. The CIA put Bezmenov on the "no entry to the United States" list because of his past membership in the Communist Party of the Soviet Union, which was a requirement for being a Soviet intelligence officer. The DIA forced me out of my job as an intelligence officer by accusing me of having communist sympathies and having a mysterious mental illness that would make my analysis susceptible to bias. Other DIA analysts with Russian analytic expertise were fired, reassigned, or otherwise forced out of their positions between 2014 and the end of 2016. One was accused of mishandling classified information and spying for the Russians. Another "failed" multiple polygraphs (which is unsettling, because every time it was a random, unsubstantiated issue raised by a speculative polygrapher, ranging from espionage to terrorism to sabotage of IT systems). Yet another was grabbed at a military base, handcuffed, and accused of espionage. I personally know these three officers. They are competent intelligence officers and patriotic Americans, two of whom served in the military and risked their lives working the Russian target.

The accusations of communist leanings against me and other former Russians are absurd and illogical. No one who survived communism would be in favor of this atrocious and oppressive system—not even Putin. Forty-five years ago, Bezmenov spoke passionately about the corrupt and inhumane communist system to American audiences. Raised in an anti-communist family, married to an anti-communist American, I don't even teach my American-born children the Russian language. Both Bezmenov and I tried to warn the U.S. government of the hostile Russian intentions towards America. DIA's accusations against me were irrational. In the eyes of my accusers, I was either a hard-core communist super-spy who

penetrated the Intelligence Community only to warn the government about Putin's war plans or a lunatic whose delusions about
the Russian threat found their way into analytic reports. Aren't
these accusations mutually exclusive? What is the logic? Obviously,
these were just tactics the bureaucracy often deploys to get rid of
employees who are not marching in lockstep with the prevailing
analytic line and policy posture.

What the bureaucracy did not want to hear from me or refused
to believe five to ten years ago is accepted fact now. Russia does want
to reverse the outcome of the Cold War by restoring its superpower
influence. Putin does have hostile intentions toward America. Having intervened in the 2016 and 2020 elections, he has shown that he
will continue repeating his tricks: it turns out that Russia really
should be America's top security concern, a fact articulated not too
long ago by top Obama- and Trump-administration intelligence and
security officials, including former secretary of defense Mark Esper.
Additionally, in March 2021, General Glen VanHerck, commander
of NORAD/USNORTHCOM, stated that "Russia…remains the most
acute challenge to our homeland defense mission" and warned that
it is "rehears[ing] strikes on our homeland."[3] The catastrophic 2020
SolarWinds cyberattack on numerous critical U.S. agencies and cor-
porations, reported only in January 2021,[4] and the Ukraine crisis of
April 2021[5] prove the general's point—the same one made in *Putin's
Playbook*—that Putin's Russia is on the move, in exactly the ways he
promised it would be. No more laughing you out of the room, the
way Barack Obama did to Mitt Romney back in 2012 when the
Republican presidential candidate said that Russia was America's biggest geopolitical foe. At last the establishment has coalesced around
a different analytic line that used to be anathema to "reset"-hopeful,
kumbaya-singing democracy promoters. No longer are there biases,
delusions, or foreign influence or communist sympathies, as alleged

by my faceless, anonymous accusers at DIA. For Trump, it was "No obstruction. No collusion." It was all hoaxes and witch hunts created by the deep-state operatives to silence and destroy unwanted opponents. Unlike former president Trump, however, I do not have the resources or influence to get back the career that I loved.

By publishing *Putin's Playbook* as it is, I am taking the significant risk of incurring the Washington security establishment's wrath. Having witnessed the government unleashing the unlimited power of the state against my former boss, DIA director and American patriot General Michael Flynn, I have no illusions about the level of further destruction that U.S. government apparatchiks can do to me and my family. It is common knowledge among intelligence and security professionals that the government can find numerous ways to silence and retaliate against former federal employees who are critical of the bureaucracy's incompetence. There are myriad ways that government apparatchiks can weaponize the various government processes against an individual. We have seen them weaponize the FISA surveillance powers against Carter Page, an American citizen and former foreign policy advisor for presidential candidate Trump.

But my America-loving, anti-communist Russian parents raised me to speak truth to power, even if the choice is between bread and freedom. My blessed mother also believed that if there was a country where justice existed, it was America. And that's why she and my father made sacrifices that many Americans can't understand to send me to one of the top Moscow universities to study English so that I could eventually find my way to the land of freedom.

The government's reaction to *Putin's Playbook* will determine whether it can stomach constructive criticism and is willing to change its ways and improve its strategic competence, at least regarding Russian strategy or whether the national security bureaucracy will choose to continue concealing its responsibility for its wrongheaded Russia policies and for the failure to protect Americans from, or at least warn them about, Putin's 2016 cyber-enabled active-measure attack.

Sadly, I have learned that under American democracy, just like under Soviet and Russian autocracy, the government bureaucrats don't like their failures exposed, as shown by the Vietnam-era *Pentagon Papers* and the more recent *Afghanistan Papers*.[6] Experience shows that the federal "executioners" will go to great lengths to wield punishment against those who choose not to play their hide-and-seek games.

It is time to pause and make course corrections in our relationship with the Kremlin. To do so, I offer five recommendations to our government officials who devise our Russia strategy and interface with Moscow leaders.

First, really know your target. Study it. Don't expect Russians to think and behave like Americans. They don't, and they won't. Listen to your intelligence briefers—the competent ones who briefed Romney in 2012. If you are an intelligence briefer, develop competence by learning the language and doing in-country field work. You will then be able not only to answer questions about who, what, when, and how, but also, and most importantly, why and what's next.

In this regard, ironically, we can learn from the Russians. Since the end of the Cold War, Russia has been able to outfox America by doing the homework, studying its "main enemy" (*glavnyi protivnik*). Since the creation of the USSR, Soviet and now Russian leaders have been preoccupied with the question "Who/Whom?" or *Kto/Kogo*? (pronounced as *kto/kovo*), which means, "Who will beat whom?" In Russia's dialectical view of the world, the country is in a perpetual deadly confrontation with America, which Moscow sees as an existential threat to be eroded. Because Russia cannot compete with the United States on merit due to its inefficient economic system with a socialist legacy, it must rely on various tricks to subvert or otherwise undermine our homeland. Studying America and the American psyche helps

Moscow figure out which tools in the toolbox are more likely to deliver the most devastating blow without causing U.S. retaliation or even Washington's knowledge of who is to blame for the wreckage.

Second, armed with the knowledge of your strategic opponent, set realistic expectations, based on the art of the possible, with security and stability being the overarching goal. America and Russia will never become BFFs, but it doesn't mean that they cannot be transactional parties. Putin is a pragmatic character. The successor whom Putin will certainly handpick by 2024, the way that Yeltsin selected him, will adopt the same approach. It will serve them well if U.S. leaders abandon an ideological approach in favor of a pragmatic and purely transactional modus operandi with Moscow. Lecturing Russia about its domestic issues or demonizing Putin or his successor, even if he turns out to be a bombastic buffoon like Vladimir Zhirinovsky, would only lead to further deterioration in the relationship.

There are areas of collaboration, albeit extremely limited, with nuclear security and non-proliferation being the most critical. There is precedent of collaboration in the counterterrorism area with Moscow's warning U.S. intelligence about the Tsarnaev brothers who staged the bombings during the 2013 Boston Marathon.[7] According to a 2017 disclosure by the Kremlin, U.S. intelligence, shared by the CIA with Russia, helped the Russians prevent an unspecified terror attack in St. Petersburg.[8]

Direct military-to-military cooperation is critical to lowering the probability of an unintended kinetic conflict. Service members, even from diverse cultures, have a way of relating to one another that civilians often do not. A former NSA colleague, who was an Air Force officer and flew long-range flights at the height of the Cold War, told me the following story. Soviet and American pilots regularly escorted each another into international airspace close to Russia or the United States if either breached the other's air-defense identification zone border (ADIZ). They would fly so close that they could see each other in the cockpit. Americans would stick pages from pornographic magazines to their warplane's windows, causing the Soviet pilots to laugh and high five toward them. Military guys and gals who stand ready when ordered to drop a couple thousand pounds of destructive munitions on the opponent or unleash nuclear ICMBs to decapitate the enemy's leadership know how to maintain a cool head and a good sense of humor when tensions are high. Sadly, there is no such mutual joking today when American fighter jets escort the Russian bombers that breach the North American ADIZ. It is way too serious and "professional" now, my Cold Warrior friend noted, with irony.

Third, stop ignoring the threat by politicizing the Russia issue. From the Mueller investigation, we learned that no American citizens conspired with Moscow operatives to "fix" the 2016 election results. It is time to move on from the fake "Trump-Putin collusion" narrative. As painful as it may be to admit, it is now clear that American intelligence and law enforcement were duped by the Russian tricksters. Worse, some rogue elements used Russian *dezinformatsiya* to try to unseat a sitting president!

Consistent with reflexive-control game theory, once the FBI and the IC fell into Putin's trap, they continued fomenting the chaos and disorder in Washington and across America by broadcasting that the Russians had infected social media by hacking DNC emails and by releasing email correspondence that the Russians knew would inflame Americans. Endless investigations, improper surveillance of U.S. citizens, and the entrapment of General Flynn that resulted in his firing created dysfunction that surely exceeded Putin's expectation. We were doing it to ourselves. Now it is time to clean up the wreckage, hold the incompetent and the malicious to account—so they cannot repeat this—and move on with putting our house in order. We have our own freedom and democracy to protect, rather than worrying about Ukraine's and Russia's.

Fourth, don't expect quick results. Americans think in hours and days, while Russians think in decades and centuries. Growing up under socialism, we waited years for a landline phone to be installed and to be able to purchase a car, and decades to obtain a separate, single-family apartment, as opposed to a communal flat where multiple families shared a tiny kitchen and a "no-toilet-paper" bathroom. We even had a joke about a Soviet man who tried to schedule installation of a phone in his apartment. When given a date by the government ten years from that day, he asked what time of the day the appointment was. "Why do you care what time," said the government bureaucrat, "it is ten years away." "Well," replied the Soviet man, "the plumber will be coming at 2:00 p.m. on that day, so I want to make sure the appointments don't overlap." The candidates who in the 2020 presidential election advocated socialist changes in the United States will not share such jokes with Americans.

Given such disparity in Russian and American time frames, patience is well-advised for Americans charged with Russia policy and strategy. Even if no other goal is achievable in the Russian-American relationship in the near term, de-escalating the crisis in the relationship is essential.

Fifth, prepare for a fight and have a war plan ready. Cultivating a transactional relationship with Moscow and trying to decrease tensions doesn't mean appeasing Putin and the Kremlin or establishing a relationship of trust. There is no such thing as trust when it comes to the Russian mentality, especially among state leaders. Russia does not adhere to the Western precepts of *pacta sunt servanda* ("agreements must be kept"). In fact, Vladimir Lefebvre, another Russian "runaway" to America, warned in the 1980s of the Soviet reflexive-control game theory, used to this day by the Russian General Staff, where the Soviets and Russians adhere to a completely different ethical system than the one dominating American and Western mentality. While the American ethical system mostly excludes "compromise between good and evil, even as a means of achieving good ends," under the Russian ethical system, the opposite is true. According to Lefebvre, the Russians welcome compromise between good and evil as a method of achieving good ends but are uncompromising in confrontations with their opponents. These cultural differences between the two countries make understanding between them difficult, since Moscow and Washington are not playing by the same ethics rules.[9]

"Don't trust your own father," my dad admonished my sister and me as he was trying to raise us in a way that would allow us to function in the Soviet socialist system. This meant that the corrupt, brutal, and oppressive government system sometimes forced children to turn on their parents and parents on their children. My late mother believed that escape from the totalitarian socialist hell was the only way to avoid the agonizing choice between bread and freedom. You will not hear from the proponents of socialism about the public executioners and psychological *komissars* who are determined to re-engineer your natural instincts by controlling your behavior. Socialists and communists are hell-bent on creating hierarchies of power to replace hierarchies of competence that are built into the capitalist system, which embraces the natural desire to compete, pursue knowledge, and strive for dignity and freedom.

Putin will continue implementing his playbook of strategic destabilization and ideological subversion of America to protect Russia from the "American threat." Here's an analytic assessment by a Kremlin-affiliated think tank of "International Threats" (*Mezhdunarodnye Ugrozy*) from 2018: "The [United States] will simultaneously weaken and dismember the rest of the world, and first of all, Big Eurasia. This strategy is pursued by the [United States] regardless which conservative or liberal administration occupies the White House or whether there is consensus regarding this policy among the elites or not. The only difference is how closely and steadfastly this course of action is pursued and which measures are adopted to make this goal a reality."[10]

My lasting fear is that Putin may cross the threshold of America's patience and resolve. He is convinced that Russia can outescalate America to win the conflict because Washington doesn't have the guts to stop Moscow's moves. In the end, the Kremlin may instead push us to the brink of cyber, space, or even nuclear Armageddon. In such a scenario, we need a solid plan that is based on a deep understanding of Russia and Putin's strengths, shortcomings, and hot buttons. What we know from George Kennan's insights is that Soviet power did "not take unnecessary risks." He said: "Impervious to [the] logic of reason, it is highly sensitive to logic of force."[11] I believe Kennan's assessment still applies to Russian leaders, including Putin.

Many established "experts" will reject my recommendations because they don't fit into the binary mentality of bureaucrats, which categorizes Russia as either a friend or a foe. It is also too much for government analysts to accept that Russia is preparing for war because Moscow has concluded that Washington seeks its destruction. It is also difficult to wrap your brain around Putin's "non-war" war that he wages in what the U.S. Army calls the "gray zone" between war and peace, undeclared, by way of cyber and information warfare, non-destructive counter-space methods, covert influence, and other non-kinetic means. How do you respond to it? I hope that *Putin's Playbook* provides a foundational knowledge of the Russian mindset and unique psychology of its leadership, allowing our American leaders to develop counterstrategies and de-escalation plans and avoid all-out war with this highly sophisticated, militarily dangerous, and security-obsessed strategic opponent.

Acknowledgments

I am most grateful to Regnery's president, Tom Spence, and former president, Marji Ross, for letting a first-time author write a book for their renowned publishing house. I am very thankful to my development editor, Dr. Stephen Thompson of Thompson Publications, for his excellent work and tremendous patience, to my amazing literary agent, Claire Gerus of Gerus Publishing, for her tireless efforts helping to shape the book proposal into a winning product, and to vice president and executive editor at Regnery Harry Crocker for believing in my proposed book. I am also thankful to my copy editor, Tadeusz Wójcik, publicist Lauren McCue, and to everyone else at Regnery who worked on this project.

It takes more than a village to write a book. Since life doesn't stop while an author is writing the book, someone else has to step up to help take care of "life stuff." I am grateful to my sister, Alyonka, and brother-in-law, Carlos Fonseca, to my in-law family, Danny and Lauren O'Neill and Jon and Annabelle Koffler, and to my incredible mother-in-law, Dr. Sandra Koffler, for her love and support. My dear friends Kate May, Tamiko and Patrick Smith, Judy Bowles, and godparents Ken and Carol de Graffenreid deserve enormous thanks for their love, encouragement, and all kinds of other help. I am very grateful to Dr. Mary Ortiz of Oakcrest School and Mr. Alvaro de Vicente of The Heights School for their many kindnesses. These schools are beacons of hope amidst our decaying educational system. I am hugely appreciative of the generosity of Mark Mejia and Linda Kintz of the Kintz-Mejia Academy of Ballet and Barry Neff of Capital Gymnastics National Training Center. There are not any finer institutions for training children in these disciplines.

A very special thank you goes to my husband and best friend, Keith Koffler, for keeping the family going and motivating me to finish the book, and to my children, Adam and Ariela, for their love and understanding. Ivan Koffler deserves special mention for his able assistance and his support. No words can express my gratitude to my late mother Valentina Pisikina, who for some unknown reason raised me with the idea that I would eventually go live in America, and to my father Vladimir Pisikin, who taught me resilience and to always move forward, even if I had to "step on dead bodies." None of this would have been possible, of course, without the Great Creator's aligning the stars in perfect (albeit not always apparent to me!) harmony. I feel blessed.

Notes

Author's Introduction

1. Robert S. Mueller, *The Mueller Report: The Final Report of the Special Counsel into Donald Trump, Russia, and Collusion* (New York: Skyhorse Publishing, 2019).

2. Jordan Fabian, "Trump Declares 'Game Over' on Mueller Investigation with 'Game of Thrones' Image," *The Hill*, April 18, 2019, https://thehill.com/homenews/administration/439496-trump-declares-game-over-on-mueller-investigation-with-game-of.

3. «Путин об итогах расследования Мюллера: гора родила мышь», Коммерсантъ (*Kommersant*), April 9, 2019, https://www.*Kommersant*.ru/doc/3938735 (in Russian).

4. «Песков сравнил расследование Мюллера с поиском черной кошки в темной комнате», Ведомости (*Vedomosti*), March 25, 2020, https://www.vedomosti.ru/politics/news/2019/03/25/797295-kreml-myullera (in Russian).

5. Mueller, *The Mueller Report*, 38.

6. *Intelligence Community Assessment: Assessing Russian Intelligence Activities and Intentions in Recent U.S. Elections* (National Intelligence Council: January 6, 2017), ICA 2017-01D, https://www.dni.gov/files/documents/ICA_2017_01.pdf.

7. Morgan Chalfant, "Former CIA Director: Don't Call Russian Election Hacking 'Act of War,'" *The Hill*, April 11, 2017, https://thehill.com/

policy/cybersecurity/328344-former-cia-director-dont-call-russian-election-hacking-act-of-war.

8.   "Russian National Charged with Interfering in U.S. Political System,"
     Office of Public Affairs, U.S. Department of Justice, October 19, 2018,
     https://www.justice.gov/opa/pr/russian-national-charged-
     interfering-us-political-system; United States of America v. Elena
     Alekseevna Khusyaynova, 1:18-MJ-464, U.S. District Court for the
     Eastern District of Virginia, September 28, 2018.

9.   Julian E. Barnes and Adam Goldman, "F.B.I. Warns of Russian
     Interference in 2020 Race and Boosts Counterintelligence
     Operations," *New York Times*, April 26, 2019, https://www.nytimes.
     com/2019/04/26/us/politics/fbi-russian-election-interference.html;
     *Intelligence Community Assessment: Foreign Threats to the 2020 US
     Federal Elections* (National Intelligence Council: March 10, 2021),
     ICA 2020-00078D, https://www.intelligence.gov/assets/
     documents/702%20Documents/declassified/ICA-declass-16MAR21.
     pdf.

10. Scott Wilson, "Obama Dismisses Russia as 'Regional Power' Acting
     out of Weakness," *Washington Post*, March 25, 2014, https://www.
     washingtonpost.com/world/national-security/obama-dismisses-
     russia-as-regional-power-acting-out-of-weakness/2014/03/25/
     1e5a678e-b439-11e3-b899-20667de76985_story.html.

11. *Intelligence Community Assessment: Assessing Russian Intelligence
     Activities and Intentions in Recent U.S. Elections* (National Intelligence
     Council: January 6, 2017), ICA 2017-01D, https://www.dni.gov/files/
     documents/ICA_2017_01.pdf.

12. Ibid.

13. Ibid.

14. "Interview of: Evelyn Farkas," House Permanent Select Committee
     on Intelligence (Executive Session), U.S. House of Representatives,
     June 26, 2017, https://www.dni.gov/files/HPSCI_Transcripts/2020-05-
     04-Evelyn_Farkas-MTR_Redacted.pdf; "Interview of: James
     Clapper," House Permanent Select Committee on Intelligence
     (Executive Session), U.S. House of Representatives, July 17, 2017,
     https://www.dni.gov/index.php/features/2753-53-hpsci-transcripts;

Brooke Singman, "House Intel Transcripts Show Top Obama Officials Had No 'Empirical Evidence' of Trump-Russia Collusion," Fox News, May 7, 2020, https://www.foxnews.com/politics/intel-transcripts-obama-officials-no-empirical-evidence-trump-russia-collusion.

15. *Intelligence Community Assessment: Assessing Russian Intelligence Activities and Intentions in Recent U.S. Elections* (Annex A), Chuck Grassley: United States Senator for Iowa, December 30, 2016, https://www.grassley.senate.gov/news/news-releases/sens-grassley-and-johnson-release-declassified-annex-intelligence-community; *Report on Russian Active Measures* (House Permanent Select Committee on Intelligence, U.S. House of Representatives: March 22, 2018), https://docs.house.gov/meetings/IG/IG00/20180322/108023/HRPT-115-1_1-p1-U3.pdf; "Sens. Grassley and Johnson Release Declassified Annex to Intelligence Community Assessment That was Based on the Debunked Steele Dossier," Chuck Grassley: United States Senator for Iowa, June 11, 2020, https://www.grassley.senate.gov/news/news-releases/sens-grassley-and-johnson-release-declassified-annex-intelligence-community.

16. «Путин не исключил, что будет баллотироваться на новый срок – Политика», TASS, May 21, 2020, https://tass.ru/politika/878212 (in Russian); «Голосование по-президентски: Поправки поддержали как Владимира Путина», Коммерсантъ (*Kommersant*), July 2, 2020, https://www.*Kommersant*.ru/doc/4399656?from=main_1 (in Russian).

17. Tim Hains, "Flynn Attorney Sidney Powell: This Whole Thing Was Orchestrated within the FBI, Clapper, Brennan, and President Obama," RealClearPolitics, May 10, 2020, https://www.realclearpolitics.com/video/2020/05/10/flynn_attorney_sidney_powell_this_whole_thing_was_orchestrated_within_the_fbi_clapper_brennan_and_president_obama.html.

18. *Intelligence Community Assessment: Assessing Russian Intelligence Activities and Intentions in Recent U.S. Elections* (National Intelligence Council: January 6, 2017), ICA 2017-01D, https://www.dni.gov/files/documents/ICA_2017_01.pdf.

19. David Aaro, "Russian Nuclear-Capable Bombers Intercepted by U.S. Aircraft Near Alaska," Fox News, June 10, 2020, https://www.foxnews. com/us/russian-nuclear-capable-bombers-intercepted-by-u-s-aircraft-near-alaska-report; The Canadian Press, "Senior Officer Warns Norad Can't Detect Russian Bombers in Time, Needs Upgrades," *National Post*, January 29, 2020, https://nationalpost.com/ pmn/news-pmn/canada-news-pmn/senior-officer-warns-norad-cant-detect-russian-bombers-in-time-needs-upgrades; Richard Weitz, "Russian Bombers Rehearse Nuclear Attacks against the United States," Hudson Institute, August 20, 2007, https://www. hudson.org/research/5180-russian-bombers-rehearse-nuclear-attacks-against-the-united-states; Mark Mazzetti and Thom Shanker, "Russian Subs Patrolling off East Coast of U.S.," *New York Times*, August 4, 2009, https://www.nytimes.com/2009/08/05/ world/05patrol.html; Bill Gertz, "New Russian Missile Threat to Homeland," *Washington Times*, February 27, 2019, https://www. washingtontimes.com/news/2019/feb/27/russian-missile-threat-to-us-homeland; "Statement of General Glen VanHerck, United States Air Force Commander United States Northern Command and North American Aerospace Defense Command before the Senate Armed Services Committee," Senate Armed Services Committee, U.S. Senate, March 16, 2021, https://www.northcom.mil/Newsroom/ Transcripts/Transcript/Article/2541921/norad-usnorthcom-commanders-senate-armed-services-committee-statement/.

20. "Russian Government Cyber Activity Targeting Energy and Other Critical Infrastructure Sectors," Alert (TA18-074A), Cybersecurity and Infrastructure Security Agency (CISA), March 15, 2018, https:// us-cert.cisa.gov/ncas/alerts/TA18-074A; Rebecca Smith, "Russian Hackers Reached U.S. Utility Control Rooms, Homeland Security Officials Say," *Wall Street Journal*, July 23, 2018, https://www.wsj.com/ articles/russian-hackers-reach-u-s-utility-control-rooms-homeland-security-officials-say-1532388110; Nicole Perlroth and David E. Sanger, "Cyberattacks Put Russian Fingers on the Switch in Power Plants, U.S. Says," *New York Times*, March 15, 2018, https://www. nytimes.com/2018/03/15/us/politics/russia-cyberattacks.html; Evan

Perez, "How the U.S. Thinks Russians Hacked the White House," CNN, April 8, 2015, https://www.cnn.com/2015/04/07/politics/how-russians-hacked-the-wh/index.html; Jamie Crawford, "Russians Hacked Pentagon Network, Carter Says," CNN, June 4, 2015, https://www.cnn.com/2015/04/23/politics/russian-hackers-pentagon-network/index.html; Christopher Bing, "Russians Impersonating U.S. State Department Aide in Hacking Campaign: Researchers," Reuters, November 16, 2018, https://www.reuters.com/article/us-usa-cyber-russia/russians-impersonating-u-s-state-department-aide-in-hacking-campaign-researchers-idUSKCN1NL2BG.

21. Герасимов В. (V. Gerasimov), «Ценность науки в предвидении», Военно-промышленный курьер (*Voenno-Promishlenniy Kuryer*), February 26, 2013, https://vpk-news .ru/articles/14632 (in Russian); Карякин В. В. (V. V. Karyakin), «Геополитика третьей войны: трансформация мира в эпоху постмодерна», Москва (Moscow) 2013, стр. 79 (in Russian).

22. «Пресс-конференция по итогам переговоров президентов России и США. Владимир Путин и Дональд Трамп сделали заявления для прессы и ответили на вопросы журналистов», July 16, 2018, http://kremlin.ru/events/president/news/58017 (in Russian); WSJ Roundup, "Excerpts from Trump-Putin News Conference in Helsinki," *Wall Street Journal*, July 16, 2018, https://www.wsj.com/articles/excerpts-from-trump-putin-news-conference-in-helsinki-1531761131.

23. «Военная Доктрина Российской Федерации», Российская Газета (*Rossiyskaya Gazeta*), December 30, 2014, https://rg.ru/2014/12/30/doktrina-dok.html (in Russian).

24. «Стратегия Национальной Безопасности Российской Федерации», Российская Газета (*Rossiyskaya Gazeta*), December 31, 2015, https://rg.ru/2015/12/31/nac-bezopasnost-site-dok.html (in Russian).

25. «Концепция Внешней Политики Российской Федерации», http://kremlin.ru/acts/bank/41451 (in Russian).

26. «Доктрина Информационной Безопасности Российской Федерации», https://rg.ru/2016/12/06/doktrina-infobezobasnost-site-dok.html (in Russian).
27. Eli Lake, Noah Shachtman, and Christopher Dickey, "Ex-CIA Chief: Why We Keep Getting Putin Wrong. Blame a Myopic Mindset—and an Intelligence Corps Focused on Terrorism, Not Moscow," Daily Beast, April 14, 2017, https://www.thedailybeast.com/ex-cia-chief-why-we-keep-getting-putin-wrong.
28. "CIA Director Gina Haspel Speaks at Auburn University," News & Information, U.S. Central Intelligence Agency, April 18, 2019, https://www.cia.gov/news-information/speeches-testimony/2019-speeches-testimony/dcia-haspel-auburn-university-speech.html.
29. «Военная Доктрина Российской Федерации», 2010 (in Russian).
30. CBSNews.com Staff, "Bush Meets Putin," CBS News, June 18, 2001, https://www.cbsnews.com/news/bush-meets-putin/.
31. Reuters Staff, "Clinton, Lavrov Push Wrong Reset Button on Ties," Reuters, March 6, 2009, https://www.reuters.com/article/idUSN06402140.
32. Daniel Coats, "The Lights Are Blinking Red," C-SPAN, July 13, 2018, https://www.c-span.org/video/?c4740341/director-coats-the-lights-blinking-red. Director of National Intelligence Dan Coats told a Hudson Institute audience that the digital infrastructure of the United States is under attack and that "the lights are blinking red." He warned that Russia continues to meddle in U.S. democracy and that their efforts are persistent and pervasive.

Prologue

1. "Recognition of the Soviet Union, 1933," Office of the Historian, U.S. Department of State, https://history.state.gov/milestones/1921-1936/ussr.
2. "Mutually Assured Destruction," *Encyclopaedia Britannica*, https://www.britannica.com/topic/mutual-assured-destruction.
3. "Soviet Nuclear Doctrine: Concepts of International Theater and War," CIA DOC_0000268107, CIA Historical Review Program, U.S. Central Intelligence Agency, June 1973, declassified December 21, 1993.

4. "The Cuban Missile Crisis, October 1962," Office of the Historian, U.S. Department of State, https://history.state.gov/milestones/1961-1968/cuban-missile-crisis.

5. John Grady, "Mattis Puts Russia on Top of His Threat List, Defends NATO," U.S. Naval Institute, January 12, 2017, https://news.usni.org/2017/01/12/mattis-puts-russia-top-threat-list-defends-nato.

6. *Meet the Press*, transcript for May 28, 2017, NBC News, May 28, 2017, https://www.nbcnews.com/meet-the-press/meet-press-may-28-2017-n765626. Information is from the part of the program with former DNI James Clapper.

7. Jeannie L. Johnson and Jeffrey A. Larson, "Comparative Strategic Culture Syllabus," SAIC, prepared for Defense Threat Reduction Agency, November 2006, https://fas.org/irp/agency/dod/dtra/syllabus.pdf.

8. Alison Gopnik, "Cultural Differences Start Early," *Wall Street Journal*, July 11, 2019, https://www.wsj.com/articles/how-early-do-cultural-differences-start-11562855707.

9. "Churchill on Russia," International Churchill Society, 2011, https://winstonchurchill.org/publications/finest-hour/finest-hour-150/churchill-on-russia.

10. «Концепция Внешней Политики Российской Федерации», 2013, www.kremlin.ru (in Russian).

11. «Концепция Внешней Политики Российской Федерации», November 30, 2016, http://kremlin.ru/acts/bank/41451 (in Russia).

12. Ibid.

13. Michael R. Pompeo, "U.S. Withdrawal from the INF Treaty on August 2, 2019," Press Statement, U.S. Department of State, August 2, 2019, https://www.state.gov/u-s-withdrawal-from-the-inf-treaty-on-august-2-2019.

14. Фахрутдинов Рафаэль (Rafael Fakhrutdinov), «НАТО подошло к нашим границам, Путин предостерег Запад от перехода «красной черты» в отношениях с РФ», May 26, 2018, https://www.gazeta.ru/army/2018/05/26/11764867.shtml.

15. «Военная Доктрина Российской Федерации», 1993, (in Russian).

16. National Security Archives, "The Charge in the Soviet Union (Kennan) to the Secretary of State," SECRET, 861.00/2–2246: Telegram, Moscow, February 22, 1946, 9:00 p.m., received February 22, 3:52 p.m., declassified.

17. Ibid.

18. "National Security Decision Directive 238," White House, September 2, 1986, declassified in part October 27, 2005.

19. "Approval Draft of the Defense Planning Guidance," Memorandum of the Secretary of Defense Paul Wolfowitz, May 5, 1992, declassified December 10, 2007.

20. Ibid.

21. National Security Archives, "The Charge in the Soviet Union (Kennan) to the Secretary of State."

22. Roger E. Kanet, *Russian Foreign Policy of the 21st Century* (London: Palgrave Macmillan, 2010), 148.

23. *National Security Strategy of the United States of America* (White House, December 2017), https://www.whitehouse.gov/wp-content/uploads/2017/12/NSS-Final-12-18-2017-0905.pdf.

24. Angela Stent, *Putin's World: Russia Against the West and with the Rest* (New York: Twelve, 2019).

25. WSJ Roundup, "Excerpts From Trump-Putin News Conference in Helsinki," *Wall Street Journal*, July 16, 2018, https://www.wsj.com/articles/excerpts-from-trump-putin-news-conference-in-helsinki-1531761131.

Chapter 1

1. Daniel Coats, *Worldwide Annual Threat Assessment of the Intelligence Community*, Statement for the Record, U.S. Intelligence Community, February 13, 2018, https://www.dni.gov/files/documents/Newsroom/Testimonies/2018-ATA—-Unclassified-SSCI.pdf.

2. "Multi-Year FBI Investigation Uncovers Network in the United States Tasked with Recruiting Sources and Collecting Information for Russia. Ten Alleged Secret Agents Arrested in the United States," U.S. Department of Justice, June 28, 2010, https://www.justice.gov/opa/pr/

ten-alleged-secret-agents-arrested-united-states; Amit Kachhia-Patel, United States of America v. Anna Chapman and Mikhail Semenko, complaint (violation of USC 371), U.S. District Court for the Southern District of New York, June 27, 2010, https://www.justice. gov/sites/default/files/opa/legacy/2010/06/28/062810complaint1.pdf.

3. Ibid.
4. Michael Sulmeyer, "Russia and Cyber Operations: Challenges and Opportunities for the U.S. Next Administration," Belfer Center for Science and International Security, December 13, 2016, https://www. belfercenter.org/publication/russia-and-cyber-operations-challenges-and-opportunities-next-us-administration.
5. "Speech and the Following Discussion at the Munich Conference on Security Policy," February 10, 2007, http://en.kremlin.ru/events/president/transcripts /24034; Thom Shanker and Mark Landler, "Putin Says the U.S. Is Undermining Global Stability," *New York Times*, February 11, 2007, https://www.nytimes.com/2007/02/11/world/europe/11munich.html.
6. Ibid.
7. «Военная Доктрина Российской Федерации» (Military Doctrine of the Russian Federation), approved by President Putin, 2010, (in Russian).
8. «Военная Доктрина Российской Федерации» (Military Doctrine of the Russian Federation), approved by President Putin, 2014, (in Russian).
9. "Russian National Security Strategy," Russian Federation Presidential Edict 683, approved by President Putin, December 2015, http://www. ieee.es/Galerias/fichero/OtrasPublicaciones/Internacional/2016/Russian-National-Security-Strategy-31Dec2015.pdf.
10. "Foreign Policy Concept of the Russian Federation," Ministry of Foreign Affairs of the Russian Federation, approved by President Putin, November 30, 2016, https://www.mid.ru/en/foreign_policy/official_documents/-/asset_publisher/CptICkB6BZ29/content/id/2542248.
11. "Russia Plans $650bn Defence Spend up to 2020," BBC News, February 24, 2011, https://www.bbc.com/news/

world-europe-12567043; "Putin Announced New Ten-Year Rearmament Plan," Interfax, January 24, 2018, (in Russian); "Rogozin Explained How to Increase Production During Wartime," January 26, 2018, gazeta.ru (in Russian). Dmitry Rogozin is vice prime minister of Russia.

12. "The IPAWS National Test," Federal Emergency Management Agency, Public Service Announcement, www.fema.gov.

13. Brian Fung, "Cell Phone Users Nationwide Just Received a 'Presidential Alert.' Here's What to Know," *Washington Post*, October 4, 2018, https://www.washingtonpost.com/technology/2018/10/03/millions-cellphone-users-are-about-get-presidential-alert-heres-what-know.

14. Garret M. Graff, "The Presidential Alert Has a Long Strange History," *WIRED*, October 3, 2018, https://www.wired.com/story/presidential-text-alert-fema-emergency-history.

15. "Russian Government Cyber Activity Targeting Energy and Other Critical Infrastructure Sectors," Alert (TA18-074A), Cybersecurity and Infrastructure Security Agency (CISA), March 15, 2018, https://us-cert.cisa.gov/ncas/alerts/TA18-074A.

16. Ibid.

17. Rebecca Smith, "Russian Hackers Reached U.S. Utility Control Rooms, Homeland Security Officials Say," *Wall Street Journal*, July 23, 2018, https://www.wsj.com/articles/russian-hackers-reach-u-s-utility-control-rooms-homeland-security-officials-say-1532388110.

18. Ibid.

19. Nicole Perlroth and David E. Sanger, "Cyberattacks Put Russian Fingers on the Switch in Power Plants, U.S. Says," *New York Times*, March 15, 2018, https://www.nytimes.com/2018/03/15/us/politics/russia-cyberattacks.html.

20. "Ukraine Power Cut Was Cyber Attack," BBC News, January 11, 2017, https://www.bbc.com/news/technology-38573074.

21. Andy Greenberg, "How an Entire Nation Became Russia's Test Lab for Cyberwar," June 20, 2017, https://www.wired.com/story/russian-hackers-attack-ukraine.

22. "Weapon Systems Cybersecurity: DOD Just Beginning to Grapple with Scale of Vulnerabilities," U.S. Government Accountability Office, October 9, 2018, https://www.gao.gov/products/GAO-19-128.

23. Brian E. Finch, "The American Arsenal Is Vulnerable to Cyberattacks," *Wall Street Journal*, October 15, 2018, https://www.wsj.com/articles/the-american-arsenal-is-vulnerable-to-cyberattacks-1539645144.

24. "U.S. Steps Up Grid Defense," *Wall Street Journal*, August 6, 2018.

25. Finch, "The American Arsenal," 2018.

26. V. I. Polegayev, *"O neyadernom sderzhivanii, ego roli i meste v sisteme strategicheskogo sderzhivaniya"* ("Regarding Deterrence and Its Role and Place in the System of Strategic Deterrence"), *Voyennaya Mysl (Military Thought)* (in Russian).

27. *Voina i mir v terminakh i opredeleniyakh: Voenno-politicheskiy slovar (War and Peace in Terms and Definitions: Military-Political Dictionary)*, 2011–2013, www.voina-i-mir.ru (in Russian).

28. XXXI Vserossiyskaya Nauchno-Tekhnicheskaya Konferentsiya Voyennoy Adademii Nauk Raketnykh Voisk Strategicheskogo Nazncheniya (Thirty-First Scientific Technical Conference of the Military Academy of Sciences of Strategic Rocket Forces), 2012 (in Russian).

29. "Treasury Sanctions Russian Cyber Actors for Interference with the 2016 U.S. Elections and Malicious Cyber Attacks," Press Releases, U.S. Department of the Treasury, March 15, 2018, https://home.treasury.gov/news/press-releases/sm0312.

30. «Послание Президента Федеральному Собранию» (President's Address to the Federal Assembly), March 1, 2018, www.kremlin.ru/events/president/news (in Russian).

31. Ibid.

32. Ibid.

33. "Radioactive Ashes of Kisilev. Kisilev Threatened USA with Nuclear War," March 17, 2014, www.journal.ru (in Russian; no longer available).

34. «Константин Сивков: США Может Остановить Только Оружие Армагеддона» (Konstantin Sivkov: USA Can Be Stopped Only with Armageddon Weapon), http://russnov.ru/konstantin-sivkov-ssha-mozhet-ostanovit-tolko-oruzhie-armageddona/ (in Russian).

35. "Statement on Russian Long Range Aviation Flights," USNORTHCOM and North American Aerospace Defense Command (NORAD), July 2015.

36. *Statement of General Lori J. Robinson, United States Air Force Commander, United States Northern Command and North American Aerospace Defense Command Before the Senate Armed Services Committee*, Senate Armed Services Committee, U.S. Senate, February 15, 2018, https://www.armed-services.senate.gov/imo/media/doc/Robinson_03-22-18.pdf.

37. Ibid.

38. *Nuclear Posture Review*, U.S. Department of Defense, February 2018, https://media.defense.gov/2018/Feb/02/2001872886/-1/-1/1/2018-NUCLEAR-POSTURE-REVIEW-FINAL-REPORT.PDF.

39. Richard Weitz, "Russian Bombers Rehearse Nuclear Attacks against the United States," Hudson Institute, August 20, 2007, https://www.hudson.org/research/5180-russian-bombers-rehearse-nuclear-attacks-against-the-united-states.

40. "Russian President's Speech and Discussion at the Munich Conference on Security Policy," www.kremlin.ru (in Russian); Shanker and Landler, "Putin Says the U.S. Is Undermining Global Stability."

41. Andrew E. Kramer, "Russia Resumes Patrols by Nuclear Bombers," *New York Times*, August 18, 2007, https://www.nytimes.com/2007/08/18/world/europe/17cnd-russia.html.

42. Ibid.

43. "Russia Tests Super-Strength Bomb, Military Says," Reuters, September 12, 2007, https://www.reuters.com/news/picture/russia-tests-superstrength-bomb-military-idUSL1155952320070912.

44. Helen Cooper and Mujib Mashal, "U.S. Drops 'Mother of All Bombs' on ISIS Caves in Afghanistan," *New York Times*, April 13, 2017, https://www.nytimes.com/2017/04/13/world/asia/moab-mother-of-all-bombs-afghanistan.html.

45. "Russia Intercepts Russian Bombers and Fighters Entering Alaskan Air Defense Identification Zone," Release No: 19-016, North American Space Defense Command (NORAD), May 22, 2019, https://www.norad.mil/Newsroom/Press-Releases/Article/1855607/norad-intercepts-russian-bombers-and-fighters-entering-alaskan-air-defense-iden/.

46. "NORAD Tracks Santa," www.noradsanta.org.

47. Brian Todd and Jethro Mullen, "July Fourth Message Not the First from Russian Bombers," CNN, July 23, 2015, https://www.cnn.com/2015/07/23/politics/us-russian-bombers-july-4-intercept/index.html.

48. Mark Mazzetti and Thom Shanker, "Russian Subs Patrolling off East Coast of U.S.," *New York Times*, August 4, 2009, https://www.nytimes.com/2009/08/05/world/05patrol.html.

49. Bill Gertz, "Silent Running: Russian Attack Submarine Sailed in Gulf of Mexico Undetected for Weeks, U.S. Officials Say," Washington Free Beacon, August 14, 2012, https://freebeacon.com/national-security/silent-running/.

50. Alina Polyakova and Filippos Letsas, "On the Record: the U.S. Administration's Actions against Russia," Brookings Institution, December 31, 2019, https://www.brookings.edu/blog/order-from-chaos/2018/09/25/on-the-record-the-u-s-administrations-actions-on-russia/.

51. Ibid.

52. Dustin Volz, "Trump, Seeking to Relax Rules on U.S. Cyberattacks, Reverses Obama Directives," *Wall Street Journal*, August 15, 2018, https://www.wsj.com/articles/trump-seeking-to-relax-rules-on-u-s-cyberattacks-reverses-obama-directive-1534378721.

53. Ibid.

54. Greg Miller, Ellen Nakashima, and Adam Entous, "Obama's Secret Struggle to Punish Russia for Putin's Election Assault," *Washington Post*, June 23, 2017, https://www.washingtonpost.com/graphics/2017/world/national-security/obama-putin-election-hacking/.

55. David Jackson, "Cybersecurity: Donald Trump's New Strategy Allows More Offensive Operations," *USA Today*, September 21, 2018, https://www.usatoday.com/story/news/politics/2018/09/20/donald-trumps-new-cybersecurity-plan-allows-more-offensive-operations/1370946002/.

56. «Современные Тенденции В Исследовании Критической Инфраструктуры В Зарубежных Странах» (Modern Tendencies in Studies of Critical Infrastructure of Foreign Countries),

Зарубежное Военное Обозрение *(Foreign Military Review)*, January 2012 (in Russian).

57. Ibid.

58. Дугин Александр (Alexander Dugin), Основы Геополитики (Арктогая), 2000 (*The Foundations of Geopolitics*, Moscow: Arctogaia, 2000) (in Russian).

59. Ibid.

60. Карякин В (V Karyakin), «Геополитика Третьей Волны: Трансформация Мира в Эпоху Постмодерна» *(Geopolitics of the Third Wave: Transformation of the World in the Era of Post-Modern)* (Moscow, 2013), (in Russian). This book was recommended for publication by the Council of the Faculty of National Security of the Russian Academy of Nation's Management and State Service under the president of the Russian Federation.

61. Zbigniew Brzezinski, *The Grand Chessboard: American Primacy and Its Geostratic Imperatives* (New York: Big Books, 1998).

62. "U.S. Relations with the USSR," National Security Decision Directive 75, 1983, declassified.

63. "Basic National Security Strategy," National Security Decision Directive 238, White House, September 2, 1986, declassified in part October 27, 2005.

64. Ibid.

65. Eduard Chesnokov, "Geopolitical Models of H. Mackinder and Spykman in U.S. Foreign Policy of the 20th and 21st Centuries," Center for Strategic Assessments and Forecasting, October 31, 2016, (in Russian).

66. Patrick J. Garrity, "Defending the Rimland," *Claremont Review of Books*, October 28, 2013, https://claremontreviewofbooks.com/digital/defending-the-rimland.

67. Ibid.

68. Chesnokov, "Geopolitical Models."

69. Brzezinski, *The Grand Chessboard.*

70. Chesnokov, "Geopolitical Models."

71. "Issues of Russia's Security in the Context of Mackinder Concept," Russian Institute of Strategic Research, May 23, 2014 (in Russian).

72. Dugin, *The Foundations of Geopolitics.*

73. *Voyennaya Doktrina Rossiyskoy Federatsii* (Military Doctrine of the Russian Federation), approved by President Putin, December 30, 2014, (in Russian); National Security Strategy of the Russian Federation, approved by President Putin, December 31, 2015, (in Russian).

74. Anton Barbashin and Hannah Thoburn, "Putin's Brain: Alexander Dugin and the Philosophy behind Putin's Invasion of Crimea," *Foreign Affairs*, March 31, 2014, https://www.foreignaffairs.com/articles/russia-fsu/2014-03-31/putins-brain.

75. Interview with author.

76. Ibid.

77. Ibid.

78. Ibid.

79. Ibid.

80. Kyle Rempfer, "'Homeland is No Longer a Sanctuary' Amid Rising Near-Peer Threats, NORTHCOM Commander Says," Military Times, August 27, 2018, https://www.militarytimes.com/news/your-air-force/2018/08/27/the-homeland-is-no-longer-a-sanctuary-amid-rising-near-peer-threats-northcom-commander-says.

81. Patricia Zengerle and Doina Chiacu, "NATO Chief Warns of Russia Threat, Urges Unity in U.S. Address," Reuters, April 3, 2019, https://www.reuters.com/article/us-usa-nato/nato-chief-warns-of-russia-threat-urges-unity-in-u-s-address-idUSKCN1RF22L.

82. Jim Sciutto, "A Conversation with the Defense Intelligence Agency Director," Interview with DIA Director General Robert Ashley, 2019 Aspen Forum, https://71314db5-9323-4688-b902-112e132cd12f.filesusr.com/ugd/93f0e1_c9f52e400dff45529f9e4d4a347a92ac.pdf.

83. Ibid.

84. Ibid.

85. «От Первого Лица,» Автобиография Путина В (*First Person: Autobiography of V. Putin*), *Public Affairs.*

86. *Russia Military Power: Building a Military to Support Great Power Aspirations* (U.S. Defense Intelligence Agency, 2017), https://www.dia.

mil/Portals/27/Documents/News/Military%20Power%20
Publications/Russia%20Military%20Power%20Report%202017.pdf.

87. Hope Hodge Seck, "Marine Leaders Highlight Norway Unit's Role as
Deterrent to Russia," Military Times, December 21, 2017, https://
www.military.com/daily-news/2017/12/21/marine-leaders-highlight-
norway-units-role-deterrent-russia.html.

88. Nathan P. Freier et al., *Outplayed: Regaining Strategic Initiative in the
Gray Zone* (Army Capabilities Integration Center, in coordination
with Joint Staff J-39/Strategic Multi-Layer Assessment Branch, June
2016), https://ssi.armywarcollege.edu/outplayed-regaining-strategic-
initiative-in-the-gray-zone-a-report-sponsored-by-the-army-
capabilities-integration-center-in-coordination-with-joint-staff-j-39-
strategic-multi-layer-assessment-branch/.

89. *Nuclear Posture Review*, U.S. Department of Defense, February 2018,
https://media.defense.gov/2018/Feb/02/2001872886/-1/-1/1/2018-
NUCLEAR-POSTURE-REVIEW-FINAL-REPORT.PDF;
«Утверждены Основы государственной политики в области
ядерного сдерживания. Президент подписал Указ «Об Основах
государственной политики Российской Федерации в области
ядерного сдерживания»», June 2, 2020, http://kremlin.ru/acts/
news/63447 (in Russian).

Chapter 2

1. "Former Secretary of State Condoleezza Rice Argues 'Putin is a
Megalomaniac,'" Former Cabinet Secretaries on Russia, Aspen
Institute, C-SPAN, August 8, 2014, https://www.c-span.org/
video/?320782-1/cabinet-secretaries-russia-ukraine.

2. Zachary Cohen, "CIA: North Korean Leader Kim Jong Un Isn't
Crazy," CNN, October 6, 2017, https://www.cnn.com/2017/10/05/
politics/cia-kim-jong-un-intelligence-profile/index.html.

3. Ray Locker, "Pentagon 2008 Study Claims Putin Has Asperger's
Syndrome," *USA Today*, February 4, 2015, https://www.usatoday.com/
story/news/politics/2015/02/04/putin-aspergers-syndrome-study-
pentagon/22855927.

4. Jerrold Post and Stephanie Doucette, *Dangerous Charisma: The Political Psychology of Donald Trump and His Followers* (New York: Pegasus Books, 2019).

5. Н. Геворкян, А. Колесников, Н. Тимакова (N. Gevorkyan, A. Kolesnikov, N. Timakova), «От Первого Лица. Разговоры С Владимиром Путиным», Вагриус, 2000, (in Russian).

6. Ibid.

7. Putin's quote is from the website dedicated to his second election campaign, www.putin2012.ru (no longer available).

8. Ibid.

9. Н. Геворкян, А. Колесников, Н. Тимакова (N. Gevorkyan, A. Kolesnikov, N. Timakova), «От Первого Лица. Разговоры С Владимиром Путиным», Вагриус, 2000, (in Russian).

10. Ibid.

11. Ibid.

12. Ibid.

13. «Путин встретился с россиянами–фигурантами «шпионского скандала»», РИА Новости (RIA News), July 24, 2010, (in Russian).

14. «Яды и Меркадеры Владимира Путина», Ежедневный Журнал, March 7, 2018, http://www.ej.ru/?a=note&id=32219 (in Russian).

15. Ibid.

16. Н. Геворкян, А. Колесников, Н. Тимакова (N. Gevorkyan, A. Kolesnikov, N. Timakova), «От Первого Лица. Разговоры С Владимиром Путиным», Вагриус, 2000, (in Russian).

17. Ibid.

18. Ibid.

19. Sol W. Sanders, "Who Is Vladimir Putin? Dealing with the Ex-Spy Who Came from Nowhere to Lead Russia," *World Tribune*, July 7, 2017, https://www.worldtribune.com/who-is-vladimir-putin-dealing-with-the-ex-spy-who-came-from-nowhere-to-lead-russia/.

20. Н. Геворкян, А. Колесников, Н. Тимакова (N. Gevorkyan, A. Kolesnikov, N. Timakova), «От Первого Лица. Разговоры С Владимиром Путиным», Вагриус, 2000, (in Russian).

21. Ibid.

22. Fiona Hill and Clifford G. Gaddy, *Mr. Putin: Operative in the Kremlin* (Washington, D.C.: Brookings Institution Press, 2013).

23. «Железный Путин», Коммерсантъ (*Kommersant*), March 10, 2000, (in Russian).

24. Н. Геворкян, А. Колесников, Н. Тимакова (N. Gevorkyan, A. Kolesnikov, N. Timakova), «От Первого Лица. Разговоры С Владимиром Путиным», Вагриус, 2000, (in Russian).

25. "Transcript: Angela Stent Talks with Michael Morell on 'Intelligence Matters,'" CBS News, May 29, 2019, https://www.cbsnews.com/news/transcript-angela-stent-talks-with-michael-morell-on-intelligence-matters/.

26. "Chris Wallace Interviews Russian President Vladimir Putin" (transcript), Fox News, July 16, 2018, https://www.foxnews.com/transcript/chris-wallace-interviews-russian-president-vladimir-putin.

27. Ibid.

28. "Grand Jury Indicts Thirteen Russian Individuals and Three Russian Companies for Scheme to Interfere in the United States Political System," Office of Public Affairs, U.S. Department of Justice, February 16, 2018, https://www.justice.gov/opa/pr/grand-jury-indicts-thirteen-russian-individuals-and-three-russian-companies-scheme-interfere.

29. "Chris Wallace Interviews," Fox News.

30. Ibid.

31. "Megyn Kelly Questions Vladimir Putin on Election Interference," NBC News, June 2, 2017, https://www.nbcnews.com/long-story-short/video/megyn-kelly-questions-vladimir-putin-on-election-interference-958705731843; «Интервью американскому телеканалу», www.kremlin.ru, June 5, 2017, (in Russian); «Интервью американскому телеканалу», www.kremlin.ru, March 10, 2018, (in Russian).

32. Ibid.

33. "Obama Tells Russia's Medvedev More Flexibility after Election," Reuters, March 26, 2012, https://www.reuters.com/article/

us-nuclear-summit-obama-medvedev/obama-tells-russias-medvedev-more-flexibility-after-election-idUSBRE82P0JI20120326.

34. David Morgan, "Putin Is Time Magazine's 'Person of the Year,'" Reuters, December 19, 2007, https://www.reuters.com/article/us-time/putin-is-time-magazines-person-of-the-year-idUSN1956834820071219.

35. "Powerful People 2018: #2 Vladimir Putin," *Forbes*, https://www.forbes.com/profile/vladimir-putin/#254aa5eb6fc5.

36. «Стенограмма: О чем рассказал Владимир Путин на пресс-конференции», Российская Газета (*Rossiyskaya Gazeta*), December 19, 2019, https://rg.ru/2019/12/19/stenogramma-bolshaia-press-konferenciia-vladimira-putina.html (in Russian).

37. Н. Геворкян, А. Колесников, Н. Тимакова (N. Gevorkyan, A. Kolesnikov, N. Timakova), «От Первого Лица. Разговоры С Владимиром Путиным», Вагриус, 2000 (in Russian).

38. Ibid.

39. «Французский философ: Что творится в голове у Владимира Путина», DW, June 14, 2016, https://www.dw.com/ru/французский-философ-что-творится-в-голове-у-владимира-путина/a-19319607 (in Russian); «В поисках мудрости: Чиновникам велено подучить философию», Журнал «Коммерсантъ Власть» (*Kommersant*) №2 от, 20.01.2014, стр. 22, https://www.*Kommersant*.ru/doc/2383840 (in Russian).

40. «Пассажиры Философского парохода: Иван ИЛЬИН (1883–1954)», Российская Газета (*Rossiyskaya Gazeta*), Родина–№ 9 (917), https://rg.ru/2017/10/02/rodina-ivan-ilin.html.

41. «Почему Путин цитирует философа Ильина?» Комсомольская Правда», July 3, 2009, https://www.kp.ru/daily/24321/513782/ (in Russian).

42. Ibid.

43. Lyubov Tsarevskaya, "Remembering 'Passionarian' Lev Gumilev," *Russia Beyond*, December 30, 2012, https://www.rbth.com/articles/2012/12/30/remembering_passionarian_lev_gumilev_21361; Alexey Timofeychev, "10 Facts about Lev Gumilev, the Famous Russian Historian Who Refused to Be Broken by the Gulag," *Russia*

Beyond, September 30, 2017, https://www.rbth.com/history/326285-10-facts-about-lev-gumilev; Charles Clover, "Lev Gumilev: Passion, Putin and Power," *Financial Times*, March 11, 2016, https://www.ft.com/content/ede1e5c6-e0c5-11e5-8d9b-e88a2a889797.

44. «Победа! Сильный Президент — сильная Россия», http://putin2018.ru.

45. «20 высказываний Путина, ставших афоризмами», РИА Новости (RIA News), May 7, 2008, https://ria.ru/20080507/106744531.html (in Russian).

46. «Путин действительно такое сказал? Разумеется», Журнал «Коммерсантъ Власть» (*Kommersant*) №45 от November 18, 2002, стр. 36, https://www.*Kommersant*.ru/doc/351346 (in Russian).

47. «Личная жизнь Путина—табу для российской прессы», Голос Америки (*Golos Ameriki*; Voice of America), April 21, 2008, https://www.golos-ameriki.ru/a/russia-putin-private-life/4936319.html; Наталья Меликова, «С президентом: Неделикатные вопросы», Независимая Газета, April 21, 2008, https://www.ng.ru/week/2008-04-21/12_president.html?mtheme=0_2 (in Russian).

48. Чинкова Елена (Elena Chinkova), «Вопрос Владимиру ПУТИНУ: Правда ли, что Вы обещали повесить Саакашвили за одно место? Наказывать агрессора будет сам грузинский народ», Комсомольская Правда (*Komsomoliskaya Pravda*), December 4, 2008, https://www.kp.ru/online/news/173476/ (in Russian).

49. «Россия должна быть сильной, чтобы избежать диктата извне – Путин», РИА Новости (RIA News), April 20, 2011, https://ria.ru/20110420/366398441.html (in Russian).

50. «Прямая Линия С Владимиром Путиным», www.kremlin.ru, June 20, 2019, http://kremlin.ru/events/president/news/60795 (in Russian).

51. Путин В. В. (V. V. Putin), «Новый интеграционный проект для Евразии—будущее, которое рождается сегодня», October 3, 2011, https://iz.ru/news/502761?page=2.

52. «Послание Президента Федеральному Собранию Владимир Путин огласил ежегодное Послание Президента Российской Федерации Федеральному Собранию», www.kremlin.ru,

December 12, 2012, http://kremlin.ru/events/president/news/17118 9 (in Russian).

53. «Концепция внешней политики Российской Федерации (утверждена Президентом Российской Федерации В.В. Путиным, 30 ноября 2016, г.)», -01-12-201630, https://www.mid.ru/ foreign_policy/official_documents/-asset_publisher/CptICkB6BZ29/ content/id/2542248.

54. Указ Президента Российской Федерации от 31 декабря 2015 года N 683, «О Стратегии национальной безопасности Российской Федерации», Дата подписания, December 31, 2015 г; Опубликован December 31, 2015 г, Вступает в силу, December 31, 2015 г, https:// rg.ru/2015/12/31/nac-bezopasnost-site-dok.html (in Russian).

55. Путин В. В. (V. V. Putin), «Россия на рубеже тысячелетий,» Независимая Газета (Nezavisimaya Gazeta), December 31, 1999, https://www.ng.ru/politics/1999-12-30/4_millenium.html (in Russian).

56. Oliver Stone, *The Putin Interviews* (New York: Skyhorse Publishing, 2017).

57. Liphshiz, Cnaan, "Putin Attends Unveiling of Moscow's First Major Holocaust Monument," *Times of Israel*, June 5, 2019, https://www. timesofisrael.com/putin-attends-unveiling-of-moscows-first-major-holocaust-monument/; "Putin Donates Month's Salary to Jewish Museum," Ynetnews (via Reuters), June 6, 2007, https://www. ynetnews.com/articles/0,7340,L-3409150,00.html.

58. Н. Геворкян, А. Колесников, Н. Тимакова (N. Gevorkyan, A. Kolesnikov, N. Timakova), «От Первого Лица. Разговоры С Владимиром Путиным», Вагриус, 2000 (in Russian).

59. Angela E. Stent, *Putin's World: Russia Against the West and with the Rest* (New York: Twelve, 2019).

60. "Russia Takes on Its Demographic Decline," Stratfor, March 27, 2019, https://worldview.stratfor.com/article/russia-takes-its-demographic-decline.

61. Juliane Helmhold, "Netanyahu Meets Putin in Moscow, Attends Victory Day Parade," *Jerusalem Post*, May 9, 2018, https://www.jpost.

com/international/netanyahu-meets-putin-in-moscow-attends-victory-day-ceremony-555925.

62. Рейтинги Президента Путина, Центр Левада, Levada.ru; «Левада-центр», зафиксировал рекордно низкий рейтинг одобрения Путина, Ведомости (Vedomosti), May 6, 2020, https://www.vedomosti.ru/politics/news/2020/05/06/829651-levada-tsentr .

63. Michael Wines, "Election in Russia: The Overview," *New York Times*, March 27, 2000, https://www.nytimes.com/2000/03/27/world/election-russia-overview-putin-wins-russia-vote-first-round-but-his-majority.html.

64. "Russia Election: Vladimir Putin Wins by Big Margin," BBC News, March 19, 2018, https://www.bbc.com/news/world-europe-43452449.

65. Н. Геворкян, А. Колесников, Н. Тимакова (N. Gevorkyan, A. Kolesnikov, N. Timakova), «От Первого Лица. Разговоры С Владимиром Путиным,» Вагриус, 2000, (in Russian).

Chapter 3

1. «Российская Внешняя Политика и Евразийство», Eurasianet, Sepptember 6, 2005 (in Russian).

2. «Передовая «фабрика» военной мысли России: прошлое, настоящее, будущее», Военная Мысль Военно-теоретический журнал *(Military Thought)*, January 12, 2018 (in Russian); «Стратегия победы от Александра Андреевича Свечина», Независимая Газета (*Nezavisimaya Gazeta*), April 22, 2011, https://nvo.ng.ru/history/2011-04-22/14_svechin.html (in Russian); Aleksandr A. Svechin, *Strategy*, ed. Kent D. Lee (Minneapolis: East View Information Services, 2004) (a translation of: Стратегия, Военный Вестник, Москва, 1927).

3. «Владимир Путин: Быть сильными: гарантии национальной безопасности для России», Российская Газета (*Rossiyskaya Gazeta*), February 20, 2020, https://rg.ru/2012/02/20/putin-armiya.html (in Russian).

4. Ibid.

5. Герасимов В. (V. Gerasimov), «Генеральный штаб и оборона страны» «Военно-промышленный курьер» (*Voenno-Promishlenniy Kuryer*), February 3, 2014 (in Russian).

6. «О перспективах развития Вооружённых Сил, других войск, воинских формирований и органов, выполняющих задачи в области обороны, на период до 2030 года», Совет Безопасности Российской Федерации, November 22, 2019, http://www.scrf.gov.ru/council/session/2688/ (in Russian).

7. «Единоначалие как момент перехода к всеобщему самоуправлению», Журнал «Пропаганда» (*Propaganda*), October 15, 2013 (in Russian); Сергей Мельков, «Что все-таки означает "единоначалие" сегодня?», Еженедельник «Военно-промышленный курьер», July 12, 2006 (in Russian).

8. «Единоначалие как момент перехода к всеобщему самоуправлению» Журнал «Пропаганда» (*Propaganda*), October 15, 2013 (in Russian).

9. Carl Van Dyke, *The Soviet Invasion of Finland, 1939–40* (London and Portland, Oregon: Frank Cass, 1997), 40.

10. «Белому дому прописано единоначалие, Структура правительства претерпела мелкие, но тектонические сдвиги», Газета «Коммерсантъ» (*Kommersant*) 90 от May 22, 2012, стр. 2, https://www.kommersant.ru/daily/67226 (in Russian).

11. X (George Kennan), "The Sources of Soviet Conduct," *Foreign Affairs* 25, no. 4 (July 1947).

12. Carl von Clausewitz, *On War* (New York: Oxford University Press, 2006), 264.

13. Anthony D. McIvor, *Rethinking the Principles of War* (Annapolis, Maryland: Naval Institute Press, 2005), 29.

14. Jason Shell, "How the IED Won: Dispelling the Myth of Tactical Success and Innovation," War on the Rocks, May 1, 2017, https://warontherocks.com/2017/05/how-the-ied-won-dispelling-the-myth-of-tactical-success-and-innovation/.

15. Frank Hoffman, "Repairing America's Strategy Bridge," War on the Rocks, July 21, 2013, https://warontherocks.com/2013/07/repairing-americas-strategy-bridge/.

16. Andrew Krepinevich and Barry Watts, "Lost at the NSC," *National Interest*, January 6, 2009, https://nationalinterest.org/article/lost-at-the-nsc-2959.

17. Susannah Sirkin, "Assad's and Russia's Bombing of Hospitals Isn't an Accident—It's a Strategy," *Boston Globe*, September 12, 2019, https://www.bostonglobe.com/opinion/2019/09/12/assad-and-russia-bombing-hospitals-isn-accident-strategy/mfXdTb1uBqfxRkl1i FKOlM/story.html.

18. McIvor, *Rethinking the Principles of War*, xi.

19. Военная Академия Генерального Штаба Военных Сил Российской Федерации, www.mil.ru (in Russian).

20. «Герасимов и Дандфорд Обсуждали Вопросы ПРО» ("Gerasimov and Dunford Discussed the Issues of BMD [Ballistic Missile Defense]"), TACC, March 4, 2019 (in Russian).

21. Center of Military-Strategic Research, Military Academy of the General Staff of the Russian Federation, Russian Ministry of Defense, www.mil.ru (in Russian).

22. Чекинов С. Г., Богданов С. А. (S. G. Chekinov, S. A. Bogdanov), «Прогнозирование характера и содержания войн будущего: проблемы и суждения», Военная Мысль, Октябрь 2015 ("Forecasting of the Character and Content of Future Wars"), *Military Thought*, October 2015 (in Russian).

23. V. V. Kruglov, "Military Forecasting: State of Affairs, Opportunities, and Achievement of Results," *Military Thought*, December 2016 (in Russian).

24. Ibid.

25. V. V. Kruglov, "On the Methodology of the Forecasting of Armed Struggle," *Military Thought*, April 2017 (in Russian).

26. International Threats 2017, Analytic Agency "Foreign Policy," 2017.

27. S. P. Tsyrendorzhiyev and B. V. Kuroyedov, "Prospective Development of the International Relations System and Requirements for Ensuring Military Security of the Russian Federation," *Military Thought*, June 2017 (in Russian).

28. "Insider Information: How Insurance Companies Measure Risk," Insurance Companies.com, http://www.insurancecompanies.com/

insider-information-how-insurance-companies-measure-risk/ (no longer available).

29. Мисник Лидия (Lidiya Misnik), «Мешают стереотипы: Путин оценил действия НАТО. Путин оценил потенциальную угрозу для России со стороны НАТО», December 3, 2019 (in Russian).

30. «Владимир Путин: «Быть сильными: гарантии национальной безопасности для России», Российская Газета (*Rossiyskaya Gazeta*), February 20, 2020, https://rg.ru/2012/02/20/putin-armiya. html (in Russian).

31. Colin Clark, "VCJCS Selva: North Korea Hasn't Demonstrated Key Tech to Nuke US Yet," Breaking Defense, January 30, 2018, https:// breakingdefense.com/2018/01/vcjcs-selva-north-korea-hasnt-demonstrated-key-tech-nuke-us-yet/.

32. «Вопрос закрыт навсегда. В Госдуме ответили на слова Зеленского о Крыме», РИА Новости (RIA News), August 6, 2020, https://ria.ru/20200826/krym-1576332274.html (in Russian).

33. "How They Reacted in Russia to Pompeo's Declaration Regarding the Return of Crimea," RIA Novosti, August 4, 2019.

34. "Threats to Crimea Are Outlined and the Limits of Russia's Patience," RIA Novosti, July 19, 2018.

35. Martin Egnash and Chad Garland, "Ukrainian Troops Keep Russia on Their Minds as They Train with U.S. Marines," *Stars and Stripes*, July 15, 2018, https://www.stripes.com/ukrainian-troops-keep-russia-on-their-minds-as-they-train-with-us-marines-1.537838.

36. Герасимов Валерий (Valeriy Gerasimov), «Ценность науки в предвидении. Новые вызовы требуют переосмыслить формы и способы ведения боевых действий», «Военно-промышленный курьер» (*Voenno-premishlenniy Kuryer)*, February 26, 2013, https:// www.vpk-news.ru/articles/14632 (in Russian).

37. Ibid.

38. Герасимов Валерий (Valeriy Gerasimov), «Векторы развития военной стратегии. Начальник Генерального штаба Вооружённых Сил РФ генерал армии Валерий Герасимов выступил на общем собрании Академии военных наук»,

Красная звезда (*Red Star*), March 4, 2019, http://redstar.ru/vektory-razvitiya-voennoj-strategii/ (in Russian).

39. von Clausewitz, *On War*, 89.

40. Ibid.

41. Герасимов Валерий (Valeriy Gerasimov), «Векторы развития военной стратегии. Начальник Генерального штаба Вооружённых Сил РФ генерал армии Валерий Герасимов выступил на общем собрании Академии военных наук», Красная звезда (*Red Star*), March 4, 2019, http://redstar.ru/vektory-razvitiya-voennoj-strategii/ (in Russian).

42. Molly K. McKew, "The Gerasimov Doctrine," *Politico Magazine*, September/October 2017, https://www.politico.com/magazine/story/2017/09/05/gerasimov-doctrine-russia-foreign-policy-215538.

43. John Kruzel, "General Mattis: U.S. Must Prepare for 'Hybrid' Warfare," Small Wars Journal, February 13, 2009, https://smallwarsjournal.com/blog/general-mattis-us-must-prepare-for-hybrid-warfare.

44. B. H. Liddell Hart, *Strategy: The Classic Book on Military Strategy*, (New York: Penguin, 1991).

45. Стратегия Непрямых Действий, "Война и Мир", Словарь Военных Терминов (in Russian).

46. Карякин Владимир (Vladimir Karyakin), Россия как цель реализации стратегий «непрямых действий» и «мягкой силы» внешнеполитических акторов», Российский Институт Стратегических Исследований, Аналитика, December 11, 2012 (in Russian).

47. Герасимов Валерий (Valeriy Gerasimov), «Векторы развития военной стратегии. Начальник Генерального штаба Вооружённых Сил РФ генерал армии Валерий Герасимов выступил на общем собрании Академии военных наук» Красная звезда (*Red Star*), March 4, 2019, http://redstar.ru/vektory-razvitiya-voennoj-strategii/ (in Russian).

48. Указ Президента Российской Федерации от 23 июля 2017 г. № 631 (Edict of the President of the Russian Federation No. 631), Вопросы

Генерального штаба Вооруженных Сил Российской Федерации, July 23, 2013, pravo.gov.ru (in Russian).

49. "Putin's Former Aid: Russia Has Been Preparing for Global War Since 2003," Delfi En, September 26, 2014, https://en.delfi.lt/politics/putins-former-aid-russia-has-been-preparing-for-global-war-since-2003.d?id=65957992.

50. Карякин Владимир (Vladimir Karyakin), «Россия как цель реализации стратегий «непрямых действий» и «мягкой силы» внешнеполитических акторов» (On Employment of Strategies of Indirect Action and Soft Power in Geopolitical Confrontation), Российский Институт Стратегических Исследований (Russian Institute of Strategic Studies), Аналитика, December 11, 2012 (in Russian). This is a think tank that was founded by President Putin's edict and serves the Russian president.

51. Герасимов Валерий (Valeriy Gerasimov), «Ценность науки в предвидении. Новые вызовы требуют переосмыслить формы и способы ведения боевых действий», «Военно-промышленный курьер» (*Voenno-premishlenniy Kuryer),* February 26, 2013, https://www.vpk-news.ru/articles/14632 (in Russian).

52. Ibid.

53. *Intelligence Community Assessment: Assessing Russian Intelligence Activities and Intentions in Recent U.S. Elections* (National Intelligence Council: January 6, 2017), ICA 2017-01D, https://www.dni.gov/files/documents/ICA_2017_01.pdf.

54. Alexa Corse, "Foreign Threats More Numerous, Sophisticated as 2020 Election Looms, Official Says," *Wall Street Journal,* January 14, 2020, https://www.wsj.com/articles/foreign-threats-more-numerous-sophisticated-as-2020-election-looms-official-says-11579042613; United States v. Internet Research Agency LLC, Criminal No. 18 USC. 2, 371, 1349, 1028A, U.S. Department of Justice, https://www.justice.gov/file/1035477/download.

55. Сушенцов Андрей (Andrey Sushentsov), «Международные угрозы 2018», www.foreignpolicy.ru.

56. Ibid.

57. Yuri Bezmenov (Tomas Schuman, pseud.), *World Thought Police 1986* (Los Angeles: NATA Almanac, 1986), https://archive.org/details/BezmenovWorldThoughtPolice1986.

58. Yuri Bezmenov (Tomas Schuman, pseud.), *Love Letter to America* (Los Angeles: W.I.N. Almanac Panorama, 1984), https://archive.org/details/BezmenovLoveLetterToAmerica.

59. Карякин Владимир (Vladimir Karyakin), «Россия как цель реализации стратегий «непрямых действий» и «мягкой силы» внешнеполитических акторов» (On Employment of Strategies of Indirect Action and Soft Power in Geopolitical Confrontation), Российский Институт Стратегических Исследований (Russian Institute of Strategic Studies), June 4, 2013 (in Russian).

60. *Intelligence Community Assessment: Assessing Russian Intelligence Activities and Intentions in Recent U.S. Elections* (National Intelligence Council: January 6, 2017), ICA 2017-01D, https://www.dni.gov/files/documents/ICA_2017_01.pdf.

61. Ibid.

62. United States v. Internet Research Agency LLC, Criminal No. 18 USC. 2, 371, 1349, 1028A, U.S. Department of Justice, https://www.justice.gov/file/1035477/download.

63. Deirdre Shesgreen, "GOP Lawmaker: Russian Agents Stirred Racial Divisions at Fatal Charlottesville Rally," *USA Today*, August 11, 2018, https://www.usatoday.com/story/news/politics/2018/08/11/russians-involved-unite-right-charlottesville-tom-garrett-jr/966669002/.

64. Floriana Fossato, "Russia: Primakov Back In Moscow as NATO Prepares to Strike Serbia," Radio Free Europe/Radio Liberty, March 24, 1999, https://www.rferl.org/a/1090871.html.

65. 2000 Military Doctrine of the Russian Federation, approved by President Putin (in Russian).

66. George W. Bush, "Joint Declaration by President George W. Bush and President Vladimir V. Putin on the New Strategic Relationship between the United States of America and the Russian Federation," May 24, 2002, https://www.presidency.ucsb.edu/documents/joint-declaration-president-george-w-bush-and-president-vladimir-v-putin-the-new-strategic.

67. "Robert Hanssen," FBI History, U.S. Federal Bureau of Invesigation, https://www.fbi.gov/history/famous-cases/robert-hanssen.

68. Reuters Staff, "Obama Tells Russia's Medvedev More Flexibility after Election," Reuters, March 26, 2012, https://www.reuters.com/article/us-nuclear-summit-obama-medvedev/obama-tells-russias-medvedev-more-flexibility-after-election-idUSBRE82P0JI20120326.

69. Brian Whitmore, "Did Russia Plan Its War with Georgia?," Radio Free Europe/Radio Liberty, August 15, 2008, https://www.rferl.org/a/Did_Russia_Plan_Its_War_In_Georgia__/1191460.html.

Chapter 4

1. "Challenges to Security in Space," U.S. Defense Intelligence Agency, February 2019, https://media.defense.gov/2019/Feb/11/2002088710/-1/-1/1/SPACE -SECURITY-CHALLENGES.PDF.

2. "About NRO," U.S. National Reconnaissance Office, https://www.nro.gov/About-NRO/.

3. "UCS Satellite Database," Union of Concerned Scientists, published December 8, 2005, updated August 1, 2020, https://www.ucsusa.org/resources/satellite-database.

4. Clifton B. Parker, "Deterrence in Space Key to U.S. Security," U.S. Strategic Command, January 24, 2017, https://www.stratcom.mil/Media/News/News-Article-View/Article/1059106/deterrence-in-space-key-to-us-security/.

5. Ibid.

6. «Космос и характер современных военных действий», Журнал «Воздушно-космическая оборона» (*Vozdushno-kosmicheskaya Oborona*), December 1, 2009.

7. "Hearing to Consider the Nomination of: Vice Admiral Charles A. Richard, USN to Be Admiral and Commander, United States Strategic Command," Senate Committee on Armed Services, U.S. Senate, October 24, 2019, https://www.armed-services.senate.gov/imo/media/doc/19-71_10-24-19.pdf.

8. Ibid.

9. Isabel Coles, "'We Could Feel the Shock Wave': How U.S. Troops Withstood Attack on Iraq Base," *Wall Street Journal*, January 13, 2020,

https://www.wsj.com/articles/we-could-feel-the-shock-wave-how-u-s-troops-withstood-attack-on-iraq-base-11578942544.

10. "Remarks by President Trump on Iran," White House, January 8, 2020, https://www.whitehouse.gov/briefings-statements/remarks-president-trump-iran/.

11. Sandra Erwin, "STRATCOM Chief Hyten: 'I Will Not Support Buying Big Satellites That Make Juicy Targets,'" Space News, November 19, 2017, https://spacenews.com/stratcom-chief-hyten-i-will-not-support-buying-big-satellites-that-make-juicy-targets/.

12. Ibid.

13. «Владимир Путин рассказал о защите России в космосе», Российская газета (*Rossiyskaya Gazeta*), December 4, 2019.

14. «Стратегическая стабильность в мировой политике: формулы академика Кокошина», Журнал Международная жизнь, Векторы развития военной стратегии, Красная звезда (*Red Star*), March 4, 2019.

15. «Лавров: РФ при любом развитии событий с НАТО сможет отстоять свой суверенитет», TASS, September 1, 2017, https://tass.ru/politika/4523873.

16. Ibid.

17. «Ядерная доктрина США», Независимое Военное Обозрение (Nezavisimoe Voennoe Obozrenie), March 22, 2002, https://nvo.ng.ru/wars/2002-03-22/1_doctrine.html.

18. *2019 Missile Defense Review* (Office of the Secretary of Defense, U.S. Department of Defense, 2019), https://www.defense.gov/Portals/1/Interactive/2018/11-2019-Missile-Defense -Review/The%202019%20MDR_Executive%20Summary.pdf.

19. "Russian Space Wars: U.S. Intelligence Claims Kremlin Made Seventh Test Of Nudol ASAT Missile," SpaceWatch.Global, https://spacewatch.global/2019/01/russian-space-wars-u-s-intelligence-claims-kremlin-made-seventh-test-of-nudol-asat-missile/; *2019 U.S. Missile Defense Review*.

20. Leonard David, "China's Anti-Satellite Test: Worrisome Debris Cloud Circles Earth," Space, February 2, 2007, https://www.space.com/3415-china-anti-satellite-test-worrisome-debris-cloud-circles-earth.html.

21. Jay Raymond, "Operations Group Blazes New Trail during Operation Burnt Frost," Peterson Air Force Base, U.S. Space Force, March 11, 2008, https://www.peterson.spaceforce.mil/News/Article/328607/ operations-group-blazes-new-trail-during-operation-burnt-frost/.

22. «Военная Доктрина Российской Федерации», Утверждена Указом Президента Российской Федерации, February 5, 2010.

23. "Laika, the Heroine of Space, Who Had No Chance of Return," BBC in Russian, November 3, 2017.

24. Ibid.

25. Robert Krulwich, "Cosmonaut Crashed into Earth 'Crying in Rage,'" NPR, March 18, 2011, https://www.npr.org/sections/ krulwich/2011/05/02/134597833/cosmonaut-crashed-into-earth-crying-in-rage.

26. AU-18, Space Primer, Air Command and Staff College, Space Research Electives Seminars.

27. Jeffrey T. Richelson, *America's Space Sentinels: The History of the DSP and SBIRS Satellite Systems* (University Press of Kansas, 1999).

28. *National Intelligence Estimate: The Soviet Space Program* (U.S. Central Intelligence Agency, 1983), declassified; *National Intelligence Estimate: Soviet Space Programs* (U.S. Central Intelligence Agency, 1985), declassified.

29. «Зато мы делаем макеты», Журнал «Коммерсантъ Власть» (*Kommersant*) №44 от, November 17, 1998, стр. 38.

30. Елисеева Марина and Томиленко Мария (Marina Eliseeva and Mariya Tomilenko), «Опередивший время. Взгляды маршала Огаркова на военную реформу оказались провидческими», Красная Звезда (*Red Star*), October 31, 2017.

31. «Сетецентричная война: чему советский маршал научил американцев», Русская семерка, Rambler News, Febrary 8, 2019.

32. «Человек, который мог разгромить НАТО: Победная доктрина маршала Огаркова», Аргументы и Факты (*Argumenty i Fakty*) (in Russian).

33. *National Intelligence Estimate: The Soviet Space Program*; *National Intelligence Estimate: Soviet Space Programs.*

34. *National Intelligence Estimate: Soviet Space Programs.*

35. J. C. Moltz, *Space.*

36. Ken Dilanian, "Why Does the U.S. Use Russian Rockets to Launch Its Satellites?," NBC News, June 9, 2016, https://www.nbcnews.com/mach/space/why-does-u-s-use-russian-rockets-launch-its-satellites-n588526; David Welna, "Why the U.S. Still Has No Viable Alternatives to Russian Rocket Boosters," NPR, February 8, 2016, https://www.npr.org/2016/02/08/465974255/why-the-u-s-still-has-no-viable-alternatives-to-russian-rocket-boosters.

37. *Challenges to Security in Space* (U.S. Defense Intelligence Agency, February 2019), https://media.defense.gov/2019/Feb/11/2002088710/-1/-1/1/SPACE-SECURITY-CHALLENGES.PDF.

38. Ibid.

39. Ibid.

40. Jared Keller, "After Experiencing Russian Jamming Up Close in Syria, the Pentagon Is Scrambling to Catch Up," Business Insider, June 3, 2019, https://www.businessinsider.com/pentagon-focus-on-electronic-warfare-after-russian-jamming-in-syria-2019-6.

41. GPS NUDET, USTI, 1993; Welna, "Why the U.S. Still Has No Viable Alternatives to Russian Rocket Boosters."

42. Raymond Limbach, "Battle of Stalingrad," *Encyclopedia Britannica*, updated October 2, 2020, https://www.britannica.com/event/Battle-of-Stalingrad

43. Todd Harrison, Kaitlyn Johnson, and Thomas Roberts, *Space Threat Assessment 2019* (Center for Strategic and International Studies, April 2019), https://www.csis.org/analysis/space-threat-assessment-2019; *Challenges to Security in Space* (U.S. Defense Intelligence Agency, February 2019), https://media.defense.gov/2019/Feb/11/2002088710/-1/-1/1/SPACE-SECURITY-CHALLENGES.PDF; Brian Weeden and Victoria Samson, eds., *Global Counterspace Capabilities* (Secure World Foundation, April 2019), https://swfound.org/media/206408/swf_global_counterspace_april2019_web.pdf.

44. Kyle Mizokami, "It Sure Looks Like Russia Just Tested a Space Weapon," *Popular Mechanics*, December 17, 2020, https://www.popularmechanics.com/military/weapons/a34992366/russia-test-space-weapon-satellite-killing-missile/.

45. Richard Sisk, "SecDef Esper: The Military's Next Big Fight May Start in Space," Military.com, September 18, 2019, https://www.military.com/daily-news/2019/09/18/secdef-esper-militarys-next-big-fight-may-start-space.html.

46. Patrick Shanahan, "Remarks by Acting Secretary Shanahan at the 35th Space Symposium, Colorado Springs, Colorado," U.S. Department of Defense, April 9, 2019, https://www.defense.gov/Newsroom/Transcripts/Transcript/Article/1809882/remarks-by-acting-secretary-shanahan-at-the-35thspace-symposium-colorado-sprin/.

47. Keller, "After Experiencing Russian Jamming Up Close in Syria, the Pentagon Is Scrambling to Catch Up," Business Insider, June 3, 2019, https://www.businessinsider.com/pentagon-focus-on-electronic-warfare-after-russian-jamming-in-syria-2019-6; Joel Gehrke, "State Department: U.S. Lags China and Russia in Development of Hypersonic Missiles," *Washington Examiner*, July 21, 2020, https://www.washingtonexaminer.com/policy/defense-national-security/state-department-us-lags-china-and-russia-in-development-of-hypersonic-missiles.

48. Rebeccah Heinrichs, "Regaining the Strategic Advantage in an Age of Great Power Competition: A Conversation with Michael Griffin," Hudson Institute, April 25, 2018, https://www.hudson.org/research/14284-full-transcript-regaining-the-strategic-advantage-in-an-age-of-great-power-competition-a-conversation-with-michael-griffin.

49. William Shelton, *Military Space Programs in Review of the Defense Authorization Request for Fiscal Year 2013 and the Future Years Defense Program* (Department of the Air Force, Presentation to the Subcommittee on Strategic Forces, Senate Armed Services Committee, U.S. Senate, March 21, 2012), https://www.armed-services.senate.gov/imo/media/doc/Shelton%2003-21-12.pdf.

50. John T. Correll, "The Counter-Revolution in Military Affairs," *Air Force Magazine*, July 1, 2019, https://www.airforcemag.com/article/the-counter-revolution-in-military-affairs/.

51. Ibid.

52. *2019 Missile Defense Review.*

Chapter 5

1. Author's performance reports from DIA.
2. Панарин Игорь (Igor Panarin), «Система информационного противоборства», Военно-Промышленный Курьер (*Voenno Promishlenniy Kuryer*), October 15, 2008, https://www.vpk-news.ru/articles/3672.
3. *A 2017 Joint Statement for the Record by Former DNI Clapper, former Director of NSA and Head of U.S. Cyber Command Admiral Rogers, and USDI Marcel Lettre at the Worldwide Annual Threat Assessment of the U.S. Intelligence Community* (Statement for the Record, Senate Select Committee on Intelligence, U.S. Senate, January 29, 2019).
4. Sean Lyngaas, "Hayden: Russian Cyber Sophistication Derives from Criminal Groups," FCW, May 24, 2016, https://fcw.com/articles/2016/05/24/hayden-russia-cyber.aspx.
5. *Meet the Press*, transcript for May 28, 2017, NBC News, May 28, 2017, https://www.nbcnews.com/meet-the-press/meet-press-may-28-2017-n765626.
6. «Доктрина Информационной Безопасности Российской Федерации», Дата подписания 5 декабря 2016 г (written December 5, 2016), Опубликован 6 декабря 2016 г (published December 6, 2016), Утверждена Указом Президента Российской Федерации от 5 декабря 2016 г, №646 (in Russian).
7. Информационное Противоборство, Война и Мир, Словарь Военных Терминов, Под редакцией Рогозина (in Russian).
8. *Russia Military Power: Building a Military to Support Great Power Aspirations* (U.S. Defense Intelligence Agency, 2017), https://www.dia.mil/Portals/27/Documents/News/Military%20Power%20Publications/Russia%20Military%20Power%20Report%202017.pdf.
9. Craig Whitlock, Leslie Shapiro, and Armand Emamdjomeh, "The Afghanistan Papers: A Secret History of the War," *Washington Post*, December 9, 2019, https://www.washingtonpost.com/graphics/2019/investigations/afghanistan-papers/documents-database/.

10. «Военная Доктрина Российской Федерации», 2014; «Стратегия Национальной Безопасности Российской Федерации», 2015; «Концепция Внешней Политики Российской Федерации», 2016.

11. «Доктрина Информационной Безопасности Российской Федерации», Дата подписания 5 декабря 2016 г (written December 5, 2016), Опубликован 6 декабря 2016 г (published December 6, 2016), Утверждена Указом Президента Российской Федерации от 5 декабря 2016 г, №646 (in Russian).

12. *Special Report: Quantifying the Q Conspiracy: A Data-Driven Approach to Understanding the Threat Posed by QAnon* (The Soufan Center, April 2021), https://thesoufancenter.org/wp-content/ uploads/2021/04/TSC-White-Paper_QAnon_16April2021-final-1.pdf.

13. *A 2017 Joint Statement for the Record by Former DNI Clapper.*

14. Ibid.

15. *Russia Military Power: Building a Military to Support Great Power Aspirations* (U.S. Defense Intelligence Agency, 2017), https://www.dia. mil/Portals/27/Documents/News/Military%20Power%20 Publications/Russia%20Military%20Power%20Report%202017.pdf.

16. "What Is Stuxnet?" McAfee, https://www.mcafee.com/enterprise/ en-us/security-awareness/ransomware/what-is-stuxnet.html; "Stuxnet," *Encyclopaedia Britannica*, updated November 23, 2016, https://www.britannica.com/technology/Stuxnet.

17. "What Is Stuxnet?" McAfee.

18. Beth Duff-Brown, "At Stanford, Secretary of Defense Ashton Carter Unveils Cyber Strategy, Calls for Renewed Partnership with Silicon Valley," *Stanford News*, April 24, 2015, https://news.stanford. edu/2015/04/24/ash-carter-talk-042415/.

19. Jamie Crawford, "Russians Hacked Pentagon Network, Carter Says," CNN, June 4, 2015, https://www.cnn.com/2015/04/23/politics/ russian-hackers-pentagon-network/index.html.

20. Danny Yadron, "Three Months Later, State Department Hasn't Rooted Out Hackers," *Wall Street Journal*, February 19, 2015, https:// www.wsj.com/articles/three-months-later-state-department-hasnt- rooted-out-hackers-1424391453.

21. Ellen Nakashima, "Cyber-Intruder Sparks Response, Debate," *Washington Post*, December 8, 2011, https://www.washingtonpost.

com/national/national-security/cyber-intruder-sparks-response-debate/2011/12/06/gIQAxLuFgO_story.html.

22. Jenny Strasburg and Dustin Volz, "Russian Hackers Blamed for Attacks on Coronavirus Vaccine-Related Targets," *Wall Street Journal*, July 16, 2020, https://www.wsj.com/articles/russian-hackers-blamed-for-attacks-on-coronavirus-vaccine-related-targets-11594906060.

23. Rebecca Ruiz, "Simone Biles and Williams Sisters Latest Target of Russian Hackers," *New York Times*, September 13, 2016, https://www.nytimes.com/2016/09/14/sports/simone-biles-serena-venus-williams-russian-hackers-doping.html.

24. Paul Elias, "Hacker Gets 5 Years for Russian-Linked Yahoo Breach," Associated Press, May 29, 2018, https://apnews.com/article/2664cefa070e470584a59bd56f8688a5.

25. Holly Ellyatt, "Russia 'Concerned' for Human Rights as It Watches U.S. Protests, Kremlin Says," CNBC, June 10, 2020, https://www.cnbc.com/2020/06/10/george-floyd-protests-russia-concerned-for-human-rights-in-us.html.

26. "VI Moscow Conference on International Security," Russian Ministry of Defence, April 26–27, 2017, https://eng.mil.ru/en/mcis/2017.htm.

27. Ibid.

28. Ibid.

29. Michael Hayden and Wesley Clark, "Russia: Cold War 2.0?" (interview), Michael V. Hayden Center for Intelligence, Policy, and International Security, George Mason University, March 5, 2018, https://haydencenter.gmu.edu/news/general-michael-hayden-discusses-russia-cold-war-2.0-with-former-nato-saceur-general-wesley-clark-at-hayden-center-event-5-mar-2018.

30. Emily Tillett, "Michael Hayden Fears Russian Meddling 'Narrative' Is Being Lost," CBS News, October 18, 2017, https://www.cbsnews.com/news/michael-hayden-fears-russian-meddling-narrative-isnt-a-top-priority/.

31. Daniel Coats, *Worldwide Annual Threat Assessment of the U.S. Intelligence Community*.

32. David E. Sanger and Nicole Perlroth, "U.S. Escalates Online Attacks on Russian Power Grid," *New York Times*, June 15, 2019, https://www.nytimes.com/2019/06/15/us/politics/trump-cyber-russia-grid.html.

33. «Уроки на все времена», Красная Звезда (*Red Star*), October 27, 2010, http://old.redstar.ru/2010/10/27_10/1_06.html.

34. Полегаев В. И. (V. I. Polegayev), «О неядерном сдерживании, его роли и месте в системе стратегического сдерживания» ("Regarding Deterrence and Its Role and Place in the System of Strategic Deterrence"), Полковник в запасе, Военная Мысль (*Military Thought*), July 2015 (in Russian).

35. Чекинов С. Г. (S. G. Chekinov), Богданов С. А. (S. A. Bogdanov), «Асимметричные действия по обеспечению военной безопасности России», Военная Мысль (*Military Thought*) № 3/2010, стр. 13-22 (in Russian).

36. *Worldwide Threat Assessment of the US Intelligence Community* (Statement for the Record, Senate Armed Services Committee, U.S. Senate, February 26, 2015), https://www.dni.gov/files/documents/Unclassified_2015_ATA_SFR_-_SASC_FINAL.pdf.

37. "Russian Government Cyber Activity Targeting Energy and Other Critical Infrastructure Sectors," Alert (TA18-074A), Cybersecurity and Infrastructure Security Agency (CISA), March 15, 2018, https://us-cert.cisa.gov/ncas/alerts/TA18-074A.

38. Catalin Cimpanu, "You Have around 20 Minutes to Contain a Russian APT Attack," ZDNET, February 19, 2019, https://www.zdnet.com/article/you-have-around-20-minutes-to-contain-a-russian-apt-attack/.

39. Ibid.

40. Adam Meyers, "Meet the Threat Actors: List of APTs and Adversary Groups," Crowdstrike, February 24, 2019, https://www.crowdstrike.com/blog/meet-the-adversaries/.

41. Michael Schmitt, ed., *Tallinn Manual 2.0 on the International Law Applicable to Cyber Operations*, 2nd ed. (Cambridge: Cambridge University Press, 2017).

42. Ellen Nakashima, "Russia's Apparent Meddling in U.S. Election Is Not an Act of War, Cyber Expert Says," *Washington Post*, February 7, 2017, https://www.washingtonpost.com/news/checkpoint/wp/2017/02/07/russias-apparent-meddling-in-u-s-election-is-not-an-act-of-war-cyber-expert-says/.

43. Daniel Coats, *Worldwide Annual Threat Assessment of the U.S. Intelligence Community*.

44. Ibid.

45. Michael Schmidt and David Sanger, "Russian Hackers Read Obama's Unclassified Emails, Officials Say," *New York Times*, April 25, 2015, https://www.nytimes.com/2015/04/26/us/russian-hackers-read-obamas-unclassified-emails-officials-say.html.

Chapter 6

1. Vladimir Putin, "A Plea for Caution from Russia," *New York Times*, September 11, 2013, https://www.nytimes.com/2013/09/12/opinion/putin-plea-for-caution-from-russia-on-syria.html.

2. George Lardner Jr., "Unbeatable Bugs: The Moscow Embassy Fiasco," *Washington Post*, June 18, 1990, https://www.washingtonpost.com/archive/politics/1990/06/18/unbeatable-bugs-the-moscow-embassy-fiasco/5bb6dcbf-0a61-4948-a953-e2d81085ed05/.

3. Putin, "A Plea for Caution from Russia."

4. Ibid.

5. Sun Tzu, *The Art of War* (El Paso: El Paso Norte Press Special Edition Books, 2011).

6. Ивахин А. И. (Ivakhin, A. I.), Прыгунов П. Я. (Prigunov P. Ya.), «Оперативная Деятельность и Вопросы Конспирации в Работе Спецслужб» (*Manual on Operational Tradecraft and Clandestine Activities of Special Services*), 2006 (in Russian).

7. Ibid.

8. Ibid.

9. Lardner Jr., "Unbeatable Bugs."

10. Interview with the author.

11. Ibid.

12. Lardner Jr., "Unbeatable Bugs."

13. Interview with the author.

14. Elaine Sciolino, "The Bugged Embassy Case: What Went Wrong," *New York Times*, November 15, 1988, https://www.nytimes.

com/1988/11/15/world/the-bugged-embassy-case-what-went-wrong. html.

15. "The Thing: Great Seal Bug," Crypto Museum, https://www. cryptomuseum.com/covert/bugs/thing/index.htm.

16. Calder Walton, "That Time the Soviets Bugged Congress, and Other Spy Tales," *Politico Magazine*, May 22, 2017, https://www.politico. com/magazine/story/2017/05/22/donald-trump-russia-soviet-union-spying-congress-bug-215174.

17. Jane Onyanga-Omara, "Suspected Russian Spy Worked at the US Embassy in Moscow for over 10 Years, Reports Say," *USA Today*, August 3, 2018, https://www.usatoday.com/story/news/ world/2018/08/03/suspected-russian-spy-worked-us-embassy-moscow/896671002/.

18. Associated Press, "U.S. Embassy in Moscow Removes a Radio Antenna," *New York Times*, November 14, 1977, https://www.nytimes. com/1977/11/14/archives/world-news-briefs-us-embassy-in-moscow-removes-a-radio-antenna-byrd.html; Lynn Rosellini, "Russians Deny the Use of Antennas for Spying," *New York Times*, December 21, 1981, https://www.nytimes.com/1981/12/21/us/russians-denny-the-use-of-antennas-for-spying.html; Joe Kukura, "Tales of Espionage at S.F. Russian Consulate," *SF Weekly*, December 15, 2017, https://www. sfweekly.com/news/tales-of-espionage-at-s-f-russian-consulate/.

19. «От Первого Лица» (in Russian).

20. Sun Tzu, *The Art of War*.

21. Ведомости (in Russian).

22. Ведомости (Vedomosti), July 27, 2010 (in Russian).

23. Christopher Andrew, *The Sword and the Shield* (New York: Basic Books, 1999).

24. Ibid.

25. Ibid.

26. Ibid.

27. Ibid.

28. "Operation Ghost Stories: Inside the Russian Spy Case," FBI News, October 31, 2011, https://www.fbi.gov/news/stories/operation-ghost-stories-inside-the-russian-spy-case; "Ten Alleged Secret Agents Arrested in the United States," Press Release, U.S. Department of

Justice, June 28, 2010, https://www.justice.gov/opa/pr/ten-alleged-secret-agents-arrested-united-states; Amit Kachhia-Patel, United States of America v. Anna Chapman and Mikhail Semenko, complaint (violation of 18 USC 371), U.S. District Court for the Southern District of New York, June 27, 2010, https://www.justice.gov/sites/default/files/opa/legacy/2010/06/28/062810complaint1.pdf; Maria Ricci, *United States of America v. Christopher Metsos et al.*, U.S. District Court for the Southern District of New York, complaint (violations of 18 USC 371 and 1956), June 25, 2010, https://www.justice.gov/sites/default/files/opa/legacy/2010/06/28/062810complaint2.pdf.

29. Ibid.

30. Rob Gillies, "Son of Russian Spies Relieved to Keep Canadian Citizenship," Associated Press, December 20, 2019, https://apnews.com/article/624c7589bc4f340da19db58e609bb7f2.

31. Ивахин А. И. (A. I. Ivakhin), Прыгунов П. Я. (Prigunov P. Ya.), «Оперативная Деятельность и Вопросы Конспирации в Работе Спецслужб» (*Manual on Operational Tradecraft and Clandestine Activities of Special Services*), 2006 (in Russian).

32. Ibid.

33. Ibid.

34. Ibid.

35. Interview with author.

36. Ibid.

37. Ibid.

38. Daniel Coats, *Worldwide Annual Threat Assessment of the U.S. Intelligence Community* (Statement for the Record, Senate Select Committee on Intelligence, U.S. Senate, January 29, 2019), https://www.dni.gov/files/ODNI/documents/2019-ATA-SFR---SSCI.pdf.

39. Ibid.

40. Mary Louise Kelly, "Director of U.S. Counterintelligence William Evanina Outlines Espionage Threats," NPR, October 2, 2019, https://www.npr.org /2019/10/02/766568786/director-of-u-s-counterintelligence-william-evanina-outlines-espionage-threats.

41. "Statement by NCSC Director William Evanina: 100 Days until Election 2020," News Release, Office of the Director of National Intelligence, July 24, 2020, https://www.dni.gov/index.php/ newsroom/press-releases/item/2135-statement -by-ncsc-director- william-evanina-100-days-until-election-2020; Dan De Luce, "Counterintelligence Chief Warns of Threat to Democracy from Foreign Hackers, Spies," NBC News, February 10, 2020, https://www. nbcnews.com/politics/national-security/u-s-counterintel-chief- warns-threat-democracy-foreign-hackers-spies-n1134476.

42. Kelly, "Director of U.S. Counterintelligence William Evanina Outlines Espionage Threats."

43. *An Assessment of the Aldrich H. Ames Espionage Case and Its Implications for U.S. Intelligence*, Senate Select Committee on Intelligence, U.S. Senate, S. Rep. No. 84-046 (1994); Stefan Pluta, *United States of America* v. *Robert Philip Hanssen*, affidavit (in support of complaint for violations of 794 (a) and (c)), U.S. District Court for the Eastern District of Virginia, February 2001, https://fas. org/irp/ops/ci/hanssen_affidavit.html.

Chapter 7

1. Vitaly Shevchenko, "'Little Green Men' or 'Russian Invaders'?," BBC News, March 11, 2014, https://www.bbc.com/news/world- europe-26532154.

2. Diddley Squat, "Nuland-Pyatt Leaked Phone Conversation Complete with Subtitles," YouTube video, April 29, 2014, https://www.youtube. com.watch?v=WV9J6sxCs5k; Jonathan Marcus, "Ukraine Crisis: Transcript of Leaked Nuland-Pyatt Call," BBC News, February 7, 2014, https://www.bbc.com/news/world-europe-26079957.

3. "Joint Duty," Office of the Director of National Intelligence, https:// www.dni.gov/index.php/careers/joint-duty.

4. Greg Miller, "CIA Looks to Expand Its Cyber Espionage Capabilities," *Washington Post*, February 23, 2015, https://www.washingtonpost. com/world/national-security/cia-looks-to-expand-its-cyber- espionage-capabilities/2015/02/23/

a028e80c-b94d-11e4-9423-f3d0a1ec335c_story.html; "A Day in the Life of a CIA Operations Center Officer," CIA News, https://www.cia.gov/news -information/featured-story-archive/2014-featured-story-archive/a-day-in-the-life-of-a-cia-operations-center-officer.html; "CIA Organizational Chart," unclassified, Federation of American Scientists, https://fas.org/irp/cia/orgchart.pdf.

5. Активные Мероприятия, Контрразведывательный словарь, Высшая краснознаменная школа Комитета Государственной Безопасности при Совете Министров СССР им. Ф. Э. Дзержинского (F. Z. Dzerzhinskogo), 1972 г (in Russian); *Soviet Active Measures in the United States—an Updated Report by the FBI. Congressional Record*, E4716, declassified and approved for release, December 9, 1987, CIA-RDP11M01338R000400470089-2.

6. Активные Мероприятия, Контрразведывательный словарь, Высшая краснознаменная школа Комитета Государственной Безопасности при Совете Министров СССР им. Ф. Э. Дзержинского (F. Z. Dzerzhinskogo), 1972 г (in Russian).

7. Richard H. Schultz and Roy Godson, *Dezinformatsia: Active Measures in Soviet Strategy* (Washington, D.C.: Pergamon-Brassey's, 1984).

8. Christopher Andrew and Vasily Mitrokhin, *The Sword and the Shield: The Mitrokhin Archive and the Secret History of the KGB* (New York: Basic Books, 2001), 122; Paul Kengor, *Dupes. How America's Adversaries Have Manipulated Progressives for a Century* (Wilmington: ISI Books, 2010), 160, 179.

9. Gary Kern, "How 'Uncle Joe' Bugged FDR," CIA Library, Central Intelligence Agency, https://www.cia.gov/library/center-for-the-study-of-intelligence/csi-publications/csi-studies/studies/vol47no1/article02.html.

10. Andrew and Mitrokhin, *The Sword and the Shield*, 122; Kengor, *Dupes*, 160, 179.

11. "Russian National Charged in Conspiracy to Act as an Agent of the Russian Federation within the United States," News, U.S. Department of Justice, https://www.justice.gov/opa/pr/russian-national-charged-conspiracy-act-agent-russian-federation-within-united-states.

12. Amit Kachhia-Patel, United States of America v. Anna Chapman and Mikhail Semenko, complaint (violation of 18 USC 371), U.S. District Court for the Southern District of New York, June 27, 2010, https:// www.justice.gov/sites/default/files/opa/legacy/2010/06/28/062810co mplaint1.pdf; Maria Ricci, United States of America v. Christopher R. Metsos, complaint (violation of 18 USC 371 and 1956), U.S. District Court for the Southern District of New York, June 25, 2010, https:// www.justice.gov/sites/default/files/opa/legacy/2010/06/28/062810co mplaint2.pdf.

13. *Soviet Active Measures in the United States—an Updated Report by the FBI. Congressional Record.*

14. Ibid.

15. Ibid.

16. Ibid.

17. Anton Troianovski, "As Bernie Sanders Pushed for Closer Ties, Soviet Union Spotted Opportunity," *New York Times*, March 5, 2020, https:// www.nytimes.com/2020/03/05/world/europe/bernie-sanders-soviet-russia.html.

18. *Soviet Active Measures in the United States—an Updated Report by the FBI. Congressional Record*; *Soviet Propaganda and Active Measures Efforts to Influence Arms Control Issues* (U.S. Central Intelligence Agency, July 22, 1986), declassified in part—sanitized copy approved for release, November 21, 2011, CIA-RDP86T01017R000101170001-0.

19. *Soviet Propaganda and Active Measures Efforts to Influence Arms Control Issues.*

20. Conversation with the author.

21. Robert Barns, "Supreme Court Passes on Case Involving Baker Who Refused to Make Wedding Cake for Same-Sex Couple," *Washington Post*, June 17, 2019, https://www.washingtonpost.com/politics/courts_ law/supreme-court-passes-on-new-case-involving-baker-who-refused-to-make-wedding-cake/2019/06/17/f78c5ae0-7a71-11e9-a5b3-34f3edf1351e_story.html.

22. Schultz and Godson, *Dezinformatsia: Active Measures in Soviet Strategy.*

23. Thomas Boghardt, *Operation Infektion: Soviet Bloc Intelligence and Its AIDS Disinformation Campaign* (Center for Strategic and Intelligence Studies), CIA Library, U.S. Central Intelligence Agency, https://www.cia.gov/library/center-for-the-study-of-intelligence/csi-publications/csi-studies/studies/vol53no4/pdf/U-%20Boghardt-AIDS-Made%20in%20the%20USA-17Dec.pdf.

24. «'Активные мероприятия' советских спецслужб: Одной из самых успешных акций Первого главного управления (внешней разведки) К» Коммерсантъ №2 (*Kommersant*), January 13, 2003, https://www.kommersant.ru/doc/358576 (in Russian).

25. Yuri Bezmenov (Tomas Schuman, pseud.), *Love Letter to America* (Los Angeles: W.I.N. Almanac Panorama, 1984), https://archive.org/details/BezmenovLoveLetterToAmerica.

26. Thom Shanker and Mark Landler, "Putin Says U.S. Is Undermining Global Stability," *New York Times*, February 11, 2007, https://www.nytimes.com/2007/02/11/world/europe/11munich.html.

27. Julian Barnes and David Sanger, "Russian Intelligence Agencies Push Disinformation on Pandemic," *New York Times*, July 28, 2020, https://www.nytimes.com/2020/07/28/us/politics/russia-disinformation-coronavirus.html.

28. Vladimir Isachenkov, "Putin Sternly Warns US against Putting Missiles in Europe," Associated Press, February 20, 2019, https://apnews.com/article/50d1cc8634214139ae73d3a45e53ef77; "US Missile Defense System Deployment May Destabilize World, Russian Security Chief Warns," TASS, September 15, 2020, https://tass.com/defense/1201069.

29. Rob Barry and Shane Shifflett, "Russian Trolls Tweeted Disinformation Long before U.S. Election," *Wall Street Journal*, February 20, 2018, https://www.wsj.com/graphics/russian-trolls-tweeted-disinformation-long-before-u-s-election/.

30. Vladimir A. Lefebvre, *Lectures on Reflexive Game Theory* (Los Angeles: Leaf & Oaks Publishers, 2010).

31. Ibid.

32. Кирюшин. А. Н. (A. N. Kiryushin), «Информационное противоборство: проблема терминологической

недостаточности», Центр анализа террористических угроз (Tsentr analiza terroristicheskikh ugroz) (in Russian); Махнин В. Л. (L. V. Makhnin), «Рефлексивные Процессы в Военном Искусстве», Журнал Военная Мысль (*Military Thought*) (in Russian).

33. Edward Jay Epstein, *Deception: The Invisible War between the KGB and the CIA* (New York: Simon and Schuster, 1989), 107.

34. Ibid.

35. David Ignatius, "Former CIA Director John Brennan Takes On Trump, and Doesn't Hold Back," *Washington Post*, October 9, 2020, https://www.washingtonpost.com/outlook/former-cia-director-john-brennan-takes-on-trump-and-doesnt-hold-back/2020/10/08/6754f6f4-0962-11eb-859b-f9c27abe638d_story.html; Alex Swoyer, "John Brennan: Trump's Press Conference with Putin 'Nothing Short of Treasonous,'" Associated Press, July 16, 2018, https://apnews.com/article/3a2b28d94251e6f8223edcb34b56cd7c; Veronica Stracqualursi, "Ex-DNI Confirms Trump Was Briefed on Putin's Involvement in 2016 Election," CNN, July 19, 2018, https://www.cnn.com/2018/07/19/politics/james-clapper-trump-russia-hacking-cnntv/index.html.

36. Stephen J. Blank and Richard Weitz, eds., *The Russian Military Today and Tomorrow: Essays in Memory of Mary Fitzgerald* (Hudson Institute, July 2010), https://www.hudson.org/content/researchattachments/attachment/795/20100630_-_blank_-_the_russian_military_camera-ready_proof_to_printer.pdf.

37. Anatoly Golitsyn, *New Lies for Old* (San Pedro: GSG & Associates, 1984).

38. Ibid.

39. Ibid.

40. Ibid.

41. Ibid.

42. Ibid.

43. Ibid.

44. Ibid.

45. "Operation 'Trust,'" Center for Intelligence Studies, U.S. Central Intelligence Agency, declassified, http://www.centerforintelligence studies.org/the-trust.html.

46. Anatoly Golitsyn, *New Lies for Old* (San Pedro: GSG & Associates, 1984).

47. Ibid.

48. Ibid.

49. Ibid.

50. Yuri Bezmenov (Tomas Schuman, pseud.), *World Thought Police* (Los Angeles: NATA Almanac, 1986), https://archive.org/details/ BezmenovWorldThoughtPolice1986.

51. Yuri Bezmenov (Tomas Schuman, pseud.), *Love Letter to America* (Los Angeles: W.I.N. Almanac Panorama, 1984), https://archive.org/ details/BezmenovLoveLetterToAmerica.

52. Ibid.

53. Ibid.

54. Ibid.

55. Ibid.

56. Politically Incorrect, "Yuri Bezmenov Interview with G. Edward Griffin," YouTube video, April 29, 2019, https://www.youtube.com/ watch?v=ZO9G4n9Uc2s.

57. Bill Miller, "KGB Defector Blames '60s Activists for Soviet Success," Redding Record-Searchlight, CIA Library, U.S. Central Intelligence Agency, March 24, 1986, https://www.cia.gov/library/readingroom/ docs/CIA-RDP90-00552R000605880003-3.pdf (search).

58. Scott Shane, "Soviet Defector Charges High-Level U.S. Betrayal, Scorns Press," *Baltimore Sun*, May 25, 1984, https://www.cia.gov/ library/readingroom/docs/CIA-RDP90-00552R000605880001-5.pdf (search). Scott Shane details Tomas Schuman and the defector's dilemma.

59. Ibid.

60. "Defector's Dilemma," *Washington Times*, February 5, 1986, https:// www.cia.gov/library/readingroom/docs/CIA-RDP90- 00552R000606130003-4.pdf (search).

61. Карякин В. В. (V. V. Karyakin), «Геополитика Третьей Волны: Трансформация Мира в Эпоху Постмодерна» (*Geopolitics of Third Wave: Transformation of the World in the Post-modern Epoch*) (in Russian).

62. Josh Christenson, "Sanders: We Must First Elect Biden, Then Keep Pushing Country Further Left," Washington Free Beacon, August 16, 2020, https://freebeacon.com/2020-election/sanders-we-must-first-elect-biden-then-keep-pushing-country-further-left/.

63. Josh Dawsey, Amy Brittain, and Sarah Ellison, "Andrew Cuomo's Family Members Were Given Special Access to Covid Testing, According to People Familiar with the Arrangement," *Washington Post*, March 24, 2021, https://www.washingtonpost.com/politics/andrew-cuomo-family-covid-testing/2021/03/24/e8f6f4a8-8cb8-11eb-aff6-4f720ca2d479_story.html.

64. Sun Tzu, *The Art of War* (El Paso: El Paso Norte Press Special Edition Books, 2011).

65. "Soviet Active Measures in the United States – an Updated Report by the FBI. Congressional Record," E4716, December 9, 1987, CIA-RDP11M01338R000400470089-2, declassified and approved for release.

66. Ibid.

67. "IG Footnotes: Serious Problems with Dossier Sources Didn't Stop FBI's Page Surveillance," News Release, Chuck Grassley: United States Senator for Iowa, April 15, 2020, https://www.grassley.senate.gov/news/news-releases/ig-footnotes-serious-problems-dossier-sources-didn-t-stop-fbi-s-page-surveillance.

68. "On Senator Kennedy's Offer to General Secretary of the Central Committee of the Communist Party of the Soviet Union Yu. V. Andropov," Memo from KGB Chairman V. Chebrikov to Comrade Yu. V. Andropov, Special Importance, declassified from Soviet Archives, May 14, 1983 (in Russian).

69. Ibid.

70. "Interview of: James Clapper," House Permanent Select Committee on Intelligence, U.S. House of Representatives, July 17, 2017, DNI

website, declassified, https://www.dni.gov/files/HPSCI_
Transcripts/2020-05-04-James_Clapper-MTR_Redacted.pdf.

71. "Operation Trust," U.S. Central Intelligence Agency; «К 85-летию
СВР России. Знаменательные операции советской внешней
разведки», http://svr.gov.ru/history/stages/znamoper.htm (in
Russian).

72. Ibid.

73. Ibid.

74. Ibid.

75. Ibid.

76. Anatoly Golitsyn, *New Lies for Old* (San Pedro: GSG & Associates,
1984).

77. "Operation Trust," U.S. Central Intelligence Agency.

78. Ibid.

79. United States of America v. Internet Research Agency LLC et al.,
indictment (for violations of 18 USC 2, 371, 1349, 1028 (a)), U.S.
District Court for the District of Columbia, February 16, 2018,
https://www.justice.gov/file/1035477/download.

80. Ibid.

81. Ibid.

82. Ibid.

83. Ibid.

84. Ibid. (The section author wrote on Russia's intelligence operations
targeting the 2016 election and preparation for the operation
targeting the 2020 election is based on the following sources); David
Holt, United States of America v. Elena Khusyaynova, complaint
(violation of 18 USC 371), U.S. District Court for the Eastern District
of Virginia, September 28, 2018, https://www.justice.gov/usao-edva/
press-release/file/1102591/download; "Open Hearing: Social Media
Influence in the 2016 U.S. Election Before the Senate Select
Committee on Intelligence," 115th Congress (2017), https://www.
intelligence.senate.gov/hearings/open-hearing-social-media-
influence-2016-us-elections# (Cited information is from handouts
given to audience members and notes taken by the author during the
hearing); Robert Mueller, *The Mueller Report: The Final Report of the*

Special Counsel into Donald Trump, Russia, and Collusion (New York: Skyhorse Publishing, as issued by the Department of Justice, 2019); *Intelligence Community Assessment: Assessing Russian Intelligence Activities and Intentions in Recent U.S. Elections* (National Intelligence Council: January 6, 2017), ICA 2017-01D, https://www.dni.gov/files/documents/ICA_2017_01.pdf.

85. Карякин В. В. (V. V. Karyakin), «Геополитика Третьей Волны: Трансформация Мира в Эпоху Постмодерна » (*Geopolitics of Third Wave: Transformation of the World in the Post-modern Epoch*) (in Russian); Герасимов В. (V. Gerasimov), «Ценность науки в предвидении», Военно-промышленный курьер (*Voenno-Promishlenniy Kuryer)*, February 26, 2013, https://vpk-news.ru/articles/14632, (in Russian).

86. Robert Mueller, *The Mueller Report: The Final Report of the Special Counsel into Donald Trump, Russia, and Collusion* (New York: Skyhorse Publishing, 2019).

87. Ibid.

88. «Путин об итогах расследования Мюллера: гора родила мышь», Коммерсантъ (*Kommersant*), April 9, 2019, https://www.kommersant.ru/doc/3938735 (in Russian).

89. *Russian Active Measures Campaigns and Interference in the 2016 U.S. Election* (Select Committee on Intelligence, U.S. Senate, S. Rep. No. 116-XX, vol. 1 2019), https://www.intelligence.senate.gov/sites/default/files/documents/Report_Volume1.pdf.

90. Bill Miller, "KGB Defector Blames '60s Activists for Soviet Success," Redding Record-Searchlight, CIA Library, U.S. Central Intelligence Agency, March 24, 1986, https://www.cia.gov/library/readingroom/docs/CIA-RDP90-00552R000605880003-3.pdf (search).

91. *Intelligence Community Assessment: Assessing Russian Intelligence Activities and Intentions in Recent U.S. Elections* (National Intelligence Council: January 6, 2017), ICA 2017-01D, https://www.dni.gov/files/documents/ICA_2017_01.pdf.

92. Ibid.

93. "Interview of: James Clapper," House Permanent Select Committee on Intelligence, U.S. House of Representatives, July 17, 2017, DNI

website, declassified, https://www.dni.gov/files/HPSCI_
Transcripts/2020-05-04-James_Clapper-MTR_Redacted.pdf.

94. *Intelligence Community Assessment: Assessing Russian Intelligence
     Activities and Intentions in Recent U.S. Elections* (National Intelligence
     Council: January 6, 2017), ICA 2017-01D, https://www.dni.gov/files/
     documents/ICA_2017_01.pdf.

95. "Interview of: James Clapper," House Permanent Select Committee
     on Intelligence, U.S. House of Representatives, July 17, 2017, DNI
     website, declassified, https://www.dni.gov/files/HPSCI_
     Transcripts/2020-05-04-James_Clapper-MTR_Redacted.pdf.

96. David Ignatius, "Former CIA Director John Brennan Takes on
     Trump, and Doesn't Hold Back," *Washington Post*, October 9, 2020,
     https://www.washingtonpost.com/outlook/former-cia-director-john-
     brennan-takes-on-trump-and-doesnt-hold-
     back/2020/10/08/6754f6f4-0962-11eb-859b -f9c27abe638d_story.html;
     Alex Swoyer, "John Brennan: Trump's Press Conference with Putin
     'Nothing Short of Treasonous,'" *Washington Times*, July 16, 2018,
     https://apnews.com/article/3a2b28d94251e6f8223edcb34b56cd7c;
     Veronica Stracqualursi, "Ex-DNI Confirms Trump Was Briefed on
     Putin's Involvement in 2016 Election," CNN, July 19, 2018, https://
     www.cnn.com/2018/07/19/politics/james-clapper-trump-russia-
     hacking-cnntv/index.html.

97. Ignatius, "Former CIA Director John Brennan Takes on Trump."

98. Mark Mazzetti and Matt Apuzzo, "Analysts Detail Claims That
     Reports on ISIS Were Distorted," *New York Times*, September 15, 2015,
     https://www.nytimes.com/2015/09/16/us/politics/analysts-said-to-
     provide-evidence-of-distorted-reports-on-isis.html.

99. William Barr, "Overview of the Counterintelligence Investigation of
     Christopher Steele's Primary Sub-Source," enclosed in a letter from
     Attorney General Barr to Chairman of the Senate Judiciary
     Committee Lindsey Graham, U.S. Federal Bureau of Investigation,
     September 24, 2020, https://www.judiciary.senate.gov/imo/media/
     doc/AG%20Letter%20to%20Chairman%20Graham%209.24.2020.
     pdf.

100. Ibid.

101. Eric Felten, "Dossier Source Was a Suspected Russian Spy, and the FBI Knew It When It Spied on Carter Page," RealClearInvestigations, September 25, 2020, https://www.realclearinvestigations.com/articles/2020/09/25/dossier_source_was_russia_spy_suspect_and_the_fbi_knew_it_125358.html.

102. "Soviet Active Measures in the United States – an Updated Report by the FBI. Congressional Record," E4716, December 9, 1987, CIA-RDP11M01338R000400470089-2, declassified and approved for release.

103. Pete Earley, *Comrade J.: The Untold Secrets of Russia's Master Spy in America After the End of the Cold War* (New York: The Berkley Publishing Group, 2007).

104. Rosemary M. Collyer, "*In Re* Accuracy Concerns Regarding FBI Matters Submitted to the FISC," U.S. Foreign Intelligence Surveillance Court, December 17, 2019, https://www.fisc.uscourts.gov/sites/default/files/MIsc%2019%2002%20191217.pdf; "Review of Four FISA Applications and Other Aspects of the FBI's Crossfire Hurricane Investigation," Office of the Inspector General, December 2019, https://www.justice.gov/storage/120919-examination.pdf.

105. "FBI Attorney Admits Altering Email Used for FISA Application During 'Crossfire Hurricane' Investigation," U.S. Attorney's Office Press Release, U.S. Department of Justice, August 19, 2020, https://www.justice.gov/usao-ct/pr/fbi-attorney-admits-altering-email-used-fisa-application-during-crossfire-hurricane.

106. WSJ Editorial Board, "The Flynn Unmaskers Unmasked," *Wall Street Journal*, May 13, 2020, https://www.wsj.com/articles/the-flynn-unmaskers-unmasked-11589411876.

107. "Closing Communication, Crossfire Razor," Washington Field Office, U.S. Federal Bureau of Investigation, January 4, 2017, https://justthenews.com/sites/default/files/2020-04/FBIFlynnCaseCloseMemo.pdf; Peter Strzok, email (recipient withheld), "Potential Qs for DD Call," January 24, 2017, https://justthenews.com/sites/default/files/2020-04/FlynnFBINotes_0.pdf; Handwritten FBI note, https://justthenews.com/sites/default/files/2020-04/FlynnFBINotes_0.pdf.

108. Call transcripts of Lieutenant General Michael Flynn, May 29, 2020, declassified by DNI Ratcliffe, Chuck Grassley: United States Senator

for Iowa, https://www.grassley.senate.gov/sites/default/files/2020-05-29%20ODNI%20to%20CEG%20RHJ%20%28Flynn%20Transcripts%29.pdf (no longer available).

109. *Russian GRU 85th GTsSS Deploys Previously Undisclosed Drovorub Malware* (U.S. National Security Agency and Federal Bureau of Investigation, August 2020), unclassified, https://media.defense.gov/2020/Aug/13/2002476465/-1/-1/0/CSA_DROVORUB_RUSSIAN_GRU_MALWARE_AUG_2020.PDF.

110. Susan Heavy and Simon Lewis, "Sanders Blasts Russia for Reportedly Trying to Boost His Presidential Campaign," Reuters, February 20, 2020, https://www.reuters.com/article/us-usa-trump-russia-idUSKBN20F01B.

111. Olivia Beavers, "U.S. Intelligence Says Russia Seeking to 'Denigrate' Biden," *The Hill*, August 7, 2020, https://thehill.com/policy/national-security/511078-top-intelligence-official-warns-of-foreign-influence-ahead-of-2020.

112. "Operation Trust," U.S. Central Intelligence Agency.

113. Edward Jay Epstein, *Deception: The Invisible War between the KGB and the CIA* (New York: Simon and Schuster, 1989).

114. Активные Мероприятия, «Контрразведывательный словарь», Высшая краснознаменная школа Комитета Государственной Безопасности при Совете Министров СССР им. Ф. Э. Дзержинского (F. Z. Dzerzhinskogo), 1972 г, (in Russian).

115. «Особая Папка», «Отчет о Работе КГБ Брежневу», 1977, https://nsarchive2.gwu.edu/NSAEBB/NSAEBB191/03-27-1978a.pdf (in Russian).

116. Активные Мероприятия, «Контрразведывательный словарь», Высшая краснознаменная школа Комитета Государственной Безопасности при Совете Министров СССР им. Ф. Э. Дзержинского (F. Z. Dzerzhinskogo), 1972 г (in Russian).

117. Andrey Soldatov and Irina Borogan, *The Compatriots: The Brutal and Chaotic History of Russia's Exiles, Emigres, and Agents Abroad* (New York: Public Affairs, 2019).

118. "Soviet Use of Assassinations and Kidnappings: A 1964 View of KGB Methods," CIA Library, U.S. Central Intelligence Agency, https://

www.cia.gov/library/center-for-the-study-of-intelligence/kent-csi/
vol19no3/html/v19i3a01p_0001.htm.

119. Ibid.

120. Andrew and Mitrokhin, *The Sword and the Shield*, 122; Andrey
Soldatov and Irina Borogan, *The Compatriots: The Brutal and Chaotic
History of Russia's Exiles, Emigres, and Agents Abroad* (New York:
Public Affairs, 2019).

121. Ibid.

122. Ibid.

123. "An Italian Investigative Commission Has Said Former Soviet Union
Leaders Ordered the Shooting of Pope John Paul II in 1981," Reuters,
March 4, 2006, https://reuters.screenocean.com/record/335554.

124. "Federal Law: On Countering Extreme Activity," July 25, 2006, www.
Pravo.ru (in Russian).

125. Ibid.

126. David Stout, "Pavel Sudoplatov, 89, Dies; Top Soviet Spy Who
Accused Oppenheimer," *New York Times*, September 28, 1996, https://
www.nytimes.com/1996/09/28/world/pavel-sudoplatov-89-dies-top-
soviet-spy-who-accused-oppenheimer.html.

127. Boris Volodarsky, *The KGB's Poison's Factory: From Lenin to
Litvinenko* (Minneapolis: Zenith Press, 2009).

128. Ibid.

129. Ann Simmons, "Alexei Navalny Hospitalized in Russia Three Weeks
into Hunger Strike," *Wall Street Journal*, April 19, 2021, https://www.
wsj.com/articles/alexei-navalny-hospitalized-in-russia-three-weeks-
into-hunger-strike-11618839052.

130. Andrey Kozenko, "Navalny Poisoning: Kremlin Critic Recalls Near-
Death Novichok Torment," BBC, October 7, 2020, https://www.bbc.
com/news/world-europe-54434082.

131. "Soviet Use of Assassinations and Kidnappings: A 1964 View of KGB
Methods," U.S. Central Intelligence Agency.

132. Robert Owen, "The Litvinenko Inquiry: Report into the Death of
Alexander Litvinenko," British House of Commons, January 21, 2016,
https://assets.publishing.service.gov.uk/government/uploads/system/

uploads/attachment_data/file/493860/The-Litvinenko-Inquiry-H-C-695-web.pdf.

133. "Novichok Nerve Agent Use in Salisbury: UK Government Response, March to April 2018," Government of the United Kingdom, March 14, 2018, last updated April 18, 2018, https://www.gov.uk/government/news/novichok-nerve-agent-use-in-salisbury-uk-government-response; "Evidence of Russia's Involvement in Salisbury Attack," Government of the United Kingdom, September 6, 2018, last updated September 7, 2018, https://www.gov.uk/government/speeches/you-dont-recruit-an-arsonist-to-put-out-a-fire-you-especially-dont-do-that-when-the-fire-is-one-they-caused.

134. "Novichok Nerve Agent Use in Salisbury: UK Government Response, March to April 2018," Government of the United Kingdom; "Evidence of Russia's Involvement in Salisbury Attack," Government of the United Kingdom.

135. Richard Pérez-Peña and Ellen Barry, "U.K. Charges 2 Men in Novichok Poisoning, Saying They're Russian Agents," *New York Times*, September 5, 2018, https://www.nytimes.com/2018/09/05/world/europe/russia-uk-novichok-skripal.html.

136. "Former Chechen Commander Gunned Down in Berlin; Eyes Turn to Moscow (and Grozny)," Radio Free Europe/Radio Liberty, August 28, 2019, https://www.rferl.org/a/chechen-commander-khangoshvili-berlin-assassination-moscow-(and-grozny)/30133813.html.

137. «Путин рассказал об убитом в Германии Зелимхане Хангошвили» (Putin Spoke About Zelimkhan Khangoshvili Killed in Germany), Российская газета (*Rossiyskaya Gazeta)*, December 19, 2019, https://rg.ru/2019/12/19/putin-rasskazal-ob-ubitom-v-germanii-zelimhane-hangoshvili.html (in Russian).

138. Mike Eckel and Carl Schreck, "Exclusive: Washington Autopsy Files Reveal Lesin Sustained Broken Bone in Neck," Radio Free Europe/Radio Liberty, March 16, 2019, https://www.rferl.org/a/lesin-autopsy-record/29824566.html.

139. "Soviet Use of Assassinations and Kidnappings: A 1964 View of KGB Methods," U.S. Central Intelligence Agency.

140. Richard Behar, "Another Anniversary of Forbes Editor Paul Khlebnikov's Unsolved Moscow Murder (But Rumors of Death of 'Project K' Are Exaggerated)," *Forbes*, July 14, 2020, https://www.forbes.com/sites/richardbehar/2020/07/14/another-anniversary-of-forbes-editor-paul-klebnikovs-unsolved-moscow-murder-but-rumors-of-death-of-project-k-are-exaggerated/.

141. Evan Perez and Alan Cullison, "FBI Helps Probe Kremlin Critic's Shooting," *Wall Street Journal*, March 5, 2007, https://www.wsj.com/articles/SB117305863029326544.

142. Josh Rogin, "Russia Is Harassing U.S. Diplomats All over Europe," *Washington Post*, June 27, 2016, https://www.washingtonpost.com/opinions/global-opinions/russia-is-harassing-us-diplomats-all-over-europe/2016/06/26/968d1a5a-3bd.

143. "Interview with The Financial Times," Kremlin News, June 27, 2019, http://en.kremlin.ru/events/president/news/60836.

144. «Что касается предателей, они сами загнутся. Владимир Путин рассказал россиянам о разведчиках и свиньях, которые их предают», Коммерсантъ (*Kommersant*), December 16, 2010 (in Russian), https://www.kommersant.ru/doc/1558806.

145. «Свежо предательство, «Ъ» выяснил, кто сдал американским спецслужбам сеть российских разведчиков-нелегалов», Газета Коммерсантъ (*Kommersant*), №208 от November 11, 2010, стр. 1, https://www.kommersant.ru/doc/1536406 (in Russian).

146. Виктор Нехезин, «Путин: 'Совсем не факт, что человека нужно убивать'», BBC News, December 17, 2015, https://www.bbc.com/russian/russia/2015/12/151217_putin_presser_wrapup (in Russian).

Chapter 8

1. Указ Президента Российской Федерации, «Вопросы Генерального штаба Вооруженных Сил Российской Федерации от», July 23, 2013 (in Russian).

2. «Военная Доктрина Российской Федерации», 2014 (in Russian).

3. Полегаев В. И. (V. I. Polegaev), «О Неядерном Сдерживании, Его Роли и Месте В Системе Стратегического Сдерживания»

("Regarding Deterrence and Its Role and Place in the System of Strategic Deterrence, Military Thought, in Russian"), Военная Мысль (*Military Thought*).

4. Vladimir Putin, "Principles of State Policy of the Russian Federation in the Sphere of Nuclear Deterrence," Pravo Publications, June 2, 2020, http://publication.pravo.gov.ru/Document/View/00012020060 20040?index=0&rangeSize=1 (in Russian).

5. «Военная Доктрина Российской Федерации», 2000 (in Russian).

6. Ibid.

7. «Военная Доктрина Российской Федерации», December 25, 2014, https://rg.ru/2014/12/30/doktrina-dok.html (in Russian).

8. «Военная Доктрина Российской Федерации», December 25, 2014, https://rg.ru/2014/12/30/doktrina-dok.html (in Russian); *Russia Military Power: Building a Military to Support Great Power Aspirations* (U.S. Defense Intelligence Agency, 2017), https://www.dia.mil/Portals/27/Documents/News/Military%20Power%20Publications/Russia%20Military%20Power%20Report%202017.pdf.

9. «Военная Доктрина Российской Федерации», December 25, 2014, https://rg.ru/2014/12/30/doktrina-dok.html (in Russian).

10. Ibid.

11. Ibid.

12. "Air Force Doctrine Document 2-1.9," U.S. Air Force, June 8, 2006, https://apps.dtic.mil/dtic/tr/fulltext/u2/a454614.pdf.

13. Matthew J. Wemyss, "The Bear's Den: Russian Anti-Access/Area-Denial in the Maritime Domain," Air Command and Staff College, Air University, May 2016, https://apps.dtic.mil/dtic/tr/fulltext/u2/1031334.pdf.

14. Герасимов Валерий (Valeriy Gerasimov), «Векторы развития военной стратегии. Начальник Генерального штаба Вооружённых Сил РФ генерал армии Валерий Герасимов выступил на общем собрании Академии военных наук,» Красная звезда (*Red Star*), March 4, 2019.

15. S. G. Chekinov and S. A. Bogdanov, "A Forecast for Future Wars: Meditations on What They Will Look Like," *Military Thought* 24, no. 4 (October 2015): 90–98 (in Russian).

16. Кириленко В. П. and Коростелев С. В. (V. I. Kirilenko and S. V. Korostelev), «К вопросу о праве государств на упреждающее при- менение военной силы», Военная мысль (*Military Thought*) no. 9 (2011): 55–60, (in Russian).

17. Герасимов Валерий (Valeriy Gerasimov), «Ценность науки в предвидении. Новые вызовы требуют переосмыслить формы и способы ведения боевых действий», Военно-промышленный курьер (*Voenno-Promishlenniy Kuryer),* February 26, 2013, https://www.vpk-news.ru/articles/14632 (in Russian).

18. Michael Fitzsimmons, "The False Allure of Escalation Dominance," War on the Rocks, November 16, 2017, https://warontherocks.com/2017/11/false-allure-escalation-dominance/.

19. Greg Miller, Ellen Nakashima, and Adam Entous, "Obama's Secret Struggle to Punish Russia for Putin's Election Assault," *Washington Post,* June 23, 2017, https://www.washingtonpost.com/graphics/2017/world/national-security/obama-putin-election-hacking/.

20. Jessica Davis, "U.K. Says Russia Was behind NotPetya Cyberattack That Shut Down Nuance, Hospitals," February 15, 2018, https://www.healthcareitnews.com/news/uk-says-russia-was-behind-notpetya-cyberattack-shut-down-nuance-hospitals.

21. Sydney J. Freedberg, "U.S. 'Gets Its Ass Handed to It' in Wargames: Here's a \$24 Billion Fix," Breaking Defense, March 7, 2019, https://breakingdefense.com/2019/03/us-gets-its-ass-handed-to-it-in-wargames-heres-a-24-billion-fix/.

22. Ibid.

23. Ibid.

24. David Sanger and Eric Schmitt, "Russian Ships Near Data Cables Are Too Close for U.S. Comfort," *New York Times,* October 25, 2015, https://www.nytimes.com/2015/10/26/world/europe/russian-presence-near-undersea-cables-concerns-us.html.

25. *Russia Military Power: Building a Military to Support Great Power Aspirations* (U.S. Defense Intelligence Agency, 2017), https://www.dia.mil/Portals/27/Documents/News/Military%20Power%20Publications/Russia%20Military%20Power%20Report%202017.pdf.

26. "Presidential Address to the Federal Assembly," Kremlin News, March 1, 2018, http://en.kremlin.ru/events/president/news/56957 (in Russian).

27. Ibid.

28. Ibid.

29. *The Military Balance* (revised edition), International Institute of Strategic Studies (2020).

30. Ibid.

31. "Presidential Address," Kremlin News.

32. Ibid.

33. Pavel Felgenhauer, "Putin Unveils Array of Nuclear 'Super Weapons' Aimed at US," Jamestown Foundation, March 1, 2018, https://jamestown.org/program/putin-unveils-array-of-nuclear-super-weapons-aimed-at-us/.

34. "Presidential Address," Kremlin News.

35. "Kh-101 / Kh-102," Missile Threat, Center for Strategic and International Studies, June 15, 2018, https://missilethreat.csis.org/missile/kh-101-kh-102/.

36. "SSC-8 (9M729)," Missile Threat, https://missilethreat.csis.org/missile/ssc-8-novator-9m729/.

37. Cheryl Pellerin, "Selva: Nuclear Deterrent Is the Joint Force Modernization Priority," News, U.S. Department of Defense, March 8, 2017, https://www.defense.gov/Explore/News/Article/Article/1107141/selva-nuclear-deterrent-is-the-joint-force-modernization-priority/; Idrees Ali, "U.S. General Says Russia Deploys Cruise Missile, Threatens NATO," Reuters, March 8, 2017, https://www.reuters.com/article/us-usa-russia-missiles/u-s-general-says-russia-deploys-cruise-missile-threatens-nato-idUSKBN16F23V.

38. Sydney J. Freedberg, "Russians in Syria Building A2/AD 'Bubble' over Region: Breedlove," Breaking Defense, September 28, 2015, https://breakingdefense.com/2015/09/russians-in-syria-building-a2ad-bubble-over-region-breedlove/.

39. *Russia Military Power: Building a Military to Support Great Power Aspirations* (U.S. Defense Intelligence Agency, 2017), https://www.dia.

mil/Portals/27/Documents/News/Military%20Power%20
Publications/Russia%20Military%20Power%20Report%202017.pdf.

40. Sydney J. Freedberg, "McMaster: Army May Be Outnumbered and
    Outgunned in Next War," Breaking Defense, April 6, 2016, https://
    breakingdefense.com/2016/04/mcmaster-army-may-be-
    outnumbered-and-outgunned-in-next-war/.

41. "Russia Rejects US Claim of Violation of Nuke Test Ban," Military
    Times, May 30, 2019, https://www.militarytimes.com/
    flashpoints/2019/05/30/russia-rejects-us-claim-of-violation-of-nuke-
    test-ban/.

42. Joseph Trevithick, "Russia's New Surveillance Plane Just Flew over
    Two of America's Top Nuclear Labs," The Drive (The War Zone),
    April 25, 2019, https://www.thedrive.com/the-war-zone/27678/
    russias-new-surveillance-plane-just-flew-over-two-of-americas-top-
    nuclear-labs; «Российские специалисты выполнят
    наблюдательный полет над территорией США», Russian Ministry
    of Defense News, April 22, 2019, https://function.mil.ru/news_page/
    country/more.htm?id=12227149 (in Russian).

43. «Путин руководил учениями стратегических ядерных сил»,
    Лента (Lenta), https://lenta.ru/news/2014/05/08/putin/ (in Russian).

44. William Burr and Sveltana Savranskaya, eds., "Previously Classified
    Interviews with Former Soviet Officials Reveal U.S. Strategic
    Intelligence Failure Over Decades," National Security Archive at
    George Washington University, https://nsarchive2.gwu.edu/
    nukevault/ebb285/.

45. «Военная Доктрина Российской Федерации», 2014, https://
    rg.ru/2014/12/30/doktrina-dok.html (in Russian).

46. Левшин В. И. (V. I. Levshin), Неделин А. В. (A. V. Nedelin), и
    Сосновский М. Е. (M. E. Sosnovskiy), «О применении ядерного
    оружия для деэскалации военных действий», Военная мысль
    (*Military Thought*), no.3 (1999): 34–37, http://militaryarticle.ru/
    zarubezhnoe-voennoe-obozrenie /1999-zvo/8995-o-primenenii-
    jadernogo-oruzhija-dlja-dejeskalacii.

47. «Посол Антонов назвал ошибочными слова о выработке РФ доктрины 'эскалация для деэскалации'», TASS, April 9, 2020, https://tass.ru/politika/6309802 (in Russian).

48. Vladimir Putin, "Principles of State Policy of the Russian Federation in the Sphere of Nuclear Deterrence," Pravo Publications, June 2, 2020, http://publication.pravo.gov.ru/Document/View/00012020060 20040?index=0&rangeSize=1 (in Russian).

49. Ibid.

50. Steven Aftergood, ed., "Strategic Command and Control," Federation of American Scientists, https://fas.org/nuke/guide/russia/c3i/.

51. Pavel Aksenov, "Stanislav Petrov: The Man Who May Have Saved the World," BBC News, September 26, 2013, https://www.bbc.com/news/world-europe-24280831.

52. Jessica Sleight, "Seven Things Mistaken for an Incoming Nuclear Attack," Global Zero, May 26, 2016, https://www.globalzero.org/updates/seven-things-mistaken-for-an-incoming-nuclear-attack/.

53. Donald P. Steury, "What Stalin Knew: The Enigma of Barbarossa," CIA Library, U.S. Central Intelligence Agency, https://www.cia.gov/library/center-for-the-study-of-intelligence/csi-publications/csi-studies/studies/vol50no1/9_BK_What_Stalin_Knew.htm.

54. «Указ Президента Российской Федерации: Вопросы Генерального штаба Вооруженных Сил Российской Федерации», July 23, 2013 (in Russian).

55. «Рогозин заявил о введении в действие 'мобилизационного плана экономики'», Интерфах (Interfax), January 14, 2014 (in Russian), https://www.interfax.ru/business/351311.

56. Ibid.

57. Counterintelligence Dictionary (in Russian).

58. «Рогозин заявил о введении в действие 'мобилизационного плана экономики'», Интерфах (Interfax), January 14, 2014 (in Russian), https://www.interfax.ru/business/351311.

59. "State Armament Programs of Russia: Dossier," TASS, February 26, 2018; "New Plan for the Mobilization of the Economy Has Come into Effect in the Russian Federation–Rogozin," RIA Novosti, www.ria.ru (in Russian); "On the Strategy of Economic Security of the Russian

Federation for the Period through 2030," Boris Yeltsin Presidential Library, https://www.prlib.ru/en/node/681513; "Russian State Mobilization: Moving the Country on to a War Footing," Chatham House, May 20, 2016, https://www.chathamhouse.org/2016/05/russian-state-mobilization-moving-country-war-footing; "Mobilization Plan: Definition," Russian Ministry of Emergency Situations, www.mchs.gov.ru (in Russian).

60. Лапик Игорь (Igor Papik), «Сердце российской армии: как работает Национальный центр управления обороной», TV Zvezda, December 19, 2019, https://tvzvezda.ru/news/forces/content/201912191737-JcWFf.html (in Russian).

61. Ibid.

62. "Putin Orders Massive Snap Russian 'Combat Readiness Check,'" Radio Free Europe/Radio Liberty, July 17, 2020, https://www.rferl.org/a/putin-orders-massive-snap-russian-military-drills-ukraine/30733189.html; Dave Johnson, "VOSTOK 2018: Ten Years of Russian Strategic Exercises and Warfare Preparation," NATO Review, December 20, 2018, https://www.nato.int/docu/review/articles/2018/12/20/vostok-2018-ten-years-of-russian-strategic-exercises-and-warfare-preparation/index.html.

63. *Russia Military Power: Building a Military to Support Great Power Aspirations* (U.S. Defense Intelligence Agency, 2017), https://www.dia.mil/Portals/27/Documents/News/Military%20Power%20Publications/Russia%20Military%20Power%20Report%202017.pdf.

64. "Bogus Notification of War between Soviet Union and United States of America," declassified, serial 2/19/2515-84 Spot Report, U.S. National Security Agency, August 15, 1984, https://nsarchive.files.wordpress.com/2015/10/kal-007-nsa-history.pdf.

65. Ibid.

66. Ibid.

67. Ibid.

68. Ibid.

69. Ibid.

70. Ibid.

71. Benjamin Fischer, "Able Archer 83," in *Cold War Conundrum: The 1983 Soviet War Scare*, CIA Library, U.S. Central Intelligence Agency, declassified, https://www.cia.gov/library/center-for-the-study-of-intelligence/csi-publications/books-and-monographs/a-cold-war-conundrum/source.htm#HEADING1-13.

72. Ibid.

73. *Nuclear Posture Review* (U.S. Department of Defense, February 2018) https://media.defense.gov/2018/Feb/02/2001872886/-1/-1/1/2018-NUCLEAR-POSTURE-REVIEW-FINAL-REPORT.PDF.

74. Michael Pompeo, "On the Treaty on Open Skies," U.S. Department of State, May 21, 2020, https://www.state.gov/on-the-treaty-on-open-skies/.

75. Ibid.

Epilogue

1. Craig Whitlock, "At War with the Truth," *Washington Post*, December 9, 2019, https://www.washingtonpost.com/graphics/2019/investigations/afghanistan-papers/afghanistan-war-confidential-documents/.

2. Rebekah Koffler, "Putin Draws a 'Red Line' on Ukraine, and He Means It," *The Hill*, April 26, 2021, https://thehill.com/opinion/international/550036-putin-draws-a-red-line-on-ukraine-and-he-means-it.

3. "Statement of General Glen VanHerck, United States Air Force Commander United States Northern Command and North American Aerospace Defense Command before the Senate Armed Services Committee," Statement for the Record, Senate Armed Services Committee, U.S. Senate, March 16, 2021, https://www.northcom.mil/Newsroom/Transcripts/Transcript/Article/2541921/norad-usnorthcom-commanders-senate-armed-services-committee-statement/.

4. "Advanced Persistent Threat Compromise of Government Agencies, Critical Infrastructure, and Private Sector Organizations," Alert (AA20-352A), Cybersecurity and Infrastructure Security Agency

(CISA), April 15 2021, https://us-cert.cisa.gov/ncas/alerts/aa20-352a; "FACT SHEET: Imposing Costs for Harmful Foreign Activities by the Russian Government," Briefing Room, White House, April 15, 2021, https://www.whitehouse.gov/briefing-room/statements-releases/2021/04/15/fact-sheet-imposing-costs-for-harmful-foreign-activities-by-the-russian-government/; Robert McMillan and Dustin Volz, "Suspected Russian Hack Extends Far Beyond SolarWinds Software, Investigators Say," *Wall Street Journal*, January 29, 2021, https://www.wsj.com/articles/suspected-russian-hack-extends-far-beyond-solarwinds-software-investigators-say-11611921601.

5. James Marson and Catherine Lucey, "Biden Proposes a U.S.-Russian Summit in Call to Putin," *Wall Street Journal*, April 13, 2021, https://www.wsj.com/articles/nato-urges-russia-to-halt-military-buildup-on-ukraines-borders-11618316598; Michael Gordon and Georgi Kantchev, "Satellite Images Show Russia's Expanding Ukraine Buildup," *Wall Street Journal*, April 20, 2021, https://www.wsj.com/articles/satellite-images-show-russias-expanding-ukraine-buildup-11618917238; Andrew Osborn and Alexander Marrow, "Russia Calls U.S. an Adversary, Warns Its Warships to Avoid Crimea," Reuters, April 13, 2021, https://www.reuters.com/world/europe/russia-warns-us-warships-steer-clear-crimea-for-their-own-good-2021-04-13/; Ann Simmons, "Russia's Putin Issues Warnings Amid Military Buildup, Pro-Navalny Protests," *Wall Street Journal*, April 21, 2021, https://www.wsj.com/articles/putin-warns-against-crossing-russias-red-line-amid-military-buildup-near-ukraine-11619009268.

6. Craig Whitlock, "At War with the Truth."

7. Reuters Staff, "Russia Warned U.S. about Boston Marathon Bomb Suspect Tsarnaev: Report," Reuters, March 25, 2014, https://www.reuters.com/article/us-usa-explosions-boston-congress/russia-warned-u-s-about-boston-marathon-bomb-suspect-tsarnaev-report-idUSBREA2P02Q20140326.

8. Andrew Kramer, "C.I.A. Helped Thwart Terrorist Attack in Russia, Kremlin Says," *New York Times*, December 17, 2017, https://www.

nytimes.com/2017/12/17/world/europe/putin-trump-cia-terrorism. html.

9. "The United States and Soviet Union Are Separated by Something More," CIA Library, U.S. Central Intelligence Agency, July 1, 1982, declassified, https://www.cia.gov/library/readingroom/docs/CIA-RDP85M00364R001001580041-5.pdf (search).

10. Международные Угрозы, Геополитическое ускорение, Университет МГИМО, 2018.

11. "The Charge in the Soviet Union (Kennan) to the Secretary of State," National Security Archive at George Washington University, February 22, 1946, declassified, https://nsarchive2.gwu.edu/coldwar/documents/episode-1/kennan.pdf.

Index